MACROECONOMICS

MACROECONOMICS

ROBERT D. CHERRY
Brooklyn College
of the City University of New York

ADDISON-WESLEY PUBLISHING COMPANY

Reading, Massachusetts • Menlo Park, California
London • Amsterdam • Don Mills, Ontario • Sydney

Library of Congress Cataloging in Publication Data

Cherry, Robert D   1944-
  Macroeconomics.

  Includes bibliographical references and index.
  1. Macroeconomics. 2. Capitalism. 3. Marxian
economics. I. Title.
HB171.C53   339   79-3130
ISBN 0-201-00911-0

ISBN 0-201-00911-0
ABCDEFGHIJ-MA-79

To three generations of Cherrys:
Jack and Jean,
Shelley,
and Sara and Joshua

PREFACE

During the 1970s, the economics profession began to seriously question the necessity for and efficacy of traditional Keynesian policies. In particular, the Keynesian contention that unemployment can be held permanently at low levels without high inflation rates has become a minority position among influential macroeconomic theorists. At the 1979 AEA Convention, Bennett McCallum noted, "Just over a decade ago, Milton Friedman's suggestion that unemployment could be kept low only by accelerating inflation seemed radical; now even many activists doubt that it can be kept low by *any* monetary stance."

Much of this shift has been a result of the monetarist counterattack begun by Friedman in the late 1960s. However, at the same time left-economists also raised theoretical explanations for the inability of market economies, using tradition policies, to sustain permanently low levels of unemployment accompanied by stable prices. Left-liberals, such as Galbraith and the post-Keynesians, claim that only planning to stabilize investment and incomes policies to determine the functional distribution of income could be effective. Radicals claim that capitalism requires an industrial reserve army in order to maintain economic and social stability. Hence, recent problems are a result of the long period of full employment during the 1960s.

The lack of consensus makes it imperative that macroeconomics textbooks present a broad spectrum of viewpoints. They should take seriously both the monetarist contentions concerning the self-regulating properties of a market economy *and* left-views concerning the functional distribution of income and the functional role of unemployment. This book presents such a spectrum of views.

In order to facilitate the presentation of this spectrum of viewpoints more effort is spent at the beginning of the book to clarify the major policy issues. For example, rather than immediately presenting income accounts, Chapter 2 details the natural unemployment rate thesis, which if uncritiquely accepted, undermines the whole thrust of Keynesian policies. By presenting the reserve army thesis and theories of the State, students realize that there may be political barriers to the maintenance of full employment.

Also, more attention is paid to the underlying assumptions made when developing models. Whenever appropriate, the value judgments underlying assumptions will be specified. For example, the underlying rationales for assuming a constant MPC and business savings equal to zero in the simple Keynesian model are critiquely discussed.

This book does not shy away from presenting technical material when it adds to the exposition of theories presented. For example, the prisoners' dilemma framework is used when discussing potential problems of decentralized decision-making, and the neo-classical theory of the firm is used to discuss bank decisions. However, by discussing policy implications in each chapter so that the material is related to the debate among conservatives, liberals, and radicals, the student is always forced to focus on important issues rather than wade through what is often viewed as irrelevant and technically difficult details.

The book is particularly attractive to students who have a social science orientation. By presenting theories of alienation, racial discrimination, managerial control, and the functional distribution of income, these students develop an understanding of the relationship of economics to the other social sciences.

Care is taken to avoid simultaneous development of competing theories. Traditional topics, such as income determination, consumption functions, IS-LM framework, and growth theory are developed independently in their usual order. However, by presenting the broader issues early and indicating the policy implications immediately, students are sensitized to the considerations involved in accepting/rejecting each theory.

It is my belief and experience that this approach, when done correctly, clarifies issues for students. They are able to separate the substantive conceptual issues from problems associated with technical manipulations. It gives them a firm background in problems associated with model building and abstract theorizing in the social sciences.

Because of the unique approach taken in this book let me briefly summarize each chapter's features:

Chapter 1 introduces the student to macroeconomics by reviewing the reasons for the breakdown of the Keynesian consensus. It also indicates why statistical testing is not capable of resoving major theoretical disputes.

Chapter 2 develops the natural unemployment rate thesis, presenting the mainstream contention that it has not been steadily rising during the last decade. The natural rate view is then contrasted with the left-liberal and radical views, including the industrial reserve army thesis, concerning the extent of involuntary unemployment in a market economy.

Chapter 3 critically evaluates the mainstream conceptions of people's capitalism and managerial control which provide the foundation for the assumption that the federal government acts in the "national interest." Alternative conceptions, such as economic class and financial control, are developed and used to explain recent political and economic events.

Chapter 4 demonstrates how income accounts can be reorganized to facilitate macroeconomic model building. It is demonstrated how, through the use of simplifying assumptions, the economic process can be reduced to a system of manageable relationships.

Chapter 5 develops the equilibrium and multiplier concepts. It indicates the important distinction between the simple and full income multiplier.

Chapter 6 emphasizes that the choice of theory of household behavior critically affects the size of the MPC. It is shown that while the permanent income and life cycle hypotheses imply a small MPC and, hence, a stable household spending pattern, other theories, such as the Paradox of Thrift model, imply a volatile pattern.

Chapter 7 systematically incorporates the functional distribution of income into the simple income determination model. It indicates that under certain assumptions the raising of profit margins during contractions could decrease both equilibrium income and equilibrium profits. Through the use of the prisoners' dilemma it demonstrates that destabilizing and counterproductive decisions by firms results from the decentralized decision-making process of market capitalism. This chapter provides the foundation for further discussions of the influence of income distribution on the Keynes Effect (Chapter 12), growth (Chapter 14), and underconsumptionism (Chapter 18).

Chapter 8 indicates that if the income multiplier is small and discretionary intervention uncertain and lagged, only government automatic stabilizers are warranted. It also demonstrates that under reasonable conditions a balanced budget expansion reduces equilibrium disposable income and, hence, there is a strong possibility that it also reduces social welfare.

Chapter 9 presents the view that the interest rate is the critical determinant of capital spending and derives the IS curve. It demonstrates that with sufficient interest elasticity of aggregate spending there exists an interest rate that is compatible with full employment regardless of the size of autonomous spending.

Chapter 10 presents theories of money demand and supply sufficient to develop an interest sensitive LM curve. The distinction between advocates of monetary policy and monetarists is highlighted. Also, while the relative effectiveness of monetary versus fiscal policy (relative slopes) is discussed, effort is made to explain why this debate is rather unimportant.

To the extent that there is interest in pursuing more detail, Chapter 11 presents a number of factors that influence the relative effectiveness of monetary and fiscal policy. Besides the usual topics, this chapter discusses the importance of choice of interest rate (shortterm versus longterm), the interest sensitivity of the consumption function, the expansion of money substitutes, and banking decisions when applying the neo-classical theory of the firm.

Aggregate supply and demand curves are developed in Chapter 12 in order to analyze the effects of price changes on equilibrium spending. The possibility of wage declines *without* compensating price declines is analyzed together with the more traditional criticisms of the Keynes Effect.

Chapter 13 emphasizes that the structural properties of investment goods —fix proportions requirements, indivisibility, and long construction period— are the foundation of most left-liberal business cycle and stagnationist models. Besides the Hicksian model, the Kondratieff and Galbraithian models are constructed. In order to demonstrate that psychological factors are also capable of explaining cyclical behavior, Katona's and Schumpeter's theories are described.

Chapter 14 emphasizes the Harrod-Domar theory of growth. Presentations include the view that income distribution determines the national savings rate. The chapter applies this model to both developed and developing countries. Also, the razor's edge is presented as a problem resulting from decentralized decision-making.

Chapter 15 contrasts the marxian and neo-classical competitive models, applying each to problems of agriculture and racial discrimination. The marxian theories of uneven development and alienation are discussed.

Chapter 16 presents the theoretical foundations of marxian crisis theory. In particular, class struggle and overinvestment theories are developed to illustrate the marxian falling rate of profit thesis.

Chapter 17 applies the radical analysis to recent U.S. experience. It contrasts Nordhaus and Feldstein explanations for profit rate declines with marxian theories.

Chapter 18 provides a full treatment of marxian underconsumptionist theories. Marxian reproduction schema are described, as well as a complete review of the history of underconsumptionist views. The Baran and Sweezy model is critically discussed.

Chapter 19 brings the discussion of inflation into the formal analysis. The Keynesian Phillips Curve analysis is presented, as well as mainstream and radical critiques. The chapter highlights the factors which influence the shape of the shortrun Phillips Curve and empirical methods of distinguishing between the natural rate and reserve army theories.

Chapter 20 indicates how each viewpoint characterizes the distributional and production effects of inflation. It also identifies and contrasts various forms of government intervention, such as TIP and wage-price control legislation.

Chapter 21 provides a unifying summary of the various viewpoints and theories presented in the book.

SUGGESTED COURSE OUTLINE

The following twelve chapters provide the core for most outlines:

1. Introduction
2. The Degree of Unemployment
4. Production, Income, and Spending
5. Simple Mainstream Macroeconomic Model
6. Consumption
8. The Government Sector
9. Capital Spending, Equilibrium, and the Interest Rate
10. The Money Market
13. Structuralist Models of Capital Spending
14. Economic Growth
16. Marxian Crisis Theory
19. Theories of Inflation

Other chapters can be added depending upon interests and skills of students. Chapters 11 and 12 complete the discussion of interest rate and price effects within the IS-LM framework; Chapters 7, 18 and 20 extend the analysis of how income shares influence and are influenced by economic performance; while Chapters 3, 15, and 17 extend the radical analysis. Regardless of the outline used, Chapter 21 provides a summary of the issues and explanations presented in this book.

A guide to symbols is presented at the back of the book so that students can quickly make sure of the notation being used regardless of the chapters covered.

Brooklyn, N.Y.   R. D. C.
August 1979

ACKNOWLEDGMENTS

Much of the analytical precision which I hope this book contains, reflects my graduate work at Purdue and Kansas, especially the training provided by my dissertation advisors James Quirk and Rubin Saposnik.

Many reviewers offered invaluable suggestions. In particular, I would like to thank James Fackler (University of Kentucky), Brian Stanhouse (Notre Dame), and Robert Murphy (University of South Florida) for their comments on the consumption function and money market chapters. The successive economics editors at Addison-Wesley, Marshall Aronson and George Abbott, were especially helpful in obtaining useful reviews and facilitating the writing process. Linda Bedell provided the continuity necessary to keep the process running smoothly and made sure that loose ends did not create distractions.

I was fortunate to have a conducive work environment at Brooklyn College. Despite the financial chaos plaguing the CUNY system, Bonnie Gustav, Ed Marcus, and Nathan Schmukler provided as much tranquility and support administratively possible. My colleagues, particularly Abe Hirsch and David Laibman, provided a sounding board for many ideas as well as many useful comments.

I would like to thank George Tzannetakis (Seton Hall) for allowing the manuscript to be student tested, and Pat Clawson (Seton Hall) for using it and providing important feedback.

David Gordon (New School) and William Tabb (Queens) provided encouragement, time, and advise during the early stages of this project. However, more than anyone else, Jim Crotty (University of Massachusetts, Amherst) made this book possible. His support, painstaking commentaries on both the general presentations and individual arguments, and his advice at every stage of the project were invaluable.

I acknowledge the permission granted by The Survey Research Center of the University of Michigan to reproduce Figure 13.5 from George Katona and

Burkhard Strumpel, "Consumer Investment Versus Business Investment," in *Challenge of Economics,* edited by Myron E. Sharpe (1977).

Finally, my wife Shelley has to adapt to the ups and downs of my academic career, and without her quiet encouragement this project would never have been started.

CONTENTS

CHAPTER ONE

INTRODUCTION

Capitalist societies, characterized by private ownership of productive assets, dominated the world during the nineteenth century. However, during the twentieth century a number of countries rejected the capitalist development path and, instead, adopted some form of socialist development. Debates over the relative efficacy of these alternative paths are more than academic; wars have been and continue to be fought over the choice of paths to be taken. Therefore, studying the workings of a capitalist society has profound philosophical as well as practical importance.

1.1 THE RISE AND FALL OF THE KEYNESIAN REVOLUTION[1]

One aspect of this debate questions the ability of capitalist societies to sustain balanced growth with full employment of labor. Conservatives contend that a capitalist society, without government intervention, is capable of such balanced growth. This viewpoint began with Adam Smith. It assumes that market mechanisms operate to quickly offset any deviations away from balanced growth. Therefore, fluctuations are viewed as minor shortrun variations which, at first approximation, may be justifiably neglected.

The Great Depression dealt this viewpoint a staggering blow. The collapse itself was "easily" explained by the faithful in a variety of ways; what was inexplicable was the fact that the system did not seem to exhibit any tendency to snap back to the "normal" full employment equilibrium. As the Depression dragged on and social unrest deepened, this laissez-faire theory fell increasingly into disrepute and Keynesian theory rapidly took its place.

Keynes attacked the orthodox notion that "supply creates its own demand" since it was this notion which led to the conclusion that capitalism

---

1. The organization of this section and some of the material comes from Anwar Shaikh, "An Introduction to the History of Crisis Theory," *U.S. Capitalism in Crisis* (New York: URPE, 1978), pp. 219–240.

tended automatically to fully utilize the available labor and means of production. Specifically, in the labor market the wage rate would adjust so that the supply of labor would equilibrate with the demand for labor. In financial markets, the funds that households were unwilling to spend (savings) would equilibrate with the funds that firms desired to borrow for capital spending through movements of the interest rate. In this way if a deviation should momentarily create unemployment and a shortage of demand, wage rates would decline, which would increase the demand for labor. And, interest rates would decline, which would increase business expenditures on capital goods.

Keynes claimed that neither the labor nor the financial markets were as smoothly equilibrating as laissez-faire advocates believed. In particular, Keynes claimed that the decision to borrow funds for capital spending purposes was only marginally affected by the cost of borrowing. Keynes believed that in a capitalist economy with decentralized decision-making it was impossible for corporations to be provided with the information about the future behavior of prices, costs, markets, technology, etc., which would be needed in order to make rational and sound judgments concerning investment programs. That is, in a capitalist society there is no way, even in principle, for a corporation (or wealthy individual) to know what composition of assets, real and financial, will be most profitable or least unprofitable. In the absence of hard information about the future, the corporation is *forced* to commit large amounts of funds into risky investments on the basis of little more than "faith" in the future, or a gambling instinct, or "animal spirits." Thus, according to Keynes, expectations (which behave like "animal spirits") are produced by the structure of capitalism inherent in it, and have nothing to do with the individual investor's psychology per se.

Two important conclusions follow from this. First, since expectations are notoriously volatile, capitalist societies are likely to have quite erratic economic movements. Second and even more important, there exists no automatic mechanism within capitalism which would make capitalists plan just the right amount of investment so as to assure full employment production. Finally, since only planning could eliminate the basis for the volatile expectations inherent in market decision-making, Keynes urged a movement towards planning at both the domestic and international level.

The so-called Keynesian Revolution was an ambivalent one, however. Much of the foundation of Keynes' analysis was the same as that of the orthodoxy he attacked: the division of society into producers and consumers (not capitalists and workers); the crucial importance of psychological propensities and preferences; the role of supply and demand; and the general reliance on equilibrium analysis. Because of this, many economists argued that Keynes' theory could be absorbed into an expanded version of neo-classical orthodoxy. Conceding that there were some problems with the market adjustment process, the neo-classical Keynesians turned to the State as the mechanism which would bring to life the society pictured in the laissez-faire parables. If the State did its job well, it would manipulate aggregate demand so as to maintain near full employment with little or no inflation. With this modification, the rest of the doctrine of the orthodoxy could be revived.

By the 1950s, the neo-classical Keynesian viewpoint was the unchallenged theory within the economic profession. It claimed that while a laissez-faire capitalist society was incapable of balanced growth, only limited government intervention was necessary to insure the fulfillment of this objective. The only question which remained was which type of government intervention was most effective. Neo-classical Keynesians were divided into two camps—monetary policy advocates and fiscalists. Monetary policy advocates claimed that the most effective instrument was government adjustments of the money supply. Fiscalists claimed that direct spending by the government or tax cuts to households was the most effective. This minor technical conflict was reduced even more when Samuelson announced his post-Keynesian synthesis, which indicated that *either* set of policies could be effective.

The dominance of the neo-classical Keynesian view reached its pinnacle during the Kennedy Administration. During the early 1960s, despite government economic deficits, the economy continued to experience a period of sluggish growth. Corporate leaders desired government stimulation, especially tax relief for businesses. Thus, the corporate community adopted the Keynesian argument because government stimulation at the time was compatible with their objectives. Kennedy accepted the neo-classical Keynesian prescription, which proposed increasing the deficit in order to stimulate growth and employment. The apparent success of Keynesian policies was hailed as the triumph of an idea whose time had come.

However, at the same time that this success was occurring, conservative laissez-faire advocates began mounting a counterattack. Milton Friedman and Anna Schwartz claimed that the duration of the Great Depression was a result of a series of government policy errors rather than the inability of market mechanisms to insure full employment.[2] According to their "evidence," each time the private market was beginning to rebound, government intervention would destabilize the economy. The conservative laissez-faire position now claimed that government deficit spending did not stimulate growth nor increase employment. Rather, deficit spending, by shifting funds from the private sector to the government, resulted in a decline in capital spending which fully offset the government stimuli. Hence, deficit spending only led to a "crowding out" of capital spending by government and/or household spending. Therefore, while government deficit spending might not hurt the economy in the shortrun, it has serious damaging effects in the longrun through its constraining effect on business capital spending.

At the same time, left-liberals began criticizing the substantial reliance on market mechanism by neo-classical Keynesians. John Kenneth Galbraith claimed that we live in the *New Industrial State* in which large corporations

---

2. Milton Friedman and Anna Schwartz, *A Monetary History of the United States* (Princeton: Princeton University Press, 1963).

dictate market conditions rather than respond to competitive forces. Pierro Sraffa demonstrated that even if markets were competitive, technological considerations make it impossible to predict the effect of market mechanisms on capital investment decisions. Also, input-output techniques which emphasize the importance of technological considerations became a popular method of planning the direct and indirect effects of government economic decisions at the industry and regional level. This group argued that ad hoc government intervention which: (1) relied on the general effectiveness of private market mechanisms, (2) ignored the role of the large corporation, (3) ignored the characteristics of modern technology, and (4) ignored the effects of income distribution among groups in society would be doomed to failure. Left-liberals claimed that widespread economic planning was both possible and necessary if capitalism was going to be able to sustain balanced growth with full employment.

During this period, responding to the anti-racist and anti-war sentiment on college campuses, there began a renaissance of interest in radical economics. This viewpoint claimed that fundamental contradictions make it impossible for a capitalist society, with or without extensive government intervention, to sustain balanced growth. According to radicals,

> The contradictions in [capitalist] systems are such that balanced, full employment growth cannot be sustained. When an economic expansion reaches the stage of relatively full employment, a whole series of distortions and imbalances develop which destroy the basis for the continuation of that expansion. For example, increased worker militancy at full employment results in an increase in wage rates and a reduction in the rate of growth of productivity. Inflation accelerates, but not by enough to prevent profit margins from starting to decline. Corporations are forced to turn increasingly to external sources in order to finance investment in plant and equipment and inventories. Debt thus accumulates just at the time when interest rates are highest. Moreover, serious balance-of-trade problems develop as the rising price of U.S. products retards exports and, aided by strong aggregate U.S. demand, stimulates imports.

> It is the economic function of the recession to correct the imbalances of the previous expansion and thereby create the preconditions for a new one. By robbing millions of people of their jobs, and threatening the jobs of millions of others, recessions erode worker militancy and end the rise of labor costs. They eventually rebuild profit margins and stabilize prices. . . . recessions are inevitable in the unplanned economy of the United States because they perform an essential function for which no adequate substitute has thus far been available.[3]

----

3. Raford Boddy and James Crotty, "Who Will Plan the Planned Economy," in *Economics: Mainstream Readings and Radical Critiques,* David Mermelstein (New York: Random House, 1976), p. 265.

The final blow to the hegenomy of neo-classical Keynesian views was the collapse of the economy in 1974 and the inability of the subsequent recovery to correct all of the underlying weaknesses—inflation, unemployment, capital spending sluggishness, and balance-of-trade deficits. Ad hoc government intervention, such as one-time tax cuts or government countercyclical job creation, fell into disrepute within government and professional circles. Increasingly, the economics profession is being polarized to support one of the alternatives to the neo-classical Keynesian view. On the one hand, laissez-faire views, as reflected in the explosion of economics textbooks from that perspective, have again become respectable and attractive explanations within the profession. Following the Friedman and Schwartz thesis, the persistence of economic problems are the result of government intervention. All would be well if the government were to stop mismanaging the economy.

On the other hand, increasing numbers of economists have been attracted to the left-liberal and radical views. For example, a group of mainstream economists, including three Nobel Prize winners, together with liberal labor leaders and corporate executives, formed the Initiative Committee on Economic Planning. Their stated objective was to create a forum for the discussion of the possibility of economic planning in the United States. Already, the energy program proposed by President Carter in 1977 attempted to incorporate some forms of economic planning.

The turn of events has created an exciting opportunity for economics students. No longer can macroeconomics be presented as a dismal science in which all of the major questions have been answered—and where the only problem is to find the correct values to place in the prescribed formulas. Macroeconomics again deals with fundamental questions, and again has conflicts which reflect broadly differing views on the role of the federal government in a capitalist society.

1.2 ECLECTICISM

This textbook takes an eclectic approach to the study of macroeconomics. Eclecticism implies much more than presenting different views. It implies that views which are in significant conflict with each other are presented. For a long time, macroeconomics has been characterized by the "conflict" between monetary policy advocates and those who advocate the use of fiscal policy. As the preceding section indicated, while these positions are different, they are not in conflict. Both the monetary policy and fiscal policy viewpoints agree that some form of government intervention to regulate aggregate spending is *necessary and sufficient* to sustain full employment. To present monetary versus fiscal policy as the only different views in economics is to ignore all of the alternative competing macroeconomic theories. On the one hand, it ignores the conservative views which claim that government intervention is *not necessary* to sustain full employment since competitive market forces automatically generate full employment. On the other hand, it ignores the left views which claim that government regulation of aggregate spending is *not sufficient* since government planning and regulation of the labor process are necessary if full employment is to be sustained.

The need for an eclectic approach can be justified for a number of reasons. First, there has been a theoretical vacuum created by the volatility of capitalist economies since the mid-1960s. Keynesian economics, at least in its widely-held version, has increasingly been criticized for its inability to explain and/or reduce this volatility. In this situation, it would be counterproductive to explore only one set of macroeconomic theories. Eclecticism can thus be justified as insurance against only concentrating on the wrong theoretical framework.

Second, eclecticism can be justified as a response to the increasing complexity of the real world. For example, it may be that each of the theoretical frameworks can give useful insights into specific issues in macroeconomics—Keynesianism into unemployment problems; conservatives into inflation problems; and left-views into balanced growth problems. Thus, eclecticism is justified in order to guard against making "simplistic one-dimensional" observations concerning complex economic issues.

Third, it is necessary to analyze differing macroeconomic frameworks if we wish to fully understand the underlying economic basis for differing political viewpoints. We will find that the major political viewpoints rely on widely-differing, often mutually exclusive, economic theories. In this textbook the major distinctions will be made between mainstream theories and left-view theories. Mainstream theories will be divided into conservative and mainstream-liberal variations. These mainstream theories are the most well-recognized views in the United States, and reflect the underlying rationales for the principal economic policies recommended by the Democratic and Republican parties. The left-view theories are divided into left-liberal and radical variations. These left-view theories are widely-held in Western Europe and by many economists in the United States. They reflect the underlying rationales most often espoused by European Social Democratic and Marxist parties, as well as by an increasingly influential group within the United States.

Statistical Testing

Economists often rely on statistical tests in deciding which theory should be emphasized in their economic models. It is assumed that these tests provide a value-free method of determining the theory which most accurately reflects reality. According to this viewpoint, the development of better data-gathering techniques and more refined statistical tests are the only roadblocks which keep economics from eliminating all value judgments—from becoming a pure science.[4]

---

4. Paul Samuelson presents economics as a value-free science in his section, "The Queen of the Social Sciences," in which he suggests that "to commemorate the com-

The problem with this conception of economics is that it ignores the central distinction between economics and pure sciences, such as chemistry. Economics differs from pure sciences in that the actual data is subject to value judgments. In chemistry there is only one measure of salt, NaCl. Regardless of the political views of the chemist, this is the one measure used. The same cannot be said for most of the critical measures used by economists, such as the measure of poverty and unemployment. Numerous studies in numerous fields of economics have demonstrated that statistical results are often extremely sensitive to the measures adopted; results would be dramatically different if alternative measures were used.

During the 1960s there developed widespread concern over the extent, causes, and solutions to poverty in the United States. One important focus was to measure the extent of poverty. If the official government measure of poverty-level income is used, we find that during the 1960s the poverty population was relatively small (15% of all households) and declining.[5] If instead, the government's higher *Moderate-but-Adequate* income measure is used, we would find that the poverty population was relatively large (more than 50% of all households) and growing.[6] Finally, if we used Victor Fuchs' relative measure,

---

ing of age of economics as a science a new Nobel Prize in economics was instituted in 1969." *Economics,* 8th ed. (New York: McGraw-Hill, 1970), p. 5.

Gunnar Myrdal, co-winner of the 1974 Nobel Prize in economics, and a long-time member of the Swedish Academy of Science, which is responsible for the designation of Nobel Prize recipients in all the natural sciences, rejects the view that economics should be considered a science. Myrdal contends that economics can never exclude value judgments. For this reason, he believes that political judgments will dictate the Nobel Prize awards in economics. In order to protect the scientific reputation of its awards in the pure sciences he proposed that the Academy terminate the economics award. Gunnar Myrdal, "The Nobel Prize in Economic Science," *Challenge* 20 (Mar./Apr. 1977): 50–52.

5. The government's poverty budget is an estimate of the amount of money required by a family of four to purchase all the necessities of life. Only if a household has less income than required to buy the poverty budget does the government consider the household to be living in "poverty." In 1968, the government's poverty budget was estimated to be about $3500. The 1974 revision estimated the budget to be about $5000. This 1974 budget allows for food expenditures of only $1.15 per person per day; and housing costs (rental, utilities, and operating expenses) of about $120 per month. Using the government official measure, the percentage of U.S. households living in poverty fell from 22% in 1959 to 13% by 1968 (and to 12% by 1974).

6. Many critics consider the government's poverty budget to be totally inadequate and instead use the government's *Moderate-but-Adequate* budget as the minimum income required to avoid poverty. According to this budget, the percentage of households living in poverty rose from 30% in 1959 to 59% in 1968. In 1968, the Bureau of Labor Statistics revised *downwards* the budget which it then characterized as *Low-Moderate-but-Adequate*. This new budget, in 1974, allowed households to spend $1.76 per person per day on food, $132 per month for rent and utilities, and similarly meager allowances for clothing, transportation, and medical care. Even using this meager budget as the cut-off for poverty, 30% of all U.S. households were considered living in poverty in 1974.

we would find that the poverty population was stable at about 25% of all households.[7]

No amount of data-gathering nor statistical refinements could help us determine which of these measures more accurately reflects poverty. These are political and philosophical questions which cannot be resolved by further technical developments. Hence, it is impossible to separate political and philosophical views through statistical testing.

The choice of measure is important because it gives a basic evaluation of economic performance. If the size of the poverty population were small and declining, we have a basically different attitude towards the free market system than if it were large and growing. It is also important because the explanations of poverty could vary dramatically with the choice of measure. This was the basic finding of a study of poverty undertaken by Oscar Ornati.[8]

Ornati attempted to explain why some metropolitan areas had relatively little poverty and others had a large amount of poverty. When Ornati used a low measure of poverty, the racial composition of the metropolitan area was the most important explanatory factor. Those metropolitan areas which had a larger percentage of nonwhites tended to have a larger percentage of their population with incomes below the poverty level. When Ornati used a somewhat higher measure of poverty, the most important explanatory factor was the average educational level. Those metropolitan areas with higher educational levels tended to have a smaller percentage of their population with incomes below the poverty level. Finally, when he used an even higher measure of poverty, he found the most important explanatory variable was the type of jobs available. Those metropolitan areas which had the greatest number of high-wage industrial jobs (auto, steel, etc.) tended to have the lowest percentage of population living below the poverty level. Thus, depending upon the measure of poverty used, race, education, or jobs available were the most important factors in explaining the extent of poverty.

In macroeconomics each viewpoint differs as to the amount of unemployment a capitalist society normally experiences. Conservatives claim that competitive market forces automatically create full employment. Mainstream liberals claim that without government intervention there will be periods of significant unemployment. Left-liberals claim that unemployment rates would be higher in unplanned economies, such as the United States, than in planned capitalist economies, such as Sweden or West Germany. Radicals claim that

---

7. Victor Fuchs and others have argued that poverty is a relative condition rather than an absolute condition. Fuchs proposed that all households which had incomes of less than one-half the national average should be considered to be living in poverty.

8. Oscar Ornati, "Poverty in the Cities," in *Issues in Urban Economics,* Harvey S. Perloff & Lowden Wings, Jr., eds. (Baltimore: Johns Hopkins, 1968), p. 351. Ornati used $3,000 as his low measure of poverty, $4,000 as his high measure, and $5,000 as his highest measure of poverty.

there must always be a significant amount of unemployment in capitalist economies and periodically it will be very high due to recurring economic crises.

It would seem then that by comparing the actual unemployment rates to each view's predictions we could make some value-free judgment as to which theories seem to be consistent and which theories are inconsistent with reality. However, as Chapter 2 demonstrates, each view can define the unemployment rate in such a way as to support its general contentions. Hence, it is impossible to use unemployment data as a means of judging in a value-free manner the relative merits of each viewpoint.

This, of course, does not mean that statistical testing is totally without value. It is meant to indicate that one cannot claim that statistical tests are value-free or that further technical advances in data-gathering and/or econometric techniques will improve the scientific nature of testing. In particular, this indicates that one cannot dismiss any of the major views developed in this textbook solely because of statistical results. Statistical results will be included where appropriate, but will never be used to "prove" the correctness or incorrectness of various macroeconomic theories.

CHAPTER TWO

THE DEGREE OF UNEMPLOYMENT

Chapter 1 indicated that there is fundamental conflict between economists over the workings of a capitalist system. Conservative and mainstream liberal economists contend that a private market economy is basically well-working, requiring at most some minor government intervention in order to guarantee full employment. Left-liberal and radical economists claim that a private market economy is characterized by recurring periods of high unemployment that only extensive government intervention can solve.

Chapter 1 also noted that the underlying analysis of each of the viewpoints differed. Conservatives emphasize individual choice. Individual decision-makers acting in a society with limited barriers, according to their psychological determined set of preferences, are able to maximize their satisfaction. Within this framework, if unemployment exists it is because individuals choose to be unemployed.

The radical outlook emphasizes the marxian concepts of class struggle and exploitation. Class struggle over the distribution of income is considered the primary factor which explains economic outcomes. This marxist view discounts psychological factors and the role of individual choice. If workers are unemployed it is a result of the profit motive of the capitalist system. Indeed, marxists contend that unemployment is inherent in a capitalist system.

Liberals, to varying degrees, consider technological and institutional factors to be of significant importance. They argue that with industrialization and urbanization, society became more interdependent and sensitive to technological change. Mainstream liberals tend to emphasize individual choice and place secondary importance on these factors. Left-liberals consider technological and institutional factors to be the primary determinants of the normal level of unemployment.

It might appear that the controversy over the size of unemployment in a capitalist society can be resolved by referring to the official measure of unemployment, published monthly by the government. To determine the unemployment rate, the government must divide the working age population (ages 16–64) into three groups: (1) employed, E; (2) unemployed but seeking work, U; and (3) unemployed but not seeking work, U'. The government then defines the unemployment rate as the ratio $U/(U+E)$ and the labor force participation rate as the ratio $(U+E)/(U+E+U')$.

A major problem with the government's measure is that it is often very difficult to make a distinction between those who are voluntarily unemployed (U') and those who are involuntarily unemployed (U).[1] The difficulty occurs because of the need to select a criteria to judge willingness to work. The government requires an unemployed worker to apply for a specific job at least once every four weeks to be considered willing to work.

A second issue concerns the relative importance of unemployment. Should we consider the unemployment of unskilled workers to be the same as skilled workers; of secondary workers the same as head-of-household workers; of teenagers the same as prime-age workers? The government official measure counts everyone who is unemployed the same.

A third issue is the treatment of part-time employment. How should we treat those workers who are unemployed but seek part-time employment; those who are employed part-time but seek full-time employment? The government official measure counts unemployed workers seeking part-time employment as unemployed, and part-time workers seeking full-time work as employed.

This chapter will discuss how each of the viewpoints evaluates the government's official measure of unemployment and detail more fully their explanations for unemployment in a private market system.

2.1 MAINSTREAM THEORIES OF UNEMPLOYMENT

The concepts of well-working markets, freedom of choice, and consumer sovereignty all require that the economy is fully employed. Only then would households have some choice over employment, income, and purchasing power. Both conservative and mainstream liberal economists accept this viewpoint as being the best generalization of the U.S. economy. For example, according to Arthur Okun, a mainstream liberal economist who was a member of the Council of Economic Advisors during the Kennedy and Johnson Administrations,

---

1. If some individuals are incorrectly shifted from the involuntary to voluntary unemployed category, the laborforce participation rate as well as the unemployment rate would be reduced. Hence, some economists, as discussed in this chapter, contend that laborforce participation rates can be used to correct inaccuracies in official unemployment rates. For example, a sudden drop in laborforce participation rates would tend to indicate that the government is overestimating the level of voluntary employment and, hence, underestimating the level of involuntary employment.

Our economic rules are meant to encourage effort and channel it into socially productive activity. In principle the best-paying jobs are those adding the greatest value to products sold in the marketplace. Pursuing their own choices, workers respond to the signals of what society values most and is willing to pay for. . . . This snapshot of capitalist economy is, of course, heavily retouched and idealized . . . Yet the resemblance between the contemporary American economy and the glorified model are more striking than the contrasts.[2]

Not surprisingly, mainstream economists contend that the official unemployment rate vastly overestimates the degree of underutilized labor in the U.S. economy. Also, they claim that government intervention in the labor market is responsible for raising the amount of unemployment in the economy.

The Natural Unemployment Rate

Mainstream economists reject the notion that any economy is necessarily underutilizing labor when unemployment exists. They claim that in any market economy there is some natural barrier to lowering unemployment. The term *natural rate of unemployment* signifies this minimum level of unemployment possible.

Historically, the most extreme justification for a natural unemployment rate was the alleged genetic inferiority of certain racial groups. At the turn of the century, conservative economists, particularly Irving Fisher and Frank A. Fetter, claimed that the United States was engaging in "race suicide" through its immigration policies. They claimed that the genetic stock of the new immigrants, rather than the economic system, was the cause of rising unemployment, poverty, and crime.[3]

Today, this view is summed up in the words of Harvard psychologist Richard Herrnstein who contends, "unemployment runs in the genes just as bad teeth."[4] The genetic view of unemployment is found in Campbell McConnell's widely-used textbook. According to the author,

Some individuals have had the good fortune to inherit the exceptional mental qualities essential to entering the . . . fields of medicine, dentistry, and law. Others, rated as "dull normal" or "mentally retarded" are assigned to the most menial and low-paying jobs or are incapable of earning income at all.[5]

---

2. Arthur Okun, "Equal Rights But Unequal Incomes," *New York Times* (July 4, 1976): p. 101.

3. For a survey of the racial views of economists at the turn of the century, see Robert Cherry, "Racial Thought and the Early Economics Profession," *Review of Social Economy* 35 (Oct. 1975): 147–161.

4. Richard Herrnstein, *I.Q. in the Meritocracy* (Boston: Little Brown, 1973).

5. C. McConnell, *Economics,* 5th ed. (New York: McGraw-Hill, 1973), p. 659.

Recently, conservative economists Gary Becker and Jack Hirshleifer have reintroduced Irving Fisher's views that not only unemployment but all social behavior is genetically determined. This view, then called *instinct theory* and now called *sociobiology,* claims that—just like ant-colonies—human social behavior is genetically programmed for survival of the family specie. *Business Week* commenting on this ideological resurgence in the economics profession said,

> *Economists are just beginning to apply the principles of sociobiology. And there is no hard evidence to support the theory. Yet, bioeconomics provides a powerful defense of Adam Smith's laissez-faire views . . . [and] other economists contend that it will be used as a rationale for conservative economic policies.*[6]

Most mainstream economists do not defend the concept of a natural rate of unemployment on the basis of genetics. Instead, they argue that the natural rate is above zero because at any point in time there will be workers between jobs and employers seeking new hires. The natural rate of unemployment is considered to be the rate at which the total number of jobseekers exactly equals the total number of jobs available—when the unemployment rate just equals the job vacancy rate. At that point, the economy has provided jobs equal to the total size of the workforce. The remaining unemployment reflects the necessary labor market selection process in a free society. According to this viewpoint, only when the unemployment rate is above its natural rate does the economy fail to provide enough jobs. Hence, it is the gap between the official unemployment rate and the natural rate which represents a measure of the underutilization of labor.

The natural rate is a critical concept for mainstream economics because it allows them to assume away a significant amount of unemployment.[7] During the 1960s, the natural rate was assumed to be 4% and, with the rise of unemployment in the 1970s, the natural rate rose to 6%.[8] If one accepts these values for the natural unemployment rate, then capitalism is indeed well-working.

Conservative Explanations[9]

Conservative economists always emphasize that individual choice dictates economic outcomes. Since the 1970s witnessed a rising unemployment rate, conservative economists began developing explanations as to why individuals were choosing more unemployment. Robert Lekachman critically observed,

---

6. "A Genetic Defense of the Free Market," *Business Week* (April 10, 1978): 100–101.

7. By *ignore* I mean that it allows them to shift the blame away from the inadequacies of the capitalist system.

8. For a radical discussion of the changes in the natural unemployment rate, see William Tabb, "Explaining Away the Crisis," *Radical Perspectives on the Economic Crisis* (New York: URPE, 1975), pp. 163–168.

*As they did in the 1950s, [conservative] economists discovered all over
again lots of people are simply unemployable, so that 5 or 6 percent
unemployment is not something to be alarmed about. The unemployed
are dumb, illiterate, immoral, lazy, or some unattractive combination
of these qualities.*[10]

Some economists claim that the rising natural unemployment rate is due
to the loss of a work ethic among the current generation of unskilled workers.
McConnell offers the following explanation,

*Most of the poor are ultimately responsible for their circumstances.
They have forfeited away their educational opportunities. They . . .
won't enroll in retraining programs. They . . . refuse to move (to
obtain better jobs). Some are poor because they are slothful or lazy.*[11]

This view follows the work of Edward Banfield who claims,

*. . . the lower-class individual lives from moment to moment. . . .
Whatever he cannot use immediately he considers valueless. His bodily
needs (especially for sex) and his taste for "action" take precedence
over everything else—and certainly over any work routine. . . . [He]
lives in the slum, which, to a greater extent, is an expression of his life-
style. . . . He is not troubled by dirt and dilapidation and he does not
mind the inadequacies of public facilities such as schools, parks, hos-
pitals, and libraries; indeed, where such things exist he may destroy
them by carelessness or even vandalism.*[12]

Others claim it is due to the rising expectations of the poor. According to
Samuelson,

*Whether black or white, [individuals] will not take dirty, low-paid jobs
the way they used to. . . . Examine the graduating class of an innercity high school. You will find in it hundreds of girls aspiring to be
typists and secretaries rather than housemaids and beauticians. Aspira-
tions are elevated, but at the same time if one examines performance
on standardized tests, only a few can type or take dictation at rates
required for successful employment. And so you have a measure of dis-
content and one explanation of unemployment.*[13]

---

9. Extreme conservatives rely on a genetic argument to justify the rising unemployment rate. Their analysis emphasizes the alleged genetic inferiority of blacks. Since
economists do not make explicit reference to this view, it will be ignored.

10. Robert Lekachman, *Inflation* (New York: Random House, 1973), p. 42.

11. McConnell, *Economics,* p. 669.

12. Edward Banfield, *The Unheavenly City Revisited* (Boston: Little Brown, 1973),
p. 63.

13. P. Samuelson, *Economics,* 8th ed. (New York: McGraw-Hill, 1970), p. 788.

The most widely-held theory of the rising natural unemployment rate is the job search theory first formulated by Edmund Phelps.[14] It claims that households potentially benefit from refusing a job and, hence, benefit from having a higher rate of unemployment. Imagine an individual being offered a job at $5 an hour. If this individual perceives that his talents are worth $6 an hour it would pay for him to wait for a more appropriate job offer. His extra time being unemployed would be more than compensated for by the higher hourly wage rate. There are, of course, costs involved with refusal so that if the individual does not find a $6 an hour job soon, he may lower his expectations. However, according to this thesis, it is quite rational and beneficial for workers to spend time searching rather than accepting the first job offer.

The job search theory is particularly attractive, because unlike the McConnell or Samuelson philosophies, it considers the natural level of unemployment to be rational and socially beneficial rather than pathological. The job search theory is capable of explaining the rise in the natural unemployment rate.

Job search time is particularly long for those workers who are entering or reentering the labor market. These workers usually have difficulty assessing accurately their market value so it takes time for them to determine their best possible job. Also, they often have less than average knowledge about possible vacancies so that it takes them longer to find their potential positions. Historically, women and teenagers have disproportionately higher numbers of new entrants and reentrants into the labor market than adult males. For example, in 1974, 21% of the adult male unemployed workforce were either new entrants or reentrants, while the figure was 44% and 68% for women and teenagers, respectively. This indicates that as the percentage of the laborforce composed of adult males decreased, the average job search time of unemployed workers increased.[15] In this way, the job search theory explains the alleged increase in the natural unemployment rate during the last twenty years.

Mainstream Liberal Explanations

Mainstream liberals claim that technological factors rather than individual choice explains the rising natural unemployment rate. They claim that technological changes have resulted in a greater mismatch between job seekers and job vacancies so that more unemployment will naturally occur. This type of unemployment is usually called *structural unemployment*. Mainstream liberals most often cite increasing automation and changing location patterns of industry as the reasons for growing structural unemployment and, hence, a rising natural unemployment rate.

---

14. See Edmund S. Phelps et al., *Microeconomic Foundations of Employment and Inflation Theory* (New York: Norton, 1970).

15. Between 1955 and 1974, the percentage of young workers and adult women increased from 40.2% to 52.6% of the laborforce.

The *Kerner Commission Report on Civil Disorders* claimed automation has resulted in an increasing mismatch between the capabilities of rural migrants and industrial skill requirements. It said,

> *When the European immigrants were arriving in large numbers, America was becoming an urban-industrial society. To build its major cities and industries, America needed great pools of unskilled labor. Since World War II . . . America's urban-industrial society has matured; unskilled labor is far less essential than before, and blue-collar jobs of all kinds are decreasing in numbers and importance as sources of new employment; . . . The Negro migrant, unlike the immigrant, found little opportunity in the city; he had arrived too late, and the unskilled labor he had to offer was no longer needed.*[16]

If skill level requirements have been rising, then any increase in the percentage of unskilled workers in the laborforce would increase the natural unemployment rate. Since adult women and teenagers have below-average skill levels, as their numbers within the laborforce have increased so has the natural unemployment rate.[17]

This indicates that both mainstream liberals and conservatives agree that the changing composition of the laborforce is the reason for the rising natural unemployment rate. They both consider the high rates of adult female and teenage unemployment to be natural and nothing to be concerned about.[18] They only disagree as to why these groups should have higher rates. Conservatives argue it is because these groups spend more time searching for the best job. Mainstream liberals argue that it is because these groups do not have the necessary skill requirements.

Besides skill mismatches, mainstream liberals also contend that technology has increased the number of locational mismatches. The development of more efficient transportation networks has decreased the attractiveness of central city locations. Moreover, technology has made it more profitable to use assembly-line techniques which require one-floor operations, making central city multi-floor industrial buildings unsuitable. For these technical reasons, an

---

16. *Kerner Commission on Civil Disorders* (New York: Bantam Books, 1968), p. 278.

17. We should note that conservatives reject this explanation. They argue that automation, by segmenting jobs and making them more narrow and repetitive, has actually *reduced* necessary skill levels. Harvard economist Thomas Sowell claims that "many jobs are becoming *simpler* to the point of boredom. . . . There is no indication that most jobs are beyond the intellectual range of anyone above the level of mental retardation." Thomas Sowell, *Black Education: Myths and Realities* (New York: MacKay, 1972).

18. Mainstream liberals, such as George Perry, have even taken to revising the unemployment rate to discount unemployment of women, teenagers, and implicitly, blacks. For Perry's method, see "Changing Labor Markets and Inflation," *Brookings Papers* (1970): 411–441.

increasing amount of industrial production has moved to suburban industrial rings rather than remain in the city business district. However, because of financial and institutional constraints, low-skilled industrial workers continue to live in the city. Thus, a mismatch between the location of job vacancies and the location of unemployed workers is created, increasing the amount of structural unemployment.

2.2 MAINSTREAM VIEWS ON GOVERNMENT INTERVENTION

Government-Induced Market Distortions

Both mainstream liberals and conservatives claim that government intervention in the labor market reduces the effective supply of labor (by distorting work incentives); thus, raising the natural unemployment rate. The two government policies most often cited are minimum wage legislation and unemployment compensation.

Minimum wage legislation In a perfectly competitive economy the unemployment caused by a mismatch of skills and jobs would not be very serious. Unskilled workers' wage rates would decline until it became profitable to hire them. Mainstream economists claim that one factor which limits the ability to lower the wage rate until this point is reached is minimum wage legislation. A higher minimum wage rate is alleged to create more unemployment because:

1. Prices would have to rise disproportionately for those firms whose laborforce is heavily unskilled labor. Consumers would then shift their demand away from these goods, thus lowering the demand for unskilled workers.

2. Firms would shift away from domestic labor to alternative sources of production, such as machinery or cheaper foreign labor.

In both cases, minimum wage legislation accelerates the declining demand for unskilled labor and thereby increases the mismatch of jobs and workers.[19]

---

19. If the demand for labor is inelastic, then a higher minimum wage raises the *total wages* paid while reducing the number of hours worked. Hence, a higher minimum wage can be beneficial to the entire group of low-wage workers because their objective is total wages, not employment. Moreover, it has often been argued that higher minimum wage rates increases purchasing power, which in turn stimulates total spending. This implies that the demand for labor would be increased as a result of an increase in the minimum wage. For example, in its *Report of the Annual Meeting* (June 20, 1974), F. W. Woolworth Company directors contend, ". . . Our experience with prior minimum wage legislation shows that our salary increases are more than offset by the increased purchasing power generated by these wage boosts to the general public."

Unemployment compensation According to the individualistic theory, as search time increases so does the natural rate of unemployment. One factor which determines the amount of time an unemployed worker will spend searching is the individual's opportunity cost—the amount of present income that must be relinquished in order to continue to search. In particular, conservative economists claim that present unemployment compensation benefits reduce the opportunity cost and encourage longer search time. This is especially true for unemployed workers who (1) usually earn about $200 per week, or (2) have employed spouses. An unemployed worker who has previously earned $200 per week usually qualifies for the state's maximum unemployment allowance, which is as high as $120 per week in many states. For this individual, the opportunity cost of remaining unemployed is substantially less than the $80 per week differential since he or she must pay taxes on wages but not on the unemployment compensation. After accounting for tax payments, the opportunity cost is probably less than $40 per week and can be as low as $26. (Once earnings rise above $200 per week, since unemployment compensation benefits are frozen at the maximum, the opportunity cost dramatically rises, reducing the disincentives it creates.)

The effect of unemployment compensation on the work incentives of unemployed low-wage female workers with working husbands is even more dramatic. Martin Feldstein estimated in 1971 that a married woman with two children and an employed husband, who earns less than $800 per month, could expect family income to decline by only $6 per month if she chooses to remain unemployed for three months rather than accept a slightly lower paying position.[20]

Feldstein believes that the disincentives to work especially affect workers on temporary lay-offs who often do not search at all but simply wait to be recalled to their old job. It also increases the amount of temporary lay-offs since firms are no longer worried that they will lose workers who, when temporarily laid-off, must seek alternative employment. Indeed, Feldstein has estimated that about one-half of all temporary lay-off unemployment can be attributed to the current average level of unemployment benefits.[21]

Government Intervention to Lower the Natural Rate

Mainstream economists claim that it is impossible for the economy to sustain an unemployment rate below its natural rate. More government spending could create jobs. However, since these jobs would be in excess of those who are willing and able to accept them, job vacancies would be in excess of the ef-

---

20. Martin S. Feldstein, "The Economics of the New Unemployment," *The Public Interest* 33 (Fall 1973): 3–42.

21. Martin S. Feldstein, "The Importance of Temporary Layoffs: An Empirical Analysis," *Brookings Papers* 6 (1975): 725–44.

fective supply of available labor. If excess demand for labor is created, then an accelerated inflation would result until the unemployment rate is lowered back to its natural rate. Therefore, government macro-policies, which are solely concerned with stimulating aggregate spending, would be counterproductive. For this reason, mainstream economists are strongly opposed to government public service job programs. They claim that public service employment is an inefficient method of lowering the natural rate since most jobs would go to individuals who are employable by the private sector as well as to nonlabor costs. They also contend that because of the relatively high wages that public service jobs would pay, they would further increase the disincentives to accepting low-wage private sector employment. For example, Charles Schultze, Carter's chief economic advisor, when testifying against the public service provisions of the Humphrey-Hawkins Full Employment Bill in 1976 argued,

> In many cases . . . the wage for a low-skill or semi-skilled municipal job is often higher than the wage paid for the same jobs in private industry. . . . An unskilled laborer earning, say $2.50 an hour in private industry can afford to quit, remain unemployed for four to six weeks (or whatever time might be needed to be eligible), then claim a "last resort" job paying (on municipal wage scales) $3.50 to $4.50 an hour, and come out way ahead.

> It is clear that in any area where municipalities pay higher scales . . . than private industry the wage scales in private industry will quickly be driven up to the higher level. . . . A new and much higher set of minimum wages would be created! . . . [Therefore] the concept of government as employer of last resort is not a workable method of pushing the overall unemployment rate down to very low levels [below 5 to 5.5 percent].[22]

Mainstream economists contend that only microeconomic policies, which increase work and hiring incentives, are capable of permanently lowering unemployment rates by lowering the natural rate. Conservatives emphasize reforming minimum wage and unemployment compensation laws.

Edward Banfield believes that the most effective way to lower the natural unemployment rate among teenagers is to lower the age of compulsory schooling to fourteen and eliminate the minimum wage altogether. He reasons that if the work ethic is instilled in young teenagers, then they will not develop antisocial habits nor lack the self-discipline that further useless schooling often encourages. Moreover, since the vast majority of these teenagers are secondary wage-earners the lower wage rates would not cause an increase in poverty.[23]

---

22. Charles L. Schultze, "Can the Full Employment-Inflation Link Be Broken?" *Washington Post* (June 7, 1976).

23. Banfield, *The Unheavenly City Revisited.*

Martin Feldstein also believes that lowering the minimum wage for teen-agers would lower the natural rate of unemployment. It would increase the number of teenage jobs available which would reduce search time. It would also give some incentive to employers to begin training programs for teen-agers. However, Feldstein does not believe this approach is politically viable, therefore, he proposed a voucher system instead.[24] Under Feldstein's plan, teenagers would be given a training voucher which entitles federal funds to any employer who hires and trains teenagers. Though firms would continue to be required to pay the current minimum wage rate, they could now receive federal subsidies if those teenagers hired were being trained.

Feldstein has also proposed a number of reforms of unemployment com-pensation.[25] To increase the opportunity cost of unemployment, he proposes that unemployment benefits be taxed at the same rate as actual wages. To dis-courage workers from remaining unemployed for long periods (as they attempt to continue to search for the best job), Feldstein would penalize the worker. When the worker returns to work, his or her take-home pay would be reduced by an amount proportional to the length of time spent collecting unemployment benefits.

Mainstream liberals agree with conservatives that reforming minimum wage and unemployment compensation laws can help lower the natural unem-ployment rate. However, they have some misgivings concerning relying on these reforms alone and, instead, propose other methods to lower the natural rate.[26] Despite Banfield's disclaimer, mainstream liberals believe that abolish-ing minimum wages would increase the amount of poverty. They agree with the intentions of the training voucher but do not think effective monitoring is possible. Without effective monitoring there is no guarantee that firms will use the subsidies for training or that they will keep teenagers after the subsidies have ended. Mainstream liberals also believe that Feldstein's proposals for reforming unemployment compensation are too punitive.

For these reasons, mainstream liberals emphasize direct government training programs and industrial location incentives as the best policies to lower the natural unemployment rate. By directly training unskilled workers, the government can reduce the mismatch between skills and jobs as well as reduce the barrier created by minimum wage laws. In order to eliminate loca-tional mismatches, the federal government could subsidize transportation of workers from central city to suburban industrial locations, subsidize subur-ban low-income housing, or subsidize the return of industry to central city locations. All of these subsidies would be justified financially when the savings

---

24. For a discussion of Feldstein's voucher plan, see Walter Guzzardi, Jr., "How to Deal with the 'New Unemployment,' " *Fortune* (Oct. 1976): 132.

25. Ibid.

26. For a more detailed discussion of mainstream liberal recommendations, see Robert J. Gordon, *Macroeconomics* (Boston: Little Brown, 1978), pp. 266–68.

in welfare, criminal justice, and unemployment insurance expenditures are included along with the expected income tax revenues resulting from the additional employment.[27]

2.3 LEFT-LIBERAL VIEWS ON UNEMPLOYMENT

Left-liberal economists contend that the U.S. economy normally has large amounts of idle labor and this is intensified by periodic business cycles. They claim that mainstream economists vastly underestimate the degree of unnecessary idleness by overestimating the natural unemployment rate and underestimating, especially during recessions, the actual rate of unemployment. Moreover, left-liberals reject the mainstream view that private market mechanisms can be expected to moderate employment shortfalls. They therefore reject the use of market schemes to improve economic performance and, instead, emphasize government planning of income distribution and corporate investments.

The Natural Unemployment Rate Myth

Left-liberals consider the concept of the natural unemployment rate to be based upon a number of myths. The first myth is that the natural unemployment rate presents a barrier to economic expansion. Left-liberals note,

> *If in fact there is some such residual [natural] level of unemployment it is not one we have encountered in the United States.* Never in the postwar period has the government been unsuccessful when it has made a sustained effort to reduce unemployment. *On several occasions, unemployment has fallen below the government target.*[28]

The second myth is that inflation and employment are closely interdependent. As already noted, this view claims that too much employment has been the cause of accelerating inflation. Left-liberals contend that unemployment and wage determination are essentially independent phenomena. According to Michael Piore,

---

27. If transportation fares do not cover costs, it is impossible for a private bus company to service central city residents who must commute to the industrial suburban locations. A private firm can only incorporate direct costs and benefits. However, the government can also incorporate externalities into the decision, such as the reduction in social costs and increased income tax revenues. If these externalities are sufficient, then it would save money for the government to subsidize the private firm. This is a typical example of how the presence of externalities can justify government intervention.

28. Michael Piore, "Unemployment and Inflation: An Alternative View," *Challenge* 21 (May/June 1978): 28.

The distinction between wage determination and unemployment arises because in most contexts the wage does not, and cannot, function to equate supply and demand. Instead wage rates perform certain basic social and institutional functions.[29]

These functions are to determine the relative position of individuals in the work community and in the family. This results in a series of fixed relationships between the wage rates of different groups. The entire set of these relationships, which adjusts quite slowly, is called the *wage contour*. When a wage breaks out of line, distorting one of the fixed relationships, pressure is created throughout the entire wage contour. If excess labor demand were the dominant explanation for the initial change in the wage contour, then the mainstream analysis would still be correct. However, the fixed relationships which make up the wage contour are not very sensitive to demand and supply considerations. For example, the automobile corporations have a policy of giving white collar workers the same percentage increase as blue collar autoworkers bargain for—regardless of the supply of or demand for white collar workers. If supply and demand considerations do not influence the wage contour, then government stimulation of employment does not necessarily create an accelerating inflation. For these reasons, left-liberals believe it is altogether possible for the United States to sustain very low rates of actual unemployment.

The third myth is that the influx of adult women and teenagers into the labor market has increased the natural unemployment rate.[30] Left-liberals altogether reject the notion that longer job search time is responsible for the higher rates of unemployment experienced by these groups, and minimize the effect of skill mismatches on unemployment rates. In particular, left-liberals note that the United States has historically had lower percentages of adult women and teenagers in the laborforce than other Western industrialized countries.[31] As Figure 2.1 indicates, many of these countries have much lower unemployment rates than the United States. Therefore, high female and teenage participation rates are not likely to be a barrier to low unemployment rates.

The fourth myth is that the natural unemployment rate is so high because of the excessive benefits provided by unemployment compensation. However, a careful study by Stephen Marston has revealed that "the U.S. unemployment insurance system may add between 0.2 and 0.4 percentage points to the U.S. unemployment rate."[32] Moreover, international comparisons support the

---

29. Ibid., p. 25.

30. The percentage of adult males in the laborforce declined from 59.8% to 47.4% between 1955 and 1974.

31. For international comparisons, see Roger Kaufman, "Why the U.S. Unemployment Rate is So High," *Challenge* 21 (May/June 1978): 40–49.

32. Ibid., p. 43.

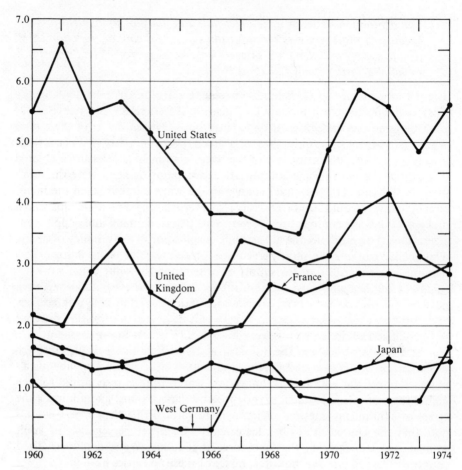

Figure 2.1   National unemployment rates, 1960–1974 (as a percentage of civilian labor force)

Source: *Economic Report of the President, 1978.*

position that unemployment benefits have little to do with work incentives. Japan, West Germany, Sweden, and France all give greater benefits to unemployed workers and yet have had much lower unemployment rates than the United States.[33]

---

33. Kaufman indicates that in the United States unemployment benefits average 50% of normal earnings while in most of Western Europe and Japan it averages over 60% of normal wages. Yet in Western Europe and Japan, unemployment rates above 3% are rare. Kaufman does not believe that different methods of data collection can explain these differences.

Actual Unemployment Rates

Mainstream liberals generally accept the official unemployment measure as being accurate or an overestimation of actual unemployment. In contrast, left-liberals contend that the official measure grossly underestimates the number of individuals who are willing to work, especially during times of economic contraction.

Conservatives usually contend that the government's willingness-to-work criterion—that persons must apply for a job at least once every four weeks—is too lenient. They often cite the case of the government counting someone who wants "a job from 10 in the morning until 2:30 in the afternoon so [she] can get home and meet the kids when they get home from school"[34] as an example of this leniency. Left-liberals agree that such cases exist. However, they claim that those cases are far outnumbered by examples of individuals who genuinely desire employment but are not counted because they have become so discouraged that they entirely give up looking for work. This is especially true during an economic contraction when many women, blacks, and teenagers believe that it is highly unlikely that they can find a job before the next expansion.

For a woman with children, the opportunity and direct costs of going to an interview are substantial. Only if there is a significant likelihood of obtaining the job would it be worthwhile to apply. If she has skills which are in oversupply relative to demand, then she might be quite rational to become extremely selective as to the interviews she pursues—possibly too selective to meet the government's measure of willingness to work.

Individuals who desire work but have given up applying for work are called *discouraged workers*. There are two methods used to estimate the number of discouraged workers. The government's method is to ask individuals currently unemployed why they are not looking for work. If they answer that it is because they don't think there are jobs available, then the government counts them as discouraged workers. However, if they give any other answer, such as, "there were no jobs available so I decided to go back to being a housewife" (or go back to school or to jail), they are not counted as being involuntarily unemployed. Indeed, the government could reduce teenage unemployment by building more prisons and detention centers to house unemployed youth who commit crimes! Despite its restrictive nature, the government's measure still indicates that there are a significant number of discouraged workers, especially during economic contractions when there are few job vacancies. For example, during the 1975 recession, the government estimated that 1.2 million workers or 1.5% of the laborforce were discouraged workers.

---

34. "Unemployment—A Story the Figures Don't Tell," *U.S. News and World Report* (Nov. 14, 1974): 44.

Most economists believe that a superior method is to compare laborforce participation rates over the course of the business cycle. For example, if the participation rate of white males, aged 55–64, declined during an economic contraction from 77% to 73%, it is likely that the change represents an estimate of the percentage of discouraged workers within that demographic group. By comparing participation rates for all demographic groupings, it is then possible to develop an estimate of the size of the discouraged workforce. One study using this procedure has conservatively estimated that the correction for discouraged workers would raise the unemployment rate by about 50%.[35] If this estimate is correct, then in 1975 when the official unemployment rate was close to 8%, the discouraged workforce would have been 4%, not the 1.5% estimated by the government.

Julius Shiskin, Federal Commissioner of Labor Statistics, seems to support the alternative method. He noted,

[In 1975] more than 9 million persons not counted as potential members of the workforce actually held jobs at some time during the preceding twelve months. That group alone is more than seven times bigger than the 1.2 million the government officially records as "discouraged" workers.[36]

Echoing these sentiments, Columbia professor Eli Ginzburg contended that "you get millions of people out of the woodwork every time there are plenty of decent jobs around."[37]

Left-liberal economists contend that the government procedure used to count part-time employment adds further to the undercounting of unemployment during recessions. When the economy contracts, many companies reduce the length of the workweek rather than lay-off part of their workforce. However, according to the government's procedure, since all workers are partially employed there is no unemployment created. During the 1975 recession, close to 3 million workers were involuntarily employed part-time.

In response to these criticisms, the federal government, while still maintaining the official unemployment rate, now also tabulates unemployment rates more consistent with the left-liberal contentions.[38] A measure, called U-7, adds the number of discouraged workers as well as one-half of the invol-

---

35. See "The Real Unemployment Rate," *Radical Perspective on the Economic Crisis* (New York: URPE, 1976), pp. 182–184.

36. A. H. Raskin, "The Changing Face of the Labor Force," *New York Times* (Feb. 15, 1976): section iv, p. 5.

37. Ibid.

38. Measures U-1 through U-4 represent estimates more in line with conservative criticisms, with U-5 being the official measure and U-6 adjusting for part-time workers but not for discouraged workers.

untary part-time workers to the official rate.[39] During the 1975 recession, U-7 was well over 10%—even with the restrictive measure of discouraged workers used by the government.

Left-Liberal Policy Recommendations

Mainstream economists claim that the economy is usually operating very close to its natural limit, therefore, government policies to stimulate aggregate spending have a limited role. Left-liberals, on the other hand, contend that there is substantial excess unemployment, which is often dramatically higher during cyclical contractions, so that a more active role is required. Left-liberals reject the claim that inflation creates a barrier to economic expansion. They argue that an incomes policy can be used to minimize any disruption to the wage contour resulting from an economic expansion. In this manner, government stimulative programs, coupled with an incomes policy, can achieve full employment and price stability.

Left-liberals stress the key role of capital spending in generating cyclical fluctuations as well as determining the growth rate of the economy. Left-liberals contend that incomes policies by regulating the distribution of income between corporate retained earnings and private sector income are also able to regulate aggregate capital spending. Therefore, incomes policies not only limit inflationary pressures, but also reduce the instability of capital spending.[40]

Incomes policies are capable of determining aggregate capital spending, but not the distribution of capital spending within various subsectors of the economy. However, many left-liberal economists believe that the present U.S. economy is too interdependent and inflexible to allow sectoral investment imbalances to occur. These economists believe that through the use of input-output data, which indicates the relationship of each sector's output to its inputs, they can accurately estimate the input requirements for specific growth rates of consumer demand. For example, if the government estimates that automobile sales must grow at 8% per year to guarantee full employment, input-output tables could estimate what this growth rate implies about the future demand for steel, tires, aluminum, and fiberglass. These economists recommend the initiation of a federal planning board which would eventually have the power to influence corporate decisions in order to sustain balanced capital spending growth rates.[41]

---

39. For consistency, this measure also subtracts one-half of unemployed workers seeking part-time employment from the government's official estimate of the number of unemployed workers.

40. For a more detailed rationale of this thesis, see John Cornwall, ''Post-Keynesian Theory: Macrodynamics,'' *Challenge* 21 (May/June 1978): 11–17.

41. For a discussion of the movement toward economic planning among U.S. economists, see William K. Tabb, ''Domestic Economic Policy Under Carter: The Imprint of Trilateralism,'' *U.S. Capitalism in Crisis* (New York: URPE, 1978), pp. 271–73.

One way in which a lack of industrial planning causes the United States to have a higher rate of unemployment than Western Europe and Japan is its effect on the rate of temporary lay-offs. Observers have often stressed that differences in international unemployment rates exist because there are dramatically fewer temporary lay-offs in Western Europe and Japan than in the United States. Recall that conservative economist Martin Feldstein contends that the high rate of temporary lay-offs in the United States is due to the excessive unemployment insurance benefits. This explanation is highly suspect since Western Europe and Japan have higher unemployment compensation benefits and lower rates of temporary lay-offs. Therefore, it is likely that his policy recommendations of decreasing unemployment compensation would only be punitive against unemployed workers and have little effect on the rate of temporary lay-offs.

Left-liberal economists stress that temporary lay-offs have little to do with individual choice; that they are determined by existing institutional arrangements. In the United States, there is limited institutional constraints on management's prerogative to initiate temporary lay-offs. In contrast, institutional constraints make it extremely difficult for Western European and Japanese corporations to initiate temporary lay-offs without the approval of the government and affected workers. Only by changing its institutional arrangements can the United States hope to reduce its unemployment rate to the levels usually found in Western Europe and Japan.[42]

This points out an important difference between mainstream and left analyses. Mainstream economists emphasize the influence of relative price changes on individual choice within a given set of institutional arrangements (which they rarely recommend changing). Left-economists, however, see progress resulting from the evolution of institutional arrangements and ignore relying on influencing individual choice.

The Western European and Japanese institutional arrangements force management to absorb a greater share of the income shortfall from cyclical fluctuations. Rather than being able to reduce costs during a contraction by laying-off workers, they must absorb more of the losses. Such a procedure can be viable only if there is an accompanying policy which limits the size of cyclical fluctuations. However, to limit cyclical fluctuations, left-liberals claim that a high degree of government intervention in corporate planning is required. Therefore, Western Europe and Japan can afford to limit temporary layoffs only because they also allow government industrial planning. In the United States there is resistance to planning which, according to left-liberals, dictates cyclical fluctuations will be frequent and often severe. In this economic environment, corporations require temporary lay-offs and this results in higher unemployment rates.

---

42. For a detailed discussion of this thesis, see Kaufman, "Why the U.S. Unemployment Rate is So High."

2.4 THE MATERIALIST CONCEPTION OF HISTORY

The radical theory of unemployment has as its foundation the marxian concept of class conflict within a capitalist society. No discussion of marxian economic concepts can begin without a description of Marx's materialist view of history from which the concepts emerge. Marx developed his materialist view of history in order to explain the transition from one historical epoch to another—from feudalism to capitalism and from capitalism to socialism—and to determine the economic foundations of each epoch.

Mode of Production[43]

Materialism begins by emphasizing the critical role in society of productive forces. Productive forces are the means of production which people use to extract goods from nature. They include machines, instruments, and raw materials, as well as the capacities of human beings. Marx wrote,

> Technology discloses man's mode of dealing with nature, the immediate process of production by which life is sustained, and thereby also lays bare the mode of formation of his social relations, and of the mental conceptions that flow from them.[44]

According to Marx's formulation, the stage of development of society's productive forces determines the social relations of production and exchange. These social relations consist of property relations—the way labor is recruited, organized, and compensated. The coming together of productive forces and its particular set of social relations is called the *mode of production.*

Class Structure

The social relations of production, in effect, determine the class structure of society. Since each historical epoch is distinguished by a different set of social relations, they are also distinguished by a different set of class relations. The slave society of ancient times was characterized by slave and master; the feudal society by serf and lord; and capitalism by capitalist and worker. In each of these societies one class exploited another. However, the conditions of the exploited and the method of extracting the fruits of his or her labor differed dramatically. According to Marx, it is these conditions and methods of extracting that fundamentally distinguish each epoch.

The marxian view differs dramatically from the mainstream conception of society. For mainstream economists, the distinguishing features of capital-

---

43. See John Gurley, *Challengers to Capitalism: Marx, Lenin and Mao* (San Francisco: San Francisco Book Co., 1976), Chapter 2.

44. Karl Marx, Capital, vol 1 (New York: International Pub., 1967), p. 372n.

ism are not characteristics of production or class relations, but the attitudes of individuals and method of exchange. According to mainstream thought, under capitalism the acquisitive behavior of man, characterized by his entrepreneurship, is unconstrained either morally or legally. He is free to pursue his narrow self-interests. Moreover, capitalism is characterized by the preeminence of exchange rather than individual self-sufficiency which dominated earlier agrarian societies. This is most apparent in mainstream theoretical models in which (1) exchange rather than production is emphasized; (2) it is usually impossible to distinguish between producers and owners; (3) consumer and producer are the primary economic agents rather than capitalist and worker; and (4) economic class is ignored.[45]

Marxists reject this notion that exchange and acquisitive behavior are the distinguishing features of capitalism. They note that both of these characteristics most identify petite bourgeois groups, such as the small merchant and independent craftsman. Both of these groups existed long before capitalism and capitalism has a strong tendency to eliminate them. Moreover, these features in no way accurately characterize the chief agent of capitalism—the industrial capitalist.

For marxists, it is labor being bought and sold at the marketplace, like any other commodity, which is the distinguishing feature of capitalism. The prerequisite for the development and maintenance of the capitalist mode of production is that ownership of the means of production is concentrated in a small group of capitalists. The majority of society has no choice other than seek employment from these owners. For capitalism to exist, there must be a hierarchical relation between capitalists and workers who impersonally meet in the market.

The Transition Process[46]

How does society transcend from one epoch to another? Mainstream thought would emphasize the role of new ideas and individual initiative. This is reflected in the concept of history being made by "great men." In studying the rise of capitalism, we learn of the writings of the great philosophers of the Renaissance period who broke with the feudal way of thinking; the great inventors who revolutionized productive methods; and the great leaders who brought democracy to mankind.

Marxists reject the notion that individuals make history. They contend that ideas are fundamentally determined by the economic structure of society. In essence, this implies that people's material lives determine their ideas and their supporting institutions. Marx summarized this viewpoint as follows:

45. For a succinct radical critique of neo-classical economics, see Duncan K. Foley, "Problems Versus Conflicts: Economic Theory and Ideology," *American Economics Review* 65 (May 1975): 231–36.

46. See E. K. Hunt, *Property and Prophets* (New York: Harper and Row, 1975), pp. 12–24.

The mode of production of material life conditions the general process of social, political, and intellectual life. It is not the consciousness of people that determines their existence, but their social existence that determines their consciousness.[47]

As productive forces grow, they come in conflict with the prevailing class structure of society. The newly developed ways that people extract a living become incompatible with the older ways they related to one another. This growing contradiction takes the form of a class struggle between the rising class associated with the new means of production and the old ruling class whose dominance was based on its control of the older, waning forces. This class struggle intensifies until, as a result of revolution, new relations of production which are compatible with the superior productive forces are established.

The growth of productive forces during the Middle Ages dictated that a new structure of social relations was necessary. New ideas, new methods of production, and freedom of movement (democracy) were all required. Only if the ideas and actions of individuals reflect these requirements could they reach fruition. During the Renaissance period, no matter how powerful they were, the feudal lords could not resist the breakdown of their social and economic structure. Nor could socialist ideas take hold during this period. The Renaissance was the period of the rise of the bourgeoisie, and only those individuals who reflected the ideas and needs of the bourgeoisie could be successful.

The feudal order rested on the ownership of land by lords of the manor and their control over the rural work processes. A set of customary relations between the serf and the lord was established. The serf was guaranteed protection by the lord and, unlike a slave, he could not be parted from either his land or his family. In return, the serf made payments to the lord, usually a portion of production.

The maintenance of the feudal society required a specific set of social relations—traditions, customs, and ideas—the divine inheritability of one's position in life. Its viability depended upon the acceptance by members of society of that tradition and set of ideas. Since acquisition threatened the stability of social relations, trade and commerce were repressed both morally and legally. Commerce could only be transacted at a "just price"—the price at which no accumulation of wealth could occur. In particular, there was condemnation of usury.

The productive forces in agriculture progressively grew, creating for the first time a surplus of food and handicrafts which then became available for the foreign market. Thus, out of the productive forces grew the ability to trade. However, as commerce expanded, a more reliable source of goods required the subordination of the independent craftsman by the merchant

---

47. Karl Marx, *Analysis of Political Economy* (Chicago: Charles H. Kerr & Co., 1908), p. 12.

capitalist. The merchant capitalist would furnish the materials and implements of production, and the craftsman (turned worker) would now produce in return for a fixed wage. In this manner, the guild system of production was replaced by the putting-out system. At the same time, through the enclosure movement,[48] masses of peasants lost their customary rights to farm the land so landowners could profit from export markets. This created a laborforce that owned little or no capital and had nothing to sell but labor. Thus, the bourgeois revolution occurred and with it a new set of social relations and ruling ideas.

Class Struggle

Marx claimed that as material forces grow they come into conflict with the existing social forces. This results in class struggle between the class of producers of material goods and the class of appropriators. In capitalism, this is a conflict between capitalists and workers. Marx claimed that besides this long-term process, capitalism was subject to periodic economic crises in which class struggle would also intensify.

Material forces thus create the conditions within which class struggle is manifested. It dictates the boundaries within which actions are feasible as well as predicts the attitudes and issues which will develop in each historical situation. However, within these boundaries, the action of the working class, the degree to which certain ideas take hold, and the cohesiveness of the capitalist class cannot be mechanically predicted. In this sense, class consciousness and class struggle are a historical force.

Marx emphasized the role of class struggle by his use of the term *tendencies*. Rather than determining universal ahistorical *laws,* which is the objective of mainstream theory, he attempted to identify economic tendencies. For example, his view that a falling rate of profit would precipitate an economic crisis is not called the *law* of the falling rate of profit (which would imply that it must always be true regardless of the particular historical circumstances). It is called the *tendency* for the rate of profit to decline. It is called the *tendency* to emphasize that while there are material factors which create certain situations in which crises are very likely to occur, there are countertendencies which can forestall and affect the degree to which a crisis develops. These countertendencies are often reflected in the shape and intensity of class struggle within each historical situation.

During the 1970s, marxists contend that U.S. capitalism entered a period of economic crisis. Mainstream economists consider the 1970s a period of somewhat larger unemployment, but nothing different than previous recessions and nothing that requires any significant changes in the organization of

---

48. For further discussion of the enclosure laws, see Marx, "The So-Called Primitive Accumulation," Capital, vol 1.

production and economic decision-making. The materialist view of history, on the other hand, claims that crises are qualitatively different from recessions in that they are manifestations of the conflict between productive forces and the social relations of production at a high level. Therefore, marxists suggest that there will be a strong tendency for the social relations of production to be changed in an attempt to resolve the crisis.[49]

Marxists generally contend that the resolution of the crisis of the 1970s requires more centralization of economic decision-making. However, there are three general forms by which centralization could take place: fascism, capitalist state planning, or socialism. According to marxists, the actual path the capitalist process takes is determined by the shape and intensity of class struggle. This indicates that, while within the marxian schema economic forces dictate the strong possibility of restructuring, it is the class struggle which determines the actual form of the restructuring.

2.5 THE RESERVE ARMY OF THE UNEMPLOYED

According to the materialist conception of history, capitalism requires a hierarchical relationship between capital and labor. Marxists contend that in order to maintain this hierarchical relationship, a reserve army of unemployed workers is necessary. According to Michal Kalecki,

> . . . under a regime of permanent full employment, "the sack" would cease to play its role as a disciplinary measure. The social position of the boss would be undermined and the self assurance and class consciousness of the working class would grow. Strikes for wage increases and improvements in conditions of work would create political tensions. . . . [The capitalists'] class instincts tell them that lasting full employment is unsound from their point of view and that unemployment is an integral part of the normal capitalist system.[50]

Marxists argue that the reserve army of the unemployed enables capitalists to not only maintain labor discipline, but also to increase their profits. They claim that with increased uncertainty, created by high unemployment rates, *each* worker would adjust his or her labor market decision so as to be willing to work the same hours at lower wages. Thus, the entire labor supplied by workers would be forthcoming at lower wage rates. It is further argued that the beneficiaries of the lower wage rates are capitalists. Hence, lower wage rates are thought to enable capitalists to increase their rate of exploitation of

49. This thesis is developed by David M. Gordon, "Up and Down the Long Roller Coaster," *U.S. Capitalism in Crisis* (New York: URPE, 1978), pp. 35–44.

50. Michal Kalecki, *Selected Essays on the Dynamics of Capitalist Societies* (New York: Cambridge Press, 1971), pp. 140–41.

workers. Consistent with this thesis, Persky and Tsang found that the higher the rate of unemployment, all other factors held constant, the greater the level of exploitation.[51]

Nonmarxist radicals also believe that unemployment is necessary in a capitalist society because it serves the interests of particular groups in society. However, unlike marxists, they identify noncapitalist groups, particularly white prime-age male workers, as major beneficiaries of unemployment. The work of Michael Piore presents examples of this line of reasoning. Piore begins by identifying the job characteristics of the workers who have a high incidence of unemployment. He finds that they form a secondary labor market in which:

> [The jobs] pay low wages, are often menial, and require little skill. In addition, many are also subject to seasonal variations, are sensitive to sudden shifts in taste and fashion, are in declining industries or marginal firms, and offer little prospect for continuous employment, let alone meaningful career opportunities.[52]

Piore contends that as long as these jobs are required, the economy must have a group of workers who will experience high rates of unemployment. Since he believes that only a fundamental change in the economic system could eliminate these jobs, Piore agrees with marxists that unemployment is a natural condition of a capitalist society. However, unlike marxists, Piore indicates three groups of white prime-age male workers who benefit from the high rates of unemployment of secondary workers.

First, Piore notes that firms which provide their workers with guaranteed employment can do so only if they can transfer fluctuations in productions to other firms. This is done by subcontracting the variable portion of demand to marginal firms—firms which are able to exist only through the use of secondary workers.[53] But as Piore notes,

> If the firms with freer hiring and firing patterns, and the sectors of the market from which they draw their labor were eliminated, all employers would be forced to absorb the flux and uncertainty of economic activity themselves, and could not afford to provide the kind of employment security which most white males enjoy at prime age.[54]

---

51. J. Persky and H. Tsang, "Piguvian Exploitation of Labor," *Review of Economics and Statistics* 56 (Feb. 1974): 52–57.

52. Piore, "Unemployment and Inflation," p. 28.

53. A similar argument is found in Harold Baron and M. Hymer, "The Dual Labor Market in Chicago," in *Problems in Political Economy,* 2nd ed., David Gordon, ed. (Lexington, Mass.: Heath, 1977), pp. 183–88.

54. Piore, "Unemployment and Inflation," p. 28.

Next, Piore claims that without a labor force willing to accept uncertainty and instability, there would be an accelerated movement abroad of declining industries, such as textiles, shoes, and garments. This would, in turn, cause increased unemployment of the higher-paid, more skilled white male workers who service these industries.

Finally, Piore contends that the secondary labor force is required to maintain cheap service help. According to this view, the price of domestic service help and leisure activities, such as restaurants and lodging, would become prohibitive for the white middle-class family if high unemployment among secondary workers were eliminated.[55]

Thus, broad sections of white society have an economic stake in the perpetuation of unemployment. White workers in strongly unionized sectors are able to obtain employment stability; those who service declining industries are able to extend their high-wage careers; and all those with moderate incomes are able to enjoy many of the benefits of leisure. For these reasons, Piore contends that unemployment has a functional role in the U.S. economy and any attempts by the government to reduce unemployment would generate opposition from those groups which have an economic stake in its perpetuation.

The radical explanation of unemployment is diametrically opposed to the mainstream view. As previously stated, mainstream economists feel that involuntary unemployment is a minor problem only seriously affecting the economy infrequently, and that it is primarily determined by the skill characteristics (mainstream liberals) and/or the values (conservatives) of individual workers. According to the radical view, unemployment is a necessary condition under capitalism and not dependent upon individual characteristics of workers. Mainstream economists believe that government policies directed at changing individual characteristics could even further reduce the already minor problems associated with unemployment. Radicals suggest that it is impossible to eliminate unemployment within a capitalist system.

We have also noted an important distinction between marxists and non-marxist radicals. Marxists claim that the persistence of unemployment is fundamentally a class question. They contend that the working class as a whole is hurt by unemployment while only the capitalist class has a longrun economic stake in its perpetuation.[56] Marxists claim that whenever one group of workers experiences unemployment, they are used as a threat against all employed workers. Moreover, the existence of racial and/or sex divisions within the working class reduces its ability to fight capital. This weakened working class

---

55. A similar argument is found in Herbert Gans, "Income Grants and 'Dirty Work,' " *The Public Interest* 6 (Winter 1967): 110–113.

56. In particular, see Michael Reich, "The Economics of Racism," in *Problems in Political Economy,* for a detailed explanation and empirical support for the view that white workers are hurt by racism.

movement hurts all workers, not just the most disadvantaged. Nonmarxist radicals, however, believe that large enough sections of the white working class benefit financially from unemployment and that its perpetuation is no longer fundamentally a class question.[57]

Many left-liberals believe that radicals overstate the degree to which groups benefit from the existence of a reserve army. Moreover, they argue that these cases are the result of greed and not inevitable in a capitalist system. They contend that the U.S. economy would be viable with substantially lower unemployment rates. They cite Western Europe and Japan as examples of capitalist countries which are able to maintain economic stability with quite low unemployment rates.

Radicals would agree that the protection of personal privileges in the United States does result in higher unemployment rates. However, they do not believe that the Western European experience proves that it is possible to maintain very low unemployment rates. For example, these countries have not eliminated the need for a secondary workforce. These countries have foreign migrant laborers rather than native workers perform these functions. Spanish, Algerian, Yugoslav, and Finnish workers, in particular, have been significantly responsible for the low unemployment rates of native labor in these countries. When these foreign migrant workers are laid-off, they simply return to their native country to await the next expansion.

Moreover, radicals claim that all capitalist countries are subject to economic crises, which require an intensification of unemployment. The Western European experience of the mid-1970s is consistent with this contention. For example, Table 2.1 indicates that unemployment rates more than doubled in the most advanced industrial countries of Western Europe. The increase in Japan would have been much higher if it were forced to curtail its aggressive exporting actions. Thus, radicals contend that it is a mistake to believe that there are capitalist economies which can maintain low unemployment rates indefinitely.

Finally, radicals contend that political factors influence the size of the industrial reserve army. In particular, radicals suggest that a workable agree-

Table 2.1
Average national unemployment rates

	France	United Kingdom	West Germany	Japan
1960–74	2.1%	2.8%	0.9%	1.3%
1975–77	4.7	6.0	3.6	2.0

Source: *Economic Report of the President, 1978.*

57. For a complete discussion of the economic effects of racism, see Robert Cherry, "Economic Theories of Racism," in *Problems in Political Economy,* pp. 170–82.

ment between organized labor and capital enabled the reserve army to be drastically reduced in all capitalist countries during the first twenty-five years of the post-World War II era. However, as will be discussed in Chapter 17, due to increased international competition and the actions of disenfranchised groups, this agreement became unworkable during the 1970s. Radicals claim that it was the breakdown of this agreement, as well as falling profit rates, which created the conditions for the worldwide economic crisis and the return in all capitalist countries to higher unemployment rates.

2.6 CONCLUSION

This chapter attempted to indicate the basic conflicts within the economics profession over the nature and extent of unemployment in the U.S. economy. The concept of a natural unemployment rate enables mainstream economists to argue that the extent of real unemployment in the United States is not serious. Moreover, mainstream economists claim that the causes of unemployment are to be found in the characteristics of individual workers. Conservatives emphasize workers' values while mainstream liberals emphasize their skill levels. Mainstream economists also contend that the higher official unemployment rate of the 1970s should not be a cause for alarm since it only reflects a rise in the natural unemployment rate. Finally, they claim that government intervention can not be relied upon since its policies, particularly minimum wage and unemployment insurance legislation, have been responsible for much of the rise in the natural unemployment rate. They especially oppose any government policies which would have the government create public works jobs.

Left-liberals reject the notion of a natural unemployment rate. They believe that there is no such thing as a barrier to sustained full employment. They claim that changes in institutional arrangements would enable the United States to drastically lower unemployment rates to those levels usually experienced in other advanced capitalist societies. Moreover, left-liberals believe that changes are necessary because actual unemployment rates far exceed the official measure. The principal reasons for this underestimation are the large number of discouraged workers not included in the official measure and the way part-time employment is treated.

Radicals claim that unemployment persists because there are groups which benefit from its existence. Marxists claim that the distinguishing feature of capitalism is the concentration of ownership of industrial capital in the hands of a small percentage of the population who are able to exploit a free proletariat. Marxists stress that in order to exploit and discipline the workforce, a reserve army of unemployed workers is required. Nonmarxist radicals contend that besides the capitalist class, broad sections of the white working class also benefit from the persistence of high unemployment when it is concentrated in nonwhite sections of the population.

CHAPTER THREE

GOVERNMENT ECONOMIC POLICIES

Throughout the 1970s there was visible dissent over the appropriate macro-economic policy. In particular, there was a continuous conflict between labor and capital regarding the pursuit of full employment. Labor supported the 1976 version of the Humphrey-Hawkins Full Employment Bill (which had extensive job-creation provisions) and the 1977 Tax-Cut Bill to stimulate consumer demand. In contrast, capital, as indicated by the *Wall Street Journal* and *Business Week,* was adamantly against any economic stimuli.

Mainstream economists usually explain this as a conflict between goals. They argue that all groups desire full employment since everyone's income is higher in a fully employed economy. However, when full employment conflicts with price stability, a choice of priorities must be made. According to this viewpoint, it is possible that differences between groups over the relative importance of price stability versus full employment could occur.[1]

This explanation of the source of the labor-capital conflict is, at best, incomplete. It is incomplete because it does not explain why capital stresses price stability to the total neglect of employment and why labor stresses employment to the total neglect of price stability.

The radical explanation of the labor-capital conflict is quite simple. Radicals reject the mainstream view that everyone benefits from full employment. Radicals contend that, in general, a sustained full employment would result in a profit squeeze and will always create political and social instability. According to this viewpoint, capitalists require a reserve army of unemployed workers. Hence, the conflict occurs.

Critical to the radical contention is the concept of economic classes—capitalists and workers. The first section of this chapter discusses mainstream theories that claim there are no longer economic classes since all workers have

---

1. This argument is found in Campbell McConnell, *Economics* (New York: McGraw-Hill, 1973), pp. 9–10.

become capitalists. It will be demonstrated that these theories are a weak and ineffective response to the radical contentions.

This chapter will also develop the major response of mainstream economists to the radical contentions—the managerial control thesis. This thesis claims that capitalists have limited power because they no longer control major corporations. Instead, it is argued that managers control individual corporations. The major radical response to the managerial control thesis has been the financial control thesis. Radicals agree that individual capitalists no longer wield decisive power in corporations. However, rather than managers, radicals contend that financial institutions have become the most powerful forces in corporate affairs. Hence, radicals contend economic power has become more concentrated within major corporate groupings centered around the larger financial institutions. Radicals contend that these financially-centered groupings are now powerful enough to directly fight over control of the federal government.

Subsequent sections of this chapter will present the radical interpretation of government actions during the 1970s. The institution of wage-price controls in the context of the historical role of the federal government to regulate labor in the interest of capital, will be discussed. Radicals argue that the adoption of controls represents the beginning of a new stage of federal labor market intervention which reflects the move towards state planning.

It is the radical contention that the 1970s witnessed the struggle between two financial groupings ("old" versus "new" money) over control of federal government economic policies. It will be argued that the unseating of Nixon and the conflict over energy legislation can only be understood within the context of this struggle.

3.1 ECONOMIC CLASSES

Marxists contend that the concept of economic class is central to understanding individual self-interest. Economic class ignores the demographic characteristics and personal views of individuals. Instead, it categorizes individuals according to their "relationship to the means of production." By this, marxists mean that individuals will be grouped according to their position in the production process. At one extreme are the capitalists—individuals who do not work (have no wage income), but instead are able to extract part of the value of production (surplus value) through their ownership of production facilities (plant and equipment). At the other extreme is the industrial proletariat—employed by the capitalist at subsistence wages in order to produce the firm's output.

Marx, of course, realized that the entire population could never fall into these two classes. He, however, felt that they were the most powerful forces in society since capitalists controlled the decisions affecting capital accumulation (investment in additional productive facilities), while the industrial proletariat was responsible for the production of output as well as the means of accumulation (profits).

Marx also identified four other less influential groups: (1) white collar labor, (2) family business owners, (3) government workers, and (4) capitalists' agents.

White collar workers, such as sales and clerical personnel, do not produce the output. Instead, they are concentrated in its distribution, what can be called the *sales effort*. Therefore, their position in the production process is intermediate between production and extraction of surplus value (profits).

Family businesses represent capitalist operations in which the individual is both the capitalist and the worker. Therefore, each individual in this situation has a dual aspect and is distinct from the industrial proletariat and the capitalist class.

Government workers do not work for a private capitalist and, therefore, do not produce an output, part of which is transformed into profits (surplus value). The principal activity of government workers is the production of services—health care, education, social services, etc.

Capitalists' agents are those sections of the workforce whose function is to directly aid the capitalists in extracting profits from workers. They include the police force, management, supervisory personnel, corporate lawyers, and corporate accountants.

Marx assumed that the capitalists and their agents represented one distinct class, while the industrial proletariat represented another. The other groups, however, cannot be easily lumped together with either of the two major classes. Marx, therefore, called them the *middle classes*. It is important to remember that the marxian middle classes are not categorized because of their income, but because of their position in the production process. Marx discounted the role of these middle classes for the following reasons:

1. They usually worked in fragmented settings as compared to the concentration of industrial proletariat in large factories. They had little power over the production process of the firm's operations. Because of their limited concentration and limited role in the production process, they would be unable to affect changes through their *independent* actions. They would only be an affective force if they allied themselves with either of the major classes.

2. Their conflicting roles result in their consistent vacillation between support of each of the major classes. They, therefore, would rarely play a leading role in affecting change.

It is commonplace today to admit that Marx fairly accurately categorized a society in its early stages of industrialization. However, according to mainstream thought, this stage of development is relatively shortlived and society becomes qualitatively transformed in successive stages. According to this view,

U.S. capitalism is now in its "post-industrial" stage; a stage where scarcity and competition over production has disappeared.[2] Society is now engaged in maximizing services and the quality of life. This is reflected by the decrease in the size and importance of the industrial proletariat and the rise in size and importance of the middle classes. Certainly, it is obvious that there is an increase in the "sales effort" (and the number of individuals engaged in its operation) and in the number of government service workers. Moreover, the industrial proletariat is seen as a member of the middle classes through its accumulation of financial assets (savings accounts, stocks, pension funds) which gives this group a stake in the profits of the corporate sector. Therefore, rather than using the outmoded Marxian classifications, it has become commonplace to categorize interest groups by (1) demographic characteristics—sex, race, age, place of residency, etc.; (2) positions on personal issues—abortion, gay rights, death penalty, school prayer, etc.; or (3) income rather than their relationship to the means of production.

People's Capitalism

The clearest assertion that there is no proletariat in the United States is advocacy of the concept of people's capitalism. People's capitalism reflects the view that today, through the wide dispersion of stock ownership, the majority of workers are also capitalists. This is the view that Texaco, through its Bob Hope commercials, has spent millions of dollars projecting. Hope notes that Texaco is owned by over 12 million households. Similarly, Samuelson claims, "The most striking feature of [the giant corporation] is the diversification of ownership among thousands and thousands of small shareholders."[3]

Is every worker, through ownership of assets, a capitalist? The number of households that own stock will not answer this question. For example, suppose society was composed of two groups—Group A, which received 99% of its income from stock ownership (and only 1% from wage income); and Group B, which received 99% of its income from wages (and 1% from stock). In such a society, both groups had some capitalist income, but it would clearly be a society of distinct economic classes. This indicates that for the concept of people's capitalism to be truly representative, the majority of workers would have to receive a *significant* portion of their income from stocks. Moreover, Samuelson's use of the number of stockholders as a measure of concentration of stock ownership is contrary to the general procedure used in economics. Economists do not determine the concentration of industrial production by the number of firms within an industry. Economists use the percentage of industry

---

2. The mainstream stage theory of economic development is found in Walter W. Rostow, *The Stages of Economic Development* (Cambridge: Cambridge Press, 1971).

3. Paul Samuelson, *Economics,* 8th ed. (New York: McGraw-Hill, 1970), pp. 89–90.

production by the largest firms. Specifically, the standard measure of industrial concentration is the percentage of industry production by the four largest firms. Following this procedure, the concentration of stock ownership should be measured by the percentage of stock owned by the wealthiest households.

By any measure of stock ownership, the United States does not approach people's capitalism. The concentration of stock ownership is exceedingly high. During the 1960s, it was estimated that 61% and 83% of all privately-held stock was owned by the richest 1% and 5% of the population, respectively.[4] The poorest 80% of households owned only 4% of the privately-held stock. Income tax returns have also shown that the vast majority of households own no significant amount of stock.[5] For example, 1973 returns indicated that the poorest 95% of households (incomes less than $25,000) received only 6% of their income from stocks (and 89% from wages). Those households with incomes over $500,000 received only 10% of their income from wages (and 75% from stocks). There is only a small percentage of families, between $50,000–500,000 annual income, who on the average receive a significant portion of their income from both wage and nonwage sources. For the vast majority of households, wages are virtually the only source of income.

Human Capital Theory

Another way in which mainstream economics attempts to justify the view that all workers are capitalists is to broaden the concept of capital. Historically, capital has been associated with the ownership of productive facilities. However, it is now argued that capital is any asset which entitles its owner to future income. This, of course, still includes stock ownership, but it also includes certain labor incomes as well. For example, a plastic surgeon may only work a few days each week and yet earn $100,000 per year. Does this mean that the surgeon is a highly over-paid worker? According to the mainstream viewpoint, the plastic surgeon previously *invested* in developing his skills. He went to medical school and absorbed information which he uses. Therefore, only part of his yearly salary reflects labor payment. The other portion represents interest payments for his past investments in "human capital."

According to this viewpoint, investment in human capital is equivalent to investment in physical capital. Each entitles the owner to future payments. However, if human capital is equivalent to stock ownership, then anyone who possesses any skill training is a "capitalist." As economists Bowles and Gintis note,

---

4. Robert J. Lampman, *The Share of Top Wealth-Holders in National Income* (Princeton: National Bureau of Economic Research, 1962). Updated by James D. Smith and Stephen D. Franklin, "The Concentration of Personal Wealth, 1922–1969," *American Economics Review* 64 (May 1974): 162–167.

5. Internal Revenue Service, *Statistics of Income, 1973: Individual Income Tax Returns,* table 4.

> *Human capital theory is the most recent and perhaps ultimate step in*
> *the elimination of class as a central economic concept. . . . [Every]*
> *worker, the human capital theorists are fond of saying, is now a*
> *capitalist.* [6]

While conservatives have been the leading proponents of the concept of
human capital, it has also been advocated by many liberals. For example,
Robert Heilbroner and John Kenneth Galbraith have argued that human
capital enables workers to control the means of production just as stock purchases do.[7] Galbraith calls those workers who possess significant human
capital "technocrats." He claims that technocrats have become so crucial to
industrial production that they now have gained control over corporate decisions. Hence, those who possess human capital now have more control over
production decisions than those who own corporate stock (capitalists).

Radicals, like Bowles and Gintis, dispute the claims that human capital
provides workers with any control over the means of production. They note,

> *. . . [Traditionally,] the concept of capital encompassed and unified*
> *two distinct aspects: the claim on future income and the ownership and*
> *control over the means of production. . . . Unless one accepts John*
> *Kenneth Galbraith's view of the hegemony of the technostructure . . .*
> *it must be admitted that educated workers do not control, much less*
> *own, the means of production. Yet it is precisely this latter . . . sense*
> *of the word which provides the ideological impact to the statement that*
> *every worker is now a capitalist.* [8] (Emphasis added)

It is certainly possible for a small number of workers to become capitalists
through the attainment of sufficient human capital. For example, some individuals who invested in economic training have become professional economic
forecasters and consultants. They have established consulting firms by selling
stock in *themselves*. The buyers of these stocks have claims on the future services and forecasts of these consultants. Another example is the experience of
a number of young golfers. They are able to sell shares in themselves where
buyers have claims on their future golf earnings. However, these examples are
rare. The vast majority of economists become university professors or salaried
employees rather than private capitalists. University professors may sometimes earn a large salary, but it is clear that they have little control over the
means of production—university decisions. Most important, the areas in

---

6. Samuel Bowles and Herbert Gintis, "The Problem with Human Capital Theory:
A Marxian Approach," *American Economics Review* 65 (May 1975): 74–89.

7. Robert Heilbroner, *Limits of American Capitalism* (New York: Harper and
Row, 1966). J. K. Galbraith, *New Industrial State* (Boston: Houghton-Mifflin,
1969).

8. Bowles and Gintis, "The Problem of Human Capital Theory," p. 79.

which human capital has succeeded in making workers capitalists—economic consultants, golf pros, etc.—are almost always in service industries. In no way, radicals argue, has human capital weakened the control of capitalists over the means of *industrial* production.

3.2 THE MANAGERIAL CONTROL THESIS

The managerial control thesis, originally formulated during the 1930s, contends that corporate power is controlled today by management rather than by stockholders. Hence, the capitalist (stockholder) may continue to earn a substantial rate of return, but is now unable to influence corporate decisions. The concept that there is a separation of ownership and control of the large corporations has become so widely accepted within the economics profession that it has become a part of the litany given to all economics students. According to Samuelson,

> *Who makes corporate decisions? Primarily the increasingly important class of profession managers. . . . In company after company, the original founder has been replaced by a new type of executive, usually having a different surname. He is likely to be a self-made man than a graduate of Harvard Business School.*[9]

Samuelson, with his sympathy with the notion of people's capitalism, claims that the increasingly wide dispersion of stock ownership reduces the power of the stockholder, thus increasing the independence of inside management.[10] Galbraith claims that capital funds are now readily available, but "the requirements of technology and planning have greatly increased the need of the industrial enterprise for specialized talent and for its organization."[11] Hence, according to Galbraith, power has passed into the hands of the techno-structure because technical skills are now the scarce productive resource. Baran and Sweezy echo Galbraith's thoughts concerning the abundance of finance capital. They note,

> *The power of the investment banker was based on the urgent need of the early corporation . . . for outside financing. Later this need declined in importance or disappeared altogether as the giants, reaping a rich harvest of monopoly profits, found themselves increasingly able to take care of their financial needs from internally-generated funds.*[12]

---

9. Paul Samuelson, *Economics,* 8th ed. (New York: McGraw-Hill, 1970), p. 89.

10. Ibid., p. 90. However, by the tenth edition of his book, Samuelson retreats from his support of people's capitalism.

11. Galbraith, *New Industrial State,* p. 57.

12. Paul Baran and Paul Sweezey, *Monopoly Capital* (New York: Monthly Review Press, 1965), pp. 17–18.

In addition, Baran and Sweezy claim that through deaths and the dispersion of inheritances among numerous heirs, foundations, and trusts, the "ownership unit which once exercised absolute control over many enterprises became increasingly amorphous and leaderless."

The primary evidence in support of the managerial control thesis has been the corporate ownership studies of Adolph Berle and Gardiner Means during the 1930s, which was updated by Robert Larner in 1965. Berle and Means analyzed the personal stockholdings of the Board of Directors of the 200 largest nonfinancial corporations in the United States.[13] They arbitrarily decided that the Board would only have to own 10% of the voting stock in order to effectively control the corporation. Ten percent was considered sufficient because (1) elections rarely have a majority of shares voted; (2) the other shares would be too widely dispersed for a competing group to coalesce; and (3) the Board would have a significant advantage through its access to confidential information in any battle. All corporations in which the Board owned less than 10% were considered controlled by inside management. Using this procedure, Berle and Means claimed that more than one-half of these corporations were controlled by inside management. Larner used the same procedure and found that over four-fifths of the 200 largest U.S. corporations were controlled by inside management.[14]

Financial Control versus Managerial Control

The managerial control thesis conjures up images of little old ladies clipping dividend coupons and spending their time on needy charities; young heirs running off and marrying some "commoner" against family wishes or going to live in some hippie commune; and invisible technicians running corporations according to slide-rule calculations. There are, however, problems with these images as well as the studies on which they are based.

To take a lack of personal holdings as an indication of lack of power, as the Berle and Means approach does, is incorrect. Individuals exert their influence today, not as personal owners of vast wealth, but as controllers of institutional holdings. For example, Henry Ford as an individual owns little Ford Motor Company stock. However, as trustee of the Ford Foundation he is able to exert control. The Rockefeller fortune is no longer held by individual members of the Rockefeller family, but by the trust department of Citibank and Chase Manhattan, as well as by the Rockefeller Brothers Foundation.

Radicals claim that capitalists exert power over corporations through their control of finance capital. This thesis of banking control of large cor-

13. A. A. Berle, Jr. and Gardiner Means, *The Modern Corporation and Private Property* (New York: Commerce Clearing House, 1932).

14. R. J. Larner, "Ownership and Control in 200 Largest Corporations," *American Economics Review* 56 (Sept. 1966): 777–787.

porations was first developed by Lenin in his work, *Imperialism*. He argued that banks exert control for two reasons. First, through their vast holdings of stock, they are able to vote their interests. Second, even when stock control is not large enough, the need for external funds makes corporate independence quite fragile. Only in times when internal funds (cash flow) are sufficient to fund capital expansions can corporations remain independent of financial institutions. However, when expansion requires external financing, corporations must often relinquish decision-making prerogatives to financial interests.

Competitive theory would have us believe that the amount of external funding required would have no effect on the independence of corporations from bank domination. After all, if there are thousands of banks in competition, firms have no problem finding a bank willing to make loans without requiring control of corporate decisions. Most studies have shown, however, that the banking community has a limited amount of competition. Except for the largest banks in the largest cities, there are virtually no independent sources of large capital funding. This was quite apparent when New York City desired to float its bonds. Without acceptance by the big New York banks, it was impossible to find sufficient buyers.[15] Similarly, the Bert Lance issue points out the power of the large banks to influence the decisions of smaller banks.[16] The Lance affair highlights the system of correspondence accounts, where smaller banks place substantial funds in noninterest-bearing accounts of large banks. In essence, the smaller banks pay the larger banks for services and, therefore, cannot be in competition with the large city banks.

In an attempt to determine the linkage between required external funds and the degree of financial control, Peter Dooley analyzed the 250 largest corporations. He found that the percentage of directors from banking interests was positively correlated with the degree of external financing. Corporations with weaker financial positions tended to have a greater percentage of their board members from the banking community.

Dooley was able to identify fifteen major banking interest groups. He then tried to identify which of the largest 250 corporations belonged to each of these groupings. If a corporation had at least four directors interlocked within any group, Dooley considered it to be part of a financial control group. However, according to Dooley, since "so many corporations interlocked with the New York group it was necessary to raise the cut-off point for membership to six or more." Using these criteria, Dooley found that of the 250 corpora-

---

15. In 1975, as part of an agreement to obtain loans, New York City agreed to allow an Emergency Control Board, composed of directors of the New York banks, to oversee all fiscal operations of the city. They had the power to veto any agreement or purchase made by New York City.

16. Bert Lance was the one member of Carter's cabinet who was a personal associate. Lance resigned under pressure when his personal financial practices were questioned for both legal and ethical reasons.

tions, 122 (49%) were controlled by the fifteen interest groups, 88 (35%) by the largest seven.

Dooley found that the largest group was the New York group. He stated,

The New York group centers around six large banks—[the numbers in parenthesis indicates the number of times the corporations interlock with others in the same group] Chase Manhattan (22), First National City (14), Chemical Bank (18), First National City (14), Manufacturers Hanover Trust (20), Bankers Trust (10), and Morgan Guarantee Trust (19), Equitable Life Assurance (23), New York Life (15), and Mutual of New York (13); and several long established industrials and utilities —AT&T (13), Consolidated Edison (15), U.S. Steel (11), General Electric (12), Union Carbide (12), General Foods (13), International Paper (11), Phelps Dodge (11), Corn Products (10), Chrysler (15), American Smelting and Refining (11), U.S. Rubber (10), and Ford Motor (10). The following corporations complete the group: National Dairy Products, Allied Chemical, IBM, Irving Trust, Goodrich, American Electric Power, Southern Railways, Union Pacific, Panhandle Eastern Pipe Lines, Socony Mobil Oil, Western Electric, F. W. Woolworth, Borg Warner, and Texaco.[17]

Implications

In recent years, within radical circles, there has been some disagreement over the extent to which the financial institutions actually dictate the operations of the corporations within each grouping. There is some evidence that corporate managers have substantial latitude and only in extreme cases are their actions countermanded by the financial elite.[18] Indeed, the mainstream response to the financial control thesis is to argue that directorships of large corporations are given to individuals as honorariums. These individuals have too little contact with and knowledge of the corporations they direct and must rely totally on the information given them by the inside managers.

Despite these alternative views, the majority of radicals still contend that there is enough cohesiveness within each of the financial groups that it is rea-

---

17. Peter Dooley, "The Interlocking Directorate," *American Economics Review* 59 (June 1969): 314–23.

18. A significant minority within the radical community believe neither the managerial control thesis nor the financial control thesis. See Edward Herman, "Do Bankers Control Corporations?" *Monthly Review* 25 (June 1973): 12–29. For support of the financial control thesis, see S. Menshikov, "Millionaires and Managers," in *Economics: Mainstream Readings and Radical Critiques,* 3rd ed., David Mermelstein, ed. (New York: Random House, 1976), pp. 407–420; R. Fitch and M. Oppenheimer, "Who Rules the Corporation?" part 1, *Socialist Revolution* 1 (July–Aug. 1970), pp. 74–108.

sonable to assume that they act together in making broad economic policy.[19] The implications of this contention are profound.[20] As long as each corporation acts separately, the potential for direct control of the federal government is small. Each corporation could only "buy" politicians and political favors in areas where it had plants and headquarters. Even in the case of the largest corporations (General Motors, AT&T, etc.), this would not be sufficient to control the federal government. However, if enough corporations act *together,* they could have sufficient power to gain control of federal government policies.

The financial control thesis is the foundation for the radical claims that there are two major corporate groupings which are contesting for control of the federal government. One is the Morgan-Rockefeller grouping ("old" money), generally located in the Northeast and Midwest and centered in metal transformation industries. The other ("new" money), centered in energy and electronics growth industries, is primarily located in the Sun Belt. The effects of this contest on federal government policies during the 1970s will be detailed later in this chapter.

3.3 GOVERNMENT AND THE LABOR PROCESS

One aspect of the economic system often neglected by mainstream economists is the degree to which the federal government influences wage rates and working conditions. When this issue is discussed, concepts of "balance between labor and capital," "protecting the national interest," and "the rule of law" are usually uncritically used to characterize the objectives of government intervention in the labor negotiating process. Radicals contend that behind these phrases has been a consistent history of federal intervention to weaken the strike and organizing activities of militant workers.

Prior to the 1970s, federal intervention can be divided into two phases. During the pre-Depression period, the federal government was openly anti-union; afterwards, it considered certain types of unions to be legitimate representatives of workers. However, during both phases, radicals contend that the federal government consistently weakened the ability of workers to strike effectively. According to radicals, the 1970s ushered in the beginnings of a third phase of government intervention—the extensive use of government compulsory arbitration and wage-price controls. In this phase, the federal

19. M. DeVroey, "Separation of Ownership and Control," *Review of Radical Political Economy* 7 (Summer 1975) indicates that the unification of an interest group does not require that banks be in control.

20. One implication, developed by Fitch and Oppenheimer, is that intercorporate purchases are determined by their effect on the overall profits of the interest group rather than of the individual corporations. Hence, firm A would purchase goods from firm B, even if B was not the lowest priced supplier, if this transaction would raise the total profits of the interest group which included both firm A and firm B.

government directly determines the labor settlements. Radicals maintain that this latest phase is a necessary part of the move towards economic planning. Following are the radical contentions concerning these three phases of government intervention in the labor negotiating process.

Attacks on Worker Militancy

With the emergence of the Industrial Revolution the number of conflicts between labor and capital increased. During the early part of the twentieth century there was a rapid growth of militant trade unionism. Thousands of anti-big business candidates were elected to local and legislative offices. Eugene Debs, running as a socialist, received over one million votes (5% of the total) in the 1916 Presidential Election while sitting in federal jail for his political activities. In general, the government sided with capital during these conflicts. The government would usually send troops to protect the orderly production in firms when labor struck. Often it involved using violence to force the strikers to return to work.

At the turn of the century, conservative and mainstream liberal economists alike considered these actions to be in the "national interest" rather than examples of the bias of government. They viewed strikes as anarchist anti-American actions which were against the "genuine" interests of both labor and capital. For example, conservative economists believed that workers who advocated anti-private market mechanisms and believed society was composed of warring classes, were genetically inferior and posed a threat to the future of democracy in America. General Francis Amasa Walker, chief administrator of the 1870 and 1880 Census and the first president of the American Economics Association, maintained that the immigrants of the 1880s and 1890s:

> . . . are beaten races; representing the worst failures in the struggle for existence. Centuries are against them, as centuries are on the side of those who formerly came to us. They have none of the ideas and aptitudes which would fit them readily and easily to take up the problems of self care and self government, such as belong to those who are descended from the tribes that met under the oak tree of old Germany to make the laws and choose a chieftain.[21]

According to Frank A. Fetter, then professor of economics at Princeton University and later president of the American Economics Association,

> The ignorant, the improvident and the feebleminded are contributing far more than their quota to the next generation. . . . Unless effective means are found to check the degeneration of the race, the noontide of

---

21. Francis A. Walker, "Restriction of Immigration," *Atlantic Monthly* (June 1896): 828.

humanity's greatness is nigh, if not passed. . . . Great changes in
thought are impending, and these will include the elimination of the
unfit . . . and the conscious improvement of the race. Under the touch
of the new science of eugenics, many of our most perplexing problems
would disappear, making possible the better democracy which we are
just beginning to seek.[22]

The major policy proposals of conservative economists were to restrict
immigration of non-Nordic peoples (eastern and southern Europeans) and to
adopt eugenical procedures, such as forced sterilization.

Among economists, the most active campaigner for these laws was Irving
Fisher of Yale University. Fisher was president of both the Race Betterment
League and the Eugenics Society. In his professional writings he recom-
mended,

. . . that by a policy of restricting immigration by excluding those unfit
to become American citizens . . . we shall help solve some of our prob-
lems, including that of distribution of wealth.[23]

Fisher believed that "the 80,000 prisoners constantly supported in the
United States are not recruited evenly from the general population, but mainly
from certain family breeds." To correct this, he recommended the "seg-
regation of defectives so that they may not mingle their family traits with
those of sound lines . . . [and] sterilization of certain gross and hopeless
defectives."[24]

Mainstream liberals did not significantly disagree with the conservative
explanation for unrest or the justification for the government to intervene on
the side of capital for the "national interest." They, too, believed that the
principal cause was defects in the immigrant population rather than the class
nature of society. Liberals, however, believed that these defects were culturally-determined and, hence, correctable.

One of the most active members of the Immigration Restriction League
was longtime Harvard economist Thomas Nixon Carver. Carver believed that
the new immigrants neither desired nor appreciated democracy. In response to
anti-private market movements, he said,

It is notable of our country, that the ideas of universality and non-
nationality abound mostly among individuals of dominated races find-
ing refuge here—Russians, Bohemians, and Polish Jews, and some
other peoples of east and south central Europe. . . . These nationless

---

22. Frank A. Fetter, "Discussant," *AEA Publications* 8 (Feb. 1907): 90–92.

23. Irving Fisher, "Some Impending National Problems," *Journal of Political Economy* 24 (1916): 710–11.

24. Irving Fisher and Eugene Fisk, *How to Live* (New York: Funk & Wagnalls, 1915), pp. 299–300.

persons, who have yet to go through the physical and spiritual conflict
which our American ancestors went through [must do so] before they
can catch a glimpse of the expanse and grandeur of democratic ideals.[25]

These thoughts were echoed by economist John R. Commons. He, like
Carver, believed that it was possible to acculturate new immigrants. Commons
especially felt that the proper type union would be instrumental to this assimi-
lation process. Of course, the type of union Commons desired was one that
stressed negotiations rather than strike activities.

If labor unrest was due to defects in the population, then it was quite
rational to recommend government intervention against such actions in the
"national interest." Indeed, it justified any means necessary to repel the
demands of workers. The period 1907–1925 saw twenty-five states pass sterilization laws directed at the high birth rates of immigrants. It witnessed the particularly harsh response of the government to the organizing activities of the
Industrial Workers of the World (IWW). This period also included the 1919
Palmer Raids directed at eastern and southern European immigrants. And
finally, the 1924 Immigration Law evolved, which was expressly intended to
terminate immigration of "undesirable" eastern and southern European
immigrants.[26]

Legal Restrictions on Militant Actions

Since the Great Depression, the philosophy of John R. Commons has dominated government policy. The federal government no longer actively supports
resistance to unionization. Instead, it has often been supportive of union organizing drives. This was especially true under the Roosevelt Administration,
when the Wager Act was passed. This act set up the National Labor Relations
Board (NLRB), which is responsible for guaranteeing union-organizing rights.
However, the government has, at the same time, consistently enacted legislation to restrict the ability of workers to undertake militant actions.

One recent example of the two-sided approach to labor of the federal
government occurred during 1977. The AFL-CIO leadership proposed two
major pieces of labor legislation. The first was to increase penalties to employers who illegally resisted union-organizing campaigns. The second was to
allow workers to picket an entire construction site if there was a strike against
any of the subcontractors working at the site. The first piece of legislation
would facilitate union organizing drives while the second would have increased
the effectiveness of militant (strike) actions. As the radical view would have

---

25. Thomas N. Carver and H. B. Hall, *Human Relations* (Boston: Little Brown,
1923), p. 77.

26. For J. R. Commons' racial views, see *Races and Immigrants* (New York:
MacMillan, 1920).

predicted, the Carter Administration supported the first but not the second piece of legislation.

Restrictions on secondary actions Secondary actions consist of actions against firms which are indirectly associated with the primary target of workers' actions. In the previous example, by picketing the entire site all other subcontractors at the site, who are indirectly associated with the primary target, would be effected. This would, therefore, be considered a secondary action. Other secondary actions are secondary boycotts and secondary strikes. A secondary boycott occurs when firms that use or sell products made by the primary target are boycotted. For example, if a grocery store was boycotted until it terminated its sales of nonunion lettuce, it would be considered a secondary boycott. Another example would be the boycott of a large department store until it terminated sales of nonunion clothing.

A secondary strike occurs when workers producing for other than the primary target strike in support of the demands of the primary target's workers. If, for example, retail workers struck department stores, demanding that they only sell clothing produced in union shops, this would be considered a secondary strike. The broadest secondary strikes are called *general strikes.* They occur when all workers in a given locality strike in support of the demands of a specific group of workers.

There have been a few examples of massive secondary actions in the United States. In 1886, 300,000 workers nationally struck for one day in support of the "eight-hour workday." Centered in Chicago, this movement is commemorated internationally as "May Day." In 1892, a general strike of all workers in New Orleans occurred in support of black dockworkers. In 1919, 100,000 workers in Seattle supported a five-day general strike in support of demands by shipyard workers. During this strike, the Metal Trades Council had total control over all productive decisions in Seattle. In 1934, there was a six-day general strike in San Francisco in support of striking longshoremen.

One of the major components of the Taft-Hartley Act of 1947 was to make it a federal crime to engage in secondary actions. For the first time, there was federal legislation which made it illegal for these kinds of actions to be used.

Restrictions on ability to strike The major way in which governments have historically restricted strike activity is through their ability to determine the legality of specific strikes. At the federal level, the Taft-Hartley Act stipulates that the federal government can issue an injunction against any strike which is against the national interest. This injunction dictates an eighty-day "cooling-off period" during which government arbitration is mandatory.

A second form of government intervention is federal intervention in *wildcat* strikes. For example, suppose foundary workers believe that the company is violating safety standards and decide to strike until they are corrected. This would only involve a fraction of the workers in the United Automobile Workers who are employed by the company. This is called a *wildcat* strike. It was decided by the Supreme Court, in 1970, that these actions are illegal and that federal judges can issue injunctions against any striking workers. Previously, the Supreme Court had ruled otherwise.

One area in which the government has been particularly severe against strikes has been the public sector. In many states it is illegal for government workers to strike. This has given courts the power to immediately issue injunctions against striking workers and to dictate heavy penalties on the union representing the striking workers. In New York, rather than ordering the strikers back to work, the court injunction stipulates, according to state law, that each worker must forfeit two days' pay for each day of the strike.

Government Direct Determination

Before 1970, the government rarely directly determined the outcome of the negotiating process. However, during the last decade this has been reversed. In 1971, the Nixon Administration instituted wage-price controls. These controls required all corporations to have all price changes and wage settlements approved by a board appointed by the President. Radicals contend that controls were overwhelmingly directed against labor (to slow down the growth rate of wages in order to enhance the profits of corporations). Price controls were added to make them politically palatable and give the impression of neutrality.

Radicals support their contention by pointing to the widespread support the initiation of controls had within the big business community. The previous two years had witnessed the largest strike activity in the post-World War II era. Also, precedent-setting construction wage settlements of over 10% in 1970 were worrisome to business because of the large number of collective-bargaining contracts which came up for renewal in 1971. According to the *Wall Street Journal,*

> *Actually, many businessmen never did favor permanent controls. Many just wanted some temporary government intervention to block what they considered to be unreasonable union wage demands.*[27]

This class bias of controls was also noted by Arnold Weber, former director of the Cost of Living Council. Weber noted,

> *Business had been leaning on [Secretary of the Treasury] Schultz and [Chairman of Economic Advisors] McCracken to do something about the economy, especially wages. The idea of the freeze and Phase II was to zap labor, and we did.*[28]

---

27. *Wall Street Journal* (March 4, 1974): 1.
28. *Business Week* (April 27, 1974): 108.

Though controls ended in 1974, government intervention in the negotiating process continued in the form of binding government arbitration. Arbitration occurs when the government appoints a third party to determine the
settlement of a labor dispute. Arbitration is binding if both sides are legally
forced to accept the arbitrator's recommendation. In these cases, the government has virtual control over labor settlements.

Radicals contend that with the move toward government economic
planning, it is necessary to directly regulate the negotiating process. Therefore,
government regulation of the negotiating process will increasingly be used to
solve more than shortrun problems of individual corporations.

3.4 "OLD" VERSUS "NEW" MONEY

Two prominent events occurred during the 1970s. In 1975, after two years of
struggle, President Nixon was forced to resign as a result of the Watergate
scandal. The second event was the inability of the Carter Administration to
pass a comprehensive energy program, especially the one which it favored.
Both these events seem to contradict the radical contention that capitalists
control the federal government. After all, Nixon was probably more sympathetic to capitalists than any President in the post-World War II period, and
the energy program was stalled for more than a year because President Carter
refused to accept an energy bill which was favored by the energy-producing
corporations. Each of these events can be reconciled with the radical thesis
when we incorporate the struggle between "old" and "new" money for control of the government.

The Watergate Episode

In 1973, four individuals from the Nixon Reelection Committee were caught
breaking into the Democratic Party offices. Over the next two years, as more
information was uncovered, the public became aware that under Nixon, the
government diverged from pursuing national objectives.

The conservative explanation relied entirely on psychological reasons for
these events. For example, Howard K. Smith, a noted television news com-
mentator, claimed that the problems stemmed from Nixon's personality
defects. Smith pictured Nixon as a basically decent, well-intentioned person
overwhelmed with a desire to have a grand place in history. This desire caused
Nixon to act irrationally. This was the contention of John Ehrlichman, one of
Nixon's aides, whose book was serialized on televison, "Behind Closed
Doors," during 1977. Moreover, this viewpoint minimizes the use of power
for economic objectives. It emphasizes that the problem was not Nixon's
objectives, but the means by which he attempted to attain these objectives.

Another variation of this psychological explanation of Watergate was
offered by Eugene McCarthy. McCarthy, too, felt that Nixon had personality
defects. He pictured Nixon as a man with a thirst for power, having a callous

and cynical attitude, if not contempt, for the public. McCarthy, however, placed most of the blame on the American public. He claimed that the American public is basically ignorant, can be easily swayed with rhetoric, and has no real regard for the protection of democratic ideals.[29] Although Smith's and McCarthy's outlooks might seem different, they are basically the same. If the problem is one of personality and values, then there is no need to change political institutions nor to believe that economic interests are the cause of governmental problems.

The mainstream liberal viewpoint, while supporting the individualistic view that psychological factors were important, also believed that certain structural factors unintentionally fostered the divergence of government objectives from serving the national interest. The major structural factor identified is the method of financing political campaigns. Politicians have historically relied on private donations for campaign funding. When the required funds were small, the method seemed to be consistent with democratic ideals. However, according to this liberal viewpoint, during the last twenty years, with the development of mass media, principally television, the cost of campaign financing escalated. With increasing costs there was an increased reliance upon large contributors. Politicians were not only under increasing pressure to make commitments to contributors but became cynical about democratic ideals. Nixon is seen as an extreme example of this problem.

This explanation relies on identifying the unintended effects of an institutional arrangement (private financing of political campaigns) which developed because of technological changes (television). Since the problem is not one of profiteering, there is no need to change the political system. Instead, mainstream liberals recommend a change in campaign funding. Rather than forcing politicians to rely on large contributors, mainstream liberals recommend that the government provide public funding of campaigns.

Radical view of Watergate Radicals argue that the Watergate episode occurred because of economic interest rather than institutional and/or psychological factors. According to the radical viewpoint, while present U.S. election procedures make it easy for corporations to buy politicians, the capitalist class has far more power over politicians than the financing of campaigns. They control the mass media, corporate jobs, and the ability to legitimate any individual by appointing him or her to prestigious committees. Radicals would argue that personal excesses have always been a part of the political process, and have never been a reason for dismissal. Radicals contend that the only time a politician will be hounded out of office by the economic elite is if the politician attempted to serve some other group in society. From this perspec-

---

29. McCarthy's attitude toward the "common man" is similar to the previously described attitude of the Progressives at the beginning of the twentieth century. Both believed that working people have no respect for democratic ideals.

tive, it is claimed that Nixon was dismissed because he attempted to serve an upstart group of capitalists against the interest of the dominant group of capitalists.

According to one radical thesis,[30] beginning in the 1950s, a number of southern and western corporations coalesced into a unified interest group. Centered in electronics, energy, and agribusiness, these corporations attempted to use the federal government for their own narrow self-interests. This "new" money group increasingly came into opposition with the "old" money group (dominated by the Morgan-Rockefeller interests).

During the 1970s, these two groups differed over the appropriate economic and military policies. New money opposed the economic slowdown that was favored by the old money grouping. Being centered in energy, new money favored deregulation of energy prices while old money opposed deregulation. Old money, reflected by Henry Kissinger's views, favored a more negotiated approach to foreign disputes and more coordination with Western European and Japanese capitalists. When Nixon began to weaken Kissinger's power and terminate wage-price controls in favor of an inflationary expansion, the radical viewpoint claims that old money decided to oust him.

"Old" Money Selects Carter

Many would argue that this radical "conspiratorial" theory is incorrect. They would claim that while the interim leadership—President Ford and Vice President Rockefeller—could be considered conscious supporters of old money, no such claims could be made for President Carter. After all, wasn't Carter the totally unexpected candidate who began with no establishment backing? Radicals contend that this view of Carter is one of the biggest myths ever invented. According to radicals, Carter more than any previous president was selected and controlled by old money.

In 1974, long before Carter decided to run for the presidency, David Rockefeller appointed him to the Trilateral Commission. This commission, funded by the Rockefeller Brothers Foundation, was composed of 180 individuals, 60 each from the United States, Western Europe, and Japan. The purpose of the Trilateral Commission was to recommend policies which would coordinate foreign trade and diplomacy between the three centers of the noncommunist world. All members of this commission were personally selected by David Rockefeller, Chairman of the Board of Chase Manhattan and titular head of the Rockefeller financial interests.[31]

---

30. Kilpatrick Sale, *The Rise of the Southern Rim and Its Challenge to the Eastern Establishment* (New York: Random House, 1973).

31. For radical analyses of the Trilateral Commission, see Sam Bowles, "Trilateral Commission," and William Tabb, "The Imprint of Trilateralism," both in *U.S. Capitalism in Crisis* (New York: Union for Radical Political Economy, 1978).

From the sixty-member U.S. delegation came not only Carter but Secretary of the Defense Brown, Secretary of the Treasury Blumenthal, Secretary of State Cyrus Vance, National Security Council chief Brzezhinsky, as well as a number of others (such as Paul Warneke, chief negotiator at the SALT talks with the USSR) who have since been appointed to high-level posts in the Carter Administration. Radicals argue that there is a direct relationship between Rockefeller's selection of these individuals in 1974 and the selection by the Democratic Party of Carter in 1976 and Carter's selection of Blumenthal, Brown, Vance, Brzezhinsky and others in 1977. Indeed, it is claimed that no other Administration in recent history can be so identified with the interests of old money.

Conflict Over Energy Program

After his inauguration in 1977, Carter proposed an energy program which reflected the move towards planning. His chief economic advisor, Charles Schultze, had previously advocated government planning in his Goodwin Lecture series delivered in 1976.[32] Schultze accepts the notion that the market may, in certain cases, not perform optimally so that state intervention is necessary. Schultze, however, rejects the traditional instruments of state planning—nationalization and wage-price controls. Instead, Schultze believes that planning can be accomplished through a system of selective taxes and subsidies. These policies would make desirable actions on the part of business profitable and nondesirable actions unprofitable.

Instead of directly determining wage settlements through either wage controls or binding arbitration, Schultze favors the use of Tax-Based Incomes Policies (TIP).[33] TIP would use tax incentives (and disincentives) to influence settlements rather than direct intervention. Under TIP, the government would indicate a "recommended" settlement. If the wage settlement exceeded the recommendation, the corporation would pay a higher tax rate on profits. If the corporation settled for less than the recommended rate, its corporate tax rate would be lowered.

Carter's energy program also made use of tax incentives and disincentives to influence industrial energy use and conversion. On the one hand, through

---

32. Schultze's lectures were reprinted in *Harper's* (May 1977) and in Charles Schultze, *The Public Use of Private Interests* (Washington, D.C.: Brookings, 1977). Secretary of the Treasury Blumenthal and Federal Reserve President Miller have also endorsed state planning. For a left-liberal assessment of the Carter Administration's attempt to initiate planning, see Robert Lekachman, "The Next Decade," *Challenge* 21 (Mar./Apr. 1978): 20–21.

33. For a detailed discussion of TIP proposals, see Sidney Weintraub, *Capitalism's Inflation and Unemployment Crisis* (Reading, Mass.: Addison-Wesley, 1978), especially Chapter 6. For a critical though sympathetic evaluation, see Laurence S. Seidman, "Tax-Based Incomes Policies," *Brookings Papers* 2 (1978): 301–348.

selective taxes, Carter's program discouraged excess use of oil and hoped to stimulate conservation and shifts to alternative energy sources. On the other hand, the Carter Administration proposed that tax revenues would be used to subsidize industrial conversions. The conflict over Carter's energy program resulted from the effect it would have had on the balance of power between old money and new money. The Carter program would have been used to subsidize the energy conversion of declining corporations in the Morgan-Rockefeller grouping and facilitate their purchases of firms in growing industries.

New money was vigorously opposed to this type of planning. They contended that if prices of oil and natural gas were set by the international market, then companies would have sufficient incentive to find new reserves of energy. Whatever the validity of this contention, the use of the free market would dramatically increase the profits of energy companies, most of which are associated with new money. Deregulation of natural gas alone could raise profits by as much as $10 billion per year. With these funds, new money could continue its ascendancy and increase the possibility of becoming the most powerful industrial grouping in the country.

3.5 CONCLUSION

This chapter has detailed the radical theory of the state. Radicals claim that society is composed of two major classes who are in conflict over full employment policies—workers and capitalists. According to radicals, capitalists dominate the state so that the government cannot be relied upon to implement full employment policies. Mainstream economists reject these contentions for a number of reasons. First, they discount any notions of a small well-defined capitalist class. Instead, many believe that concepts of people's capitalism and human capital more accurately reflect reality.

Even those mainstream economists who agree that capital ownership is concentrated in a few percent of American families discount the notion of a powerful capitalist class. These economists argue that the managerial revolution has led to a separation of ownership and power. We found that radicals reject this managerial control thesis. Instead, they claim that the financial control thesis is correct. This thesis claims that economic power is held by corporate groupings centered around major financial interests.

Also covered in this chapter was the radical contention that the form of government intervention in the negotiating process has entered a third phase. During the first two phases, government intervention was indirect—its primary objective was to weaken the effectiveness of labor strikes. In this third phase, which began with the adoption of wage-price controls during 1971–1974, the federal government has moved to directly settle labor disputes. Radicals contend that this third phase reflects the move towards state planning.

The financial control thesis is the basis for the radical contention that two groupings—old and new money—are in fierce competition for control of the federal government. It was argued that Nixon was ousted by old money because he began to support the economic and political objectives of new money. In his place, old money picked Carter and his major advisors, all of whom served on the Rockefeller-appointed Trilateral Commission. It was argued that Carter's energy program, which included a method of state planning, supported the economic objectives of old money against those of new money. It was this conflict which explained the inability of Carter to have his energy program accepted by Congress.

If one accepts the major contentions of this chapter, it is impossible to perceive of the government as a body which acts in the national interest. Also, it is extremely unlikely that the government would automatically act to eliminate unemployment. Only a political movement which is independent of politicians is capable of successfully pressuring the government to act against unemployment.

CHAPTER FOUR

PRODUCTION, INCOME, AND SPENDING

Macroeconomics is the study of *aggregate* employment, production, spending, and price changes. For example, total production, as measured by Gross National Product, was $1288 billion in 1973. Macroeconomics would be concerned with explaining why it was that level and try to predict what its future level would be. Microeconomics, on the other hand, is concerned with the production of specific industries and firms within industries. There certainly is some relationship between production in specific industries and total production. However, it is felt that they can be discussed separately.

Each of the major outlooks described in Chapter 2 has its own way of describing the macroeconomy. However, before identifying the macromodels based on each of the outlooks, it would be useful to describe in detail measures of these aggregates,[1] as well as properties common to all macromodels.

We begin with a measure of aggregate production, called Gross National Product (GNP).

DEFINITION GNP is the market value of total production of marketable goods and services produced in one year for final use.

This definition is very precise and merits comment.

4.1 THE MEASUREMENT OF GNP

GNP is a Monetary Measure

If society produced only one good, then we could look solely at physical production to measure the economic performance of the economy. Societies, however, produce a multitude of goods and services. In order to obtain one

---

1. An analysis of price level changes will be left until later. Unless stated otherwise, we will assume that prices will remain constant at some level.

measure of total production we would have to combine all outputs. For simplicity, suppose that society produced only two outputs: mink coats (luxuries) and chopped meat (necessities). Let us assume that in year 1 our society produced 10 mink coats and 150,000 pounds of chopped meat, while in year 2 it produced 14 mink coats and 140,000 pounds of chopped meat. Only if we could combine the outputs of mink coats and chopped meat could we evaluate the overall economic performance in each year and make some comparison.

Mainstream economists argue that market prices reflect the relative value to society of the last units produced of each good.[2] Therefore, market prices are a way of comparing the value of outputs of different products. If we multiply physical output by market price we can obtain the market value to society of each good produced. If we sum up the market values of production in each year of all goods we would have a single measure of overall economic performance. Let the price of mink coats equal $3000 and the price of a pound of chopped meat equal $1. In this case, the market value of total production in year 1 would be $(3000 \times 10) + (1 \times 150,000) = \$180,000$. The market value of total production in year 2 would be $(3000 \times 14) + (1 \times 140,000) = \$182,000$, if we assume that the prices are unchanged. The value of total production increased because the market value of the increased mink production (3000×4), was greater than the loss in market value of production of chopped meat $(10,000)$.

GNP Ignores Income Distribution

If we look closer at the process which brought about this change in production, it may not be true that society is better off due to the increase in market value of total production. Suppose that the shift in production was brought about because of a shift in income distribution towards more inequality. The fall in income of lower-income groups explains the decrease in production of chopped meat, while the increase in income of upper-income groups explains the increase in the production of mink coats. If this were the cause of the production changes, it would be a mistake to attempt to interpret society's well-being from changes in the market value of production. We would have to discuss the economic well-being of different groups rather than society.

This is not to say that the resulting increase in the market value of production could not have benefited most people (everyone) in society. For example, it is possible that everyone's income had increased. However, only if we knew

2. If consumers would buy items according to the *additional* utility they receive per dollar spent on the last unit of each good bought, then at equilibrium the ratio of the prices of any two goods equals the ratio of the additional utility received from the last units consumed of each good. According to this formulation, the additional utility from the 14th mink coat is 3000 times more than the additional utility from the 150,000th pound of chopped meat. Relative prices cannot, however, be used to compare the *total* utility from 14 mink coats compared to the *total* utility from 150,000 pounds of chopped meat.

something about the distribution of income could we judge whether or not higher market values reflected an increase in society's material well-being.

In an interesting example, Hunt and Sherman[3] also demonstrate that social well-being is dependent upon income distribution. They hypothesize an island economy which is periodically struck by a disease which only affects children. From past experience, the island has found that 80% of the children become afflicted with the disease. There is an antidote available. It has been found that when no doses are administered, 90% of the victims die; when one dose is given, the chance of death is reduced to 10%; two doses reduce fatality to 8%; three doses to 6%; and four doses to 5%. Beyond four doses the antidote has no effectiveness.

Let us assume that there are 1000 children on the island and the people are able to store 1000 doses of the antidote. We will find that the number of children who will die from an outbreak varies according to the distribution of the antidote. If the antidote was rationed with each child given one dose, then only 10% of the 800 children afflicted would die. However, suppose that the market is used to allocate the antidotes. The price would be bid up until only the wealthiest 250 families would be able to compete for the antidote.[4] Each of the families would give four doses of the antidote to each of their children. In this case, only 5% of the wealthy children afflicted (10 out of 200) would die, while 90% of the poorer children afflicted (540 out of 600) would die. Hunt and Sherman imply that this represents the results of having medical care in the United States being administered through the private market system.[5]

GNP is a Rough Index of Employment

In the example we are using, it is not necessarily true that the number of jobs created by the additional mink coats produced is greater than the number of jobs lost through the decrease in chopped meat production. The mink industry is a relatively high-wage industry—designers, salespeople, cutters, and piecers; while the meat industry is a relatively low-wage industry—agricultural laborers, food processors, and packers. The increased production of mink coats may create a few high paying jobs while the decrease in chopped meat production could mean the loss of numerous lower paying jobs. So even if total wages increased, the number of jobs could decrease.

In order to estimate the employment effects of changing production, we would need to know the labor (input) requirements per unit of production of

---

3. E. K. Hunt and H. Sherman, *Economics* (New York: Harper & Row, 1973), pp. 197–98.

4. Defenders of the market system would claim that by allowing the price to be bid up, a greater supply would be induced. Hence, the rationing system actually causes deaths by restricting supply.

5. See, for example, D. Schorr, *Don't Get Sick in America* (Nashville, Tenn.: Aurora Publishers, 1970).

each good or service (output). This approach is called *input-output analysis,* and is being increasingly used by governments around the world. In the United States, the leading promoter of input-output analysis is Wassily Leontief, a recent winner of the Nobel Prize in economics. Leontief has shown that shifts in government spending would have substantial effects on total employment. He found that if the government would decrease its military production by 20% and increase all other government spending by 20% (hence, keeping the total level of government spending unchanged), there would be a net loss of 200,000 jobs.[6] This would occur because $1 million spent on military goods creates more jobs than $1 million spent on nonmilitary production. So while the total level of spending remains unchanged, the number of jobs in the economy is reduced. Hence, GNP is a very rough index of employment. If we wish to more accurately assess the employment results of various combinations of output, we should use input-output analysis rather than GNP statistics.

GNP and Price Changes

For better or worse, the measure of GNP used will weigh each output by its market price. However, since prices of goods vary, we have a choice of prices to use. Table 4.1 has market prices listed for three years—1968, 1970, and 1975; and production levels for two years—1970 and 1975.

Table 4.1
Outputs and prices

Good	Production Q 1975	Unit price P 1975	Production Q 1970	Unit price P 1970	Unit price P 1968
Auto	3	$2000	4	$1800	$1700
Radio	40	50	30	50	50
Meat	10,000	1.10	8,000	1.00	0.90

DEFINITION **Money GNP (GNP$_m$) is equal to the quantity of output multiplied by its current market price.**

GNP$_m$ for 1975 is 1975 production (Q_{75}) multiplied by 1975 prices (P_{75})
$= (3 \times 2000) + (40 \times 50) + (10,000 \times 1.1) = \$19,000$.
GNP$_m$ for 1970 is Q_{70} multiplied by $P_{70} = (4 \times 1800) + (30 \times 50) + (8000 \times 1.0) = \$16,700$.

---

6. W. Leontief, "Impact of Government Expenditures," *Scientific American* (Feb. 1965).

In our example, money GNP increased by $2300 between 1970 and 1975. We would be interested in knowing how much of this increase was due to production changes and how much to price changes. To make this separation, we could attempt to calculate GNP in 1975 if prices hadn't changed since 1970. In this way we could estimate how much of the increase was solely due to production changes.

$$P_{70} \times Q_{75} = (1800 \times 3) + (50 \times 40) + (1.0 \times 10{,}000) = \$17{,}400$$

We find that only $700 of the increase was due to changes in production, while $1600 reflects changes due solely to price increases.

In general, if we select some set of prices and hold them constant, we can compare changes in production independent of price changes. The set of prices selected is called the *base year prices*. In the previous example we used 1970 prices as the base year prices, but we could just as easily use 1968 prices.

DEFINITION **Real GNP (GNP$_r$) is equal to the quantity of each output multiplied by its base year price.**

In our example, using 1968 prices as base year prices,

GNP$_r$ for 1975 $= P_{68} \cdot Q_{75} = (3 \times 1700) + (40 \times 50) + (10{,}000 \times 0.9) = \$16{,}100$
GNP$_r$ for 1970 $= P_{68} \cdot Q_{70} = (4 \times 1700) + (30 \times 50) + (8000 \times 0.9) = \$15{,}500$

GNP Ignores Changes in Quality of Products

Another factor, besides price or quantity changes, that can explain changes in GNP$_m$ is the changes in the quality of goods. In our example we implicitly assumed that the entire increase in prices was due to changes other than production. If, however, some of the price increases were due to changes in quality of goods, then we should include that portion as part of the increase in real GNP.

It is quite difficult to make accurate adjustments for quality changes, particularly in services such as education and medical care. Since quality changes increase over time, comparisons of real GNP between years becomes meaningless when the time span is more than 15 to 20 years. Many people are beginning to argue that the quality of goods and services, especially government-provided services, are deteriorating. If this is true, then real GNP estimates not adjusted for quality changes would inflate the actual level of real production.

Double Counting

When totaling production, we want to make sure to count each unit of output once and only once. A problem of double counting arises because many goods are produced for other products rather than directly for consumption. These goods are called *intermediary goods*. For example, much of the steel produced in the United States is sold to automobile producers. If we count all the steel produced and all the automobiles produced, then we would be counting the steel which was used in the production of automobiles twice. One way to solve the problem is to only count each item when it is sold for final use, not if it is to be used for further processing or manufacturing.

Production for final use would measure only sales directly to consumers. Consumers, as households, buy household goods and services directly at the marketplace and, as taxpayers, government goods and services. Businesses also consume a part of production. The plant and equipment (physical investment), unlike intermediary goods, are not processed as part of a good to be resold. Instead, physical investment remains with the firm and facilitates the production of the finished good. Over time, investment goods wear out and must be replaced. Hence, investment goods are, in a sense, consumed by the production process.

Value-Added Method

Another method of eliminating double counting is to only count the value-added to the value of the processed good at each stage of production. A full example is illustrated in Table 4.2.

Table 4.2
Value-added in a four stage production process

Stage of production	Market value of production	Value-added
Wheat Production	$15	$15
Flour Production	40	25
Bread Production	80	40
Retail Production	85	5
		$85

In this example, production goes through four stages. At each stage producers increase the market value of production through the processing of intermediary goods. Let us assume that wheat, flour, and bread production is bought entirely by the next stage in production so that the only production for final use is the $85 worth of bread bought at the retail store by households. Flour producers buy $15 worth of wheat and process it into $40 worth of flour, thus adding $25 to the market value of finished goods. Similarly, the flour is bought by the bread producer who adds $40 to the market value and the retailer, in turn, adds $5 to the market value of the finished good which is then sold to the consumer for final use. When we add up the value-added at each stage of production, we find that it totals $85.

If we look in detail at the financial statement of the bread-producing firm (Table 4.3), we can see what happens to the $40 of increased value generated at that stage of production. All of it is distributed among the firm's cost for productive resources as well as necessary government expenses (property tax).[7] The difference between the total cost and revenue becomes the firm's profits.

Table 4.3
ABC bread producing company

Revenues		Costs	
Sales	$80	Processed goods purchased	
		• flour	$40
		Payments for labor	
		• wages and salaries	20
		• supplements (pension)	2
		Payments for land	
		• rent	5
		Payments for capital funds	
		• interest	6
		Payment for government services	
		• business property taxes	4
			$77
		Residual Profits	3
	$80		$80

DEFINITION **The value-added of a firm is the market value of the firm's production minus the market value of finished goods purchased. It is the sum of the firm's payments to all factors of production, including government indirect business taxes, as well as the firm's profits.**

There are two principal benefits from using the value-added method to eliminate double counting rather than the final use method.

1. It allows us to isolate the amount of inflation generated at each stage of production. Suppose that the retail price of bread increases by 20%. The $85 worth of bread would then sell for $102. In Table 4.4, we have three possible cases where the final selling price would increase to $102. In each case, the source of inflation is in different sectors. In Case I each sector has 20% inflation; in Case II the bread sector is the only source of inflation; while in Case III the wheat sector is the only source. If we only used the final-use approach, we would be unable to find out which of the three cases was the actual reason for the 20% increase in the final selling price.

7. Indirect taxes are a direct cost to businesses that must be paid independent of income earned.

Table 4.4
Value-added at each stage of production

Stage of production	Initial	Case I	Case II	Case III
Wheat	$15	$ 18	$ 14	$ 40
Flour	25	30	24	23
Bread	40	48	60	35
Retail	5	6	4	4
	$85	$102	$102	$102

2. The value-added approach enables us to calculate the effects of changes in spending on income distribution. Table 4.5 presents a hypothetical distribution of income resulting from the final purchase of $1000 worth of each of three goods.

Table 4.5
Distribution of value-added

Income payment	Radio	Clothing	Food
Wages and salaries	$ 700	$ 750	$ 800
Non-wage income	260	220	180
Business taxes	40	30	20
	$1000	$1000	$1000

If society would shift its spending by $1000 from food to radios, wage payments would fall by $100 while nonwage payments and business taxes would increase by $80 and $20, respectively. Moreover, these distributions may vary according to changes in technology and/or power relationships between capital and labor. Only by using the value-added approach could we be able to identify and explain these changes. If we believe that the distribution of income between wages and nonwages has an important effect on the economy, then value-added should be used.

GNP Excludes Nonproductive and Nonmarket Transactions

GNP only includes those market transactions which involve the production of a good or service. This requirement implies that purely financial transactions, such as the sale or purchase of a bond, would be ignored. Suppose that the government obtains money to build a new school by selling a bond. If we count the actual building materials purchased by the local government to construct the school, then it would be double counting to also count the value of the actual bond sale.

Another group of financial transactions which are not counted in GNP are transfer payments. For example, most stock transactions represent a transfer of income from one individual to another.[8] Production is unaffected. Similarly, welfare payments, unemployment insurance, and gambling all involve the transferring of income from one individual to another. We do, however, include payments of wages to stockbrokers, jockeys, and welfare workers in GNP since they all provide services.

We also exclude from GNP the value of goods being resold, such as used automobiles. We do this because we have already counted the value of the good when it was purchased new. To count it again would be a form of double counting. We do, however, include the income of the used car and antique dealer since they both provide services to shoppers for used merchandise.

A second group of goods and services excluded from GNP are those which are not sold at the marketplace. This includes all home production, such as home repairs, child care, and housework. Because of this procedure, any shift from home production to market production falsely increases the official measure of production. For example, suppose that a mother of two small children decides to go to work assembling TV sets for $150 per week. In order to go to work, she has to spend $60 per week in child care for her children. GNP statistics would increase by $210 per week, since both the increase in TV production and child care would be included. The actual increase in production is only the TV sets since the child care was previously being done by home production. A recent study (Table 4.6) found that the market value of the services provided by an average housewife in 1974 was $257 per week. Therefore, any substantial shift away from home production would significantly inflate GNP as a measure of total production.

This is exactly what has happened in the last fifteen years. During the 1960s, there was a dramatic increase in the laborforce participation of women. For example, in 1960 only 15% of women living with husbands and having children less than six years old worked. By 1970, the figure had risen to 32%. Thus, increase was necessarily accompanied by a decrease in home production which was replaced by an increase in home services (meals and child care) purchased at the marketplace. GNP statistics counted the increased purchase of home services at the marketplace as part of aggregate production. For this reason, many economists believe that the rapid increase in GNP during the 1960s seriously overestimated the *actual* increase in production. This may explain why, despite significant rises in family income during this period, many families did not consider themselves to be better off.

---

8. Some stock sales are used by corporations to finance capital investments. However, we are already including in GNP the capital investment, so to include the stock sales would be double counting.

Table 4.6
Value of a housewife's services (1973–74)

Job	Hours per week	Rate per hour	Value per week
Nursemaid	44.5	$2.00	$89.00
Housekeeper	17.5	3.25	56.88
Cook	13.1	3.25	42.58
Dishwasher	6.2	2.00	12.40
Laundress	5.9	2.50	14.75
Food buyer	3.3	3.50	11.55
Chauffeur	2.0	3.25	6.50
Gardener	2.3	3.00	6.90
Maintenance man	1.7	3.00	5.10
Seamstress	1.3	3.25	4.22
Dietician	1.2	4.50	5.40
Practical nurse	0.6	3.75	2.25
	99.6		$257.53

Source: Chase Manhattan Bank of New York. Data based on rates paid in the New York area for the occupations listed.

4.2 NATIONAL INCOME ACCOUNTS

We have found that the market value of production is exactly equal to the value-added at each stage of production. Moreover, the value-added represents the income payments made to factors of production as well as to the government (indirect business taxes) and to owners (profits). Therefore, the value of production is exactly equal to the income payments generated by production. This identity between *total production* and *total income* is the basis of national income accounts.

Components of Production for Final Use

One side of the national income accounts identifies the components of production for final use. There are four sectors that buy goods and services for final use: the household, business, government, and foreign sectors.

Consumption expenditures This includes all purchases by households for goods and services, except the purchase of residential units (housing). We shall use the letter C to designate the total of these expenditures.

Private investment This includes all the physical investment made by society, such as purchases of capital equipment, plant, and residential and office facilities. It does not include the purchase of intermediary goods or financial investment (stocks and bonds). In this sector we also include the changes in the value of business inventory. Private investment is divided into three broad categories: replacement investment, net investment, and changes in value of inventory. We will use the letter I to designate the total of these expenditures.

Replacement investment represents the amount of investment that would be required to replace worn-out plant and equipment. The value of this investment is assumed to be equal to the government's capital consumption allowance. This represents only a rough approximation for several reasons. First, the timing of government capital consumption allowances has little to do with the timing of losses in productive ability of plants and equipment. Indeed, capital consumption allowances were accelerated (moved up in time) in 1962 in an attempt to stimulate capital investment rather than to reflect changes in the depreciation rate of capital equipment. Second, depreciation allowances are based upon original purchase prices. Hence, in a period of rapid inflation, replacement costs are substantially higher than the government's allowances.

Net investment includes all those purchases of plant and equipment which *add* to the productive capacity of the firm. It is equal to the total investment in plant and equipment minus replacement investment. It is possible for net investment to be negative. This would occur if total investment in plant and equipment is less than the investment required to replace all worn-out capital stock. For example, in 1933, total investment in plant and equipment was $1.4 billion, while the value of worn-out capital stock, as measured by capital consumption allowances, was $5.5 billion.

Government expenditures This component includes the purchases of goods and services by all levels of government—federal, state, and local. It is important to remember that government expenditures on welfare *services,* such as caseworkers, is included but that the amount of welfare payments, which is a nonproductive transfer payment, is excluded. We shall use the letter G to designate the total of these expenditures.

Foreign expenditures Some of the value of U.S. produced goods and services are purchased by foreigners. This is called *exports* and should be included as part of the value of goods and services produced. We will not include the value of stocks and bonds purchased by foreigners. For reasons to be discussed, we will subtract the value of imported goods and call this category *net* exports and use the term X_n to designate the total of these expenditures.

Necessary Adjustments

There are two important adjustments which have been made in order for the sum of these four expenditures to exactly equal the total market value of production for final use (GNP).

1. Some of the purchases of the first three sectors are imported goods. Therefore, we must subtract imported goods from the total of $C + I + G$. The accounting procedure adopted is to subtract all imported goods from the total of exported goods. This is the reason for using the term *net exports* for the fourth component.

2. The manner we have used would give us an accurate measure of *total sales* of domestic production. It is possible, however, for a portion of current production to remain unsold. National income accounts *must* include this unsold current production for it to be a measure of current production (GNP). It makes this correction by assuming that unsold production is purchased by firms as *investments* in their future sales. For this reason, we included changes in the value of inventory, which reflects this unsold production, as a component of private investment.

It is also possible for total sales to exceed current production. This would occur when firms sell out of their stock of previously produced but unsold inventories. Again, by including changes in the value of inventory, in this case negative, in our income accounts we can correct for any disparity between sales and production.

Income Generated by GNP

We found that the market value of production for final use could also have been calculated using the value-added approach. Value-added indicates the income generated by production. These income payments are to each of the factors of production, as well as government business expenses and residual profits.

Indirect business taxes A number of government taxes are costs to the firm that are passed on to the consumer. These include property taxes, excise taxes, license fees, and customs duties. These taxes should be differentiated from personal and corporate income taxes, which are taxes on income earned rather than business expenses. For this reason, income taxes are not included as a component of indirect business taxes.

Employee compensation This category includes all the expenses of the firm that are compensations for hired labor. It includes *gross* wages and all supplementary expenditures, such as the firm's social security contributions, unemployment insurance tax, and fringe benefits (medical insurance, pension fund, etc.).

Rents This component includes all income payments received by households that supply property resources. On the expenditure side, we include *all* residential construction under investment. The rationale for this procedure is that much of residential construction goes into the rental housing market. Therefore, it should be treated as an investment good rather than personal consumption. Even those units which are used for personal consumption are treated as investment goods since households have the opportunity to rent or sell their housing. In order to be consistent, income accounts include the income that could have been earned by households if they had rented out their housing. This is called *imputed rents*.

Interest payments Interest payments include all moneys which are paid by private businesses to the suppliers of money capital. It does not include interest payments to money suppliers made by households (consumer interest payments) or government (government interest) because only business interest payments represent a direct expense of production.

Payment to owners After firms make their payments to the government, labor, renters, and money suppliers, they are left to pay themselves. Part of this payment is reimbursements for the value of capital equipment which was used up during production. This component, which is measured by the capital consumption allowance, is not considered a part of the firm's profits. All payments to the firm minus capital consumption allowances are considered the *gross* profits of private businesses. Income accounts measure separately the profits received by corporations and the profits received by unincorporated businesses. The category corporate profits is then subdivided into three subcategories: corporate profit taxes, dividends, and undistributed profits. Undistributed profits are the funds that corporations do not pay out to stockholders and, instead, are retained for possible investment purposes. They are sometimes called *retained earnings*. Since the firm also has available its capital consumption allowances for investment, economists group retained earnings and capital consumption allowances together and call this category *cash flow*. A full national income account is shown in Table 4.7.

Components of Income

On the income side of the national income accounts we have a measure of the total costs of production to businesses. This, however, is not a measure of the actual money available to households for spending—disposable personal income (DPI). In order to obtain a measure of DPI, we will develop various other measures of income besides GNP.

Net national product GNP measures the market value of all goods and services produced. Part of this production is used to replace used up capital goods. If we subtract the value of production necessary to replace all used up capital goods, we obtain a measure of net national product.

DEFINITION Net national product (NNP) is the market value of goods and services produced for society's consumption and for adding to the stock of capital equipment.

Table 4.7
National income account

Receipts: Expenditure approach	Income: Business cost approach
Consumption	Business indirect taxes

Private investment
• Change in value of inventory
• Capital investment
  replacement investment
  net investment
	Employee compensation
	• wages and salaries
	• supplementary compensation

	Rents • actual rental payments
Government	• imputed rental self-payments
Net export • exports minus imports	Interest

	Employer income
	• depreciation allowances
	• gross profits
	  unincorporated profits
	  corporate profit taxes
	  dividends
	  retained earnings

National income NNP includes a number of payments that households do not have available for spending. If we subtract indirect business taxes from NNP, we have a measure which indicates the sum of all payments earned by resource owners.[9] This new measure is called national income.

DEFINITION **National income (NI) is the total of all income earned by the factors of production—the sum of wage, rent and interest payments to owners of productive resources plus profits.**

Personal income NI would be a measure of household income if all income earned at the marketplace was received by households. However, some corporate income is never received by households (retained earnings), while some income received by households, such as welfare, social security, and interest on government bonds is not "earned."[10] Also, household security contributions are earned but not received income. If we subtract from NI all earned income not received by households—corporate profits tax, undistributed profits, and all social security contributions—while adding all government transfer payments, we obtain a measure called personal income.

9. The term *earned* is used very loosely. It only means payment for non-labor resources supplied.

10. Businesses also receive transfer payments, such as depletion allowances, but here we are only concerned with income received by households.

DEFINITION **Personal income (PI) is the total income received by households from all sources.**

Disposable personal income PI is a measure of total income payments received by households. However, households have to pay income taxes out of their income. If we subtract from PI all income taxes paid by households, we obtain a measure of the actual income available to households for spending.

DEFINITION **Disposable personal income (DPI) is the income received by households net of all taxes.**

The national income account in Table 4.8 summarizes the chain of measure leading to DPI.

Table 4.8
Gross national product and related accounts*

Chain of measure	1960	1965	1970	1973
Gross National Product	$504	$685	$977	$1288
Minus:				
Capital Consumption Allowance	43	60	87	110
Equals:				
Net National Product	460	625	890	1179
Minus:				
Indirect Business Taxes	45	63	93	118
Equals:				
National Income	415	564	800	1054
Minus:				
Income earned but not received				
• Corporate Income Taxes	23	31	35	56
• Undistributed Profits	13	27	15	42
• Social Security Contributions	21	30	58	92
Plus:				
Income received but not earned				
• Transfer Payments	42	58	110	177
Equals:				
Personal Income	401	539	808	1036
Minus:				
Personal Taxes	51	66	117	153
Equals:				
Disposable Personal Income	350	473	692	883
Out of which:				
Personal consumer outlays +	333	445	636	829
Personal savings	17	28	56	54

*   Discrepancies in totals are due to the omission of minor items.
+   Includes household interest payments on consumer outlays.

4.3 CIRCULAR FLOWS AND ECONOMIC MODELS

Money flows through the economy period-by-period. Production generates income, which, in turn, generates spending. The *desired* level of spending will then determine the actual level of production in the next period. For example, suppose that current production (= current income) = 1000, while the current level of desired spending is only 980. Since desired sales are 20 less than current production, the value of business inventories builds up by 20. By including the change in the value of inventories in capital investment we find that *actual* spending would equal current production. However, noting the increase in the value of inventories[11] of 20, firms would decide to cutback their production. Let us assume that firms cutback their production by the exact amount of their change in value of inventories.[12] The next period's production would then equal the current level of desired spending (980). This new level of production would generate income and spending in the following period. The "production-income-spending chain" will continue period after period. The purpose of macroeconomics is to build models which can accurately predict these flows, explain changes in decisions, and recommend policy alternatives which would attain specified goals.

In order to develop a macromodel, data must be organized appropriately and consistent patterns must be observable.

Reorganize National Income Accounts

National income accounts aren't organized in the most suitable manner for macromodels. The income side of the national income accounts are organized from the point of view of a business statement. All incomes are costs of production to businesses—rents, gross wages, interest, business indirect taxes, and residual profits. Macromodels are interested in predicting spending done by various sectors of the economy. If we assume that spending of each sector is dependent upon, among other factors, its current level of income, then we would desire to reorganize income accounts according to spending sectors. National income accounts would have to be reorganized to show the income received by each spending sector. For example, not all of the business income listed in national income accounts remains with businesses. Businesses must pay corporate income taxes to the government and dividends to its stock-

---

11. If the firms actually desired to increase their inventories by at least 20, then production would not exceed sales. Here we are assuming that firms always desire to keep inventories at the same level so that if the value of inventories increases, it means production was higher than desired spending.

12. This is a simple assumption which can be made more sophisticated. All that is necessary for our general argument is that if the change in the value of inventories is positive, production is cut back by some amount; while if the change in the value of inventories is negative, then production is increased.

holders. Similarly, part of rental income, wages, and interest must be paid to governments in the form of taxes. With this in mind, we would reorganize the income flows of national income accounts as depicted in Table 4.9. We note that household income is divided into two distinct categories—wage and non-wage income. Radicals, as we will discuss later, have argued that different groups of households earn wage and nonwage income. If this is true, then four distinct groups of spending units exist: (1) the government, receiving taxes and social security contributions, labeled T; (2) businesses receiving net business income, labeled B; (3) nonwage households receiving net nonwage income, labeled NW; and (4) wage households receiving net wage income, labeled W. Unless stated otherwise, we will ignore the foreign sector, which receives income (money spent by the United States on imported goods) and spends (on U.S. exports).

Table 4.9 reorganizes the national income accounts so as to highlight the money flows to the four distinct domestic spending sectors. We can visualize the production-income-spending chain as a circular flow, where income flows into the four sectors and money flows back into the production process through the spending decisions of these four groups. Figure 4.1 is a representation of this circular flow.

Table 4.9
National income accounts from the point of view of spending sectors

Government Income (T)

    Indirect business taxes
    Income taxes
    Social security contributions minus government transfer payments

Business Net Income (B)

    Undistributed profits
    Capital consumption allowances
    Government transfers to businesses

Net Nonwage Income (NW)

    Net rental income
    Net interest income
    Net dividends
    Net unincorporated business profits
    Net capital gains

Net Wage Income (W)

    Net wages and salaries
    Government transfers to households

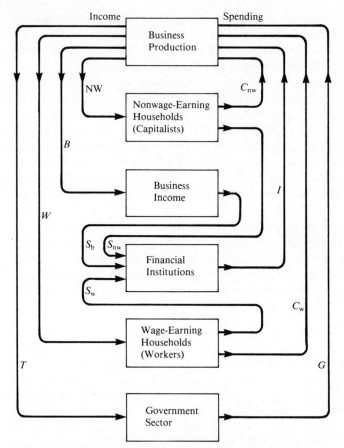

Figure 4.1 Production-income-spending circular flow

It should be noted that we have included financial institutions in the circular flow in Figure 4.1. Financial institutions such as savings banks, commercial banks, pension funds, mutual funds, life insurance companies, and business investment accounts take in savings and attempt to find, among other things, capital investment outlets for these funds. Savings consists of three components: business savings (S_b), wage-earning household savings (S_w), and nonwage-earning household savings (S_{nw}). Since all business income is available for capital investment, S_b will always be equal to business income. Also, since we have divided households into two groups, then consumption will consist of two components: wage-earning household consumption (C_w) and nonwage-earning household consumption (C_{nw}).

Consistent Patterns

The circular flow diagram identifies the flow which must be predicted in order to estimate aggregate spending. There are two sets of predictions which must be made. First, we would like to predict the distribution of income between the four spending sectors given the total level of production (GNP). That is, if we knew the present level of GNP, could we predict NW, W, B, and T? Second, we would hope to be able to use the distribution of income to predict the level of desired spending. That is, if we knew NW and W, could we predict $C = C_w + C_{nw}$? If we knew T, could we predict G? If we knew B, could we predict I? We will call the first set of predictions *production-income predictions* and the second set *income-spending predictions*.

The accuracy of predictions is determined by the consistency of responses in the economy. If there are certain patterns, which we will call *relationships,* that consistently repeat, then we can make good predictions. If, however, some relationships are volatile, then it is not possible to make accurate predictions.

DEFINITION Suppose that we can predict the value of B once we know the value of A. We would then say that there is a relationship between A and B.

One of the production-income relationships stated previously was the relationship between GNP and W. To determine whether or not a relationship exists between GNP and W, statisticians look at a set of past data. In Figure 4.2 we have plotted the combination of W and GNP for ten years (hypothetical data). For example, in 1965, GNP equaled 1200 and W equaled 624. In 1966, GNP equaled 1250 and W equaled 650. When we connect all of the ten combinations, they lie on a straight line going through the origin. This is because in each year wage income (W) was exactly 52% of total production (GNP). Suppose the level of total production in 1977 is predicted to be 1500. We would say that from past experience we expect wage income to be 52% of total production or 780. We would be pretty confident of this prediction because of the extreme consistency of the relationship between W and GNP.

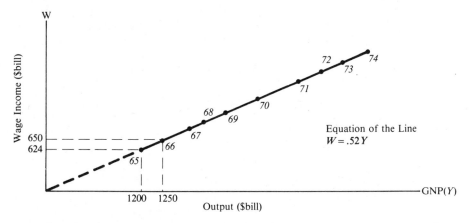

Figure 4.2   Relationship between W and GNP

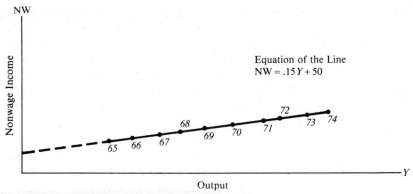

Figure 4.3   Relationship between NW and GNP

Similarly, suppose that the data for NW and GNP is as depicted in Figure 4.3. Here, too, we would have a consistent relationship, though a little more complex since the straightline does not go through the origin. We would say that NW is 15% of GNP plus 50. Again, we would be very confident of being able to predict NW if we knew GNP. If the level of GNP is expected to be 1500, then we would predict that from past experience NW would be $(.15 \times 1500) + 50 = 275$.

However, suppose that the data for NW and GNP is as depicted in Figure 4.4. In this case, $NW = .15Y + 50$ is again the *best* simple relationship between NW and GNP.[13] However, this best possible simple relationship is not very

---

13. A simple relationship is where one variable is related to only one other variable. Statistical methods of "least squares" are used to determine the best simple relationship. A more complex relationship would be to say that NW is a function of the level of Y and also the level of unemployment (Un). This would be a way of incorporating the *reserve army* thesis. A numerical example of this more complex relationship would be: $NW = .15Y + 6(\%Un) + 20$ so that

$$
\begin{aligned}
\text{if } \%Un = 6.0 \quad &\text{then} \quad NW = .15Y + 6(6.0) + 20 = .15Y + 56 \\
\text{if } \%Un = 8.0 \quad &\text{then} \quad NW = .15Y + 6(8.0) + 20 = .15Y + 68 \\
\text{if } \%Un = 5.5 \quad &\text{then} \quad NW = .15Y + 6(5.5) + 20 = .15Y + 53
\end{aligned}
$$

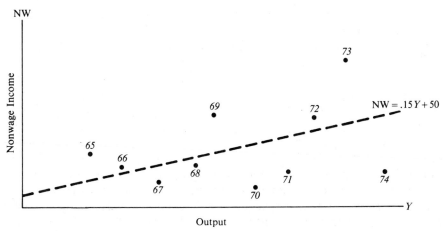

Figure 4.4 Relationship between NW and GNP

consistent, hence we would not be very confident in using it to predict future levels of NW.

Macroeconomics assumes that consistent patterns, such as in Figures 4.2 and 4.3, exist for each of the subdivisions of income. Production-income relationships imply that we can predict the distribution of income between spending sectors if we know the level of production (GNP).[14] An example of a set of production-income relationships is:

$$W = .52Y, \text{ NW} = .15Y + 50, \text{ } B = .08Y - 20, \text{ } T = .25Y - 30$$

If GNP equaled 1500, we would predict that it would be distributed as follows:

$$W = 780, \text{ NW} = 275, \text{ } B = 100, \text{ and } T = 345.$$

Predicting the distribution of income is only the first step in predicting the current level of desired spending. We must be able to predict the level of each sector's spending, given the distribution of income. The relationship between each sector's spending and its income will be called *income-spending relationships*. As with production-income relationships, we would hope that the past experience forms a set of consistent relationships.

For the two household sectors we would expect to find consistent relationships between their consumption and their income. We expect this because most households cannot spend independent of their income for very long. A set of income-spending relationships for the two household sectors is:

$$C_w = .9W \text{ and } C_{nw} = .6(\text{NW}) + 20 \text{ so that}$$
$$C = C_w + C_{nw} = .9W + .6(\text{NW}) + 20$$

---

14. These relationships may not be linear. For example, $\text{NW} = .15Y - .00001Y^2 + 10$ is a simple nonlinear relationship.

Business and government spending are much more independent of their current incomes. Businesses can borrow for long periods, can print new stock to raise money, and can go bankrupt without individual liabilities. The federal government can directly print money as payment for purchases. For these reasons we would not expect to find a simple relationship between income and spending for these two spending sectors. This does not necessarily mean that investment and/or government spending are unpredictable or not dependent upon current income. It may just mean that the relationship is more complex and more information is needed. For example, capital investment may follow consistent patterns if we incorporate information on the rate of interest, the expected rate of profit, and/or the rate of aggregate spending along with the current level of business income (B). For the time being, let us assume that investment and government spending are determined by factors outside our model and will remain constant at some predetermined level. For example, suppose $I = 200$ and $G = 400$.

If we combine the production-income and income-spending relationships we can predict aggregate spending ($C + I + G$) once the current level of GNP is known. This information is shown in Figure 4.5.

Suppose that the initial level of GNP is 1500. Given the set of production-income relationships in Figure 4.5, we can predict the distribution of income. Next, given the income-spending relationships, we can predict the level of consumption once we know the distribution of income. Finally, if we incorporate the exogenously determined level of nonhousehold spending, we can predict aggregate spending ($C + I + G$). We could say that if all the relationships continue to hold, total spending would be 1457 when the initial level of GNP is 1500.

Note that we are able to predict the savings flows. *Savings* is defined as all income available for investment. Therefore, $S_w = W - C_w$ and $S_{nw} = NW - C_{nw}$ since households can either spend their money on consumption or save it.

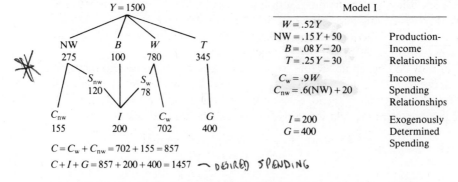

Figure 4.5 Income and spending flows (Model I) if initial GNP = 1500

1500 − 1457 = UNINTENDED INVENTORIES

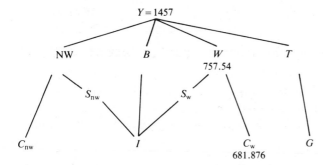

Figure 4.6 Income and spending flows (Model I) if initial
GNP = 1457

Business savings (S_b) is equal to business income since all business income is available for investment purposes. We find that the total savings available for investment is 298.

If we were interested in predicting spending in the following period, we would start by assuming that the next period's total production (GNP) would be exactly equal to the current level of desired spending. Given this level of GNP, which we would predict to be 1457, we would again use the production-income and income-spending relationships to predict the expected level of the next period's desired aggregate spending ($C+I+G$). For example, if $Y=1457$, we would predict that $W=.52 \times 1457 = 757.64$. Given this value, we would predict that $C_w=.9 \times 757.64 = 681.876$. Complete the missing income, spending, and savings flows in Figure 4.6. (Assume the same information from Model I listed in Figure 4.5.)

The relationships specified in Figures 4.5 and 4.6 represent *one* model of the economy. Starting with a given set of information (Y, G, I, production-income relationships, and income-spending relationships), this model predicts future levels of production, income, and spending.

At the undergraduate level it is argued that the macromodel should be simplified so that the major factors are highlighted. Therefore, it is considered justifiable to sacrifice some exactness if it improves clarity. We will find that the competing outlooks disagree over which component of this first model can be sacrificed because they are less important. Also, when we attempt to explain investment instead of assuming that it is exogenously determined, we will find that the competing outlooks disagree over which factors are most important.

Possible Simplifying Assumptions

There are three major simplifying assumptions which underlie some of the differences between the competing outlooks. They are:

1. Assume that we can analyze the private economy by ignoring the government sector. In this case, we would assume that $T = G = 0$.

2. Assume that all savings is done by households. In this case, we would assume that $B = S_b = 0$.

3. Assume that we can combine the nonwage-earning and wage-earning household sectors with little loss in our ability to predict total consumption. In this case, we would not have to predict the distribution between W and NW.

Ignoring the government sector Government decisions are mainly *reactions* to the private sectors. Therefore, preliminary to understanding government tax and spending decisions we must understand the workings of a private economy without a government sector. Moreover, especially conservatives would claim that a private market economy is fully capable of maintaining full employment without government intervention. Therefore, by ignoring the role of government spending and taxation we can evaluate this viewpoint. Figure 4.7 illus-

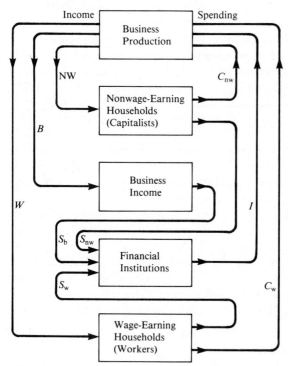

Figure 4.7 Production-income-spending circular flow (Model II)

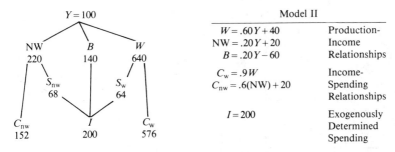

Model II

$W = .60\,Y + 40$	Production-
$NW = .20\,Y + 20$	Income
$B = .20\,Y - 60$	Relationships
$C_w = .9\,W$	Income-
$C_{nw} = .6(NW) + 20$	Spending
	Relationships
$I = 200$	Exogenously
	Determined
	Spending

Figure 4.8   Income and spending flows (Model II) if initial GNP = 1000

trates the production-income-spending circular flow when we ignore the government sector. We could also use production-income and income-spending relationships to predict spending flows, given an initial level of GNP. This is illustrated in Figure 4.8, where we have selected a hypothetical set of relationships and a predetermined level of I.

Ignoring business income We are primarily interested in predicting total spending. We only predict income subcategories if it significantly improves our spending predictions. If we assume that business income is small and has little effect on spending decisions, then it would be justified to simplify the model by assuming business income equals zero.

By eliminating business income we are assuming that all investment is externally funded. This emphasizes the role of banks as providing funds for investment. We also note that by eliminating business income we are assuming that all savings is done by households. This implies that the role of banks is to absorb household savings and attempt to find investment outlets for these funds.

Figure 4.9 illustrates the production-income-spending circular flow when we ignore both the government sector and business income. We could also use production-income and income-spending relationships to predict spending flows, given an initial level of GNP. This is illustrated in Figure 4.10 where we have selected a hypothetical set of relationships and a predetermined level of I. This will be considered Model III of the macroeconomy.

Ignoring the distribution of income between households Suppose that the income going to all households is $500. Does it make a difference how this income is distributed between wages and nonwages if we desire to predict total consumption? Let us assume that the actual income-spending relationships are:

$$C_w = .9\,W \quad \text{and} \quad C_{nw} = .6 \times NW + 20$$

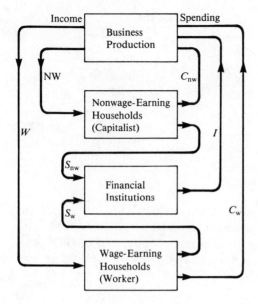

Figure 4.9 Production-income-spending circular flow (Model III)

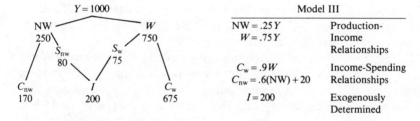

Figure 4.10 Income and spending flows (Model III) if initial GNP = 1000

Using these relationships we can see what effect changing the distribution of the 500 between W and NW would have on total consumption. In Table 4.10 we have chosen a few possible distributions.

The relationship between an individual's change in consumption in response to a change in income is called the *marginal propensity to consume* (MPC).

DEFINITION MPC equals the ratio of the change (Δ) in consumption to a change in income.

$$\text{MPC} = \Delta C / \Delta \text{Income}$$

There are a number of properties of the MPC which we should identify:

Table 4.10
Effect on consumption of changes in the distribution of total income between W and NW

| Distributions | | | | | |
Wages	Nonwages	Level of C_w	Level of C_{nw}	Total C	Change in C
500	0	450	20	470	
400	100	360	80	440	-30
300	200	270	140	410	-30
200	300	180	200	380	-30
100	400	90	260	350	-30
0	500	0	320	320	-30

1. The MPC will always be the slope of the income-consumption relationship. Only if this relationship is a linear equation would the MPC remain constant for all levels of income.

Suppose that the relationship between W and C_w is nonlinear. It can be represented by the equation:

$$C_w = .5W - (.0001 \times W^2) + 100$$

Table 4.11 shows the changes in C_w as a result of changes in W, given this relationship.

Table 4.11
The MPC out of wages with income-consumption relationship $C_w = .5W - .0001W^2 + 100$

Wages	Consumption out of wages	MPC out of wages
0	100	—
100	149	.49
200	196	.47
300	241	.45
400	284	.43
500	325	.41

2. The MPC is not necessarily equal to the average propensity to consume (APC).

DEFINITION APC equals the ratio of consumption to income.
$$APC = C/\text{Income}$$

For example, let us look at the income-consumption relationship for nonwage-earning households we have been using; $C_{cw} = (.6 \times NW) + 20$. From Table 4.12 we find that the MPC out of nonwages (MPC_{nw}) is always equal to 0.6, while the APC out of nonwages (APC_{nw}) varies and is never equal to the MPC_{nw}.

Table 4.12
The MPC and APC out of nonwages
($C_{nw} = .6NW + 20$)

Nonwages	C_{nw}	MPC_{nw}	APC_{nw}
0	20	—	—
100	80	.6	.8
200	140	.6	.7
300	200	.6	.667
400	260	.6	.65
500	320	.6	.64

The APC will only be equal to the MPC if the income-consumption relationship is linear and goes through the origin; i.e., only if consumption equals zero when income equals zero. We have an example of this with the income-consumption relationship for wage-earning households we have been using; $C_w = .9W$. From Table 4.13 we find that not only is the MPC out of wages (MPC_w) equal to 0.9, but so is the APC out of wages (APC_w).

Table 4.13
The MPC and APC out of wages
($C_w = .9W$)

Wages	C_w	MPC_w	APC_w
0	0	—	—
100	90	.9	.9
200	180	.9	.9
300	270	.9	.9
400	360	.9	.9
500	450	.9	.9

3. The marginal propensity to save is directly related to the MPC. Since all changes in income must be entirely reflected in changes in either savings or consumption, the MPC plus MPS must equal one.

DEFINITION **MPS equals the ratio of the change in savings to a change in income.**

$$MPS = \Delta S/\Delta\text{Income}$$
$$MPS = 1 - MPC$$

Using our knowledge of the MPC_w and MPC_{nw} let us return to our example (Table 4.10) and try to explain precisely why total consumption fell whenever we shifted income away from W to NW. We defined

$$MPC_w = \Delta C_w/\Delta W \quad \text{and} \quad MPC_{nw} = \Delta C_{nw}/\Delta NW$$

These equations convert to

$$\Delta C_w = (MPC_w)(\Delta W) \quad \text{and} \quad \Delta C_{nw} = (MPC_{nw})(\Delta NW)$$

The total change in consumption equals

$$\Delta C = \Delta C_w + \Delta C_{nw}$$
$$= (MPC_w)(\Delta W) + (MPC_{nw})(\Delta NW)$$

In our example, we have a pure redistribution (ΔR) so that

$$\Delta W = -\Delta NW = \Delta R$$

Substituting for ΔW and ΔNW in the above equation

$$\Delta C = (MPC_w)(\Delta R) + (MPC_{nw})(-\Delta R)$$
$$= (MPC_{nw} - MPC_w)(\Delta R)$$

This shows that as long as the MPC out of nonwages is less than the MPC out of wages, the change in total consumption will be negative whenever income is redistributed (ΔR) away from wages to nonwages. In our specific example, where $MPC_w = .9$, $MPC_{nw} = .6$, and $\Delta R = 100$,

$$\Delta C = (.6 - .9)(+100) = (-.3)(100) = -30$$

Suppose that we assume wage-earning households are poorer than non-wage-earning households. We could then use the previous information to predict the effects on consumption (and savings[15]) from a redistribution of income between rich and poor families. If the MPC of poor families is higher than the MPC of rich families, then any redistribution from the rich to the poor *increases* total consumption (and decreases total savings).

Suppose we find, except in extreme cases, that the MPC of households does not vary dramatically and that fluctuations in income distribution between income classes is not large. In this case, as a reasonable first approxi-

---

15. Since the sum of income is unchanged, if $\Delta C = -30$, then $\Delta S = +30$. This means that a redistribution of income leads to a redistribution between C and S. Also, note that $S_{nw} = MPS_{nw}(\Delta NW)$ and $S_w = MPS_w(\Delta W)$.

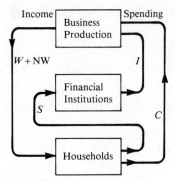

Figure 4.11 Production-
income-spending circular flow
(Model IV)

mation, we could assume that all disposable income is distributed to one household sector. Figure 4.11 illustrates the circular flow when we ignore the government sector, business income, and the distribution of income between W and NW.

If we use Model IV, it is no longer necessary to know the distribution of total income so that *no* production-income relationships are required. All income is distributed to one household sector. If we continue to assume that I is exogenously determined, we not only would be ignoring the role of (capitalist) business decisions, but also the role of capitalist (nonwage) income in determining total spending. Instead, Model IV isolates the role of household decisions between savings and consumption as a determinant of total spending. In this model the only information necessary to predict total spending, given the initial level of GNP, is a single income-consumption relationship (for all households) and the predetermined level of I. This is illustrated in Figure 4.12 where we have arbitrarily chosen the single income-consumption relationship and the level of I.

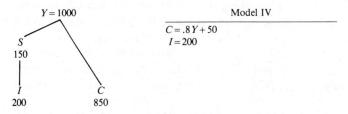

Figure 4.12 Income and spending flows (Model IV) if initial GNP = 1000

4.4 CONCLUSION

This chapter has developed a measure of total production, GNP, which will be used throughout this book as the principal measure of economic performance. By using GNP, a direct measure of *unemployment* is avoided. Moreover, it assumes that effects on employment can be inferred from changes in GNP. This latter assumption is reasonable though, as Table 4.5 indicates, different outputs can create different numbers of jobs per dollar spent.

We also found that GNP has severe weaknesses as a social welfare measure. It does not account for effects of the distribution of income on social welfare; it has difficulty adjusting for changes in quality; it is biased towards market transactions; and it uses market prices rather than a direct measure of need as the measure of value. These weaknesses will not be of significant importance since our central purpose is to explain marketplace employment and production, not social welfare.

Next, we found that GNP can be calculated by either summing up total production, making sure to avoid double counting, or by summing up incomes derived from production. Total income always equals total production. However, total spending will always equal total production only if we include the change in value of inventories in the capital investment category. There is no guarantee that *desired* spending will always equal total production. In fact, because there is no guarantee of this equality, macroeconomics spends a great deal of time attempting to predict the desired level of spending, given the current level of total production.

The second half of this chapter initiated the development of economic model building. The production-income-spending chain reflects the order in which money flows through the economy. Economic predictions are made by analyzing *previous* data, identifying stable patterns, and using these patterns to predict future behavior. In the most complete models we must find stable relationships between total production and the distribution of income. These patterns are called production-income relationships. Then, given the income of each spending group, we require income-spending relationships to be stable in order to predict aggregate desired spending ($C+I+G$).

CHAPTER FIVE

SIMPLE MAINSTREAM MACROECONOMIC MODEL

Model IV of the previous chapter is a simple model of the economy. This model is the standard model presented in all mainstream principles courses. This model was constructed by making some value-laden assumptions concerning which economic factors can be ignored as a first approximation of reality—business decisions and income distribution. In order to eliminate the role of business decisions, it was assumed that business income is zero and that capital investment is exogenously determined. In order to eliminate the effects of income distribution, it was assumed that each household has virtually the same MPC so that income distribution would only have a minor effect on aggregate consumption. Left economists fundamentally reject both assumptions since they believe that business decisions and the distribution of income are the two most important determinants of the macroeconomy. This chapter will present some of the basic properties of the standard mainstream model.

5.1 EQUILIBRIUM INCOME DETERMINATION

Chapter 4 indicated an adjustment process for the economy. Beginning at some production level, the resulting income would generate the desired level of spending. Firms would sell from their production and, if necessary, from their inventories. They would then adjust their next period's production. At all times during this adjustment process, actual production, as measured by GNP accounts, must equal total income.

$$C + I_a = Y$$

with

$$I_a = I + I_i$$

where

I_a = actual investment
I_i = unintended inventory investment
I = desired inventory investment
    plus purchases of plant
    and equipment

Since all income goes to households who either save or consume

$$Y = C + S$$

so that at all times

$$I_a = S$$

Only if $I_i = 0$, would the *desired* level of spending $(C + I)$ equal actual production. In this case, since aggregate demand equals aggregate supply, the economy is said to be at *equilibrium*. In the following period, aggregate production would remain the same, and as long as household and business behavior is unchanged, desired spending would equate with actual production each period.

Similarly, if $I_i = 0$, desired investment must equal savings. This is also a statement of equilibrium. It indicates that all of the current income that households have set aside find their way back into the spending stream through desired capital spending. We will now demonstrate that when the economy is characterized by the standard mainstream model, it will always gravitate to equilibrium.

The Spending Schedule

This model assumes a single household sector with a constant MPC so that $C = b(Y_d) + a$, where b equals the MPC and a equals the level of consumption which would occur independent of the level of income; i.e. even if $Y = 0$. Since all income is distributed to this household sector, $Y_d = Y$, so that $C = bY + a$.

Let us assume that our model of the economy is represented by

$$C = .8Y + 100$$

and the predetermined level of investment

$$I = 200$$

DEFINITION **The spending schedule is the relationship between Y and total spending. It indicates the expected level of aggregate spending at each level of Y.**

If we combine the assumed consumption and investment schedules in the simple model, we derive the spending schedule[1]

$$C + I = .8Y + 300$$

Figure 5.1 graphs the consumption function and the spending schedule. Note that the consumption function and the spending schedule are parallel,

---

1. In general, if $C = bY + a$ and $I = I_0$, the spending schedule $C + I = bY + (a + I_0)$. If $I = iY + j$ and $C = bY + a$, then the spending schedule $C + I = (b + i)Y + (a + j)$.

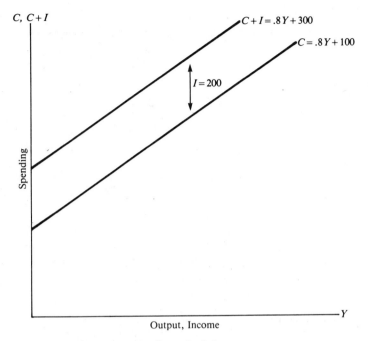

Figure 5.1   Aggregate spending schedule

with the difference equal to 200, reflecting the constant level of capital investment.

The slope of the spending schedule is defined as the marginal propensity to spend.

DEFINITION The marginal propensity to spend, MPSP, indicates the amount of additional spending which would occur if the level of Y increased by one unit. It is the ratio of the change in spending to the change in Y.

$$\text{MPSP} = \Delta \text{Spending}/\Delta Y$$

If capital investment is independent of Y, then the MPSP = MPC in a model with no government or foreign sectors. However, suppose that capital spending was positively correlated with Y. There would then be a marginal propensity to invest.

DEFINITION The marginal propensity to invest, MPI, indicates the amount of addition investment that would occur if the level of Y increased by one unit. It is the ratio of the change in investment to the change in Y.

If MPI > 0, then MPSP = MPC + MPI. This is illustrated in Table 5.1 where different models of the economy are selected, all having the same spending schedule $C + I = .8Y + 300$. Models A and B have the same MPC, but with dif-

Table 5.1
Calculated aggregate spending in different specific models all having the same spending schedule

GNP	Model A $C=.8Y+100$ $I=200$			Model B $C=.8Y+50$ $I=250$			Model C $C=.7Y+200$ $I=.1Y+100$		
	C	I	$C+I$	C	I	$C+I$	C	I	$C+I$
400	420	200	620	370	250	620	480	140	620
600	580	200	780	530	250	780	620	160	780
800	740	200	940	690	250	940	760	180	940
940	852	200	1052	802	250	1052	858	194	1052

ferent constant consumption terms. Model C has an entirely different consumption function. In each of the models, despite different consumption functions, different MPCs, as long as the spending schedule remains the same, aggregate spending $(C+I)$ at any level of Y will be the same.

Solving for Equilibrium Income

Equilibrium income is the level of income at which desired spending equals total production. In Figure 5.2, the 45°-line schedule $C+I=Y$ indicates all of the combinations for which desired spending just equals income. Given the spending schedule $C+I$, we find that there is only level of income, Y_e, for which desired spending just equals total income. If the economy is at any $Y_1 > Y_e$, desired spending is less than current income and the economy would be contracting. If $Y_2 < Y_e$, desired spending would be greater than income and the economy would be expanding. This indicates that regardless of the initial level of income, the economy would gravitate to its equilibrium value.[2] In the specific model being used $(C+I=.8Y+300)$ $Y_e = 1500$.

We could have also found the equilibrium Y by using the alternative equilibrium condition—the sum of leakages equals the sum of injections. In the simple model, where the government, foreign, and business sectors are ignored, the alternative equilibrium condition reduces to household savings equals capital investment, $S=I$.

In order to calculate savings we must know the specific consumption function. For example, suppose that the spending schedule $C+I=.8Y+300$ was derived from Model A of Table 5.1, where $C=.8Y+100$ and $I=200$. Since all income in this model is received by households who can only consume or save, $S=Y-C$. By substituting the specific consumption function $S=Y-C=Y-(0.8Y+100)=0.2Y-100$, which represents the savings sched-

---

2. If $C+I=(b+i)Y+(a+j)$, then at equilibrium $(b+i)Y+(a+j)=Y$ so that equilibrium $Y=(a+j)/(1-b-i)$. If $a=100$, $b=0.8$, $i=0$, and $j=200$ $(C=0.8Y+100$ and $I=200)$ then equilibrium $Y=(100+200)/(1-0.8)=300/0.2=1500$.

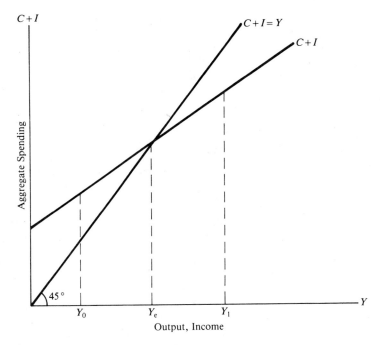

Figure 5.2   Income determination

ule in our chosen model,[3] the amount of savings at each level of Y is indicated. Figure 5.3 graphs both the savings schedule and the investment schedule ($I = 200$). Savings equals investment when GNP equals 1500.[4]

If $Y < 1500$, then businesses would be putting more back into the economy than households were leaking out.[5] Therefore, the economy would be expanding. On the other hand, if $Y > 1500$, household leakages are not being offset by investment. In this case the economy would be contracting.

5.2 THE INCOME MULTIPLIER

Let us assume that the macroeconomy is at equilibrium. The economy will remain at equilibrium Y as long as the spending schedule remains the same. However, what happens if the spending schedule changes? This could occur if either capital spending changed or households decided to change their distribution of income between savings and spending. For example, suppose that capital investment increased by 10. Now, at the existing equilibrium Y, aggregate

---

3. In general, if $C = bY_d + a$, then $S = Y_d - C = Y_d - (bY_d + a) = (1-b)Y_d - a$.

4. If $S = .2Y - 100$, then at equilibrium $S = I$ or $.2Y - 100 = 200$ or $Y = 1500$.

5. Note that the identification of households with leakages is correct if all savings is done by households.

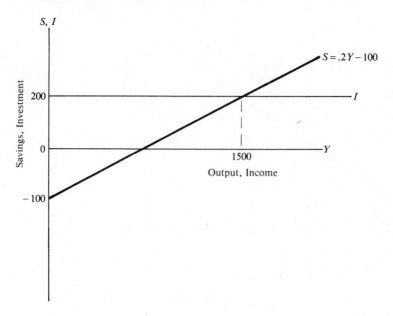

Figure 5.3   Income determination

spending would be increased by 10. We will call this an *autonomous shift* in spending.

DEFINITION **An autonomous shift in spending, ΔA, occurs when, at the same level of GNP, aggregate spending changes.**

The increase in aggregate spending of 10 results initially in sales from inventories. However, in the next period, firms in the capital goods industries where the autonomous shift occurred, adjust their production upwards. As production increases so does the employment of resources. Owners of resources having more income will increase their spending in response to the increase in their incomes. Hence, an income rise induces further spending increases.

DEFINITION **An induced change in spending, ΔY_I, occurs when aggregate spending changes in response to changes in Y.**

In each round, however, spending increases by less than the previous round because of the leakages out of income into savings each time. Income and spending continue to rise, but by smaller amounts each time. Eventually, the economy "peaks" at some new value of Y. This new value will be the new equilibrium Y. The pattern of adjustment from an old to new equilibrium is illustrated in Figure 5.4.

Similarly, if capital investment had fallen by 10, firms would not have been able to sell their current production. Inventories would increase, causing

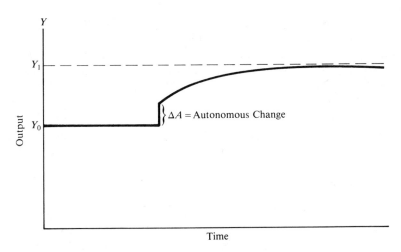

Figure 5.4 Aggregate income multiplier process

firms to cut back their production in the following period. Production declines cause income declines which induce spending declines. Decreases in production, income, and spending are generated each period. However, since part of the declines in income are absorbed by declines in savings, the decreases in each successive period diminish. Eventually, the economy "bottoms" at a new equilibrium Y.

Whatever the direction of the autonomous shift in spending, it will be multiplied by further changes in aggregate spending. If we add together the sum of all induced changes, ΔY_I, with the initial autonomous shift, ΔA, we will have the total change in spending, ΔY_T, resulting from the initial autonomous change.

$$\Delta Y_T = \Delta A + \Delta Y_I$$

$$\Delta Y_T = \text{new equilibrium } Y - \text{old equilibrium } Y$$

DEFINITION **The size of the simple income multiplier effect, M_y, equals the ratio of the total change in GNP to the initial autonomous shift.**
$$M_y = \Delta Y_T / \Delta A$$

A Numerical Example

Let us assume that the macroeconomy can be represented by $C = .8Y + 100$, $I = 200$. If we are at equilibrium $Y = 1500$, ($C = 1300$ and $I = 200$). Suppose that in period 1, investment increases to $I = 210$. Now at the same Y, (1500), aggregate spending increases to 1510, ($C = 1300$, $I = 210$). In the next period, total production and total income rise by 10 inducing further increases in spending. Since we are assuming that the MPC $= 0.8$, in response to the initial change in income, households would increase consumption by 8 and savings by 2. Spending rises to 1518, ($C = 1308$, $I = 210$), which becomes the level of production in the following period. The additional production increase of 8 induces still further spending increases as households distribute their increased income between consumption and savings. Once more, the increase in spending by households will be 80% of the increased income. This increase of $8(.8) = 6.4$ corresponds to the increase in next period's production. Table 5.2 shows the predicted increases in spending and production over the first ten periods.

Table 5.2
Production and spending increases

Period	GNP	C	I	Spending	ΔC	ΔI	ΔSpending
0	1500	1300	200	1500	—	—	—
1	1500	1300	210	1510		10	10
2	1510	1308	210	1518	8	—	8
3	1518	1314.4	210	1524.4	6.4	—	6.4
4	1524.4	1319.5	210	1529.5	5.1	—	5.1
5	1529.5	1323.6	210	1533.6	4.1	—	4.1
6	1533.6	1326.9	210	1536.9	3.3	—	3.3
7	1536.9	1329.5	210	1539.5	2.6	—	2.6
8	1539.5	1331.6	210	1541.6	2.1	—	2.1
9	1541.6	1333.3	210	1543.3	1.7	—	1.7
10	1543.3	1334.7	210	1544.7	1.4	—	1.4

We can solve immediately for the new equilibrium by using the new spending schedule, $C + I = .8Y + 310$. At equilibrium,

$$C + I = Y$$
$$.8Y + 310 = Y$$
$$1550 = Y$$

Therefore, if we had carried out the production-income-spending chain past ten periods, the economy would have approached 1550. In this example, the size of the simple income multiplier is:

$$M_y = \Delta Y_T / \Delta A$$
$$= (1550 - 1500)/10 = 50/10 = 5$$

Properties of the Simple Multiplier

In our simple model the only induced changes are a result of changes in Y, as measured by the MPSP. In later chapters we will find that changes in Y induce spending changes in an indirect fashion—through its effect on interest rates and prices which, in turn, affect spending decisions. For this reason, it will become important to differentiate between the simple multiplier and the full multiplier.

The simple multiplier (M_y) is the ratio of the total change in equilibrium income to the autonomous change, *assuming there are no changes in the interest rate.* The full multiplier (M_y^*) is the ratio of the total change in equilibrium income to the autonomous change in spending, including interest rate price effects.

Let us explore some of the properties of the simple income multiplier developed in this chapter.

PROPERTY 1 The size of the simple income multiplier is the same for an autonomous shift in any sector.

In the numerical example we used, the initial autonomous shift was in the capital spending sector. Investment rose by 10, independent of the level of GNP. Suppose, instead, that the initial autonomous shift occurred in the household sector; that is, households decided to shift 10 from savings to consumption, independent of their level of income. This autonomous shift in household spending would be reflected in a parallel shift of the consumption function to:

$$C' = .8Y + 110$$

According to the new consumption function, at each level of Y, consumption is 10 higher than when household responses were represented by the old consumption function. This is illustrated in Figure 5.5.[6]

In this case, at the old equilibrium $Y = 1500$, consumption would rise to 1310 and aggregate spending to 1510. The only difference from the previous example is that now the initial catalyst would be production increases in the consumer goods industries rather than the capital goods industries. The increases in production and spending would be exactly the same as in Table 5.2 except that in period 1 the change in spending would be in consumption rather than investment. We should have expected this since in both examples the spending schedule is shifted to $C + I = .8Y + 310$. Since the spending schedule is the sole determinant of the equilibrium level of Y, then in both cases the new equilibrium Y must be the same; $Y = 1550$. Since the size of the total increase (50) and the initial increase (10) will be the same, so will the size of the simple multiplier.

PROPERTY 2 The size of the simple income multiplier is determined by the size of the MPSP.

---

6. We will ignore the possibility of households changing their MPC.

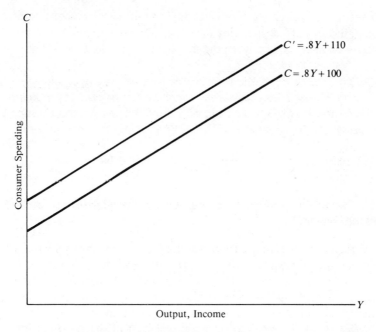

Figure 5.5 Shift of the consumption schedule

The size of the multiplier chain is dependent upon the size of the induced changes in spending. The size of the induced changes are determined by the size of the MPSP. In Table 5.3 we have three different models, each having the same size MPSP. In each case we assume that there is an initial autonomous increase in investment of 10.

In each model, since the MPSP = 0.8, the change in aggregate spending is 80% of the change in GNP. In the simple model, where it is assumed that investment is exogenously determined, there are no induced changes in investment. In this case, Model D, all of the induced changes are in consumption and it may seem that the size of the income multiplier is determined by the size of the MPC. However, in the other two models, where investment responds to increases in production, we find that even if the MPCs are different, as long as the MPSPs are the same, the size of the simple income multiplier will be the same.

PROPERTY 3 **If the MPSP remains constant, then the size of the simple income multiplier remains constant regardless of the size of the autonomous shift in spending.**

In each of the previous examples we have used an autonomous shift of 10 to start the process. In each case we found that the eventual increase in GNP

Table 5.3
Production and spending increases

Period	ΔY	ΔC	ΔI	$\Delta(C+I)$
		Model D		
1	0	—	10	10
2	10	8	—	8
3	8	6.4	—	6.4
4	6.4	5.1	—	5.1
		Model E		
Period	ΔY	ΔC	ΔI	$\Delta(C+I)$
1	0	—	10	10
2	10	7	1	8
3	8	5.6	0.8	6.4
4	6.4	4.5	0.6	5.1
		Model F		
Period	ΔY	ΔC	ΔI	$\Delta(C+I)$
1	0	—	10	10
2	10	6	2	8
3	8	4.8	1.6	6.4
4	6.4	3.8	1.3	5.1

Model D represented by $C=.8Y+20$, $I=240$.
Model E represented by $C=.7Y+15$, $I=.1Y+10$.
Model F represented by $C=.6Y+10$, $I=.2Y+20$.

totaled to 50 and the multiplier was necessarily 5. Table 5.4 shows that regardless of the size of the autonomous shift, the simple income multiplier remains the same, as long as the MPSP remains constant.

Table 5.4
Adjustment process when autonomous spending changes vary

Period	ΔY	$\Delta(C+I)$	ΔY	$\Delta(C+I)$	ΔY	$\Delta(C+I)$
1	10	8	20	16	40	32
2	8	6.4	16	12.8	32	25.6
3	6.4	5.1	12.8	10.2	25.6	21.4
4	5.1	4.1	10.2	8.2	20.4	16.4
5	4.1	3.3	8.2	6.6	16.4	13.2

In each case when we double the size of the autonomous shift (from 10 to 20 to 40), we double the size of the induced changes in spending. Hence, we double the size of the total change in spending. If both the autonomous shift and the total change are doubled, then the size of the simple income multiplier will be unchanged.

The stability of the size of the simple income multiplier enables us to quickly calculate the predicted total effect of any autonomous change in spending. Recall that if $M_y = \Delta Y_T / \Delta A$, then

$$\Delta Y_T = (M_y)(\Delta A)$$

Therefore, if we know both the size of the income multiplier and the autonomous change in spending, we could immediately predict ΔY_T. For example, if we know the size of the simple income multiplier is 6 and the initial autonomous change in spending is -9, then we could immediately predict that $\Delta Y_T = 6(-9) = -54$.

PROPERTY 4 The size of the simple income multiplier is directly related to the size of the MPSP.

Table 5.5 shows the adjustment process for three models, each having a different MPSP. In each model we assume that in the initial period, investment autonomously increases by 10.

The larger the adjustment in spending in *each* period, the larger the MPSP. Hence, the larger the *cumulative* change in spending, the larger the MPSP. For example, after five periods, the total effect of an autonomous increase in spending of 10 is 41 when the MPSP $=0.9$, but less than 12.5 when the MPSP $=0.2$. Since the simple income multiplier is just the sum of the cumulative changes divided by the autonomous initial change, the larger the MPSP, the larger the size of the simple income multiplier.

Table 5.5
Adjustment process in models each having a different MPSP

Period	Model G MPSP = .9 ΔY	$\Delta(C+I)$	Model H MPSP = .5 ΔY	$\Delta(C+I)$	Model J MPSP = .2 ΔY	$\Delta(C+I)$
1	—	10	—	10	—	10
2	10	9	10	5	10	2
3	9	8.1	5	2.5	2	0.4
4	8.1	7.3	2.5	1.3	0.4	0.08
5	7.3	6.6	1.3	0.6	0.08	0.016
		41.0		19.4		12.496

PROPERTY 5 The size of the simple income multiplier will always equal the inverse of (1 – MPSP)

$$M_y = 1/(1 - \text{MPSP})$$

The income multiplier has a particular form. The change in spending in each successive period is always the same percentage of the change in spending of the previous period. The percentage change is always equal to MPSP. Let $m = \text{MPSP}$ and the initial autonomous change in spending equal K. Then in the first period the change in spending $= K$. In the next period the change in spending $= mK$. In the next period the change in spending $= m(mK)$. In the next period the change in spending $= m(m^2K)$.

We then have a simple geometric series to represent the sum of the changes in spending over time

$$\Delta Y_T = K + mK + m^2K + m^3K + m^4K + m^5K + \ldots$$

The algebraic sum equals $K/(1 - m)$. Therefore, the size of the simple income multiplier effect would be

$$M_y = \Delta Y_T/\Delta A = [K/(1 - m)]/K = 1/(1 - m)$$

Alternative Explanation

An autonomous shift in spending, ΔA, creates an equivalent difference between leakages and injections. As Y changes, induced changes in leakages and injections close this gap until equilibrium is reestablished with total leakages equal to total injections. In the model with no induced investment, leakages and injections are brought closer together by the size of the induced savings, $\text{MPS}(\Delta Y)$. Therefore, for any autonomous change in spending, ΔA, the economy will return to equilibrium when MPS $(\Delta Y) = \Delta A$ or, equivalently, when $\Delta Y_T = (\Delta A)/\text{MPS} = \Delta A/(1 - \text{MPC})$. However, in a model with no induced investment, $\text{MPC} = \text{MPSP}$ so that $\Delta Y_T = \Delta A/(1 - \text{MPC}) = \Delta A/(1 - \text{MPSP})$.

If there was some induce investment $(\text{MPI} > 0)$, it would take a larger increase in Y to close the gap between leakages and injections. As before, we have induced savings equal to $\text{MPS}(\Delta Y)$, but now it is somewhat offset by induced investment $\text{MPI}(\Delta Y)$. Therefore, the gap is only closed by $(\text{MPS} - \text{MPI})\Delta Y$. Equilibrium is reestablished when $(\text{MPS} - \text{MPI})\Delta Y = \Delta A$ or, equivalently, whenever $\Delta Y_T = \Delta A/(\text{MPS} - \text{MPI}) = \Delta A/(1 - \text{MPC} - \text{MPI}) = \Delta A/(1 - \text{MPSP})$.

5.3 CONCLUSION

This chapter has introduced the standard mainstream model. The model implies that there are significant tendencies towards equilibrium in a private market economy. Moreover, the standard model implies that movements away from equilibrium are unpredictable. In later chapters, left-models will be developed which contend that economic fluctuations are not only predictable but self-generating.

Since the mainstream model assumes that the fluctuations are begun by unpredictable shocks, their major focus is on predicting the size of the cumulative adjustments resulting from these shocks. The simple income multiplier concept was developed to highlight this focus. The simple income multiplier ignores interest rate and price adjustments that are incorporated in the full income multiplier. If the income multiplier is large, then small shocks can set off large cumulative movements, resulting in sharp declines or expansions—a boom or bust economy. In this case, government intervention is necessary to limit the size of fluctuations. These government policies are called *stabilization* policies. They should be distinguished from government economic planning which attempts to anticipate and avoid fluctuations altogether. Chapter 6 will present mainstream views on the size of the income multiplier. We will find that conservatives contend that the income multiplier is so small that government intervention is not necessary, whereas mainstream liberals contend that it is sufficiently large so that some government stabilization is required.

CHAPTER SIX

CONSUMPTION

In Chapter 5 we assumed that household spending was dependent upon the current level of disposable income. This specific view of household behavior approximates the view advanced by Keynes in the *General Theory*. It is called the absolute income hypothesis because it assumes consumption is determined by the absolute level of income.

This chapter will present alternative views which are in the mainstream tradition. It will be shown that other measures of income—permanent and relative—are more plausible and more accurately correspond to actual observations. Next, it will be shown that factors other than income can play an important role in determining household spending. The two factors discussed in this chapter are interest rates and household expectations.

Chapter 5 developed the income multiplier concept. The alternative theories of household behavior developed in this chapter have differing implications for the size of the full income multiplier and, hence, the need for government intervention. Specifically, we will find that the permanent income and life cycle hypotheses imply a small full income multiplier, while the expectations hypothesis implies that it would be large. Therefore, it is of some importance which theory dominates.

6.1 SHORTRUN VERSUS LONGRUN CONSUMPTION SCHEDULE

Chapter 4 indicated that past data is analyzed to determine the best estimate of the consumption schedule. By plotting each year's observation of consumption and disposable income, we can determine if a stable relationship between the two variables exists. Statistical methods can then be used to derive the best estimate of that relationship. Economists, using longterm data (1910–74), have found that the fraction of disposable income saved has been almost constant. The only way that savings could remain a fixed proportion of disposable income is if consumption is a fixed proportion of disposable income; i.e., if

$C = bY_d$. In particular, $C = 0.94Y_d$ gives the best estimate of the consumption schedule during the entire period.

This seems to indicate that the MPC $= 0.94$ so that induced changes in consumption would be large and, hence, the income multiplier effect in a private market economy would be large. If this is correct, then the case for government intervention to avoid large fluctuations would be strong. However, many economists, beginning with Keynes, have felt that the MPC obtained from longterm data greatly overestimates the size of induced consumption resulting from an autonomous shift in disposable income. In particular, these economists claim that the *shortrun* change in consumption is slight because changes in savings would absorb most of the change in disposable income.

Figure 6.1 illustrates the kind of data that would support the contention that the shortrun MPC is smaller than the MPC obtained from longterm data. Let LC represent the longterm consumption schedule ($C = 0.94Y_d$). However, if only the data from the period 1960–1967 is used, SR_0 would represent the

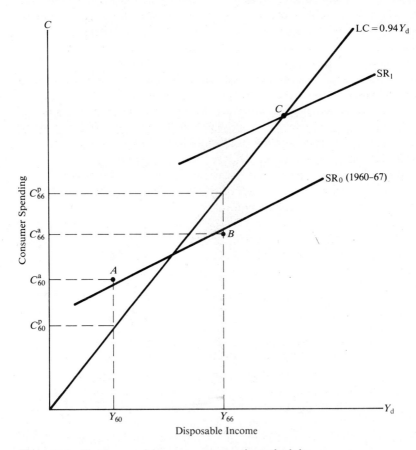

Figure 6.1 Shortrun and longrun consumption schedules

consumption schedule for that period. It indicates that in recession years, such as 1960 (point A), actual consumption (C_{60}^a) is above the level of consumption predicted by the longterm schedule (C_{60}^p). However, in periods of expansion, such as 1966 (point B), actual consumption is below that predicted by the longterm schedule.

The shortrun consumption schedule SR_0 indicates that while in the longrun consumption is proportional to disposable income, the deviations are systematic over each complete economic cycle (recession and expansion). Hence, consumption would be above the trend during recessions and below during expansions. This indicates that shortrun consumption schedules, which have a smaller MPC, should be used for predictive purposes. For example, suppose that the economy is at point C and the government desires to predict consumption changes which would occur if there was an autonomous change in spending. The government should superimpose shortrun consumption schedule SR_1 on the longrun schedule and use it for predictive purposes.

If the data presented for 1960–67 is representative of the shortrun pattern, then for a theory of consumption to be complete it must be able to explain why:

1. In the longrun total consumption is proportional to total disposable income—the longrun national savings ratio is constant.

2. In the shortrun the MPC is smaller than predicted by the longrun consumption schedule—in the shortrun the national savings ratio varies directly with total disposable income.[1]

Relative Income Hypothesis

The simple consumption function specified in Chapter 5 (in which consumption was equal to a constant plus a fixed proportion of disposable income) is not capable of explaining both the longterm and shortrun consumption behavior. For this reason, economists have usually rejected the thesis that consumption could be predicted by the *absolute* level of disposable income and, instead, developed alternative theories of household behavior.[2] The first popularized alternative theory was the relative income hypothesis (RIH), developed by James Duesenberry.[3]

---

1. In addition, any theory of household behavior should explain why, at any point in time, individual upper-income households have a lower consumption ratio than individual lower-income households. This point will be discussed in Chapter 7.

2. The simple consumption function is called the *absolute income hypothesis* to distinguish it from the *relative income hypothesis*.

3. James S. Duesenberry, "Income-Consumption Relations and Their Implications," in *Income, Employment and Public Policy Essays in Honor of Alvin H. Hansen* (New York, W. W. Norton, 1948).

Duesenberry believed that in order to predict consumption, a relative measure of disposable income—the ratio of current disposable income to the previous highest level—was necessary. Specifically, Duesenberry claimed that

$$C = a_0 Y_\mathrm{d}(Y_\mathrm{d}/Y^*) + a_1 Y_\mathrm{d}$$

where

$Y^* = $ highest previous level of disposable income

would be able to explain the shortrun and longterm consumption schedules. If we divide both sides by Y_d:

$$C/Y_\mathrm{d} = a_0(Y_\mathrm{d}/Y^*) + a_1 \quad \text{where } a_0 < 0$$

This indicates that according to Duesenberry's formulation the consumption ratio varies inversely with the relative income ratio Y_d/Y^*.

If the economic growth rate is constant at its longrun rate, then Y_d/Y^* is constant and, hence, the consumption ratio will be constant. Duesenberry's relative income hypothesis is therefore able to predict that the longrun consumption schedule will be proportional to disposable income.

During recessions, Y_d/Y^* is below its longterm trend so that, according to the relative income hypothesis, the consumption ratio would be above the longrun consumption schedule. Similarly, during an expansion, Y_d/Y^* is above its longterm trend so that the consumption ratio would be below the longrun consumption schedule. This indicates that Duesenberry's formulation was also able to predict the deviations of consumption from its longterm trend during recessions and expansions.

Duesenberry believed that household spending decisions were based on purely psychological factors. His "fundamental psychological postulate [was] it is harder for a family to reduce its expenditures from a high level than for a family to refrain from making high expenditures in the first place."[4] This echoed Keynes' view that, "A man's habitual standard of living has first claims on his income. . . ."[5]

The relative income hypothesis was an advance over the simple absolute income hypothesis since it could be adapted to explain both the shortrun and longrun consumption schedules. There were, however, two important weaknesses. First, the relative income hypothesis, while being able to predict the deviation of the expansion in consumption when disposable income increases from the longterm trend, had no explanation for this occurrence. Indeed, owing to the recent Depression, Duesenberry only used the relative income hypothesis to explain the rise in the consumption ratio during the Great Depression. Therefore, he had an incomplete explanation of the shortrun consump-

---

4. Ibid.

5. John Maynard Keynes, *General Theory of Employment, Interest and Money* (London: MacMillan, 1936), p. 97.

tion schedule.[6] Second, his consumption schedule implies that if a decline in disposable income would prevail for an extended period of time, since Y_d/Y^* would remain constant, there would be no further downward adjustment of consumption. However, it is more reasonable to assume that households would eventually adjust their spending habits downward to fully reflect their new level of income and, thus, return to the longrun consumption schedule.

Permanent Income Hypothesis

Suppose a salesperson, whose income is based upon commissions, has annual incomes of $9,000, $20,000, $12,000, and $19,000 over a four-year period. Furthermore, suppose this individual desires to save 10% of her income during the period. What should we expect her consumption pattern to be during the period? According to the permanent income hypothesis, formulated by Milton Friedman,[7] individuals desire a stable consumption pattern. Rather than consuming 90% of current income each year ($8,100, $18,000, $10,800, and $17,100), the individual would choose to have a stable pattern by consuming 90% of her *average* income over the four-year period. Since, during this period, her average income is $15,000, the individual would choose to consume $13,500 each year. In general, Friedman claims that each household, in attempting to stabilize its consumption pattern, would consume each year a fixed percentage of its *permanent* income.[8] Let us now describe how the permanent income hypothesis (PIH) interprets the income-consumption relationship.

If the economy was experiencing steady growth, then it would be likely that the deviation households have between their permanent income and actual income would be slight. Moreover, it would be likely that the number of households experiencing income shortfalls (incomes below their permanent income) would be balanced by households receiving windfalls (incomes above their permanent income). In this situation, aggregate disposable income would be an accurate estimate of aggregate permanent income. Since the PIH assumes all households consume a fixed percentage of their permanent income,

---

6. Indeed, it is usually felt that according to the RIH, the Y/Y^* ratio only takes on values below the longterm trend. In this case, the shortrun schedule is only operational in recessions; while during the expansion, consumption follows the longrun schedule. However, Duesenberry never makes any statement to this effect.

7. Milton Friedman, *A Theory of the Consumption Function* (Princeton, N.J.: Princeton University Press for NBER, 1957).

8. Friedman defines permanent income as *some* weighted average of past incomes. If a special set of weights, called Almon weights, are used, then $C=bY_p$ can be transformed into $C_t = b(Y_d)_t + c(C_{t-1})$. Also, note that one can agree that permanent income is the relevant income variable, but not agree that consumption is proportional to permanent income.

the data would indicate that consumption was a fixed percentage of aggregate disposable income. Hence, the PIH is able to explain the constant longrun consumption ratio.

The PIH is also able to explain the shortrun fluctuations of the consumption ratio. During recessions, a majority of households experience economic shortfalls. For these households, permanent income is above current income. Since this is not offset by households having windfalls, aggregate permanent income is above aggregate disposable income. Hence, the consumption ratio would rise during recessions. The PIH also indicates that if the lower level of disposable income persists, then households would continuously adjust downward the estimate of their permanent income so that the consumption ratio would tend towards its longrun ratio.

The PIH also predicts that during the early phases of expansions the consumption ratio would decline since households only slowly adjust upwards their permanent income. However, as the expansion sustains the higher income levels, the consumption ratio rises towards its longrun ratio.

This indicates that the PIH is able to explain the deviation between short-run and longrun household behavior. Moreover, it is able to avoid the criticisms made of the relative income hypothesis. The PIH is able to explain why household consumption rises slowly during economic expansions. It is also able to explain why as an economic contraction persists, household consumption approaches its longrun ratio rather than implying it would remain above its longrun ratio.

6.2 THE PERMANENT INCOME HYPOTHESIS AND ECONOMIC POLICY

As already indicated, the PIH implies that induced consumption in response to economic fluctuations would be lower than predicted by the longrun MPC and, hence, the income multiplier would be smaller. A small income multiplier weakens the case for government intervention because it implies that private sector mechanisms cushion the economy from any sharp contractions or expansions. Second, the PIH assumes that household spending only responds to changes in permanent income. Therefore, the PIH implies that *temporary* tax changes would have little or no effect on spending and are ineffective policy instruments.

The PIH and the Size of the Income Multiplier

Let us begin with a simple model of the economy

$$C = 0.8 Y_p \qquad I = 300$$

where

$$Y_p = \text{permanent income}$$

In the longrun, $Y_p = Y_d$, and since we are still assuming that there is no government sector, $Y_d = Y$. In this case, longrun equilibrium occurs when $Y = 1500$.[9] Let us assume, for simplicity, that Y_p is the unweighted average of income in the previous 10 periods and predict the period-by-period adjustment process from an autonomous investment decline of 10.

Table 6.1
Adjustment process when households respond to changes in their permanent income

Period	Y	Y_p	ΔY_p	ΔC	ΔI	$\Delta(C+I)$
0	1500	1500	—	—	-10	-10
1	1490	1499.	-1.00	-0.80	—	-0.80
2	1489.20	1497.92	-1.08	-0.86	—	-0.86
3	1488.34	1496.76	-1.26	-1.01	—	-1.01
4	1487.33	1495.49	-1.27	-1.02	—	-1.02
5	1486.31	1494.12	-1.37	-1.10	—	-1.10
6	1485.21	1492.64	-1.48	-1.18	—	-1.18
7	1484.03	1491.04	-1.60	-1.28	—	-1.28
				-7.25		

In the initial period in Table 6.1, aggregate spending declines by 10, which results in a decline of total production and total income to 1490 in the following period. However, the decline in Y_p is only to 1499 since

$$Y_p = \frac{\overbrace{1490 + 1500 + 1500 + \ldots + 1500}^{\text{last 9 periods}}}{10} = 1499$$

Therefore, their induced decrease in consumption in the second period would only be $.8(-1) = -0.8$. In the third period, Y_p only declines to 1497.92 since

$$Y_p = \frac{\overbrace{1489.2 + 1490 + 1500 + 1500 + \ldots + 1500}^{\text{previous 8 periods}}}{10} = 1497.92$$

Hence, the decline in Y_p in the third period is only 1.08 (1499–1497.92) so that the decline in C is only $.8(-1.08) = 0.86$. Table 6.1 indicates that the cumulative induced changes in C after seven periods is only -7.25, whereas if households had responded solely to changes in their current income (see Table 5.2) C would have declined by 31.62.

---

9. $C = 0.8Y$ and $I = 300$ so that at equilibrium $0.8Y + 300 = Y$ or equilibrium $Y = 1500$.

The PIH and Temporary Tax Changes

When the government initiates federal tax changes, there are two approaches which could be taken. The government could institute permanent changes, such as *permanent* changes in the income tax tables or it could initiate *temporary* changes, such as a one-time tax rebate or surcharge. According to the PIH, the effects of permanent and temporary tax changes are different. Specifically, since temporary changes have no effect on Y_p, one-time rebates or surcharges would have little or no effect on consumer spending. If it is a temporary tax increase, such as the 1968–70 tax surcharge,[10] then households would respond by lowering their savings rate. Similarly, when the government enacts a one-time tax rebate, such as in 1975, households would just increase their savings without significantly increasing their consumption. PIH advocates, therefore, claim that only permanent changes in taxes can affect consumer spending.

Liberal opponents of this position contend that there is little difference in household behavior when persons view the tax change as temporary as against when they view it as permanent. One argument given is that temporary tax changes are concentrated in lower income groups. These groups have little opportunity to adopt a spending stream which is significantly different from their income stream. For example, more prosperous households can obtain credit when, due to a temporary decline in income, they wish to maintain their current level of spending. However, lower income groups, with limited access to consumer credit, must adjust their spending in accordance with their changing current income.

A second argument claims that even if households will allocate any temporary income fluctuation to their savings, they may change their pattern of savings. Specifically, most economists distinguish between consumer spending on durable goods and nondurable goods. It is argued that the purchase of a durable good, such as an automobile or furniture, is really an "investment" in future consumer services. In this regard, the purchase of a durable good is really equivalent to a financial investment since both provide claims on future consumption. In the case of the financial investment, the derived income can buy future goods and services while, in the case of a durable good, its purchase gives the owner claims on the future service of the purchased item. Hence, when the government initiates a temporary tax rebate, it might very well be correct that the one-time income may be allocated to savings. However, the household may decide that it is more advantageous to save (provide for future consumption) by purchasing a durable good, rather than a financial instrument. If this occurred, then while the PIH is technically correct, the tax rebate would indeed have a substantial stimulus.

---

10. The tax surcharge required each taxpayer to add 10% to their federal tax liability. The rebate was a one-time tax credit.

One of the problems in trying to use statistical methods to determine the effect of a temporary tax rebate on consumer spending is that there are always other factors which change household income and spending decisions.[11] For example, in 1975 the federal government not only enacted a temporary tax rebate of $8 billion, but also reduced taxes permanently at a rate of $12 billion per year. Two months later, the federal government gave recipients a one-time social security increase of $1.7 billion and three months later a permanent increase of $6 billion per year in social security payments was enacted. Besides the direct changes in income, households had potentially as important changes in their expectations. Between 1974 and 1975, the economy experienced its sharpest decline in the post-World War II period which, along with the Watergate scandal and the Nixon resignation, may have changed household views from optimism to pessimism.

For these reasons, it is not surprising that there are widely different results. For example, strong advocates of the PIH have used statistical models which claim that only 15% of the tax rebate went to additional consumer spending during the first six months after its enactment.[12] On the other hand, other models claim that more that 60% of the rebate went to additional consumer purchases.[13] Indeed, some have argued that the 60% is an underestimation since, in their estimations, it does not include change in consumer sentiment.[14] Despite all the technical sophistication available, an elite panel of economists was unable to collectively decide which results were correct. Therefore, while it can be argued that, according to the PIH, temporary tax changes are ineffective, there is no proof.

6.3 THE MARKET INTEREST RATE AND MARKET EXPECTATIONS

The induced changes only explain household adjustments to changes in disposable income. However, it is possible that households respond to other factors.

---

11. At a superficial level, we could compare the savings rate during the temporary tax change with the savings rate before and afterwards. In 1967, the savings rate was 7.5%. It fell to 6.5% in 1968 and to 5.6% in 1969—the two years of the surcharge. After the surcharge was over in 1970, it rose to 7.4%. During 1975, in the quarter before the rebate the savings rate was 7.5%. During the rebate quarter it rose to 10.6% and did not decline back to the 7.5% level until three quarters later. These figures seem to be supportive of the permanent income hypothesis since during the period of the surcharge the savings rate was lower and during the period of the rebate the savings rate was higher.

12. See the study by Thomas Juster discussed in Franco Modigliani and Charles Steindel, "Is a Tax Rebate an Effective Tool for Stabilization Policy?" *Brookings Papers* 1 (1977): 175–209.

13. See the Michigan Model quoted in Ibid., p. 187.

14. See the discussion of Modigliani and Steindel quoted in Ibid., pp. 205–208.

Two such factors are changes in the market interest rate and household expectations.

Consumer Spending and the Market Interest Rate

A purely individualistic theory contends that financial savings is dependent upon the psychologically-motivated time preference of individual households. It also claims that individual choice responds to changing market prices. Suppose that the market interest rate fell. Some households would now consider the market rate of return on their financial savings to be too small and would shift some of their resources to present consumption. In particular, this shift would be made to consumer durables, such as houses and cars.

If interest rates move in the same direction as economic fluctuations, then, according to this theory, induced consumer spending declines are somewhat offset by households shifting some resources from financial investments to consumer durables. If the economy is expanding and interest rates rise, household expenditures on durable goods would be discouraged and the size of the expansion would be smaller.

There is still another way in which interest rate changes affect household spending on durable goods—through the effect of interest rate changes on the value of household wealth. The most widely accepted theoretical foundation for this viewpoint is the life cycle hypothesis (LCH), developed by Franco Modigliani and his collaborators.[15] The LCH assumes that households desire to stabilize consumption over their lifetime. As illustrated in Figure 6.2, this indicates that during early years and retirement, households have negative savings. During their middle years, households save to pay off youth debts and to save for retirement.

The LCH implies that households would allocate any temporary income change to their lifetime spending (and savings) streams. In a boom, most of the increase would go to savings for future consumption. On the other hand, a recession would not lower current consumption significantly, because households would distribute the shortrun loss over their lifetime consumption stream. Therefore, the LCH is able to explain the shortrun variation of the national consumption ratio.

Under certain assumptions, the LCH is capable of explaining the longrun constant consumption ratio. If in each generation the distribution of households between young, middle, and retired remains constant and each age

---

15. For a current exposition of the Life Cycle Hypothesis, see Franco Modigliani, "The Life Cycle Hypothesis of Savings Twenty Years Later," in *Contemporary Issues in Economics,* Michael Parkin and A. R. Nobay, eds. (Manchester Press, 1975).

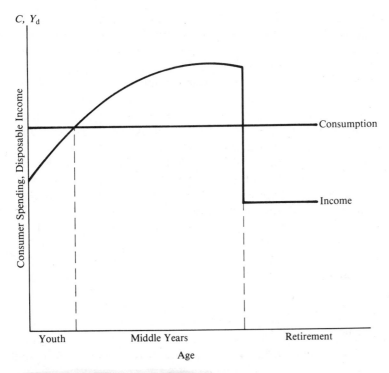

Figure 6.2 The life cycle hypothesis

group's spending behavior remains unchanged generation after generation, then the consumption ratio should remain constant.[16]

The LCH implies that wealth is an important determinant of consumption. If wealth appreciates, the value of future income rises and households allocate part of this increase to present consumption. Some recent events seem to support this contention. During the 1970s, the value of single-family suburban homes increased dramatically. Homes bought in the early 1960s for $20,000 were selling for $60,000 during the late 1970s. As the LCH would have predicted, many households took out second mortgages so that part of the increased wealth could be used for present consumption.

Let us now analyze the relationship between the market interest rate and the value of wealth. Households can allocate their savings to either an interest-

16. The significant change in the age distribution during the 1970s towards young adults and retirees should have lowered the savings ratio if the LCH is correct. Since the savings ratio was actually above its longterm trend during this period, there is some reason to doubt that the LCH is the major determinant of household behavior. See also Betsy Buttrill White, "Empirical Tests of the Life Cycle Hypothesis," *American Economics Review* 68 (Sept. 1978): 547–60.

bearing asset such as bonds, which pay the market interest rate, or to stocks, which pay dividends. Due to the uncertainty involved with stock purchases, households require a risk premium to purchase stocks. Let us assume that the risk premium remains constant at 3% and determine the effect of interest rate changes on the price of stocks. Suppose a certain company was paying $8 per year in dividends per share. If the market interest rate was 7%, then the price of a share of stock in this company would be selling for $80 since at that price investors would be receiving a 10% rate of return. This would just cover the market interest rate plus the risk premium. If the market interest rate fell to 5%, investors would purchase stocks as soon as the rate of return on the company's stock was above 8%. Hence, the company's stock price would rise to $100. This indicates that there is an inverse relationship between the market interest rate and the value of household wealth.

If during recessions interest rates decline, then the rise in the value of wealth would encourage some additional consumption, which would somewhat offset the downturn. On the other hand, if during booms interest rates rise, then the decline in the value of wealth would reduce consumption, which would limit the expansion.

This brief presentation indicates two channels—an income and substitution effect—by which interest rate induced shifts in consumption can reduce the size of the income multiplier. During recessions, lower interest rates induce households to *substitute* durable goods for financial savings. Also, during recessions, lower interest rates raise the value of household wealth and part of this additional *income* would be allocated to present consumption.

Household Expectations

So far we have explored the possible effects that changes in various measures of income—relative, permanent, and lifetime—may have on household spending decisions. It is also possible that households adjust their spending patterns to changes in future expectations. According to this view, a recession creates pessimistic attitudes which, in turn, cause households to postpone some purchases. Therefore, changes in household expectations worsen the downturn. On the other hand, a boom creates optimistic attitudes which accelerate the purchase of goods and thus increases the expansion. Since households have some discretion as to the timing of the replacement of durable goods, these purchases are considered the most sensitive to changes in household expectations. For these reasons, expectations may have a destabilizing effect on the level of spending on consumer durables—deepening recessions and accelerating booms.

Figure 6.3 illustrates this expectations hypothesis. Let us assume that after an autonomous spending decline, the savings and investment schedules are S_0 and I_0, respectively. This indicates that the economy would contract until equilibrium is reestablished at Y_0. If households, due to increased pessimism,

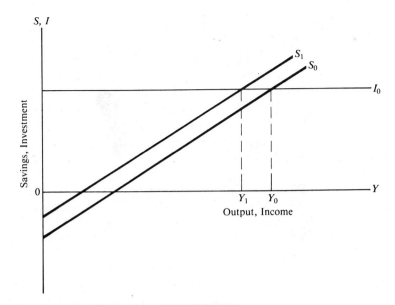

Figure 6.3   Autonomous change in savings

now decide to increase savings independent of income, the savings schedule would shift to S_1. Now at the expected equilibrium Y_0, savings is greater than investment. Therefore, the economy would contract past Y_0 until equilibrium savings equals investment at Y_1. Hence, the downturn is deepened by the pessimism it engenders.

The results of the expectations thesis are called the Paradox of Thrift because they indicate a number of paradoxes:

1. What may be good for an individual household may not be good for society as a whole. If everyone saved more and consumed less, aggregate spending is lowered and unemployment is increased.

2. The process will be reinforced even though it is against the interests of individuals. That is, after individuals increased their savings and unemployment increased, they will believe that they were right to save for adversity. The next time the economy begins to decline, households remembering the last time, will say, "I better be smart enough to again increase my savings."

3. While households attempt to increase their savings, they end up saving the exact same amount but at a lower level of income if investment remains constant.[17]

---

17. If the MPI > 0, then, since the simple income multiplier is larger, there will be a decline in equilibrium S.

6.4 EVALUATION OF ALTERNATIVE
THEORIES OF HOUSEHOLD BEHAVIOR

This chapter began by arguing that the absolute income hypothesis was inadequate because it was unable to differentiate between shortrun and longrun household behavior. The relative income hypothesis, while an advance, also was found wanting. Today, the PIH is considered to be the best explanation. We also found that the LCH is capable of explaining the relationship between interest rate adjustments and household spending. Both the PIH and LCH imply that the full income multiplier is quite small. The PIH assumes that households would not change their consumption significantly in response to shortrun variations of income. The LCH implies that the adjustment of consumer spending to economic fluctuations is even less severe if we include the countercyclical changes in consumption due to interest rate adjustments. According to the LCH, when the economy declines so do interest rates. As interest rates decline, some households accelerate their purchases of consumer goods, particularly durable goods. As will be shown in Chapter 9, under certain assumptions the increased purchase of consumer durables is large enough to completely offset not only the induced declines in spending, but also the initial autonomous spending decline. In this special case, the full income multiplier would be zero!

There seems to be conflict between the PIH/LCH thesis and the expectations hypothesis. The PIH and expectations hypotheses seem to have conflicting views of household sentiment during recessions. The PIH implies that households are *optimistic* during recessions—they perceive the downturn as shortlived and do not significantly adjust their spending. On the other hand, the expectations hypothesis claims that households become *pessimistic* during recessions and adjust downward their consumption independent of income. The expectations hypothesis and LCH are in conflict over the fluctuations in consumer durable purchases during recessions. According to the LCH, households *accelerate* their purchases because of interest rate induced income and substitution effects. On the other hand, the expectations hypothesis claims that households *postpone* the replacement of consumer durables.

One difficulty in selecting the appropriate theory to use for generalizations is that there are prototype individuals who fit each theory.[18] There are laid-off workers who only slightly cut back their consumption; there are workers with substantial seniority and no reason for pessimism who take advantage of lower interest rates by accelerating their purchase of consumer durables; and there are employed workers who postpone replacement of consumer dur-

---

18. Another difficulty is that the PIH assumes durable goods are a form of savings because they represent investments in future consumption. The PIH claims that in recessions, savings is reduced, and can argue that part of the reduction is a decline in durable goods purchased. In this manner, the PIH would predict a decline in consumer durable purchases in recessions just as the expectations hypothesis.

ables because they fear that future lay-offs and/or cutbacks in overtime would adversely affect them. Therefore, the problem of generalization seems to arise because during a recession there are three distinct groups—those who are laid-off; those who have some objective uncertainty about their immediate future income; and those who have little uncertainty about their income.

Mainstream liberal and conservative economists consider the choice of generalizations to be of great importance. To the extent that induced changes in consumption are small and interest rate adjustments create countercyclical consumption changes, the full income multiplier is small and the case for government intervention is weakened. On the other hand, if consumer purchases of durable goods are volatile and destabilizing, then the case for government intervention is strengthened.

In general, conservatives tend to support the view that household adjustments are the most predictable responses to economic shocks and that these responses are strongly stabilizing. As already mentioned, extreme conservatives claim that these responses are capable of fully offsetting the entire shock so that the full income multiplier is zero.

Mainstream liberals are not as confident as conservatives that the private market can completely stabilize the economy. Mainstream liberals note that the PIH requires that all households have access to debt instruments during periods of economic contractions. Without such access, they would be unable to borrow in order to sustain their former living standards. Mainstream liberals suggest that for many households at the lower end of the income spectrum, this is an unrealistic assumption. For these households, regardless of their desires, debt limitations make it impossible for them to sustain their former consumption patterns when their current income declines. Mainstream liberals also tend to place some emphasis on the destabilizing effects of expectations on consumer spending. They also place more emphasis on the possibility that investment adjustments would also have a destabilizing influence on the economy. However, because they reject the notion of business cycles, they reject the need for government planning and instead only recommend *stabilization* policies.

Left-liberals consider the choice of consumer motivation to be relatively unimportant for a number of reasons. They suggest that psychological motivation has little to do with the actual decisions of households because the MPC for workers is probably very close to one. In this case, all savings is derived from profits and, hence, the amount of savings is determined by the distribution of income between wages and profits. This thesis, called the *income shares hypothesis,* will be developed in Chapter 7.

Leftist-economists also believe that investment decisions are the most pivotal in any evaluation of the economic process. Therefore, they believe it impossible to make important judgments concerning the economic process from only evaluating household decisions. Finally, by only discussing the effects that these theories have on the size of the full income multiplier, the analysis is still embedded in an equilibrium framework. As pointed out in Chapter 5, leftist-economists believe that the economic process is subject to continuous and predictable cyclical behavior, rather than being dominated by equilibrating tendencies.

6.5 CONCLUSION

This chapter began by indicating that the shortrun response of households to changes in current income is smaller than the longterm trend. Duesenberry's RIH was the first attempt to explain this distinction. However, the dominant explanation is the PIH which claims that consumption is a fixed proportion of a household's permanent income. The PIH implies that the simple income multiplier is small, particularly when income changes are perceived to be short-run, such as temporary federal tax changes. The smaller the income multiplier, the weaker the case for government intervention.

Modigliani's LCH, by implying that interest rate adjustments would induce countercyclical spending, weakens the case for government intervention still further. According to the LCH, as the economy declines (expands), interest rates decline (rise), which induce an expansion (contraction) of household spending. Thus, interest rate induced changes counter the movement of the economy and reduce the size of the full income multiplier effect.

The only destabilizing influence discussed in the chapter was the expectations hypothesis. It claimed that an economic decline (expansion) creates pessimism (optimism), which causes households to delay (accelerate) purchases of replacements for old durable goods. Thus, it is argued that the movement of the economy is accelerated when household expectations are included.

CHAPTER SEVEN

INCOME DISTRIBUTION AND MACROECONOMICS

Chapter 6 indicated that depending upon the psychological motivation selected, mainstream economists find household behavior stabilizing or destabilizing. It was noted that left-economists find this debate over household motivation to be diversionary. Most left-economists assume that all wages are consumed. Thus, all savings is derived from profits. This view can be characterized as the *income shares hypothesis* (ISH) since it claims that the shares of income going to wages and profits determine the consumption ratio.[1]

This chapter will indicate that the ISH is theoretically defensible, can explain the shortrun and longrun consumption schedule, and has empirical support. It will demonstrate that one implication of the ISH is that wage-cutting tendencies of corporations during recessions, which must be undertaken regardless of consequences, have a fundamentally destabilizing influence on consumption. Hence, unless profits have a significant effect on capital spending, class conflict over income shares can have serious adverse consequences for the economy.

7.1 THE INCOME SHARES HYPOTHESIS

Let us describe the macrodynamics resulting from an income redistribution, ΔR, to wages from profits. The rise in wages would raise consumption by $MPC_w(\Delta R)$, while the lowering of profits would lower consumption by $MPC_p(\Delta R)$, where MPC_w and MPC_p are the marginal propensities to consume out of wages and profits respectively. This indicates that the redistribution towards wages would raise aggregate consumption if $MPC_w > MPC_p$.

---

1. Income shares models have their foundation in the work of Michal Kalecki. See his *Selected Essays on the Dynamics of the Capitalist System* (Cambridge, U.K.: Cambridge Press, 1971).

Let us assume that profits (P) are proportionally divided between household nonwage income (NW) and business income (B) so that

$$\text{NW} = (1-q)P \qquad B = qP$$

where

$$0 \le q \le 1$$

Since all business income goes to savings, the change in consumption resulting from a change in profits

$$\Delta C_p = \text{MPC}_{nw}(\Delta \text{NW}) = \text{MPC}_{nw}(1-q)\Delta P$$

where MPC_{nw} equals the marginal propensity to consume out of nonwage household income. Therefore,

$$\text{MPC}_p = \Delta C_p / \Delta P = \text{MPC}_{nw}(1-q)$$

This indicates that the $\text{MPC}_p < \text{MPC}_w$ if either $\text{MPC}_{nw} < \text{MPC}_w$ or $q > 0$.

The MPC$_w$ and MPC$_{nw}$

All data indicates that nonwage income goes disproportionately to upper income households. For example, according to 1973 tax returns, households with incomes less than \$25,000 received only 6% of their income from corporate profits; 20% for households with incomes of between \$50,000 and \$100,000; and 75% for households with incomes over \$500,000. Therefore, if $\text{MPC}_{nw} < \text{MPC}_w$, we would expect the MPC to be inversely related to household income; i.e., the MPC of the rich is lower than the MPC of the poor.

Chapter 6 discussed the consumption patterns for society as a whole. It presented time series data on how total consumption varied as total household income changed from one time period to the next. In order to determine the effects of a change in the consumption of an individual household as its income varied, we can compare the consumption patterns of individual households at *one point in time*. This is a cross-sectional approach. Virtually all cross-sectional studies find an inverse relationship between the MPC and income levels, which is exactly what we would have expected if $\text{MPC}_{nw} < \text{MPC}_w$.[2]

Before we accept the results from cross-sectional studies as proof that the $\text{MPC}_{nw} < \text{MPC}_w$, let us see how the PIH and LCH can also explain these results. According to the PIH, at any point in time there are many households among the poor that are having a bad year. This includes farmers having a poor crop, ballplayers having an off year, or college professors who have just been fired. Because a disproportionate number of poor households have

---

2. For one such study, see *Studies of Consumer Expenditures, Incomes, and Savings,* Wharton School of Finance and Commerce, University of Pennsylvania, 1957, p. 2.

current incomes below their permanent income, the average consumption for the group would be high.

On the other hand, among the rich are many households having a good year. This includes movie stars having a successful film, executives receiving record bonuses, and workers with unexpected overtime. Since a disproportionate number of the rich have current incomes above their permanent income, the average consumption for the group would be low.

According to the LCH, the group of households with high incomes includes a disproportionate share of middle-age households who have below-average consumption. The group of households with low incomes includes a disproportionate number of young households who have a high consumption ratio. This makes it appear that as income rises the MPC declines because it only shows that middle-aged households (who happen to have high incomes) save more than young households (who happen to have low incomes).

If these alternative explanations of cross-sectional data are correct, then a redistribution of income from the rich to the poor would have no effect upon total consumption since both the LCH and PIH assume that all households have the same MPC. This indicates that there is no general agreement within the economics profession as to the effects that income redistribution between rich and poor households would have on total consumption. There have certainly been studies which have found that incorporating income distribution into macro-models have increased their explanatory power. However, the results have been mixed.[3] Therefore, it is not possible to make a strong case that the MPC of high income households is lower than the MPC of low income households once we include permanent income and life cycle considerations.[4]

Business Income (B)

If we assume $B = 0$, then all savings is done by households. Moreover, by eliminating business income from consideration, this assumption implies that internal funding of capital spending is not an important consideration. It also implies that fluctuations in total savings are primarily a result of fluctuations in household savings. As noted in Chapter 5, these views have significant ideological importance. They reinforce consumer sovereignty views and minimize the role of corporations in determining economic fluctuations.

---

3. For a discussion of studies, see Michael Evans, *Macroeconomic Activity* (New York: Harper & Row, 1970), pp. 44–45. The most recent work by Paul L. Menchik, "The Inheritance of Wealth: Like Parent Like Child?" *Focus* 2 (Spring 1978): 8–11, offers strong support for the thesis that there is a significantly larger MPS for upper-income households than for lower-income households and that a redistribution would significantly affect equilibrium income.

4. Steve Marglin, writing from the radical perspective, claims that virtually all households have an MPC = 1, so that all capital spending is financed from business income. See his "What Do Bosses Do? Part II" *Review of Radical Political Economy* 6 (Winter 1974).

Assuming $B = 0$ is quite a weak assumption. Business savings is always greater than household savings. For example, during the period 1965–76, business savings averaged 71% of total savings, with a range of 65–80%. If any simplifying assumption should be made, it is that *all savings is done by businesses*. This indicates that $q > 0$ and, therefore, it is more than reasonable to assume that the $MPC_p < MPC_w$.

The ISH and Variations in the Consumption Ratio

The ISH is capable of explaining the distinction between the longrun and shortrun consumption schedule. According to the ISH, the consumption ratio is dependent upon the distribution of income between wages and profits and the proportion of profits going to dividends.[5] If both these determinants remain constant in the longrun, then the consumption ratio would also remain constant. Thus, the ISH is consistent with the observation of a constant longrun consumption ratio.

While the shares of income going to wages and profits could remain constant in the longrun, it is possible that they vary systematically over the cycle. In particular, if profits are more volatile than wages, we would expect the share of profits to rise during booms and to decline during recessions.[6] Since the consumption ratio is inversely related to the share of income going to profits, this implies that the consumption ratio would decline during booms and rise during recessions. Thus, the ISH is consistent with the shortrun cyclical variation of the consumption ratio.

7.2 INCOME DETERMINATION

Let us assume that the ISH is correct and analyze the effects an income redistribution from profits towards wages would have on equilibrium production, wages, and profits. Let profits and wages each be a fixed proportion of total income, $P = (1 - k)Y$ and $W = kY$. At the initial equilibrium income Y_0 (Figure 7.1), $W = W_0$ and $P = P_0$. Now assume that there is a lump sum redistribution, ΔR, from profits to wages. This would be reflected by an upward parallel shift of the wage schedule to $W' = kY + \Delta R$ and a downward parallel shift of the profit schedule to $P' = (1 - k)Y - \Delta R$.

At the initial equilibrium income Y_0, the redistribution would lower profits by ΔR and increase wages by the same amount. However, since the redistribution is in favor of the group with the higher MPC, the economy will expand. The total effect of the redistribution on wages is clearly positive. Total wages

---

5. There is evidence that income shares have remained relatively constant in the longrun with 75% going to wages and 25% to profits.

6. This in fact occurred during the first four post-World War II recessions. See Evans, *Macroeconomic Activity,* pp. 287–89.

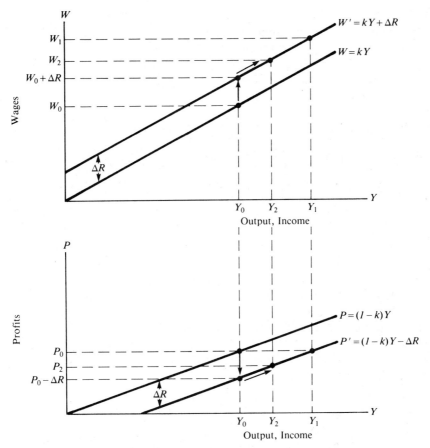

Figure 7.1   Effects of income redistribution from profits to wages

initially increase from the redistribution and grow still further, by $k(\Delta Y)$, as the economy expands. The total change in wages is:

$$\Delta W^{T} = \Delta R + k(\Delta Y)$$

The outcome for profits is not as clear cut. Initially, profits decline by the size of the redistribution. Subsequently, as the economy expands there is an induced increase in profits of $(1-k)\Delta Y$. Therefore, the total change in profits is:

$$\Delta P^{T} = -(\Delta R) + (1-k)(\Delta Y)$$

If the economic expansion is to Y_1, then profits would return to their original level, P_0. The entire expansion would go to wages. (Equilibrium wages increase from W_0 to W_1.)

However, what if the economic expansion was only to Y_2? In this case, the redistribution policy, while expanding the economy, reduces equilibrium profits. At Y_2, profits are only P_2, while wages have increased to W_2. Similarly, if there was a redistribution from wages to profits, it is possible that even though the economy declines, profits would still be higher than before the redistribution. For these reasons, let us look more closely at a model with two distinct sectors each having a different MPC.

Capitalist-Worker Model

Let us continue to assume that there are two distinct groups, one receiving only wages, and the other controlling and/or receiving all the profits. Furthermore, let us continue to assume that total income is initially proportionately distributed between wages and profits.

$$W = kY \qquad P = (1 - k)Y$$

where

$$0 < k < 1$$

We will continue to assume that I is exogenously determined

$$I = I_0$$

Note that this assumes that changes in profits have no effect on capital investment decisions.

Next, assume that the income-spending relationship of each sector is a simple consumption schedule

$$C_w = b_w(W)$$
$$C_p = b_p(P)$$

where

$$b_w = MPC_w, \; b_p = MPC_p, \text{ and}$$
$$b_p < b_w$$

Let us assume that $b_w = 1$ so that all wage income goes to consumer spending. Figure 7.2 illustrates the total consumption $(C_p + C_w)$ and total spending schedules in this model.

Capitalist households receive a portion $(1 - k)$ of total income so that the capitalist consumption schedule is

$$C_p = b_p(1 - k)Y$$

The slope of the capitalist consumption schedule, $b_p(1 - k)$,[7] reflects the change in capitalist consumption which would occur if *total* income increased by one unit.

---

7. For example, suppose $b_p = 0.50$ and $k = 0.75$. Then for each unit of Y, profits rise by 0.25 units and the consumption of capitalists by $0.5(\Delta P) = (.5)(0.25) = 0.125 = b_p(1 - k)$.

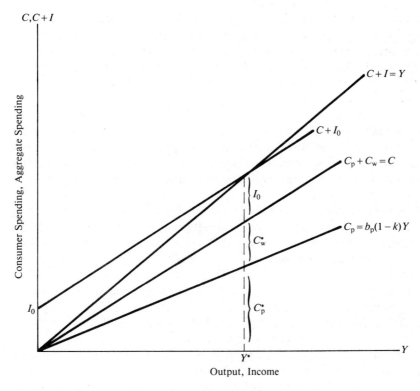

Figure 7.2   Income determination in income shares model

Since wage-earning households consume all their income and since $W = kY$, then

$$C_w = kY$$

The total consumption schedule is

$$C = C_p + C_w = b_p(1 - k)Y + kY = [b_p(1 - k) + k]Y$$

If we add the investment schedule, we obtain the total spending schedule

$$C + I = [b_p(1 - k) + k]Y + I_0$$

Figure 7.2 indicates that at equilibrium income Y_e, $C_p = C_p^*$ and $C_w = C_w^*$.[8]

Let us now analyze the effect of an income redistribution of size, ΔR, from profits to wages. The initial autonomous change in spending would be an

<hr />

8. If $C_p = .5P + 100$, $C_w = W$, $W = .75Y$, and $I = 100$, then $C_p = .5(0.25Y) + 100 = .125Y + 100$. $C_w = .75Y$ so that $C = C_w + C_p = .875Y + 100$. $C + I = .875Y + 200$ so that equilibrium occurs when $.875Y + 200 = Y$ or equilibrium $Y = 1600$. Equilibrium $P = .25$(equilibrium Y) $= .25(1600) = 400$.

increase of total consumption of $(1 - b_p)(\Delta R)$. This occurs because while wage-earning households spend all the additional income, ΔR, part of the decline in capitalist income would be absorbed by a decline in savings. Hence, capitalist consumption declines by only $b_p(\Delta R)$. When we include the subsequent multiplier effect, the total change in equilibrium Y is

$$\Delta Y = (1 - b_p)(M_y)(\Delta R)$$

As we have already seen, the size of the increase in equilibrium income will be critical in determining the effect on equilibrium profits. It will be shown that the increase in equilibrium Y will be just sufficient to keep profits unchanged. In this case, the redistribution only increases total and wage income.

This can be shown by analyzing the effect of the income redistribution on equilibrium income through the savings-investment approach (Figure 7.3). In our model, since all wages go to consumption, there is no savings out of wages. Hence, total savings is the savings out of profits. Given the initial savings schedule, Figure 7.3 indicates that equilibrium income is at Y^*. Now suppose that the income distribution, ΔR, from profits to wages occurs. At each level of total income, profits is lowered by ΔR so that savings would be lowered by $(1 - b_p)(\Delta R)$. Therefore, the savings function is lowered to S_p'. At the initial equilibrium, $S < I$ so that an expansion occurs.

As Figure 7.3 indicates, as long as investment is constant, savings must return to its original level before equilibrium is reestablished. This occurs at Y_1. But how has equilibrium profits fared?[9] Since equilibrium savings is unchanged and all savings is derived from profits, this could occur only if profits return to their original level. Hence, as long as investment is held constant and there is no savings out of wages, equilibrium profits are unchanged.

Referring again to Figure 7.3, suppose that the redistribution was in the other direction, from wages to profits. Initially, profits at Y^* would increase by ΔR and savings would increase by $(1 - b_p)\Delta R$. Since this is a lump sum redistribution, $(1 - b_p)\Delta R$ is the change in savings at each level of Y so that the savings schedule shifts to S_p''. Since $S > I$, a contraction begins and will continue as long as profits are above their original level. Hence, equilibrium is reestablished, at Y_2, only when profits return to their original level.

This exercise has shown that in our model, as long as investment is held constant and all savings is done by capitalists, the multiplier effect is just large enough to fully offset any attempts to change profits through a redistri-

---

9. Before the shift, according to note 8, $C_p = .125Y + 100$ and $C_w = .75Y$ so that $C = .875Y + 100$. If $\Delta R = 10$ so that $W' = .75Y + 10$ (and $P' = .25Y - 10$), then $C_p = .5(.25Y - 10) + 100 = .125Y + 95$ and $C_w = .75Y + 10$. Hence, $C = C_p + C_w = .875Y + 105$. This indicates that the redistribution results in an autonomous increase of consumption of 5. The new spending schedule is $C + I = .875Y + 205$ so that the new equilibrium occurs when $.875Y + 205 = Y$ or equilibrium $Y = 1640$. Equilibrium $P = .25$ (equilibrium Y) $- 10 = .25(1640) - 10 = 410 - 10 = 400$.

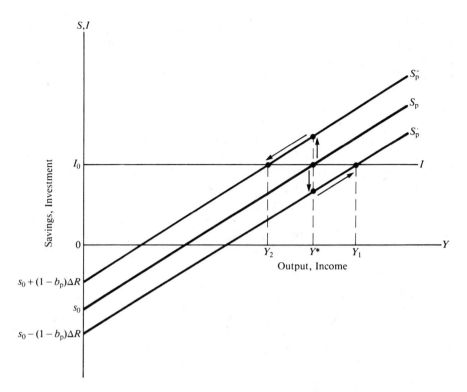

Figure 7.3 Effect of income redistribution on equilibrium income

butional policy. Any attempt to raise profits will be completely offset by the resulting economic contraction while any attempt to lower profits would only induce a fully compensating expansion.

7.3 IMPLICATIONS OF ISH

Paradox of Profits

The result just described can be called a "Paradox of Profits" since any attempt by capitalists to increase their profits at the expense of wages would only lead to a decline in production. Equilibrium profits are unchanged. If, in fact, there was some induced investment (MPI$>$0), the multiplier effect would be larger so that equilibrium profits would decline. There are important similarities and dissimilarities between the Paradox of Profits and Paradox of Thrift results of Chapter 6.

The major similarity is that both the Paradox of Profits and Paradox of Thrift results indicate that if society attempts to increase savings at the expense of spending, it will induce economic declines which will fully offset the initial increase in savings, as long as I is constant. However, the explanation and the policy implication of this process are dissimilar. The Paradox of Thrift results from a psychologically-motivated shift in savings patterns of individual households. Offsetting household pessimism is the corrective policy implication of this viewpoint. On the other hand, the Paradox of Profits results from a redistribution of income with *no* change in individual savings patterns. This viewpoint indicates that attempts to change household attitudes will have no effect on spending. Finally, the Paradox of Profits model highlights the possibility that the nature of savings may be as important as its sum.

This framework implies that downward wage flexibility can have a destabilizing effect on the economy. For example, suppose that the economy begins to decline, resulting in lower equilibrium profits and wages. According to the reserve army thesis, when unemployment exists capitalists are able to exploit workers by lowering wages with no compensating decline in prices. Each firm (industry) acting individually would choose to lower wages, regardless of its total effect on sales. However, the shift of income from wages to profits would contract the economy still further.

It is important to realize that while the reserve army thesis implies that initially profits rise, it does not necessarily mean that equilibrium profits rise. Indeed, according to the capitalist-worker model developed in this chapter, it might actually result in a decline in equilibrium profits. This would be a case where capitalists' greed kills the goose (workers' purchasing power) that laid the golden eggs (sales).

Fragmentation of Decison-Making

Let us assume that there is some induced investment (MPI = 1/60) so that if firms reduce wages in order to increase profit margins, there will be a decline in equilibrium profits. It can be demonstrated that even if this result was known to individual capitalists, they must still attempt to lower wages. Moreover, it will be shown that this result is due to the lack of economic planning—fragmentation of decision-making—rather than the pressures of competitive forces.

The fragmentation of decision-making is what Marx described as the anarchy of capitalist production. Individual profit objectives rather than resulting in the socially optimum outcome, à la Adam Smith's invisible hand, leads to socially suboptimum outcomes for *both* capitalists as a group and workers. Here, Marx's critique of capitalism is not primarily moral (workers exploited by the greedy capitalist), for he believed that the anarchy of the capitalist system created systemic contradictions which individual capitalists could neither control nor overcome. The crisis just described is what Marxists call the realization problem. It is so called because after the capitalist redistributes income, he has the ability to raise his profits if he maintains sales. However, he cannot realize these profits because the redistribution, by lowering workers' purchasing power, dictates a sales decline.

Market Decision-Making Process

To demonstrate this let us assume that the economy is composed of two in-dustries, A and B. In order to avoid the effects of competition, assume that all firms in each industry make the same wage decision. This eliminates the effects of *intra*-industry competition. Further assume that regardless of the wage decision of each industry, both industries always equally divide sales. This eliminates the effects of *inter*-industry competition. Furthermore, in order to eliminate the effects of price changes, we will assume that each industry can make only two choices: cut wages and take higher profits or don't cut wages.[10] There are then *four* possible outcomes: both cut wages, both don't cut wages, only industry A cuts wages, and only industry B cuts wages. In each of the four boxes of Table 7.1 we have the results of each outcome. The numbers in the upper-righthand corners indicate Industry A's sales and, in parentheses, Industry A's profits. The numbers in the lower-lefthand corners indicate Industry B's sales and, in parentheses, profits.

Table 7.1

Industry B   *Industry A*

	Cut Wages	Don't Cut
Cut Wages	1125 (296) 1125 (296)	1163 (291) 1163 (306)
Don't Cut	1163 (306) 1163 (291)	1200 (300) 1200 (300)

Suppose we are initially at equilibrium at $Y = 2400$. Both industries would have sales of 1200 and if we assume that each industry's mark-up is 25%, they will both have profits of $\frac{1}{4}(1200) = 300$. This represents the results if they both maintain wages.

Suppose both industries decided to cut wages by 15.[11] From our previous analysis we would expect an autonomous decline in consumption. If the $MPC_p = 2/3$ for all capitalists, then the redistribution of 30 would decrease total consumption by $(1 - MPC_p)(30) = (1/3)(30) = 10$. With $MPI = 1/60$, the

---

10. Here we are ignoring the conservative contention that all cost decreases are reflected in price decreases with profits remaining constant at their "normal" level.

11. Each industry's profit schedule shifts to: $(1/4)(\text{sales}) + 15$.

$M_y = 15$.[12] Therefore, the new equilibrium income would be 2250. Each industry's sales would decline by 75, so that the induced decline in profits would be $1/4(75) \cong 19$. For each industry, the total change in profits (equal to the initial change plus the induced change) would be $+15 - 19 = -4$; i.e., equilibrium profits would decline to 296 for both industries.

This is the strong case of the Paradox of Profits. The induced decline is large enough to more than offset the initial increase in profits. It would seem irrational for both industries to choose to lower wages. However, let us look at the effects if only one industry lowers wages.

Suppose Industry A chooses to lower the wages of its workers while Industry B chooses to maintain wages. Now the autonomous decline in consumption is halved to $(1/3)(15) = 5$. If the multiplier remains 15, then the decline in equilibrium income is also halved to $5(15) = 75$. Each industry's sales are only lowered by 37.5 so that the induced decline in profits for both is only $\frac{1}{4}(37.5) \cong 9$. Since Industry A had an initial increase in profits of 15, its equilibrium profits actually rise to 306 while Industry B's profits decline to 291. The results would be the opposite if it had been Industry A which had maintained wages while Industry B cut wages.

In a private market economy each industry makes its decisions separately. Let us now determine the decision each industry will make, assuming that they are aware of each of the four possible outcomes of Table 7.1.

Industry A's decision Suppose Industry B maintains wages. According to the known outcomes, it would pay for Industry A to lower wages since it could have equilibrium profits of 306. Industry A's induced profit decline results from the lost purchasing power of its own workers alone since the other industry maintains the purchasing power of the other workers.[13] The lost purchasing power and resulting multiplier effect are small enough so that the induced decline is less than the initial gains from a wage cut.

Suppose Industry B cuts wages. Again, it would be in the best interest of Industry A to also lower wages. It realizes that when both lower wages, each industry's profits decline to 296 (Paradox of Profits). However, it calculates

---

12. Recall that the slope of the total consumption schedule is $MPC = b_p(1 - k) + k$. Since $b_p = 2/3$ and $k = 3/4$, $MPC = 11/12$. Hence, $MPSP = MPC + MPI = 11/12 + 1/60 = 14/15$ so that $M_y = 1/(1 - MPSP) = 15$.

13. In a perfectly competitive economy each industry assumes that all others will maintain wages. Therefore, each industry's sales are hurt by only the direct purchasing power loss of its own workers plus the induced effects of the resulting multiplier process. The smaller the industry, the smaller this sum would be. In the extreme, where each industry is so small that its own workers make up an insignificant fraction of the entire workforce, each industry would assume that cutting its own workers' wages would have *no* effect on its sales. Therefore, if we would expand this 2-industry case to a 300-industry case, each industry would lower wages whenever possible.

that if it maintains wages when the other industry does not, its profit decline would be still greater (to 291).

This indicates that as long as Industry A must decide independently, it would always lower wages. If Industry B lowers wages, then its profits would be 296; and if Industry B maintain wages, its profits would be 306.

Industry B's decision Since the results are symmetrical, regardless of Industry A's actual choice, Industry B would attempt to maximize its profits by lowering wages.

This analysis has made use of the "prisoners' dilemma" framework (see appendix to this chapter). It emphasizes that individual decisions result in sub-optimal solutions when outcomes are interdependent. Each industry's decision to lower wages occurs even though both are aware this will probably result in an inferior outcome. However, each industry cannot risk maintaining wages without a guarantee that the other industry would do likewise. Without a guarantee they risk having the worst outcome (profits equal to 291). On the other hand, they realize that by lowering wages there is a chance that if the others maintain wages they could maximize profits (of 306). Indeed, this last case indicates that even if some voluntary agreement is reached, it would be in the interest of each industry to break the agreement.

Class Differences Over Incomes Policies

The Paradox of Profits result assumed that all savings was done by capitalists ($b_w = 1$). Suppose, however, that $b_p < b_w < 1$.

Let us begin with a redistribution from profits to wages, ΔR. As previously shown,

$$\Delta C_p = b_p(-\Delta R) \text{ and } \Delta C_w = b_w(\Delta R)$$

so that the autonomous change in spending,

$$\Delta A = \Delta C_w + \Delta C_p = (b_w - b_p)(\Delta R) < (1 - b_p)(\Delta R)$$

when $b_w < 1$.

Hence, the initial autonomous change in spending is less than when $b_w = 1$. The size of the income multiplier is also smaller since one of the spending sector's MPC is reduced.[14] If both the income multiplier and autonomous change in spending are reduced, then so must the change in equilibrium income. If the change in equilibrium income is reduced, then so must the induced change in profits [$(1-k)\Delta Y$]. When $b_w = 1$, the induced change exactly offsets the initial redistribution so that equilibrium profits are unchanged. If now the induced

---

14. In general, MPC $= b_p(1 - k) + b_w k$. Therefore, the smaller b_w, the smaller the MPC and, hence the smaller M_y.

changes are smaller, then they will not be enough to offset the initial profit decline; equilibrium profits would be lowered by a redistribution of income away from profits. Similarly, if income is redistributed away from wages (to profits), there would be an economic contraction. However, this contraction would be sufficiently small so that equilibrium profits would be improved.

This implies that if $b_w < 1$, income redistribution policies which improve total income would conflict with the economic interests of capitalists. In this case, it is impossible to identify the "national interest," for the proposition so widely accepted that everyone benefits from policies which stimulate economic growth is not true. Capitalists would actually benefit from a redistribution away from wages even though it would reduce equilibrium income.

There are other reasons to believe that equilibrium profits may increase when income is redistributed away from wages towards profits. First, the subsidy to firms may improve the competitive position of U.S. corporations. This could be reflected in higher exports and/or lower imports. If this occurs, the downward multiplier effect would be reduced, thus reducing the induced profit decline. Second, as we will find in Chapter 8, when the government collects its taxes proportionately the size of the income multiplier is reduced. A smaller multiplier lessens the contraction and, again, the induced profit decline is smaller. This, of course, must be balanced with the possibility that the inclusion of induced investment, as reflected in Table 7.1, would increase the income multiplier. Therefore, one should consider it possible, even quite likely, that raising profits at the expense of wages can raise equilibrium profits.

Investment and Profits

The Paradox of Profits indicates that if profits have *no* effect on capital spending, the economy would be adversely affected by shifting income from households to corporations. Consumer spending would be adversely affected by such a redistribution and there would be no compensating increase in capital spending. For example, Michael Evans believes that profits have only a negligible effect on capital spending. Using the Wharton Econometric Model, he estimated that raising corporate profits by $1 billion would only increase equilibrium income by $600 million.[15] On the other hand, lowering personal income by $1 billion would lower equilibrium income by more than $1.6 billion.[16] Therefore, Evans estimated that shifting $1 billion from households to corporations would decrease equilibrium income by more than $1 billion. This indicates that corporations would benefit in the longrun from such a redistribution even though it would lower production and employment.

---

15. Evans, *Macroeconomic Activity,* p. 571.

16. Ibid., p. 570.

Evans' estimates should not be accepted uncritically. Other mainstream economists[17] and radicals[18] contend that profits have a significant effect on capital spending. Evans' results only indicate that income distribution *can* have a large effect on equilibrium income *if* capital spending is not significantly affected by the level of profits.[19]

7.4 CONCLUSION

This chapter demonstrated that equilibrium income can be significantly affected by the distribution of income between wages and profits. We found:

1. If either part of additional profits is undistributed or the $MPC_w >$ MPC_{nw}, then the $MPC_w > MPC_p$, and any redistribution towards wages increases equilibrium income.

2. Since a redistribution towards profits lowers equilibrium income, downward wage flexibility can have a destabilizing effect on the economy. Specifically, if in a declining economy wages are lowered to increase profit margins, the economy would be accelerated further downward. This contradicts the mainstream contention that downward wage flexibility has a stabilizing effect on the economy.

3. If $MPC_w = 1$, then equilibrium profits are unaffected by redistributions of income. Therefore, capitalists as a group do not benefit from wage-cutting policies. However, we found that due to the "anarchy of production decisions," all firms would lower wages regardless of the long term consequences on profits.

---

17. Profits as a determinant of capital spending are emphasized by W. W. Heller, "The Anatomy of the Investment Decision," *Harvard Business Review* (Mar. 1951): 95–103 and in J. R. Meyer and E. Kuh, *The Investment Decision* (Harvard University Press, 1957), Chapters 8 and 12.

18. Radicals contend that the banking community through its control of external financing can gain control of corporations (financial control thesis of Chapter 3). Therefore, many corporations may decide to invest only out of internal funds (undistributed profits and depreciation allowance) in order to maintain their independence from the banking community.

19. In his study of the 1964 tax cut, Arthur Okun obtains results which are in sharp contrast with those of Evans. According to Okun, raising corporate profits by $1 billion would increase equilibrium income by $3.45 billion, while lowering personal income by $1 billion would only lower equilibrium income by $2.58 billion. Thus, Okun estimates that a shift of $1 billion from wages to profits would actually *raise* equilibrium income by almost $1 billion. Critical to Okun's findings is his assumption that each additional dollar of profits would increase capital spending by $0.75. For a discussion of Okun's findings, see Rudiger Dornbusch and Stanley Fischer, *Macroeconomics* (New York: McGraw-Hill, 1978), pp. 304–313.

4. There are a number of situations, such as if $MPC_w < 1$, in which a redistribution towards profits could increase equilibrium profits. In this case, a conflict over macro-policy will emerge. Capitalists would benefit from a redistributional policy even though it would cause a decline in production and employment.

5. These results are critically dependent upon the assumption that capital spending is not significantly affected by the level of profits.

APPENDIX

PRISONERS' DILEMMA MODEL

The decision-making process described in Table 7.1 is called the prisoners' dilemma framework. It analyzes situations in which individual outcomes discourage trust and lead to suboptimal choices. In Table 7.1 each industry realizes that if it would trust the other industries to cooperate by maintaining wages, they all would be better off. However, even if the industries were legally allowed to enter into *non*binding agreements, fears and greed would undermine their group interest. Its name is derived from the following classical illustration.

Let us assume that there have been two similar crimes committed. Two suspects are captured in the act of the second offense (armed robbery) and the district attorney, though having no evidence to directly connect them with the first offense, decides to indict them for both crimes. The district attorney indicates to each of the suspects that if they both plead guilty each will receive 10-year sentences. If they both plead not guilty there is only enough evidence to convict them of one count so they would each receive a 5-year sentence. The district attorney also indicates that he would look very favorably upon either individual if they pleaded guilty while the other pleaded not guilty. In this case, the one who pleads guilty would receive a 2-year sentence, while the other suspect, who would be incriminated, would receive a 20-year sentence. The alternative outcomes that each suspect faces are indicated by Table 7A.1. The district attorney says that they can discuss their choices collectively, but that each suspect's final decision must be made individually without the other's knowledge. The best outcome seems to be if both plead not guilty. However, as in the previous example, neither decision-maker can afford to make the "best" decision without a guarantee that the other decision-maker will make the same decision. Here, pleading not guilty runs the risk of a 20-year sentence if the other suspect turns state's evidence. This is a reasonable possibility since by turning state's evidence the suspect may receive only a 2-year sentence.

Table 7A.1

2nd Suspect   *1st Suspect*

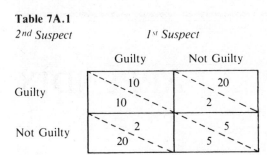

	Guilty	Not Guilty
Guilty	10 \ 10	20 \ 2
Not Guilty	2 \ 20	5 \ 5

Both suspects will plead guilty. (Note that this occurs *regardless* of whether or not either person actually committed the second offense.)

Another classical example is the decision on nuclear disarmament when there is no way of monitoring compliance. Suppose two adversary countries, A and B, have equal access to the growth of scientific knowledge. They can both choose to limit nuclear armament, which would result in a military stalemate. Another choice would be for both nations to drastically increase their armament. They would again be stalemated, but this time substantial resources would be diverted away from socially useful production, and if war occurs, the losses to both countries would be devastating. This second possible outcome (increasing armament) is clearly inferior to the first possibility (disarmament).

The problem is that with no ability to monitor compliance, each country must rely on mutual trust. Trust, however, can break down when the other possible outcomes are denoted. For example, suppose that each country views outsmarting the other as the *best* possible outcome (arming while the other country disarms) and views being outsmarted as the worst outcome (disarming when the other arms). The choices in this situation are denoted in Table 7A.2.

Given the information in Table 7A.2, when each country decides individually, they would both choose the inferior solution (arming). The reasons are (1) neither can afford to risk disarming and ending up with the worst outcome, and (2) each realizes that by arming there is the possibility of the best outcome if the adversary chooses disarming.

Table 7A.2

Country B   *Country A*

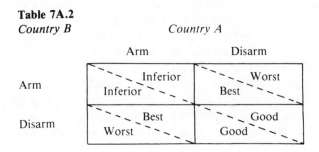

	Arm	Disarm
Arm	Inferior \ Inferior	Worst \ Best
Disarm	Best \ Worst	Good \ Good

CHAPTER EIGHT

THE GOVERNMENT SECTOR

Chapter 6 indicated that there is a continuum of opinions from conservative to left-economists on the stabilizing/destabilizing effects of consumer behavior on the economy. Conservatives, emphasizing the PIH and LCH, claim that consumer behavior has a stabilizing influence; liberals, emphasizing the expectations hypothesis, claim that household durable goods decisions have a destabilizing effect. Chapter 7 indicated that, according to left-economists, because the distribution of income significantly affects aggregate consumption, wage-cutting tendencies of corporations during contractions can have a destabilizing effect on the economy. We will find that this same pattern of opinion will be duplicated when business investment decisions are discussed. Conservatives will claim that business behavior has a stabilizing effect, left-economists a destabilizing effect, and mainstream liberals in between.

If the private sector has substantial stabilizing influences, then government intervention is unnecessary. A laissez-faire economy can sustain full employment. Indeed, conservatives argue that economic fluctuations are caused by government intervention. Left-economists contend that government intervention is necessary due to the volatility of the private sector. Moreover, since it is considered an important determinant of spending, left-economists claim that government intervention must influence the structure of income distribution between wages and profits. Policies to influence income distribution are called *incomes policies,* the most important example being wage-price controls. Chapter 7 also indicated that competitive forces can have a destabilizing effect on the economy. We found that it was possible for situations to develop in which individual corporations, making interdependent decisions, resulted in suboptimal outcomes. In order to avoid these negative externalities associated with individual decision-making, many left-economists claim that national planning is necessary.

Mainstream liberals reject both the conservative and left positions. They do not believe the private sector is stable enough to be totally relied upon, hence, they favor government intervention. However, they do not believe that either incomes policies or national planning is warranted because they reject the left contentions that income distribution significantly affects aggregate spending and/or significant negative externalities are present.

Mainstream liberals favor limited government intervention. The two major forms of intervention they recommend are discretionary actions and automatic stabilizers to reduce the size of economic fluctuations. *Discretionary actions* are decisions by the government in direct response to economic conditions. The 1975 tax rebate and 1977 fiscal stimulus are examples of discretionary *fiscal* actions to combat high unemployment rates. *Automatic stabilizers* are government policies which have already been institutionalized to respond to economic fluctuations and, therefore, require no new government actions. Examples of automatic stabilizers are unemployment insurance, food stamps, welfare, and the federal tax system.

We have yet to fully develop the theoretical constructs that each viewpoint uses to support their contentions concerning government intervention. In particular, we have yet to explore the left-theories which underly their contention that national planning is necessary. Also, we have yet to develop the ways in which government control of the money supply can affect spending. Therefore, this chapter will only discuss issues raised by the mainstream liberal/conservative debate concerning the form and effectiveness of government *fiscal stabilization* policies.

8.1 SIMPLE MODEL WITH A GOVERNMENT SECTOR

Let us begin with a private sector model,

$$C = .8Y_d + 100 \qquad I = 200 \qquad G = T = 0$$

Since $T = 0$, $Y_d = Y$, so that the consumption schedule is $C_0 = .8Y + 100$, and the spending schedule is $C_0 + I = .8Y + 300$. Figure 8.1 indicates that equilibrium $Y = 1500$.[1]

Now suppose that there is some government spending, $G = 100$, but we continue to have $T = 0$. Since there are no taxes there would be no change in the consumption schedule. However, now at each level of Y, there is an additional spending of 100 so that the new aggregate spending schedule is shifted upward by the amount of government spending, $C_0 + I + G = .8Y + 400$. When a government sector is added, the equilibrium condition, reflecting the equality between aggregate demand and aggregate supply, becomes

$$C + I + G = Y$$

The new equilibrium $Y = 2000$.[2]

---

1. Duplication of Figure 5.2.

2. $0.8Y + 400 = Y$ so that equilibrium $Y = 2000$. In this model the only induced change is consumption MPSP = MPC and $M_y = 1/(1 - \text{MPC})$ so that, with MPC = 0.8, $\Delta Y_T = 5(\Delta A)$.

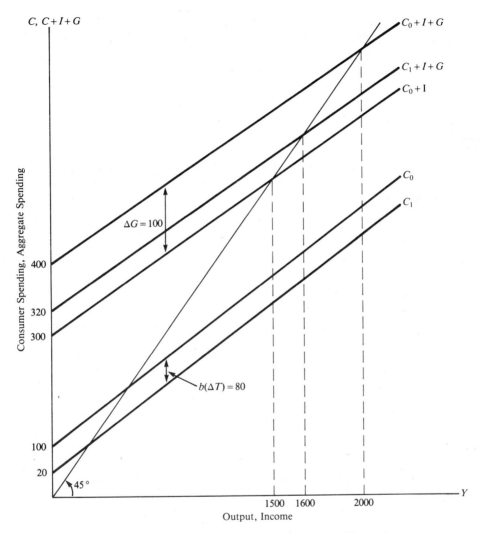

Figure 8.1 Effect of government spending and taxation on equilibrium income

Now let us add a tax schedule, $\overline{T} = 100$. This indicates that regardless of Y, taxes are a constant amount. This is called a *lump sum tax*. The property tax is the principal example of a lump sum tax. Disposable income is no longer equal to Y. Instead, disposable income is now reduced by the size of the tax at each level of income.

$$Y_d = Y - T$$

This indicates that if a lump sum tax $T = \overline{T}$ is imposed, then at each Y, $\Delta Y_d = -\overline{T}$ and the change in consumption $\Delta C = -b\overline{T}$. In our example, since $\overline{T} = 100$ and $b = 0.8$, $\Delta C = -80$.

The decline of consumption by 80 at each level of Y is reflected in the new consumption schedule $C_1 = .8Y + 20$ and the new spending schedule $C_1 + I + G = .8Y + 320$. Equilibrium $Y = 1600$.

Note that the new equilibrium (1600) is above the old equilibrium before the inclusion of a government sector (1500). This indicates that if government spending and tax receipts are simultaneously increased by the same amount, the economy would expand. This occurs because while the government is spending the full amount, if MPC < 1, part of the tax increase comes from savings so that the decline in consumption is smaller. The process of changing both taxes and government spending by the same amount is called the *balanced budget process* and will be discussed later in this chapter.

Equilibrium income determination can also be analyzed through the leakage-injection framework. With a government sector, total leakages are savings plus taxes and total injections are investment plus government spending. At equilibrium,

$$S + T = I + G$$

Once again, let us begin with a private sector economy represented by a savings schedule S_0 and investment schedule I_0. Figure 8.2 indicates that in this model equilibrium income is established at Y_e (point A).[3] If we add government spending, $G = \overline{G}$, then the total injection schedule becomes $I_0 + \overline{G}$ and equilibrium is reestablished at Y_e^g (point B).[4] Now add a tax, $T = \overline{T}$, which is just equal to government spending. Due to the tax, savings is reduced by $(1 - b)\overline{T}$ at each level of Y so that the new savings schedule becomes S_1.[5] Therefore, the new total leakage schedule, $S_1 + \overline{T}$, is only $b\overline{T}$ above the private sector leakage schedule S_0 since part of the tax is offset by the decline in savings. Equilibrium is reestablished at Y_e^{g+t}.[6] Note again that the effect of simultaneously raising government spending and taxes by the same amount is to raise equilibrium income ($Y_e^{g+t} > Y_e$).

8.2 CRITICAL EVALUATION OF DISCRETIONARY FISCAL POLICIES

The preceding example indicates that dollar for dollar additional government spending would have a greater effect on the economy than a tax cut. This result follows from the assumption that part of the tax cut goes to additional savings (MPC > 1). However, as long as M_y^* and the MPC are known, either

3. $C = 0.8Y_d + 100$ then $S = Y_d - C = 0.2Y_d - 100$. With $Y_d = Y$, $S_0 = 0.2Y - 100$. If $I_0 = 200$ at equilibrium $S_0 = I_0$ or $0.2Y - 100 = 200$ so that equilibrium $Y = 1500$.

4. With government spending but no taxes at equilibrium $S_0 = I_0 + G$ or $.2Y - 100 = 300$ (with $G = 100$) and $Y_e^g = 2000$.

5. $S = 0.2Y_d - 100$. If $Y_d = Y - 100$ then $S_1 = 0.2(Y - 100) - 100 = 0.2Y - 120$ so that $S_1 + T = 0.2Y - 20$.

6. $0.2Y - 20 = 300$ or $Y_e^{g+t} = 1600$.

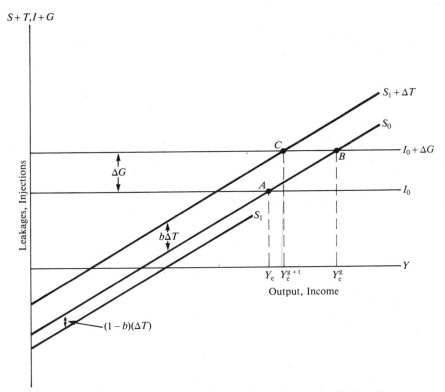

Figure 8.2   Effect of government spending and taxation on equilibrium income

policy could be used to fulfill any objective. For example, suppose that the federal government desired to increase equilibrium income by $50 billion. If $M_y^* = 5$ and MPC = 0.8, then the objective could be fulfilled through either a tax cut of $12.5 billion or a direct government spending increase of $10 billion.

There are two major criticisms of the use of discretionary fiscal policy. First, it is argued that we really have no firm knowledge as to the size of either the M_y^* or MPC so that we cannot reliably estimate the effects of government fiscal policies. Second, our numerical example assumed that the recognition and implementation of fiscal policy can occur quickly. Critics argue that there is a two-year lag between the actual economic fluctuation and the effects of government fiscal policies.

Effect of Government Intervention

Once a government stimulus is initiated, it creates a multiplier process. According to the Brookings Model, a $1 billion increase in government spending would increase aggregate spending by $2.4 billion within six months and by $2.8 billion by the end of one year. Thereafter, aggregate spending actually

neutrality.

begins to decline somewhat. At the end of three years, the Brookings Model indicates that aggregate spending would have increased by $2.5 billion. This would indicate that a good approximation of M_y^* would be 2.5, if we uncritically accept the Brookings Model.

Figure 8.3 indicates the period-by-period cumulative change in aggregate spending resulting from a $1 billion increase in government spending, according to some of the leading macroeconomic models. These results indicate that it is not possible to uncritically accept the Brookings results. For example, the St. Louis Federal Reserve Bank Model (SLF) claims that the rise in aggregate spending is never more than $1 billion and by the beginning of the second year private sector mechanisms have completely offset the effects of the government stimulus. The SLF Model is based upon the extreme conservative view that all spending shocks can be fully compensated for by private sector adjustments. Thus, in the SLF Model, the effective $M_y^* = 0$!

Even those models within the mainstream liberal perspective have a wide difference in the effect of a fiscal stimulus. The predicted effect after three years differs between the models, from $2.6 billion in the Wharton Model to $1.0 billion in the MPS Model. Moreover, there is disagreement over the timing of the impact. While the Brookings Model and the Wharton Model have agreement over the longrun predicted effect, they have substantial differences in the timing of the impact. In the Brookings Model the increase is in the first year with a decline thereafter. In the Wharton Model the increase is much smaller in the first year but the expansionary effects continue throughout the entire three years.

The Brookings/Wharton difference would be of particular importance if you were most interested in the shortrun (first year's effects). For example, if you wanted to increase aggregate spending by $50 billion in the first year, according to the Brookings Model, a government spending stimulus of $21 billion would be required. However, according to the Wharton Model, the stimulus would have to be closer to $30 billion.

One of the features of all of the models, except the Wharton Model, is that after some point the economy begins to decline back towards its original level. This indicates that these models incorporate certain market forces which will at least partially offset any autonomous shift in spending. Part of these stabilizing influences have to do with price changes, which will be explained in Chapter 12. Part of the stabilizing influences result from interest rate changes. Recall from Chapter 6 that according to the LCH, there is an inverse relationship between the market interest rate and consumption. In Chapter 10 we will find that, according to the individualistic theory of investment, there will be an inverse relationship between the market interest rate and capital spending. Therefore, if interest rate adjustments are in the same direction as the initial stimulus, then they will induce countercyclical changes in spending.

The two stages of the full multiplier process can be described as follows. During the first year the initial stimulus, by generating higher levels of employ-

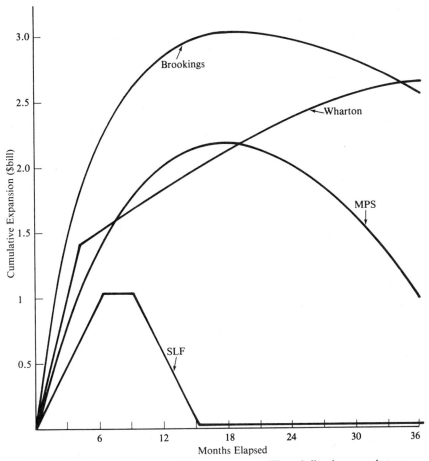

Figure 8.3   Various effects on GNP from a one billion-dollar increase in government nondefense spending

ment and production, induces an expansion of consumer spending. This reflects the simple multiplier component. However, the expansion also brings higher interest rates, which discourage spending. By the second year these interest rate effects begin to dominate so that aggregate spending begins to decline.[7] The MPS model has a dramatic decline because it assumes that spending is very sensitive to interest rate changes. On the other hand, the Wharton Model has no decline because it assumes spending is not very sensitive to interest rate changes.

---

7. The Wharton Model does include a lagged interest rate induced spending contraction. However, it also has a lagged inventory investment expansion which is of a larger magnitude. Therefore, there continues to be an expansion during the second and third years.

Time Lags[8]

A second problem with fiscal policy is that there is a substantial lag between the beginning of an economic downturn and the actual initiating of a fiscal stimulus. This lag has four components: data, recognition, legislative, and transmission lags.

Data lag Suppose that the economy began to decline during April. The quickest reporting index is 10-day automobile sales reports. If we could base government policy on this index, then there would be no lag between the beginning of the downturn and data reporting this event. However, government policy should be based on broader indices, such as monthly figures on industrial output and retail sales. If these indices were used, only after the release of figures in *mid-June,* indicating that May's figures were below April's, would we have data indicating an economic decline. The most inclusive index is quarterly GNP figures. Using these figures, it would not be until *mid-July,* three months after the beginning of the decline, when quarterly figures reveal a decline betwen the first and second quarter, that data would recognize the contraction.

Recognition lag Unless the initial contraction is severe and immediately identifiable, the data would show a slight decline with no clear explanation. It would be wise for policy-makers to wait to see if this was the beginning of a trend, a statistical error, or just a momentary pause. Policy-makers could wait until there is a set of three consecutive months of production and sales declines, which would occur in *mid-August,* or for a second consecutive decline in quarterly GNP estimates, which would be released in *mid-October.*

Legislative lag Once policy-makers recognize the contraction they must adopt a suitable fiscal stimulus. If it is a tax cut, a decision must be made on the allocation between corporations, middle-income taxpayers, and low-income taxpayers. If it is a spending stimulus, then policy-makers must decide which regions (rural versus urban, Northeast versus Southwest) and which industries (consumer versus producer goods industry, construction versus service) should be emphasized. Next, these bills must be written and passed by both branches of the legislature, and signed by the President. If there are differences, then it must go into conference committee and be voted upon again. If the disagreements are minor and the urgency appreciated, then the legislative lag could be as short as four months. However, if the disagreements are substantial (like during the 1970s), the delay can be more than a year. Therefore, it could be more than a year between the actual contraction's beginning and the passage of legislation to counteract the economic slump.

---

8. The discussion of time lags follows R. J. Gordon, *Macroeconomics* (Boston: Little Brown, 1978), pp. 511–514.

Transmission lag Once a bill is passed, the government has to implement it. In the case of a tax cut, this only takes a few weeks—time to print and distribute the new tax schedules to employers. However, in the case of government spending, the lag can be considerable. Government spending requires allocation of specific amounts to specific agencies in specific locations. Moreover, once these allocations have been made, hiring and purchasing must then be made through a competitive procedure. Therefore, the transmission lag is from two months, in the case of a tax cut, to over six months, in the case of government spending.

Fiscal Policy—Stabilizing or Destabilizing?

When we combine the four components, the beginning of the fiscal stimulus is from 12 to 24 months after the actual beginning of the contraction. If the economy is subject to short fluctuations, government fiscal policy could actually destabilize rather than stabilize the economy.

Suppose that the economy begins to contract at the start of the year. Somewhere during the following year the government stimulus would be initiated. However, it still takes some time for the multiplier process to fully stimulate the economy. Hence, it is only two years or more after the beginning of the contraction that fiscal policy would significantly stimulate the economy. However, suppose at that point the private sector begins to rebound on its own. Then fiscal policy would accelerate the private sector expansion, creating too rapid a growth rate to maintain stable prices. In this case, the effect of fiscal policy is to generate an inflationary spiral.

Next, suppose that fiscal policy to limit the expansion is initiated after a two-year lag. If by that time the private sector adjustments have begun to contract the economy, then fiscal policy would only accelerate the contraction. Hence, the lagged effect of fiscal policy could result in a more volatile economy—generating inflationary spirals and deep contractions.

These problems are, of course, compounded by the uncertainty of the timing and size of the stimulus once the fiscal policy is initiated. For these reasons, many mainstream liberals are increasingly arguing that discretionary fiscal intervention should be reserved for only severe fluctuations.

8.3 AUTOMATIC STABILIZERS

Automatic stabilizers do not require a time lag. They have already been legislated and require no formal decisions. When a slump begins, laid-off workers automatically receive unemployment compensation, welfare, and/or food stamps with a lowering of their tax liabilities. Hence, automatic stabilizers immediately reduce fluctuations in disposable income. Regardless of the model, if fluctuations in disposable income are reduced, then induced consumption and, hence, M_y^* will be smaller. We shall now see how the federal tax system and transfer payments act as automatic stabilizers.

Federal Tax System

If all taxes were collected through a lump sum tax, then the fluctuations in disposable income and total income would be exactly the same. Therefore, we found that when the government collects its revenues through a lump sum tax there is no reduction in induced consumption and, hence, in M_y^*. However, suppose the government collected its revenues as some proportion of income. Now if the economy slumped, household taxes would be reduced proportionally. If taxes are lowered, then the decline in disposable income would be less than the decline in total income. On the other hand, if total income rises, household taxes rise so that the expansion in disposable income is somewhat reduced. In this way, a proportional tax (by reducing the fluctuations in disposable income) reduces the size of M_y^*.[9]

DEFINITION **The marginal propensity to tax (MPT) equals the change in taxes as a result of a unit increase in total income.**

In general, the induced change in consumption is $MPC(1-MPT)$ since for each unit change in total income, $\Delta Y_d = (1-MPT)\Delta Y$. Therefore, the change in consumption $\Delta C = MPC(\Delta Y_d) = MPC(1-MPT)\Delta Y$ so that $\Delta C/\Delta Y = MPC(1-MPT)$. With no induced investment the simple income multiplier

$$M_y = \frac{1}{1-b(1-t)}$$

where

$$b = MPC \text{ and}$$
$$t = MPT$$

These results are also demonstrated in Table 8.1, where the effects of an autonomous increase in government spending of 10 are indicated for Model I ($b=0.8$) and Model II ($b=0.8$ and $t=0.25$). In Model I, when only additional savings are generated, equilibrium income must rise by 50 before additional leakages of 10 are induced. In Model II, where both additional savings and taxes are generated, equilibrium income must rise by only 25 in order to induce additional leakages of 10; 6.25 of additional taxes and 3.75 of additional savings.

---

9. We have found that as the MPT increases, so does the stabilizing influence of the federal tax system.

$$MPT = \Delta T/\Delta Y = (T/Y)[(\Delta T/T)/(\Delta Y/Y)]$$

where

$$(\Delta T/T)/(\Delta Y/Y) = E_Y^t = \text{income elasticity of the tax system.}$$

It indicates the ratio of the percentage change in tax receipts to the percentage change in GNP. If taxes are collected in a proportional manner, both tax receipts and GNP increase by the same percentage so that $E_Y^t = 1$ and $MPT = T/Y$. However, if taxes are progressive, then the percentage change in tax receipts is greater than the percentage change in GNP ($E_Y^t > 1$) so that $MPT > T/Y$. Hence, if taxes are progressive the MPT increases.

Table 8.1

		Model I: with $t=0$ and $b=0.8$					
Period	ΔY	ΔT	ΔY_{d}	ΔC	ΔS	$\Delta(I+G)$	ΔSpending
0	0.0	0.0	0.0	0.0	0.0	10.0	10.0
1	10.0	0.0	10.0	8.0	2.0	0.0	8.0
2	8.0	0.0	8.0	6.4	1.6	0.0	6.4
3	6.4	0.0	6.4	5.1	1.3	0.0	5.1
4	5.1	0.0	5.1	4.1	1.0	0.0	4.1
5	4.1	0.0	4.1	3.3	0.8	0.0	3.3
Total	50.0	0.0	50.0	40.0	10.0	10.0	50.0

		Model II: with $t=0.25$ and $b=0.8$					
Period	ΔY	ΔT	ΔY_{d}	ΔC	ΔS	$\Delta(I+G)$	ΔSpending
0	0.0	0.0	0.0	0.0	0.0	10.0	10.0
1	10.0	2.5	7.5	6.0	1.5	0.0	6.0
2	6.0	1.5	4.5	3.6	0.9	0.0	3.6
3	3.6	0.9	2.7	2.2	0.5	0.0	2.2
4	2.2	0.5	1.6	1.3	0.3	0.0	1.3
5	1.3	0.3	1.0	0.7	0.2	0.0	0.7
Total	25.0	6.25	18.75	15.0	3.75	10.0	25.0

Government Transfer Payments

If we include government transfer payments, R, in our model, $Y_{\mathrm{d}} = Y - T + R$. For government transfers to stabilize the economy, they must vary inversely with total income—increase when the economy is falling and decline when the economy is expanding. This can be represented by

$$R = R_0 - rY$$

where

$R_0 =$ amount of transfer payments independent of Y.
$r =$ the additional transfer payments resulting from a *decline* of total income by one unit.

If the tax schedule is proportional to income $(T = tY)$, then

$$Y_{\mathrm{d}} = Y - T + R = Y - tY + (R_0 - rY) = (1 - t - r)Y + R_0$$

In effect, government transfers act as an additional tax on households. When total income rises, households pay more in taxes and at the same time receive less in transfer payments.

8.4 BUDGET SURPLUSES

A government budget program is the choice of G_0 and T_0 where $G = G_0$ and $T = tY + T_0$.[10] For any government program, the operating surplus $T - G = tY + T_0 - G_0$. Therefore, whatever the budget program, the government could be operating with a surplus or a deficit, depending upon the level of income. For example, with government budget program, P_0, there would be a surplus at $Y = Y_2$ but a deficit at $Y = Y_1$ (Figure 8.4a).

The change in a government budget program can easily be illustrated. Let the government budget program be initially P_0 and the current equilibrium income Y_1 (point A). Now suppose the government decides to increase government spending by 10. At any level of income, this new budgetary program, call it P_1, would have a greater deficit (smaller surplus) of 10 more than program P_0. At the initial equilibrium Y_1, the government would have an increased budget deficit of S_1 (point B). However, as Table 8.1 indicated, as the economy expands, higher incomes generate more tax revenues so that at the new equilibrium income Y_3, the actual deficit is only S_3 (point C).

It should be clear that budget programs cannot be accurately characterized as expansionary (contractionary) if the government is operating with a deficit (surplus). For example, suppose in one year the government is operating with budget program P_0 at $Y = Y_1$ while the next year it operated with program P_1 at income $Y = Y_4$. We would incorrectly characterize the first year's budget program as expansionary and the second year's as contractionary if we used this superficial procedure. The confusion occurs because the *actual* budget position is determined by *both* the budget program and the actual level of income. In order to accurately evaluate budget programs, we must hold Y constant. This procedure indicates that the first year's program, P_0, was less expansionary (more contractionary) than the second year's budget program, P_1. The government is able to make accurate comparisons by measuring the full employment budget surplus (deficit) of each budget program.

DEFINITION **The full employment surplus for any budget program is the *projected* budget surplus of that program if the economy was operating at full employment.**

According to Figure 8.4b, budgetary program P_3 has a surplus at full employment; P_4 is balanced; and P_5 is in deficit. Mainstream economists consider budget program P_4 (balanced at full employment) to be fiscally neutral since if the economy was at full employment the government budget would neither stimulate nor contract the economy.[11] On the other hand, budget program P_3 would cause a contraction at full employment while P_5 would expand the economy.

---

10. This ignores the possibility that the government could change the MPT.
11. Conservatives do not support this characterization because they contend that fiscal policy has no effect on equilibrium production.

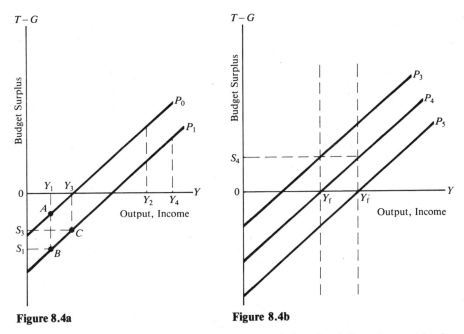

Figure 8.4a   **Figure 8.4b**

Figure 8.4   Effect of changing budget programs and changing full employment levels on the budget surplus

The full employment surplus is helpful in distinguishing between the effects of the government budget program on the economy and the effects of the economy on the government's budget. For example, in 1958, the government had an actual budget deficit of over $10 billion. Since the full employment surplus that year was over $2 billion, the deficit was not a result of the government's attempt to expand the economy but due to the effect of the economy on the government's budget. On the other hand, the 1966 actual budget was in surplus while the full employment *deficit* was projected. In this case, the government was attempting an expansionary program. However, when the economy expanded past its full employment level, the actual budget was in surplus, giving the mistaken impression that the government was trying to contract the economy.

Another implication of the full employment surplus is that any budget program, if maintained, becomes increasingly contractionary (less expansionary). For example, suppose that at current full employment Y_f, the government selects budget program P_4. The full employment surplus equals zero and the government would be considered to have selected a fiscally neutral program. Now suppose that the productive capacity of the economy expands so that in the following year full employment increases to Y_f'. If the government maintains budget program P_4, there would be a full employment surplus S_4. Only by changing to budget program P_5 could the government maintain fiscal neutrality.

During the period 1958–63, the government maintained essentially the same budget program.[12] As a result of the expansion of productive potential, the full employment surplus grew from $2 billion to over $13 billion. In 1964, the government initiated a new budget program to stimulate the economy. This new program had a full employment surplus of only $2 billion. Therefore, the economy was stimulated not because the 1964 program was expansionary but rather it was less contractionary than the previous budget program.

8.5 THE GOVERNMENT BALANCED BUDGET PROCESS

Deficit financing, through either tax cuts or government spending increases, can stimulate the economy. However, these actions result in a permanent deficit, although its size may be reduced somewhat through induced government revenues. Since permanent budget deficits are often considered undesirable because of monetary implications (to be discussed in future chapters), one alternative seems to be to expand the economy through the balanced budget multiplier process.

While the choice of using a balanced budget increase avoids the problem of deficit financing, another problem arises. The problem arises because while the balanced budget process will always increase equilibrium income, its overall effect on disposable income is uncertain. Suppose we begin at equilibrium and the government undertakes a balanced budget process of size ΔL. At the equilibrium income, disposable income would decline by ΔL as a result of this policy. However, since the economy expands, there would also be an expansion of disposable income. Therefore, the overall effect on disposable income is unclear. If the expansion is small, then disposable income would remain below its original level. If the expansion is somewhat larger, then disposable income could rise back to its original level. If the expansion was even stronger, then household disposable income would eventually rise above its original level.

This is illustrated in Figure 8.5. For any tax program, disposable income is an increasing function of total income. Suppose we begin with tax program TP_0. At Y_0, given tax program TP_0, disposable income is Y_d^0. The adoption of a balanced budget program changes the government's tax program to TP_1 since at every level of Y the government is collecting ΔL more in taxes and, hence, disposable income is ΔL smaller. Therefore, at Y_0, disposable income declines to $Y_d^1 = Y_d^0 - \Delta L$. However, as the economy expands, Y_d begins to rise back to its original level. According to Figure 8.5, total income would have to rise to Y_1 before disposable income, under the new tax program, would be back to its original level, Y_d^0. If the expansion was only to Y_2, then disposable

---

12. In 1962, a new government investment tax credit somewhat reduced the full employment surplus.

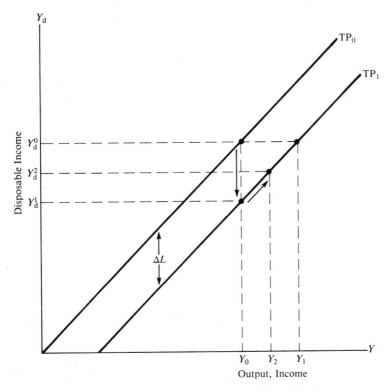

Figure 8.5 Effect of balanced budget shift on disposable income

income would not increase back to its original level. The decline would be less than the original tax but this may be small consolation to private sector households. In this case, the economic expansion to Y_2 may create jobs and production but not necessarily raise social welfare. Indeed, if household welfare was dependent upon disposable income alone, then the balanced budget process, while raising total production, lowers social welfare. Only if the balanced budget process raised total income to at least Y_1 would households perceive benefits to their welfare from the government balanced budget policy.

Social Welfare and Government Income

During the 1950s, Paul Samuelson popularized public good theory.[13] According to this theory, certain goods have the property that each individual's consumption of it leads to no subtraction from any other individual's consumption of that good. These goods are called public goods since there is no reason

13. Paul A. Samuelson, "The Pure Theory of Public Expenditures," *Review of Economics and Statistics* 36 (Nov. 1954): 387–389.

for individual ownership. Each household would obtain the same benefits as if the good was individually purchased but its cost would now be divided among all the households using that good. Many government services, such as recreation facilities, fire and police protection, schooling, and highway systems, strongly exhibit this property. Therefore, independent of externality arguments, households would desire government production of these goods and services.

According to this view,[14] households by their freedom of location can choose the amount and distribution of public goods they prefer. Within each metropolitan area some suburbs spend a large portion of revenues on education; others on fire; and still others on recreation. Households could then choose to live in the suburb which reflects the size of government purchases in accordance with their personal preferences. We could then add to this the role of the electoral process, through bond issues, in allowing government spending to reflect the personal preferences between public and individual goods.

Suppose we assume that all government purchases reflect the desire of households for public goods. Then households would purchase additional government goods, by paying taxes, until the value of the last dollar given to the government just equals the value of the last dollar of disposable income. In this case, social welfare would be determined by total income and would be independent of its distribution between government (T) and private households (Y_d). Since the balanced budget process ($\Delta G = \Delta T > 0$) always increases total income, the public good assumption implies that the balanced budget process would always increase social welfare, regardless of its effect on disposable income.

The public good assumption is highly questionable. Let us reject it and assume instead that social welfare is dependent upon both the sum and the distribution of total income between the government and private households.[15] It will be shown that under this assumption, the balanced budget process does not always result in increased social welfare even though it always raises total income.

Lump Sum Tax Model

Suppose that all government taxes are collected through an exogenously determined lump sum tax. When the government initiates its balanced budget process, the initial effect on disposable income is to lower it by ΔL. As the expansion begins, since taxes are collected in a lump sum, all subsequent changes in

---

14. Charles Tiebout, "The Pure Theory of Local Expenditures," *Journal of Political Economy* 66 (Oct. 1956): 416–424.

15. Few government projects are determined through voter approved bond issues. Moreover, while with local expenditures households can vote with their feet (move to more favorable localities), this is not very feasible with most state expenditures and not a possibility with federal expenditures.

total income will result in the same size changes in disposable income. Hence, the total effect of the balanced budget process on disposable income

$$\Delta Y_d^T = -\Delta L + \Delta Y$$

Recall that when interest rate effects are ignored, the change in equilibrium income $\Delta Y = (1-b)M_y(\Delta L)$ when a balanced budget process, ΔL, is undertaken. We also know that for a model with a lump sum tax $M_y = 1/(1-b)$, so that the change in equilibrium total income, $\Delta Y = (1-b)M_y(\Delta L) = (1-b)(\Delta L)/(1-b) = \Delta L$. This result, which we found previously, indicates that when the government collects its taxes through a lump sum tax, the increase in equilibrium income, resulting from a balanced budget process, will just equal the size of the change in the level of the budget, ΔL.

This indicates that the balanced budget multiplier process expands equilibrium income by just enough to return disposable income back to its original level. This result becomes clear when we look at the leakages-injections approach to equilibrium income.

The economy begins at equilibrium with $S + (T - G) = I$. Since the lump sum tax model specifies that MPT = MPI = 0, then only induced savings occurs. The expansion begins because of an autonomous decline in savings due to a decline in disposable income.[16] Equilibrium will be reestablished only when savings again equals its original level since $T - G$ and I are unchanged. This will occur only when disposable income returns to its initial value. Hence, as long as I and $T - G$ remain constant, equilibrium disposable income is unchanged.

If there is no change in disposable income, then the only effect of the balanced budget process on social welfare is that a change in government spending, ΔL, has occurred. This result has some important implications:

PROPOSITION 8.1 If the government collects its revenues through a lump sum tax, then households cannot change their equilibrium disposable income by adjusting the level of the government budget.

This proposition indicates that attempting to improve disposable income through cuts in the level of the government will have only transitory benefits. Initially, disposable income will rise. However, the gain is only shortrun since the resulting decline in production will decrease disposable income back to its original level. This is quite similar to the Paradox of Thrift. In both cases, as long as investment is constant, equilibrium savings cannot change. Here, as long as equilibrium savings is constant, equilibrium disposable income must also be unchanged. We can characterize the attempts of households to improve their disposable income by lowering the level of the government budget as the Paradox of Privacy.

---

16. Since $\Delta T = \Delta G$ and $\Delta I = 0$, the only uncompensated change is $\Delta S = (1-b)(\Delta Y_d)$ $= (1-b)(-\Delta L)$.

PROPOSITION 8.2 **In the lump sum tax model, if households do not benefit from the additional government income, then society is no better off when the economy is expanded through the balanced budget process.**

It has often been argued that government production of military goods is valuable, not because of its intrinsic worth but because it creates jobs. Our analysis demonstrates that if the spending was financed through taxes, disposable income does not increase but is only redistributed. Some households pay taxes so that other households can receive income from defense jobs and jobs created by the multiplier process. If military production has no direct value, then the same redistribution could have been accomplished much more efficiently through either direct income transfers or by shortening the length of the working day. In either of these alternatives, there would be no loss of leisure or natural resources through worthless production. Similarly, if the government created tax-financed jobs which are considered "make work," society is justified in rejecting this alternative to solving unemployment. Only when the additional government spending has direct social value can the balanced budget process with the lump sum tax model increase social welfare.

Proportional Tax Model

In the case of the lump sum tax model, we found that the multiplier effect on this initial autonomous change in spending was sufficient to raise equilibrium income by ΔL. In the case of the proportional tax model, the resulting increase in equilibrium income would be less since the multiplier effect is smaller. Not only will the rise in total income be less than ΔL, but since part of this additional income goes to additional taxes, the induced increase in disposable income is still smaller. However, if the rise in disposable income induced by the economic expansion is less than the initial tax rise, ΔL, equilibrium disposable income would be reduced by the balanced budget process. Hence, whenever the government collects its revenues through a proportional tax, the overall effect of the balanced budget process is to reduce disposable income despite the rise in total income.

The decline in equilibrium disposable income is implied from the leakages-injections approach to equilibrium income. As with the lump sum tax model, equilibrium occurs when $S + (T - G) = I$. When the balanced budget process creates an initial decline in savings, the economy expands. However, in the proportional tax model, government savings $(T - G)$ increases. If $T - G$ increases while I remains constant, then equilibrium savings must be lowered. If equilibrium savings is lowered, then equilibrium disposable income must be lower.

This indicates that in the proportional tax model it is not enough for government spending to have some positive value for society to benefit from the balanced budget process. Government spending must have a greater positive value than the value households place on the lost disposable income. The necessary minimum value for government spending in order for the balanced budget process to improve social welfare is not insignificant. For example, if $t=0.25$ and $b=0.8$ (values in Table 8.1), then an additional unit of government spending has to be at least 5/9 the value of an additional unit of disposable income for the balanced budget process to improve social welfare.[17]

8.6 CONCLUSION

This chapter formally demonstrated that changes in tax programs or government spending would change equilibrium income. It was also noted that conservatives claim that government fiscal policy is unreliable because there is wide disagreement over its effects, and it is potentially destabilizing because of the long time lags required before implementation.

Government policies which have already been instituted and occur automatically are considered by many mainstream economists to be the ideal form of government intervention. These programs, which include the federal tax system and transfer payments (unemployment insurance and welfare), stabilize the economy by reducing the size of fluctuation of disposable income.

Since tax receipts tend to grow as the economy expands, the concept of the full employment budget surplus was developed so that the economic effects of specific government budget programs could be analyzed. It was demon-

---

17. The change in equilibrium disposable income
$$\Delta Y_d = -\Delta L + (1-t)\Delta Y$$
where
$$\Delta Y = M_y(1-b)\Delta L \text{ and } M_y = 1/(1-b+bt)$$
Therefore,
$$\Delta Y_d = [t/(1-b+bt)]\Delta L$$
The change in equilibrium government income
$$\Delta T = \Delta L + t(\Delta Y)$$
$$\Delta T = [(1-b+t)/(1-b+bt)]\Delta L$$

If we ignore the effects of the balanced budget process on leisure, then the benefits to society are the social value of the additional government income $(\Delta T)\text{MU}_G$ and the costs are the loss of disposable income $(\Delta Y_d)\text{MU}_{YD}$ where $\text{MU}_G =$ the value of an additional dollar of government spending and $\text{MU}_{YD} =$ the value of an additional dollar of disposable income. Therefore, social welfare is improved if

$$(\Delta T)\text{MU}_G > (\Delta Y_d)\text{MU}_{YD}$$

$$\frac{(\Delta L)\,(1-b+t)\text{MU}_G}{(1-b+bt)} > \frac{(\Delta L)t\text{MU}_{YD}}{(1-b+bt)}$$

$$\text{MU}_G/\text{MU}_{YD} > t/(1-b+t)$$

If $t=0.25$ and $b=0.8$, then $t/(1-b+t)=.25/.45=5/9$.

strated that all budget programs tend to become contractionary with time because of "fiscal drag." For this reason, the federal government must periodically either raise government spending and/or lower the tax rates if it desires to maintain economic growth.

It was demonstrated that if MPC < 1, then simultaneously increasing taxes and government spending by the same amount would expand the economy. Since this balanced budget process can increase equilibrium income without requiring a government deficit, it appears to be an attractive alternative policy. However, it was shown that this expansion does not necessarily increase equilibrium disposable income or social welfare.

1. Only if the additional government spending was on public goods could we guarantee that, regardless of the effect of the balanced budget process on equilibrium disposable income, social welfare would be improved.

2. If taxes are collected by a lump sum method, then equilibrium disposable income will be unaffected by the balanced budget process. If equilibrium income is unchanged, then:

   • As long as government spending has some positive value, the balanced budget process improves social welfare.

   • Household welfare is not improved by lowering the level of the government budget.

3. If taxes are collected by a proportional method, then equilibrium income is lowered by the balanced budget process. If equilibrium income is lowered, then:

   • Government spending must have some minimum satisfaction for the balanced budget process to improve social welfare.

   • If government spending does not have this minimum level, then household welfare is improved by lowering the budget level, even though an employment decline results.

CHAPTER NINE

CAPITAL SPENDING, EQUILIBRIUM, AND THE INTEREST RATE

In previous chapters we have largely ignored incorporating theories of capital spending into our model. Capital spending is divided into three major components: (1) investment in plant and equipment, (2) investment in residential construction (housing), and (3) changes in the value of inventory. In Chapter 6, the decision to purchase housing was discussed in the context of household spending on durable goods. In later chapters we will discuss changes in the value of inventory. This chapter will be restricted to discussing the decision to invest in plant and equipment.

This chapter will analyze the capital spending decision from the conservative perspective. According to this viewpoint, firms, just as households, have to decide the allocation of income between current and future spending. Business income can be allocated to present spending, in the form of capital goods, or reserved for future spending by being allocated to some financial asset.

In Chapter 6 we found that the market interest rate, under certain assumptions, can affect equilibrium income. In this chapter we will more formally develop this relationship. We will find that inclusion of this *individualistic* theory of capital spending reinforces the general contentions of laissez-faire advocates.

9.1 INDIVIDUALISTIC THEORY OF INVESTMENT

According to the individualistic theory, producers have wide discretion over the technology to use and the timing of replacement of capital equipment. The critical determinant of these choices is the interest rate. For example, as the interest rate declines, it becomes more profitable for firms to automate, since the cost of reorganizing production is less expensive. Similarly, if firms have discretion over the timing of replacement of equipment and expansion of their capital stock, they will choose the time when costs are minimized. Therefore, they will tend to replace equipment and expand capacity when interest rates are low rather than when they are high. Finally, there are always many projects, such as new ventures, which are marginally profitable. These projects are quite sensitive to the interest rate since firms can choose to place their profits in financial assets rather than purchase capital goods. If the interest rate rises, financial investments become more profitable than these marginal projects. However, if the interest rate declines, more of these marginal projects become profitable. In summary, a decline in the interest rate increases capital spending by (1) making automation cheaper, (2) inducing an earlier build-up of capital stock, and (3) encouraging investment in marginal projects.

Let us determine how the market interest rate affects business allocation between financial investments and the purchase of capital goods. Suppose that there is a capital spending project which entails an initial outlay, C_0. The capital goods purchased will last exactly one year and have no scrap value. They will produce revenues R_1 at the end of the year, net of all costs except the full cost of the capital goods purchased. The alternative for the firm is to financially invest C_0 at the market interest rate.

In order to compare these two alternatives we might ask how much income must be financially invested today in order to obtain the net revenue equivalent to the capital investment project? For any value, P_0, which is financially invested at the market rate of interest, i_0, at the end of one year the investor would obtain interest payments $i_0(P_0)$ plus the principal invested, P_0. Total income equals $P_0(1 + i_0)$. For this sum to be equivalent to the net revenue derived from the capital spending project, $P_0(1 + i_0) = R_1$ so that $P_0 = R_1/(1 + i_0)$.

DEFINITION **The present value of a revenue stream equals the income which must be financially invested now at the market interest rate to obtain that same revenue stream.**

If $R_1 = 2200$ and $i_0 = 5\%$, then the present value equals $R_1/(1 + i_0) = 2200/1.05 = 2096$. If the owner of this investment project tried to sell future claims on its revenues for more than $2096, no one would buy it. For example, if the owner tried to sell it for $2100, the buyer could have taken the money, invested it at the market rate of interest, and received $2100(1.05) = \$2205$ the following year, which is larger than the future income claims ($2200) from the investment project. On the other hand, the owner would be foolish to sell future income claims for less than $2096. If he sells the claims for less than $2096 and reinvests the proceeds at the market interest rate, he would end up with less than $2200 the following year. Therefore, the value of future income claims on the investment project must be $2096, its "present value." Figure 9.1a indicates the present value of $2200 as the market interest rate is varied. If the cash outlay for the project $C_0 = \$2000$, then the firm should invest in the spending project if the interest rate is less than 10%; however, it should make a financial investment if the interest rate is above 10%.

The present value can be calculated for any future revenue stream. For example, suppose we had an investment project which had a single net revenue

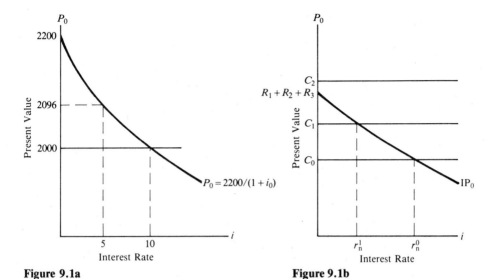

Figure 9.1a   **Figure 9.1b**

Figure 9.1   Effect of interest rate changes on present value

payoff of R_2 at the end of two years. A financial investment P_0 today would be worth $P_0(1+i_0)^2$ at the end of two years so that the present value of the revenue payoff must be $P_0 = R_2/(1+i_0)^2$. In general, if in n years a net revenue payoff R_n is obtained, its present value, $P_0 = R_n/(1+i_0)^n$. Finally, for any net revenue stream R_1, R_2, R_3, . . . , R_n where R_j is the net revenue obtained in the jth year, the present value

$$P_0 = \frac{R_1}{(1+i_0)} + \frac{R_2}{(1+i_0)^2} + \frac{R_3}{(1+i_0)^3} + \ldots + \frac{R_n}{(1+i_0)^n}$$

Businesses can then compare the present value of the investment project with the initial cash outlay, C_0, required. If the present value is higher than C_0, then the investment project should be undertaken.

This result is unchanged if we assume that firms, instead of financing capital projects internally, have distributed all earnings to shareholders and must borrow funds when capital investment projects are undertaken. This would be the situation under the assumption that no net business income exists—all income is distributed to households. In this case, the firm must borrow C_0 in order to undertake the investment project and must pay back $C_0(1+i_0)$ at the end of the first year. The investment project would be undertaken if this payback is less than the net revenue, R_1, obtained. That is, investment projects will be undertaken (the money borrowed) if $R_1 > C_0(1+i_0)$. If we rearrange terms—divide both sides by $(1+i_0)$—we obtain the same decision rule, $R_1/(1+i_0) = P_0 > C_0$, as in the case when internal funds were used.

An alternative decision rule can be obtained by calculating the internal rate of return of investment projects.

DEFINITION **The internal rate of return of an investment project, r_n, equals the interest rate at which the present value of the net revenue stream just equals the initial cash outlay.**

If the internal rate of return equals the market rate of interest, then the returns from the investment project would exactly equal the returns from a financial investment. In our numerical example (Figure 9.1a), the internal rate of return was shown to be 10%.

For any investment project where the actual value of the revenue stream exceeds the cash outlay, there exists some positive internal rate of return. For example, for an investment project, net revenues R_1, R_2, and R_3 are obtained over the next 3 years. In Figure 9.1b, IP_0 shows the relationship of the present value of this net revenue stream to the market interest rate. Note when $i_0 = 0$, the present value is $R_1 + R_2 + R_3$. If the initial cash outlay is C_0, the the internal rate of return is r_n^0. If, due to a rise in the price of capital goods, the initial cash outlay rose to C_1, then the internal rate of return would fall to r_n^1. If the cost of capital goods rose still further to C_2, then even at a zero interest rate the sum of the revenue stream would be less than the cash outlay. In this case the internal rate of return would be negative.

The alternative decision rule is to calculate each project's internal rate of return and undertake all projects which have an internal rate of return higher than the market interest rate. Any firm can then order its capital investment projects according to its internal rate of return. Each firm could then determine at any interest rate the amount of capital investment projects which should be undertaken. In Figure 9.2a, MEC_A and MEC_B are the investment schedules for firm A and firm B, respectively. They indicate that firm A has $1000 of investment projects having an internal rate of return greater than 5%, while firm B has $5000 investment projects. These schedules are called the *marginal efficiency of capital* (MEC) because they indicate the economic efficiency of the marginal (last) investment project undertaken. That is, they indicate that the rate of return for firm A of its $1000th of capital investment is 5%. The MEC schedules represent the demand curves for capital goods for each individual firm.

It would seem logical to conclude that the demand for investment for the entire economy can be calculated by summing up the demand (MEC) of each firm. For example, if the economy was composed of only firm A and firm B, the total demand for capital when $i_0 = 5$%, using this method, would be $6000. We label the summation MEC_T (Figure 9.2b). However, this schedule exaggerates the actual sum of capital investment projects which could be profitably undertaken in the entire economy if the cost schedule for the capital goods industry is sloping upward. Each individual firm's MEC schedule assumes that no other firm is undertaking investment projects. Besides the fact that this may, therefore, reflect duplication of projects, it also underestimates the price that firms must pay for capital goods. For example, if both firm A and firm B

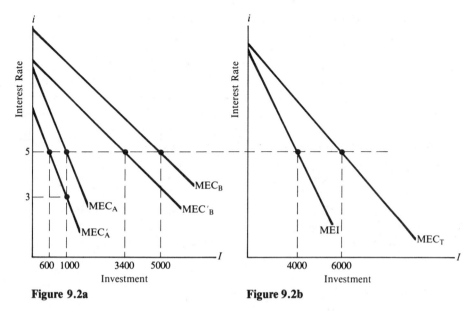

Figure 9.2a   Figure 9.2b

Figure 9.2   Aggregation of firm MEC schedules

undertook investment projects, the cost of capital goods would rise above the anticipated cost. As our previous discussion indicated (Figure 9.1b), this would lower the internal rate of return of each investment project. For example, the 1000th invested would only return 3% to firm A instead of the previous 5%. This is reflected in the shifting downwards of each firm's MEC schedule to MEC'_A and MEC'_B (Figure 9.2a). Now at $i_0 = 5\%$, each firm would find fewer profitable investment projects. Firm A would only invest $600 in capital goods while firm B would invest $3400. The new summation is represented by the MEI schedule in Figure 9.2b. It indicates that the response of businesses to lower interest rates is not as great as the MEC_T schedule implies. (The slope of the MEI schedule is steeper than the MEC_T schedule.) It is the MEI schedule which is the relevant investment schedule since it indicates the actual response of the entire economy to changes in the market rate of interest.

The MEI Schedule and Other Variables

Inclusion of the individualistic theory of capital spending reinforces the general contentions of the laissez-faire models. In Chapter 6 it was noted that laissez-faire advocates claimed interest rate reductions induce household spending to rise, thus offsetting any economic contraction. In this section, we find that interest rate reductions induce capital spending to rise. Hence, claims of strong countercyclical tendencies being present in a private market economy are strengthened by the inclusion of the individualistic theory of capital spending.

At closer inspection, there may be reasons to believe that it is unlikely for capital investment to counter economic downturns. The individualistic theory implies that firms, despite a *declining operating capacity*, would begin to expand their productive capacity; despite *declining profits*, would finance automation; and despite *declining aggregate spending*, would invest in new ventures. This indicates that for capital spending to counter economic contractions, the effects of changes in the interest rate must be more powerful than the combined influences of operating capacity, profit levels, and aggregate spending.

Let us suppose, instead, that aggregate spending had a significant effect on the level of capital spending.[1] After all, it seems reasonable to expect that current sales not only affect the immediate decision on how much to produce in the next period but also how much capacity will be required in the future. This viewpoint is illustrated in Figure 9.3. Given any interest rate, the MEI schedule shifts as the level of Y changes.

Let us assume that the economy is initially at full employment with an interest rate of 5%. Assume that for some reason the economy contracts to Y_1, which results in an interest rate decline to 4%. The interest rate decline stimulates capital spending but this is more than offset by the negative effect of the spending decline.[2] The effect is for capital spending to decline (from I_0 to I_1). Similarly, it can be argued that if the decline in profits had a more powerful effect on capital spending than the interest rate, then an economic contraction would induce declines rather than expansions of capital spending.[3] In these cases, changes in capital spending accelerate rather than dampen economic fluctuations.

Laissez-faire advocates note that capital investment projects take many years to complete. Therefore, they contend that the current level of sales (aggregate spending) will have little relationship to the level of sales when the project is completed. This is especially true if firms have confidence that peri-

---

1. For studies which emphasize the effect of aggregate spending on capital investment, see W. J. Baumol, *Business Behavior, Value and Growth,* rev. ed. (New York: Brace & World, 1967), Chapter 12.

2. Recall in Chapter 5 that it was stated MPSP = MPC + MPI. Therefore, if MPI > 0 and there is no interest rate induced changes in capital investment, then the income multiplier is increased.

3. For studies which emphasize the role of profits, see W. W. Heller, "The Anatomy of the Investment Decision," *Harvard Business Review* (Mar. 1951): 95–103 and J. R. Meyer and E. Kuh, *The Investment Decision* (Cambridge, Mass.: Harvard Press, 1957), Chapters 8 and 12. However, since profits are dependent upon the level of spending, it is hard to distinguish between the effects of profits from the effects of sales on capital spending.

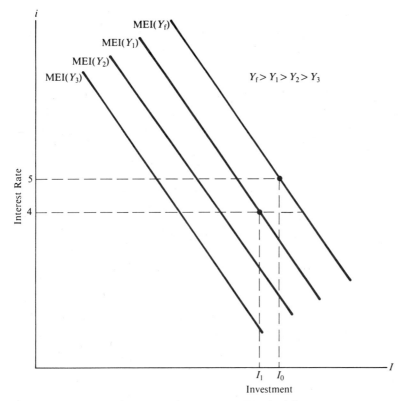

Figure 9.3 Effect of aggregate income on MEI schedule

ods of contractions are shortlived. In this case, firms would be anxious to begin their projects so that they will be completed by the time the expansion begins.

Laissez-faire advocates also contend that since most firms expect to continue to expand in the longrun, they are mainly concerned with the cost of expanding capacity rather than cyclical fluctuations in their utilization rate. This is especially true if firms believe that it is more costly to have insufficient capacity during times of expansion than having underutilized capacity during economic downturns. For example, when the economy is expanding there is a great opportunity to expand sales and *market shares* away from firms which did not plan ahead. Firms with insufficient capacity risk losing their market shares. On the other hand, little is lost by having excess capacity during downturns as the costs can be substantially offset by corporate tax reductions.

Finally, laissez-faire advocates contend that the level of profits should have no effect on capital spending decisions. They reason that if the interest rate is above the rate of return on capital projects, then it would be foolish to buy capital goods with profits. Higher future earnings could be obtained through financial investments. On the other hand, if the interest rate is below the rate of return on capital projects, firms would be quite willing to borrow money if profits were not sufficient to finance the projects.

The laissez-faire model of investment makes some quite special assumptions concerning the money market. It assumes that during economic contractions all firms have access to debt instruments at the market interest rate. This is certainly true of the larger firms, which can issue longterm bonds to finance their capital spending. However, it is not necessarily true of the smaller firms. These firms must go through financial institutions which often are unwilling to make loans to them during economic contractions.

The laissez-faire view that capital spending is independent of current sales also assumes that firms are not concerned with shortrun problems. It implies that firms have little concern that the current contraction could cause their bankruptcy. Again, this is a reasonable assumption for the larger firms but not the smaller ones. For the smaller firms, a longterm view is a luxury which they cannot afford. They realize that during a contraction could be the best time to expand productive facilities, but also realize that without survival, future growth potentials are meaningless. These firms often decide to curtail current capital spending during periods of economic contractions, regardless of interest rates, so that they can maintain financial stability and avoid bankruptcy.

The laissez-faire model of investment and the permanent income hypothesis are similar in that both assume decision-makers can take a longterm viewpoint. Both theories assume that decision-makers have little concern that they may go bankrupt. Moreover, these theories assume that all decision-makers have access to debt instruments at the market rate of interest. Both of these models, then, are most relevant to a middle-class prosperous society in which momentary shortfalls are a minor inconvenience to which decision-makers hardly adjust.

9.2 EQUILIBRIUM INCOME AND THE INTEREST RATE

We are now ready to demonstrate how changes in the interest rate induce changes in equilibrium income. In Quadrant 1 of Figure 9.4, the MEI schedule is plotted. It is drawn so that at rates below 7% the influence of interest rate changes on capital investment is reduced. In this range the elasticity of investment demand is small.[4] We will assume that the interest rate is the only determinant of investment projects.

---

4. Price elasticity is defined as the % change in demand divided by % change in price. In this case, we are describing the demand for capital investment. Its price is the interest rate since $1 of capital goods can be purchased if the firm is willing to borrow that $1 at the market rate of interest. Therefore, the price elasticity of demand for capital investment is % change in I divided by % change in i_0. In our numerical example, when i increases from 7% to 8% (a 15% change in the interest rate), I declines from 100 to 60 (a 50% decline in I). Therefore, the price elasticity in this range $= -.50/.15 = -3.33$.

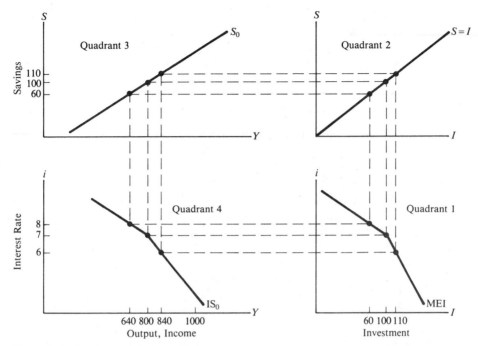

Figure 9.4   Product market equilibrium

In Quadrant 2, the equilibrium condition, $S=I$, of a private economy is plotted. We will further assume, in keeping with the individualistic model, that all savings is done by households.

In Quadrant 3, the household savings schedule is plotted. We will initially assume that it is not dependent upon the interest rate. Therefore, at each level of Y we can predict savings, regardless of the interest rate. In our model we will assume that the MPC $=3/4$ so that $M_y=4$.

Let us assume that the initial rate of interest, $i=7\%$. According to Quadrant 1, at this interest rate $I=100$. According to Quadrant 2, equilibrium $S=100$. According to Quadrant 3, $S=100$ when $Y=800$. This indicates that one combination of interest rate and total income, which results in equilibrium in the output market, is $i=7\%$ and $Y=800$.

Suppose that $i=8\%$. This is the range in which I is quite interest elastic. Quadrant 1 indicates that $I=60$. For equilibrium $S=60$ to occur, then $Y=640$. In this range, an increase of the interest rate by 1% lowers equilibrium Y by 160.[5]

If, instead, the interest rate had been lowered to 6%, we would be in the interest inelastic range. The lower interest rate only results in raising I by 10 to 110. Equilibrium $S=110$ and Quadrant 3 indicates that this will occur when

---

5. This assumes that in the range $i>7\%$, for each point the interest rate rises, I decreases by 40.

$Y=840$. In this range, each time the interest rate is lowered by 1%, equilibrium Y rises by 40.[6]

If we trace out all of the combinations of interest rate and equilibrium income we obtain a schedule called the "IS curve."

DEFINITION **The IS curve is all the combinations of total income and interest rate which result in equilibrium in the output market.**

The IS curve must be negatively sloped since interest rate declines imply increases in I and, hence, increases in equilibrium Y. However, how steeply the IS curves is crucial to our evaluation of the laissez-faire model. If it is steep, then interest rate declines have only a slight inducement to stimulating equilibrium income and the laissez-faire model would be unrealistic.

From the preceding analysis, the change in equilibrium income is determined by the slope of the MEI schedule and the size of the income multiplier (slope of the savings schedule). When the interest rate was raised from 7% to 8%, I declined by 40. Since $M_y=4$, the change in equilibrium income, $\Delta Y_T = -160$. On the other hand, when the interest rate fell to 6%, I increased by 10 so that $\Delta Y_T = M_y(\Delta A) = M_y(\Delta I) = 4(10) = 40$. If $Y_f = 1000$, then only if the interest rate fell to 2% would full employment equilibrium occur. If $Y_f = 1100$, then because of the interest inelasticity of the lower part of the MEI schedule, no decline in the interest rate would be sufficient to generate full employment spending.

Laissez-faire advocates would argue that we should also include the effects of changes in the interest rate on household savings decisions. They would claim that at each level of Y, savings would be directly related to the interest rate. This is reflected in the shifting of the savings schedule as the interest rate changes in Quadrant 3 of Figure 9.5.

Let us assume, for comparison purposes, that the savings schedule when $i=7\%$ is the same as the previous case so that $Y=800$ continues to be the equilibrium Y at that rate. When $i=8\%$, I declines again to 60. According to the individualistic outlook, each household shifts some of its income from consumption to savings. S_1, the new savings schedule, indicates that savings increases by 15 as a result of the interest rate increase.[7] The decline in equilibrium income must now be greater than 160 since at 640 savings is 75, not the previous 60. Only when income declines by 220, to 580, is equilibrium attained. In the upper range ($i>7\%$), the IS curve is more interest elastic as each rise of the interest rate by one percentage point lowers equilibrium income by 220 rather than the previous 160.

If, instead, the interest rate was lowered to 6%, I would again rise to 110. Now savings is lowered as each household redistributes more of present

---

6. This assumes that in the range $i<7\%$, for each point the interest rate declines, I increases by 10.

7. We will assume that for each point the interest rate changes, savings changes by 15.

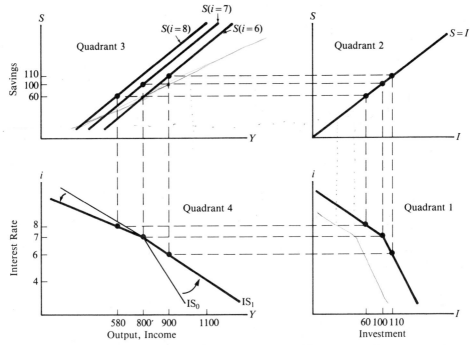

Figure 9.5   Product market equilibrium with interest sensitive consumption

income to consumption. This is reflected in the new savings schedule S_2 where at each level of Y savings is lowered by 15. The economy must expand to 900 in order to attain equilibrium with $S = I = 110$. The IS curve is also more elastic in this lower range as each percentage point decline in the interest rate raises equilibrium income by 100. There is now sufficient interest elasticity for full employment spending to be generated, even if $Y_f = 1100$.

The Government Sector and Equilibrium Income

Let us add a government sector to our model. To simplify the exposition, assume savings is interest insensitive and that the MEI schedule is linear. Such a model is illustrated in Figure 9.6.

Equilibrium in a model with a government sector occurs when total leakages, $S + T$, equal total injections, $I + G$ (Quadrant 2). In Quadrant 1, we begin with the MEI schedule. The total injections schedule, $(I + G)$, is constructed by shifting parallel from the MEI schedule by the level of G. In this example, $G = 40$.

In Quadrant 3 we must construct the total leakage schedule. Let us assume that the government decided to collect a lump sum tax, $T = 40$. S_0 represents the total private sector leakages (savings) before the imposition of the tax. According to our previous analysis (Figure 8.1a), the lump sum tax would reduce consumption by $b(\Delta T)$ and savings by $(1 - b)(\Delta T)$. Since $b = \frac{3}{4}$

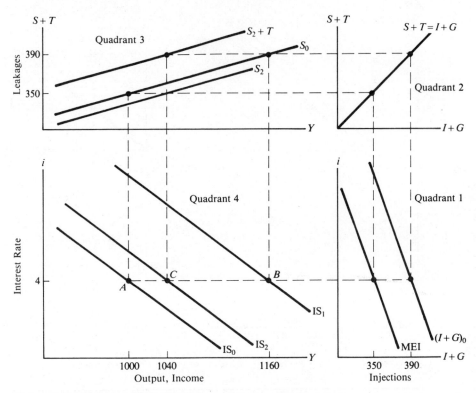

Figure 9.6 Product market equilibrium with government sector

and $T = 40$, savings is reduced by $\frac{1}{4}(40) = 10$ at each level of Y. This is reflected in savings schedule S_2. The total leakage schedule is constructed by adding the lump sum tax to the private household savings schedule after the imposition of the tax. The total leakage schedule, $S_2 + T$, is 30 higher than the initial leakage schedule S_0 before the imposition of the tax.

If there was no government sector, then the MEI schedule would be the total injections schedule and S_0 would be the total leakages schedule. Using these two schedules, we can construct IS_0, which is the IS curve before the imposition of either government taxes or spending. Let us assume that the current market interest rate, $i = 4\%$. IS_0 indicates that in a laissez-faire economy equilibrium $Y = 1000$ would be attained at that interest rate (point A).

Now suppose we add government spending, $G = 40$, but continue to assume no government taxation. The total leakages schedule would remain S_0 but the total injections schedule would be $(I + G)_0$. At $i = 4\%$, total injections now equal 390. The total injections schedule indicates that equilibrium income must rise by 160 to offset the additional injections (point B). Since at each interest rate we now have 40 more of total injections, then at each interest rate the equilibrium income must rise by 160. This result follows from our previous multiplier analysis. As long as the interest rate is unchanged, equilibrium Y

must rise by the initial autonomous change in spending (ΔA) times the simple income multiplier (M_y). In this model, $\Delta A = 40$ and $M_y = 4$ so that $\Delta Y_T = (\Delta A) M_y = 4(40) = 160$. Hence, the new IS curve, IS_1, is shifted by 160 from IS_0 at each interest rate.

Next assume a lump sum tax, $T = 40$, is imposed so that the total leakages schedule becomes $S_2 + T$. At $i = 4\%$, $S_2 + T = 390$ when $Y = 1040$. The 120 decline in equilibrium income reflects the tax multiplier. When households are taxed 40, they lower consumption by $b(\Delta T) = (\frac{3}{4})(40) = 30$ and equilibrium income $\Delta Y_T = M_y(\Delta A) = M_y(\Delta C) = 4(-30) = -120$. Since this shift occurs at every interest rate, the entire IS curve, denoted by IS_2, is shifted by 120 from IS_1. Also, note that the shift from IS_0 to IS_2 is 40, which would have been predicted by the balanced budget multiplier.

The Multiplier Effect and the Interest Rate

The preceding analysis indicates that given any autonomous shift in spending, the IS curve shifts by the simple income multiplier $M_y(\Delta A)$. For example, suppose that initially the economy is at full employment equilibrium, with $i = 5\%$ (Figure 9.7), and there is an autonomous decline in spending. The IS curve shifts from IS_0 to IS_1. If the interest rate is unchanged, then equilibrium income declines by the simple income multiplier effect, from Y_f to Y_1. However, to the extent that this will induce an interest rate decline, the size of the full multiplier effect would be reduced. For example, if the interest rate declined to 4%, then the income decline would only be to Y_2. According to the laissez-faire viewpoint, money market and price adjustments would lower the interest rate to 3% so that the effect of the autonomous change in spending would be completely offset.

9.3 CONCLUSION

This chapter has developed the individualistic theory of capital spending. It implies that expenditures on plant and equipment are inversely correlated with the interest rate due to the effect of changes in the market interest rate on automation, production capacity, and new ventures. It assumes that the effects of interest rate changes are more powerful than the effects of other factors, such as sales, capacity utilization, and profit levels.

The inclusion of the individualistic theory of capital spending implies that there is a relationship between equilibrium income and the interest rate. This relationship is known as the IS curve. We found that the more sensitive capital investment is to interest rate changes, the more sensitive equilibrium income is to interest rate changes.

We found that any autonomous change in spending would shift the IS curve by the simple income multiplier effect. However, there is no guarantee that the *actual* change in equilibrium income would be as large. Indeed, if the interest rate moves in the same direction as the economy, then the actual

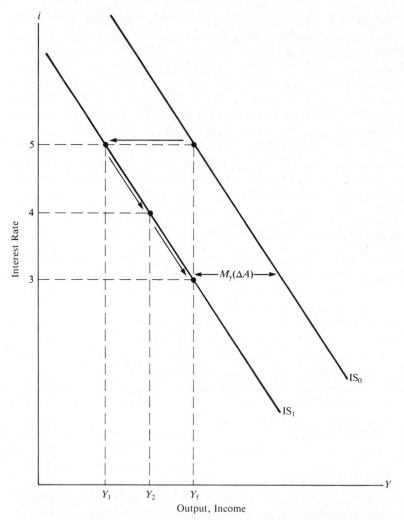

Figure 9.7   Effect of autonomous spending decline on equilibrium income

change in equilibrium income would be reduced. In the extreme case, changes in the interest rate result in capital adjustments, completely offsetting the initial autonomous change in spending. Since our ability to determine the effects of an autonomous change in spending relies on an assessment of money market adjustments, we will next detail theories of money. We will find that under assumptions other than those adopted by laissez-faire advocates, shifts in spending will result in changes in equilibrium income, and that these changes may be quite substantial even after accounting for interest rate adjustments.

CHAPTER TEN

THE MONEY MARKET

Previous chapters highlighted the potentially powerful influence money market adjustments can have on equilibrium income. To the extent that unemployment induces interest rate declines which, in turn, induce additional spending, natural market adjustments can offset autonomous shifts in spending (shocks to the economic system). Indeed, under a certain set of assumptions, made by laissez-faire advocates, these adjustments are so powerful that shifts in spending are completely offset so that private market adjustments would always guarantee full employment.

This chapter will detail the underlying money market assumptions made by laissez-faire advocates. It will be seen how the monetary policy advocacy position (only government monetary policy is effective) results from a subset of the laissez-faire model and is one of the reasons for popular confusion between the two positions. It will also detail the simple Keynesian model, which both reduces the power of monetary influences on equilibrium income and increases the effects of autonomous spending changes. Since one of the causes of autonomous changes in spending is government fiscal policy, Keynesian monetary assumptions result in an emphasis on fiscal rather than monetary intervention.

10.1 THE MONETARY POLICY ADVOCACY MODEL

Chapter 9 noted that if the market interest rate would decline sufficiently, then the full effect of a spending shift would be completely offset. In this case, attempts by the government to use fiscal policy to stimulate the economy would induce completely offsetting private sector declines. The $M_y^* = 0$. Monetary policy advocates believe this is the general case and that only monetary policy influences equilibrium income. Let us begin our analysis of the money market by describing the monetary advocacy model.

Money Supply

Money is an asset which is instantaneously and universally convertible into any good or service at a known rate of exchange. Money is considered a *liquid* asset because, like liquids, it has the ability to immediately change into the shape of any other object. The simplest form of money is legal currency which is universally accepted and exchanged for any good or service at the current market price. Economists assume that checking account balances, known as demand deposits, also have this property. The narrowest measure of the supply of money, called M_1, is equal to the total amount of pocket currency plus demand deposits.

There are, of course, other assets which have some but not all the properties of M_1. For example, savings accounts in commercial banks can almost instantaneously be used to transact expenditures. Many banks now switch funds automatically from savings account balances, called time deposits, to demand deposits. Therefore, a second broad measure of assets which can almost immediately be used for universal purchases is $M_2 = M_1 + $ commercial bank time deposits.

Near Money

Besides M_2, there is a number of assets that have some liquidity and, therefore, can act in certain circumstances as money. For example, many individuals have credit cards or government shortterm securities. Both of these assets have some degree of liquidity. Credit cards are good as money for some purchases but not all. Government shortterm (90-day) securities can be immediately exchanged *with a penalty* or one only must wait until its maturity date for exchange. Each of these assets, therefore, can be substituted for money but are by no means *perfect* substitutes.

Traditionally, the measure most used is M_1. This implies that, in practice, other assets are only limited and weak substitutes for M_1. Let us assume that M_1 is the best measure of the money supply at this point.

Determinants of the Money Supply

The money supply is the total of pocket currency (PC) and demand deposits (DD). Demand deposits, in turn, are composed of two factors: the currency (CU) that households have deposited in commercial banks, called high-powered money (H), and loans made by commercial banks. Since the money supply is dependent upon the amount of loans made by commercial banks, let us proceed to determine the size of these loans.

Ignoring time deposits, the total liabilities of a commercial bank are its DD. The government requires that a certain proportion of the bank's assets to offset these liabilities, called the reserve requirement (RR), be held in currency.

DEFINITION **The reserve requirement is the minimum allowable ratio of high-powered money to total liabilities.**

The bank's high-powered money is, therefore, composed of the legal reserves (LR) and the excess reserves (ER).

$$RR = LR/DD$$
$$ER = H - LR$$

Assuming that commercial banks always loan out their excess reserves, let us analyze the effect of households shifting $100 from pocket currency to demand deposits with $RR = 0.2$.

Table 10.1
Bank A's balance sheet after new deposit

Assets		Liabilities	
Additional LR	+20	New Deposit	+100
Additional ER	+80		
Additional H	+100	Additional DD	+100

Table 10.1 indicates the effect of the new deposit on Bank A's balanced sheet. Since it only requires $20 to cover its new liabilities, the bank has ER = $80. According to our assumption, the bank lowers its interest rate sufficiently to attract the necessary additional customers to loan out the entire excess reserves. Let us assume that the loans are spent and then deposited in Bank B. After the transfer of currency from Bank A to Bank B, each bank's balance sheet is illustrated in Table 10.2.

Table 10.2

Bank A's balance sheet after loan paid out			
Assets		Liabilities	
Additional LR	+20	New Deposit	+100
Additional Collateral	+80		
Additional Assets	+100	Additional DD	+100

Bank B's balance sheet after new deposit			
Assets		Liabilities	
Additional LR	+16	New Deposit	+80
Additional ER	+64		
Additional H	+80	Additional DD	+80

With the $80 withdrawal, Bank A is completely loaned up. It no longer has any excess reserves. However, after the deposit, Bank B has excess reserves equal to $64. Again we assume the bank lowers the interest rate until additional customers borrow the entire excess reserves. After these loans are paid out they will appear in Bank C's balance sheet. Bank C would then have excess reserves of $0.8(64) = \$51.20$, which will generate new loans. Table 10.3 indicates that through this process the additional $100 of H would eventually generate $400 in additional loans, or a total of $500 in additional DD.

Table 10.3
Total money creation in the banking system

Bank	Additional DD	Additional loans	Additional LR
Bank A	$100.00	$80.00	$20.00
Bank B	80.00	64.00	16.00
Bank C	64.00	51.20	12.80
Bank D	51.20	40.96	10.24
Bank E	40.96	32.77	8.19
Bank F	32.77	26.22	6.55
Total	$500.00	$400.00	$100.00

This indicates that if commercial banks would always loan out their excess reserves by lowering the interest rate, the money supply

$$M_s = (1/RR)H + PC$$

Let us define the bank currency ratio, $CR = H/CU$, and since $CU = PC + H$, $PC = (1 - CR)CU$. Therefore,

$$M_s = (1/RR)(CR)(CU) + (1 - CR)CU$$
$$= [(1/RR)(CR) + (1 - CR)]CU$$

For simplicity we will assume that the private sector keeps all its currency in commercial banks ($CR = 1$) so that

$$M_s = (1/RR)CU$$

However, as the interest rate declines, in the event that commercial banks are either unwilling and/or unable to loan out all excess reserves, M_s would be less. Monetary policy advocates contend that because of competition all commercial banks would be fully loaned up. This specifically implies that M_s would be unaffected by changes in the interest rate.

Money Demand

At any point in time, households must decide upon the allocation of their wealth among a number of assets. Besides money, households could store their wealth in income earning financial assets (bonds, stocks, and time deposits) or consumer durables. Both of these alternative assets provide benefits to households, either in the form of a stream of income or a stream of consumer services. Therefore, households will only allocate a portion of their wealth to money if it, too, provides some benefits. The main benefit that households derive from money is its ability to facilitate transactions. Assuming that this transactions motive is the only demand for money, let us determine the size of this demand by analyzing the behavior of a typical household.

Suppose that all payments could be made by check, and households are paid $100 on the first of each month. If households spend the entire $100 in a continuous stream, then each household would have a checking account balance of $100 on the 1st of the month, $67 on the 10th, $50 on the 15th, $33 on the 20th, and $0 on the 30th (assumed to be the last day of the month). The average cash balance for the typical household would be $50. This average balance is the transactions demand for money for the typical household that would be transacting $1200 of expenditures during the entire year.

DEFINITION **The transactions velocity of money, V, is equal to the average number of times that the quantity of money demanded, (M_d), is exchanged each year for final demand.**

In our numerical example, $V = 1200/50 = 24$. Let us change the institutional arrangement so that each household is paid twice each month—$50 on the 1st and 16th of each month. Household income and yearly expenditures remain at $1200. However, with the institutional change, average household cash balances would be reduced to $25. Now $V = 1200/25 = 48$.

According to this formulation,

$$V = pY/(M_d)$$

where

$$p = \text{price level}$$

Solving for the real demand for money,

$$m_d = M_d/p = (1/V)Y$$

Historically, monetary policy advocates assume that institutional factors adjust very slowly so that V is constant.

Money Market Equilibrium

The previous analysis indicates that monetary policy advocates make three major assumptions concerning the money market:

MP1—The real transaction demand ($m_t = M_t/p$) is equal to the real total demand for money m_d.

MP2—The real transaction demand for money $m_t = (1/V)Y$, where V is assumed to remain constant.

MP3—The nominal money supply, M_s, is unchanged by interest rate adjustments.

DEFINITION **The LM curve represents all the combinations of total income and interest rate which result in money market equilibrium.**

The money market is at equilibrium when $M_s = M_d$. According to assumptions MP1-3, at equilibrium $M_s = (1/V)pY$. Therefore, equilibrium Y in the money market occurs when $Y = M_s(V)/p$. In the monetary policy advocate model, V and M_s are unchanged by changes in the interest rate. If the price level is also held constant, the LM curve is perfectly interest rate inelastic. If, for example, $M_s = 500$, $V = 4$, and $p = 2$, then money market equilibrium occurs at $Y = 1000$, regardless of the interest rate (LM$_0$ in Figure 10.1).

The LM curve will shift if any of the parameters change. For example, suppose that there is a change in the nominal money supply to $M_s' = 520$. Then money market equilibrium income becomes $Y = M_s(V)/p = (520)(4)/2 = 1040$, regardless of the interest rate (LM$_1$ in Figure 10.1).

Note that the same effect on the LM curve could have been brought about by a decline in the price level to $p' = 25/13$. In each case, the real money supply, $M_s/p = m_s$, increases to 260.

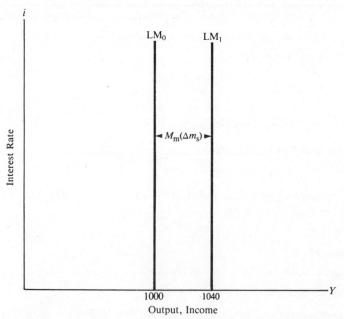

Figure 10.1 Money market equilibrium under assumptions MP1-3

DEFINITION The money market multiplier, M_m, is the ratio of the change in equilibrium income in the money market and the initial change in the real money supply Δm_s, holding the rate of interest constant.

Since $Y=(M_s/p)(V)$, with V a given constant, then a unit change in the real money supply, M_s/p, will change money market equilibrium spending by V. Therefore, $M_m = V$. In this numerical example, the change in the real money supply $(\Delta M_s)/p = 20/2 = 10$ so that $M_m = 40/10 = 4$, which also happens to be the size of V.

Equilibrium Income and Interest Rate

We can combine the money market equilibrium schedule LM_0 and the goods market equilibrium schedule IS_0 in one diagram (Figure 10.2). It indicates that one combination (point A) exists which results in equilibrium in both markets. This IS-LM framework, first proposed by Sir John Hicks,[1] has become the standard method used by economists to analyze the interaction of monetary and real phenomena. It can easily be demonstrated that under as-

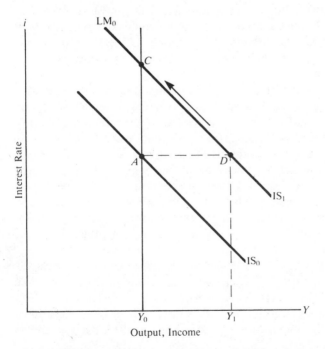

Figure 10.2 Income effect of autonomous spending change under assumptions MP1-3

---

1. J. R. Hicks, "Mr. Keynes and the 'Classics': A Suggested Interpretation," *Econometrica* 5 (1937): 147–159.

sumptions MP1–3, an autonomous shift in spending, whether through private market adjustments or fiscal policy, would have no effect upon equilibrium income.

Now suppose an autonomous shift in spending results in a new equilibrium schedule IS_1. According to the simple income multiplier, if there was no change in the interest rate equilibrium, income would rise to Y_1 (point D). However, as long as the real money supply dictates money market equilibrium schedule LM_0, this higher level of spending is not sustainable. At point D, since there is no additional funds to finance the expansion, $m_s < m_d$. The excess demand for money creates upward pressure on the market interest rate. As the interest rate rises, private sector spending is discouraged. A movement along IS_1 occurs until at point C the equilibrium in the money market is reestablished at the original income level Y_0. This indicates that if assumptions MP1–3 hold, the full income multiplier $M_y^* = 0$.

Instruments of Monetary Policy

The beginning of this chapter indicated that the determinants of the nominal money supply were RR and CU. Government policies can affect either of these determinants. The Federal Reserve can raise RR which, with a given CU, would cause banks to reduce their liabilities. Banks would contract their loans by raising the interest rate to discourage borrowing. If the Federal Reserve lowers RR, banks would lower their interest rate in order to attract additional customers.

The most widely used instrument of monetary policy is open market operations. Open market operations represent the buying or selling of government bonds by the Federal Reserve. If the Federal Reserve desired to expand the money supply, it would buy bonds from the public. Households who sold bonds to the Federal Reserve would receive currency in exchange. When deposited in the bank, the additional currency would generate an expansion of the money supply. If the Federal Reserve desired to contract the money supply, it would sell additional bonds to the public. Households would purchase these bonds by withdrawing currency from the banking system. As funds are withdrawn from the banking system, banks must contract their liabilities, thus reducing the money supply.

If assumptions MP1–3 hold, the LM curve would be interest rate inelastic. Given the nominal money supply, M_s, the money market equilibrium schedule is LM_0 (Figure 10.3). If the Federal Reserve expanded the money supply to M_s', then the money market equilibrium schedule would shift to LM_1. Regardless of the IS schedule, equilibrium income would increase by the full money multiplier effect, from Y_0 to Y_1.

Assumptions MP1–3 imply that only changes in the real money supply affect equilibrium income. Laissez-faire advocates by and large also contend that these assumptions hold. However, they make an additional assumption that the price level declines whenever the economy is at less than full employment. Thus, rather than requiring government management of the nominal money supply, laissez-faire advocates claim that natural market forces regulate m_s in order to insure full employment. In contrast, monetary policy advocates believe that the downward movement of prices during periods of unemployment is not sufficient to be relied upon. Hence, they contend government manipulation of the nominal money supply is necessary to insure full employment.

Timing of Monetary Policy

We found that discretionary fiscal policy seemed to suffer because of the long lag between the start of an economic fluctuation and the initiation of the fiscal stimulus. The monetary policy lag is much shorter. Unlike discretionary fiscal policy, which requires legislative action, monetary policy can be initiated immediately by the Federal Reserve once the fluctuation is recognized. Hence, only relatively short data and recognition lags occur with monetary policy.

The potential timing problem with monetary policy is its transmission lag—the time between its initiation and effect on the economy. When a tax cut is legislated, there is only a two-week transmission lag—the time it takes for the government to mail the new withholding tables to businesses. Most economists believe that because monetary policy must work through money supply and interest rate adjustments, the transmission lag is over a year. Laissez-faire advocates like Milton Friedman contend that the transmission lag associated

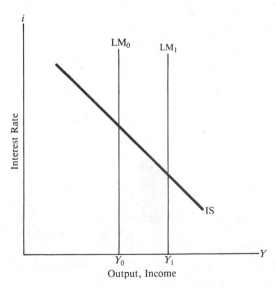

Figure 10.3   Income effect of monetary supply change under assumptions MP1–3

with monetary policy is long and variable. However, there is an increasing tendency among mainstream liberals to minimize the monetary policy transmission lag. They, therefore, claim that monetary policy does not suffer a long timing lag.

10.2 THE KEYNESIAN MONEY MARKET MODEL

The monetary policy advocacy model indicates that if the LM curve is perfectly interest rate inelastic, the economy expands through monetary policy and not fiscal policy. In order to sustain a fiscal expansion, new money must be made available without causing private spending to contract. However, assumptions MP1-3 make it impossible for the government to obtain the necessary additional funds without causing a compensating decline in private sector spending. The government spending forces the interest rate to increase until sufficient private sector units cut back their spending, making funds available to the government. This process has been called "crowding out" since it implies that government spending is accomplished by crowding private sector units out of the money market.

In order for at least a portion of the fiscal expansion to be sustained, the LM curve must be interest rate sensitive. If the LM curve is interest rate sensitive, then as the expansion forces interest rates up, the money market can find additional funds to support a higher level of equilibrium spending. One such viewpoint, which rejects MP3, claims that banks always have some excess reserves. In this case, higher interest rates induce banks to make these excess reserves available. Thus, new money is made available to finance at least part of the expansion. Another viewpoint, which rejects MP2, claims that V is sensitive to the interest rate. As the interest rate rises, households begin to use money more efficiently, raising V. As V rises, the same money supply can support a larger volume of expenditures. Again, a rise in the interest rate induces additional funds to finance at least part of the expansion.

Chapter 11 will detail how dropping assumptions MP2 and MP3 generates an interest rate sensitive LM curve. One of Keynes' breakthroughs was to develop an interest sensitive LM curve by rejecting assumption MP1.

Keynesian Speculative Demand for Money

According to the monetary policy advocacy model, since markets are smoothly and rapidly adjusting, and since all decision-makers have perfect knowledge of the future, there is no reason, other than for transactions purposes, to hold money. If markets rapidly adjust, then all assets sell at their true market value, and if perfect knowledge of the future existed, then there would be no risk in purchasing any asset. Therefore, since all interest-bearing assets would have no risk, they would be a superior asset to money.

Keynes rejected the contention that markets were rapidly adjusting and that decision-makers had perfect knowledge of the future. He claimed that risk and uncertainty were fundamental aspects of a capitalist society. If there is uncertainty, then it is possible to invest in an asset that is worth less than estimated. If markets are not smoothly and rapidly adjusting, then investors may not be able to quickly shift out of such an investment without considerable losses. For example, one might invest in a new industry and overestimate the potential market. Without instantaneous adjustments, the investor may not be able to extract himself from this project without a severe loss. This would be especially true if highly specialized capital goods had been purchased. Any investor contemplating such a risky venture may wish to postpone his decision until better information or a better investment climate is present. In this situation, our investor would desire to hold his wealth in some financial form that could be immediately convertible when he is ready to choose.

Let us assume that our investor has two alternative financial forms in which to hold his wealth: (1) idle cash balances in his checking account, or (2) a government guaranteed bond. Let us assume that the government bond is a consol. A consol is a bond which guarantees a fixed payment each year for perpetuity. It is, in a sense, a very longterm bond in that it never matures; it never must be paid off by the government. As any financial asset, a consol should sell at its present value. If R equals the guaranteed yearly payment and i_0 equals the market rate of interest, then the present value,

$$P_0 = \frac{R}{(1 + i_0)} + \frac{R}{(1 + i_0)^2} + \frac{R}{(1 + i_0)^3} + \ldots = \frac{R}{i_0}$$

If our investor chose to hold his wealth in the interest-bearing consol, he must be willing to sell it at its market price when he wishes to convert it into some other asset. If the market interest rate changes from its value at the time of the consol purchase, then its present value and, hence, its market value would change. Therefore, the actual selling price of the consol varies. Keynes assumed that each investor had some notion of the normal rate of interest, i_n. When our investor purchases the consol, if $i_0 > i_n$, then our investor expects the market interest rate to decline. A decline in the market rate of interest to i_n would raise the market value of the consol. In this case, by holding his wealth in consols, besides earning interest, our investor expects to have capital gains when he sells the consols. Our investor would always choose to buy consols rather than hold his wealth in idle cash balances when $i_0 > i_n$.

If, instead, $i_0 < i_n$, then the choice between the two assets is not so clear cut. On the one hand, the consol yields a fixed stream of interest payments, R each year. On the other hand, the consol's market value is expected to decline from its original purchase price, R/i_0, to R/i_n. Therefore, whenever our investor chooses to convert his consol into some other asset, he can expect to have capital losses $R/i_n - R/i_0$. The consol is the best alternative only if the stream of interest payments received before conversion are larger than the expected capital loss. If the market interest rate is quite close to the normal rate, then the interest payments would be larger than the capital losses. However, as the market rate is lowered, the capital losses increase. There will exist some critical interest rate, i_c, at which the capital losses just equal the interest payments received. At any market rate below i_c, our investor would expect his capital losses to be greater than interest payments received, making the purchase of consols unprofitable.[2] Our investor would then decide to hold his wealth in idle balances. These idle balances are what Keynes called the speculative demand for money.

Keynes assumed that all investors had a different notion of the normal rate of interest so that each investor has a different critical rate, i_c, below which he would shift his wealth from consols to idle balances. Keynes noted that at high market rates of interest, the fear of capital losses and, hence, the demand for idle cash balances would be minimal. However, as the market rate is lowered, some individuals begin to perceive the market rate to be below their critical rate and start shifting their wealth from consols to idle balances. As the market rate is lowered, increasing numbers of investors perceive the market rate falling below their critical rate and the demand for idle balances would increase dramatically. This is reflected in an increasingly interest elastic demand for idle balances. Finally, Keynes assumed that there would be a low interest rate at which so many investors would perceive the market rate falling below their critical rate that virtually all wealth would be shifted from consols to idle balances. This point is called the liquidity trap since all funds would be trapped in idle rather than active balances.

Implication of the Keynesian Speculative Motive

According to Keynes, there is a source of funds available to the government which would not restrict private sector spending. As before, a government spending expansion would initially create an excess demand for money. This will cause the market interest rate to rise. Higher interest rates will induce individuals to lower their speculative demand, allowing funds to be shifted to the expanding transactions demand. To the extent funds can be shifted from the

---

2. Suppose we had to hold onto funds for one year and must decide on whether or not to buy a consol with the idle funds. Suppose that the consol paid R interest each year and that the current interest rate was i_0. Let i_n equal the expected interest rate when the consol would be sold (the next year). Therefore, the income "earned" (E) by buying the consol would be the interest payment, R, plus any capital gains.

$$E = R + [(R/i_n) - (R/i_0)] = R[1 + (1/i_n) - (1/i_0)]$$

Hence, earnings will be positive as long as $1 + (1/i_n) - (1/i_0) > 0$. This occurs as long as $i_0 > [i_n/(1 + i_n)]$. For example, if $i_n = 10\%$, then $i_0 > .1/1.1 = 9.1\%$ for it to be worthwhile to buy a consol. If $i_0 < 9.1\%$, the investor has better expectations by placing funds in his checking account rather than the consol.

speculative motive to transactions purposes, government spending can expand without causing a contraction of private sector spending.

Just as important, the Keynesian money market model implies that an autonomous spending contraction will not be completely offset by an interest rate induced spending expansion. Recall that if, for any reason, there was an autonomous spending decline, an excess supply of money would result. If the LM curve is perfectly interest rate inelastic, then transaction demand must increase back to its original level. Since V is assumed to remain constant, transactions demand will rise back to its initial level only when spending returns to its initial level. In this case, the interest rate will continue to decline until it induces the necessary amount of additional spending.

If we include a speculative money motive, then the adjustment process would differ. In this case, as the market interest rate declines, individuals increase their speculative demand for money. Therefore, a portion of the excess supply is absorbed by additional speculative holdings. If some additional funds are absorbed by the speculative motive, then equilibrium will be attained with a smaller transactions demand. If the transaction demand is lower so, too, will be equilibrium spending. Hence, at the completion of the adjustment process, the economy will still be below its initial level.

Money Market Equilibrium

Figure 10.4 depicts equilibrium in the money market when we include the Keynesian speculative motive, m_{sp}. At $i \geq 12\%$, $m_{sp} = 0$. This region is called the classical range because since no speculative demand exists the only demand for money is for transaction purposes, which was the assumption of the classical laissez-faire model.

When $12\% < i \leq 6\%$, some individuals begin to shift some of their wealth to idle balances. However, interest rates are still too high for there to be a substantial movement. For each one percentage point change in the interest rate, m_{sp} increases by 10. When $6\% < i < 2\%$, a substantial movement of wealth occurs. For each one percentage point interest rate decline, m_{sp} increases by 40. Finally, when $i = 2\%$, the fear of capital losses on consols is so great that virtually all investors desire to liquidate their remaining consols. This is called the Keynesian liquidity trap region because any change in the money supply would be held as idle balances by investors. All money, therefore, would be trapped in idle balances rather than being attracted into transactions demand for expanded output. Banks would never lower the market interest rate below this level since any money available would be attracted to idle balances.

In Quadrant 3 of Figure 10.4, we have the usual transaction demand as a function of the *real* level of spending

$$m_t = (1/V)Y$$

In our example we assume $V = 2$ so that $m_t = \frac{1}{2}Y$.

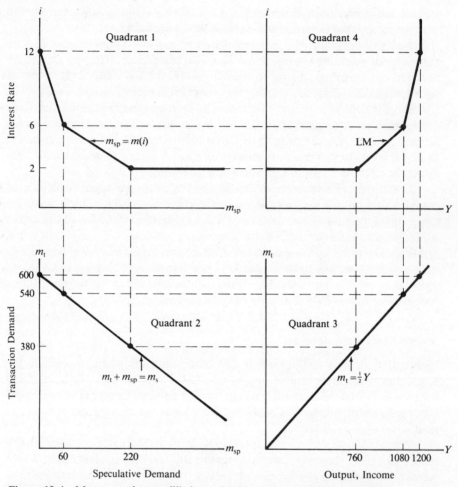

Figure 10.4 Money market equilibrium with Keynesian speculative demand

Quadrant 2 presents the money market equilibrium condition that the real money supply, M_s/p, must equal the real money demand, $m_t + m_{sp}$. This indicates that once the real money supply is specified, equilibrium when the real money demand sums to this amount. In our example, we assume that $M_s/p = 600$.

If $i \geq 12\%$ then, according to Quadrant 1, $m_{sp} = 0$. According to Quadrant 2, money market equilibrium can occur only when the entire real money supply is absorbed by transactions demand. According to Quadrant 3, $m_t = 600$ when $Y = 1200$. Therefore, for any $i \geq 12\%$, equilibrium $Y = 1200$.

If i declines to 11%, according to Quadrant 1, $m_{sp} = 10$. Therefore, m_t must equal 590 for money market equilibrium to occur. According to Quadrant 3, $m_t = 590$ when $Y = 1180$. Within the range $12\% < i < 6\%$, for each one percentage point interest rate decline, m_{sp} increases by 10. If m_{sp} increases by

10, then money market equilibrium requires m_t to decline by 10 which, in turn, requires Y to decline by 20. Therefore, (10%, 1160), (9%, 1140), (8%, 1120), (7%, 1100), and (6%, 1080) are other money market equilibrium combinations of interest rates and real income, respectively.

If $i = 5\%$ then $m_{sp} = 100$. Money market equilibrium requires $m_t = 500$ which occurs when $Y = 1000$. Within the range $6\% < i < 2\%$, each one percentage point decline in the interest rate increases m_{sp} by 40. If m_{sp} increases by 40, then money market equilibrium requires m_t to decline by 40 which, in turn, requires Y to decline by 80. Therefore, (4%, 920), (3%, 840), and (2%, 760) are other money market equilibrium combinations.

At $i = 2\%$, the Keynesian liquidity trap is assumed to occur so that it is possible for any sum of money greater than 220 to be demanded for idle balances and, hence, any sum of money less than 380 to be demanded for transactions purposes. Therefore, it is possible for any value of $Y \le 760$ to be equilibrium in the money market.

The LM curve constructed has a shape which mirrors the shape of the speculative demand schedule. In the range $i \ge 12\%$, m_{sp} is perfectly interest rate inelastic and so, too, is the LM curve. In the range $12\% < i < 2\%$, the LM curve is interest elastic to the degree of the interest elasticity of the speculative demand schedule. In the Keynesian liquidity trap region, the LM curve is completely interest rate elastic just as the speculative demand schedule.

10.3 POLICY EFFECTIVENESS IN THE KEYNESIAN MODEL

The Keynesian money market model enables us to analyze the relative effectiveness of monetary and fiscal policy within a broad range of situations.

Monetary Policy

Let us assume that we begin with money market equilibrium schedule LM_0 (Figure 10.5) and analyze the effect of a money supply expansion on equilibrium income. At each interest rate the speculative demand for money remains the same. The entire additional money supply must be absorbed by new transactions demand. Therefore, at each interest rate the money market equilibrium schedule shifts by the size of the money multiplier effect, $M_m(\Delta m_s)$. If $V = 2$ and $\Delta m_s = 60$, then the LM curve would shift by 120 to LM_1. In the liquidity trap region ($i = 4\%$), since all excess funds would be willingly absorbed by m_{sp}, any $Y < Y_1$ would be compatible with money market equilibrium.

1. If the IS curve (IS_0) cuts the LM schedules in the Keynesian liquidity trap region, the additional money supply would be immediately absorbed by speculative demand. No excess money supply would be generated, so there would be no reason for banks to lower the interest rate. If there is no change in the interest rate, there would be no change in spending and, hence no change in equilibrium income. Therefore, when the IS curve cuts the LM schedule in this region, monetary policy is completely ineffective.

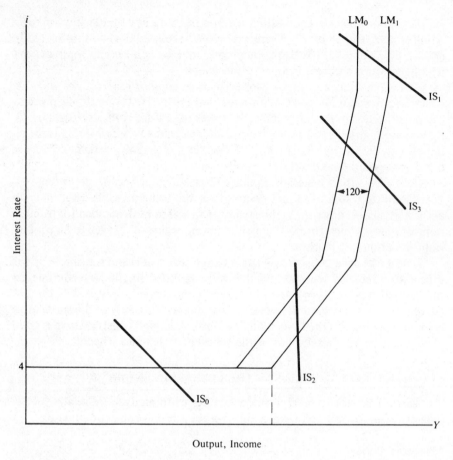

Figure 10.5 Effect of monetary policy on equilibrium income

2. If the IS curve (IS_1) cuts the LM schedules in the classical region, the additional money supply initially creates an excess supply of funds. Banks lower their interest rate. However, since m_{sp} is unchanged, all of the additional funds have to be absorbed by an increase in m_t for money market equilibrium to be reestablished. Therefore, the interest rate would decline until equilibrium income expands sufficiently to absorb the additional money supply. Since all additional funds are absorbed by m_t, the economy expands by the full money multiplier effect (120).

3. Suppose the IS curve (IS_2) cuts the LM schedules in the intermediate range. A monetary expansion initially creates an excess supply of funds. Banks lower their interest rate in order to increase the demand for money. If the IS curve were completely interest rate insensitive (vertical), then declining interest rates would have no effect upon spending or m_t. However, the declining interest rate would increase m_{sp}. Eventually interest rates would decline sufficiently so that all the additional funds were absorbed in m_{sp}. In this case, the money expansion would have no effect on equilibrium income.

However, if the IS curve is interest sensitive, like IS_3, then the declining interest rate induces additional spending and a rise in equilibrium income and m_t. In this case, a portion of the additional funds find their way into active balances so that the monetary expansion has some effect on equilibrium income.

The monetary expansion raises equilibrium income to the extent that additional funds are absorbed by m_t rather than by m_{sp}. Suppose money demand is interest sensitive (flat LM curve), while aggregate spending is not interest rate sensitive (steep IS curve). As the interest rate declines, there would be little increase in spending or m_t. However, since m_{sp} is interest rate sensitive, there would be a large increase in m_{sp}. Because most of the additional funds would be absorbed in m_{sp}, monetary policy would be ineffective in this case.

Suppose money demand is interest rate insensitive (steep LM curve), while aggregate spending is very interest rate sensitive (flat IS curve). As the interest rate declines, there would be only a slight increase in m_{sp} but a large increase in m_t. Because most of the additional funds would be absorbed in m_t, monetary policy would be quite effective in this case.

Fiscal Policy

Let us assume that fiscal policy takes the form of deficit spending of 30, funded by private market borrowing. This shifts the IS curve by 120 if $M_y = 4$.

1. If the IS curves cut the LM curve in the classical region, then fiscal policies have no effect on equilibrium income. This is illustrated by the shifting of IS_0 to $IS_{(0+g)}$ in Figure 10.6. This corresponds exactly to the monetary policy advocacy model. The government, in order to attract the necessary funds, must raise the interest rate enough to discourage the same exact amount of private sector spending. Therefore, the only effect of fiscal policy is to raise the interest rate and "crowd out" private sector spending.

2. In the Keynesian liquidity trap region, if fiscal policy shifts the IS curve from IS_1 to $IS_{(1+g)}$, equilibrium income would increase by its full simple multiplier effect (120). In this region, since only an infinitesimally small increase in the interest rate would release all the funds the government desired from idle balances, there would be no discouragement of private sector spending necessary.

3. Suppose the fiscal policy expansion, which shifts IS_2 to $IS_{(2+g)}$, occurs within the intermediate range of the LM curve. This implies that the interest rate has no effect on spending. Initially, government spending cess demand for money. As the interest rate rises, private spend

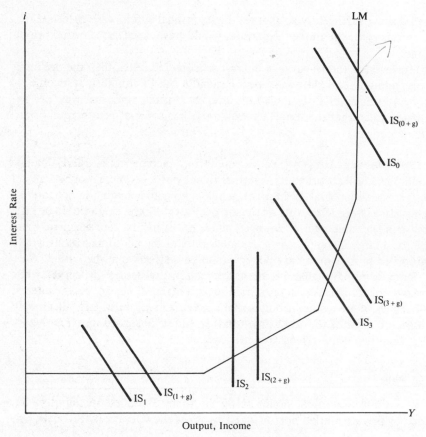

i

Interest Rate

Output, Income

LM

$IS_{(0+g)}$

IS_0

$IS_{(3+g)}$

IS_3

IS_2

$IS_{(2+g)}$

IS_1

$IS_{(1+g)}$

Y

Figure 10.6   Effect of fiscal policy on equilibrium income

affected. However, at higher interest rates m_{sp} declines, releasing funds to finance the government's deficit spending. Eventually, the interest rate rises sufficiently so that the entire government expansion is financed from released idle balances. Since no private spending was discouraged, the economy expands by the full simple income multiplier effect (120).

Suppose the fiscal expansion is represented by a shift from IS_3 to $IS_{(3+g)}$. Since the IS curve is interest sensitive, when the interest rate increases, private sector spending is discouraged. In this case, a portion of the needed funds comes at the expense of private sector spending so that the expansion is by less than the simple multiplier effect.

The fiscal expansion raises equilibrium income to the extent that additional funds are released from m_{sp} rather than m_t. Suppose m_{sp} is not very interest rate sensitive (LM curve is steep), while aggregate spending is interest rate sensitive (IS curve is flat). In this case, as the interest rate rises, there will be little funds released from m_{sp} but m_t declines as substantial private sector spending is crowded out. Since most of the funds are released from m_t, fiscal policy would be quite ineffective.

Suppose that m_{sp} was very interest rate sensitive, while aggregate demand was quite interest rate insensitive. This case is characterized by a flat LM curve and a steep IS curve. As the interest rate rises, there would be little decrease in spending, and hence, little decrease in m_t. However, because m_{sp} is interest rate sensitive, there would be a large decrease in m_{sp}. Since most of the additional funds would be released from m_{sp}, fiscal policy would be quite effective.

To summarize, the effectiveness of monetary and fiscal policy is dependent upon the range in which the IS curve cuts the LM curve.

1. In the classical range, monetary policy has a full money multiplier effect, while fiscal policy is completely ineffective.

2. In the liquidity trap region, monetary policy is completely ineffective, while fiscal policy has a full money multiplier effect.

3. In the intermediate range, both policies have some effect on equilibrium income. The relative effectiveness depends upon the interest sensitivity of the demand for money (slope of the LM curve) and the interest sensitivity of aggregate spending (slope of IS curve). Two situations have clear implications:

    • If the LM curve is steep (interest rate inelastic), and the IS curve is flat (interest rate elastic), then fiscal policy is less effective than monetary policy.
    • If the LM curve is flat (interest rate elastic) and the IS curve is steep (interest rate inelastic), then fiscal policy is more effective than monetary policy.

10.4 THE MONETARY-FISCAL POLICY DEBATE

For many years the monetary-fiscal policy controversy was considered the major area of disagreement within the economics profession. Often this controversy was considered the basis of discussing the "entire spectrum of macroeconomics."[3] However, in the late 1970s, it became increasingly clear that this debate, centering on the expected shapes of the IS and LM curves, could only identify the spectrum of opinion among mainstream liberal economists. It does not include the conservative, left-liberal or radical viewpoints. The monetary-fiscal policy debate becomes a purely mainstream liberal viewpoint, re-

3. This is the position taken by F. Glahe, who claims that the IS-LM framework enables us to examine the "entire spectrum of macroeconomic thought, from the views of the extreme Keynesians to those of the extreme monetarists." *Macroeconomics* (New York: Harcourt Brace, 1973), p. viii.

gardless of whether the advocate favors emphasis on monetary or fiscal policy, because of the level of agreement between the adversaries. They all agree:

1. There is no systematic explanation of economic turning points.

2. The private market does not have sufficient flexibility to automatically guarantee full employment.

3. Government discretionary intervention is an effective approach to problems of deficient aggregate spending.

4. Both fiscal and monetary policy are effective and can be used in a coordinated fashion.

5. Aggregate demand objectives are sufficient in order to insure full employment. No more detailed objectives, such as those which might determine the distribution of total income (income policies) or the distribution of production (government investment planning), are necessary.

Monetarists and Monetary Policy Advocates

Conservatives, such as Milton Friedman, are not included in this framework because they reject point 2. Specifically, Friedman contends that market forces are sufficiently strong and stabilizing so that no government intervention is necessary in order to insure full employment. Since the conservative position is often called monetarist, it is confused with that of extreme monetary policy advocates.

The monetarist position is in disagreement with that of monetary policy advocates for two reasons:[4]

1. Unlike monetary policy advocates, Friedman does not believe that government monetary policy is necessary to insure full employment. Monetarists contend that even if the economy is momentarily below full employment, private market forces would be sufficient to expand the economy back to full employment. Specifically, they claim that in an underemployed economy the price level would decline so that the real money supply would increase *without* the use of government monetary policy. Moreover, as already mentioned, monetarists question the effectiveness of monetary policy because of the transmission lag involved.

The mistaken belief that the monetarist position claimed that monetary policy was necessary and effective was somewhat fostered by Friedman's own work (with Anna Schwartz) on the monetary history of the United States.[5]

---

4. See M. Friedman, "Comments on the Critics," *Journal of Political Economy* 80 (Sept./Oct. 1972).

5. M. Friedman and A. J. Schwartz, *A Monetary History of the United States, 1867–1960* (Princeton, N.J.: Princeton Univ Press, 1963).

Their work attempted to demonstrate that changes in real GNP and the real money supply occurred in coordination. Their work seemed to imply that monetary policy determined equilibrium income, while fiscal policy was completely ineffective. Friedman argues, however, that their work is only an indication that in the *shortrun*—before private market forces have fully corrected for economic shocks—monetary policy can have a large effect on real GNP. He, of course, believes that these effects are not lasting, as private market forces would eventually self-correct the economy.

2. During the 1970s, Friedman clarified his position further. He admitted that fiscal policy could also have some effect in the *shortrun* on equilibrium real GNP (by accepting the view that money demand was interest rate sensitive). However, Friedman rejects the use of fiscal policy because of the extensive time lags between the beginning of an economic contraction and government policy implementation. Moreover, since fiscal policy is determined by elected officials, Friedman and other monetarists fear that short-run political objectives (reelection) will take precedence over longterm economic requirements.

In summary, the major characteristic of monetarists is their faith in the ability of a private market economy to self-correct for any deviations from full employment. In particular, monetarists contend that movements in the price level would automatically adjust the real money supply so that full employment is insured. If, due to an external shock, unemployment occurs, the price level would decline, raising the real money supply, lowering the interest rate, and expanding aggregate spending. If a shock shifts the economy so that excess spending occurs, the price level would rise, lowering the real money supply, raising interest rates, and contracting aggregate spending. Thus, flexible prices are sufficient to insure a fully employed economy. Chapter 12 will explore in detail the possibilities and effects of price flexibility on equilibrium income.

Monetarists reject government stabilization policy for a number of reasons. First, as discussed in Chapter 6, they contend that in the absence of government intervention the private sector is quite stable. Second, as previously discussed, they believe that flexible prices are sufficient to insure full employment. Third, though they admit that *both* monetary and fiscal policy can influence equilibrium income, they contend that because of time lags and political pressures, government stabilization policy would be ineffective.

Franco Modigliani, in his 1976 AEA Presidential Address, attempted to correct the mistaken view of monetarism which was widespread within the economics profession. He said,

> The difference between the two "schools" [monetarist and fiscalist] is generally held to center on whether the money supply or fiscal variables are the major determinant of economic activity and hence the most appropriate tool of stabilization policies. My central theme is that this

view is quite far from the truth, and that the issues involved are of far greater practical import . . .

In reality the distinguishing feature of the monetarist school and the real issues of disagreement with non-monetarists is not monetarism [monetary policy] but rather the role that should be assigned to stabilization policies. Nonmonetarists accept what I regard to be the fundamental practical message of The General Theory: *that a private enterprise economy using an intangible money* needs *to be stabilized,* can *be stabilized, and therefore* should *be stabilized by appropriate monetary and fiscal policies. Monetarists by contrast take the view that there is no serious need to stabilize the economy; that even if there were a need, it could not be done, for stabilization policies would be more likely to increase than to decrease instability; and, at least some monetarists would, I believe, go so far as to hold that, even in the unlikely event that stabilization policies could on balance prove beneficial, the government should not be trusted with the necessary power.*[6]

Conservative economists are laissez-faire advocates who are sometimes labelled monetarists. Because the term monetarist is so confusing, in the remainder of the text, the terms conservative or laissez-faire advocates will be used rather than monetarist to describe this viewpoint. It should be remembered that conservatives are *not* monetary policy advocates. Monetary policy advocates are those mainstream economists who believe that monetary policy tools are the most effective and necessary form of government intervention.

Left-Liberals

To characterize left-liberals as extreme fiscalists might be useful if one's objective is to maintain that the monetary-fiscal policy controversy is the essence of macroeconomics, but substantially distorts the implication and intention of their views. It implies that the essential thrust of the left-liberal view is that only fiscal policy must be used since monetary policy is totally ineffective. Left-liberals only enter the monetarist-fiscalist debate to argue against the position that monetary policy can be an effective macro-tool.[7] They do not believe that aggregate demand control can be effective if the government solely

---

6. F. Modigliani, "The Monetarist Controversy, or, Should We Forsake Stabilization Policy?" *American Economics Review* 67 (Mar. 1977): 1.

7. Both left-liberals and conservatives reject the assumption of stable income and money multipliers. See Paul Davidson, *Money and the Real World* (London: MacMillan, 1973) for a forceful defense of the thesis that Keynes' conception of speculative demand was not that it was interest rate sensitive, but that it was highly unstable. Hence, it would shift sporadically and each shift would change the velocity of money. Any change in the velocity of money changes the size of the money multiplier.

attempted to change total spending. Almost all left-liberals believe that the government must be concerned with the distribution of both income and production. They therefore favor incomes policies to attain income distribution objectives and capital investment planning to attain production distribution objectives. Moreover, they reject point 1 since they believe that economic fluctuations are subject to systematic movements so that economic planning can be effective at stabilizing the economy.

In summary, the fiscal-monetary policy controversy participants agree that government interventionist policies to effect aggregate spending are necessary and sufficient to maintain a fully employment economy. A conservative approach rejects the *need* for government interventionist policies, while a left-liberal approach rejects the *sufficiency* of government manipulation of only aggregate spending. Left-liberals contend that a more detailed set of fiscal objectives would be sufficient to maintain a fully employed economy. Marxists claim that certain contradictions are sufficiently strong that no amount of government intervention can avoid the prolonged periods of stagnation that the United States and other private market economies have been experiencing since the early 1970s.

Monetary-Fiscal Coordination

There is another sense in which this debate over how much to emphasize monetary versus fiscal policy is not very crucial. As long as the money and simple income multipliers are stable at known values, monetary and fiscal policy can be coordinated to obtain predictable changes even when we may not know the effects of either policy.

If the money multiplier is known, we could then shift the LM schedule by a predicted amount. If the simple income multiplier is known, then we can shift the IS schedule by the same predicted amount. Figure 10.7 indicates the effect if fiscal and monetary policy, which shifts the money market and goods market equilibrium schedules by the same amount (ΔY_T), are undertaken simultaneously. Because both schedules are shifted by the same amount, the new equilibrium (point B) is at the same interest rate as the initial equilibrium (point A). Equilibrium income increases by the size in the shift of the schedules, ΔY_T. Since the controversy is really over the size and effects of interest rate changes (when either policy is undertaken separately), this conflict is avoided by maintaining the *same* interest rate.

10.6 CONCLUSION

The Hicksian IS-LM framework was completed as a means of evaluating the relative effectiveness of government monetary and fiscal policy. The analysis was able to demonstrate that the monetary policy advocacy model—only money matters—is derived from a subset of the laissez-faire model. The mone-

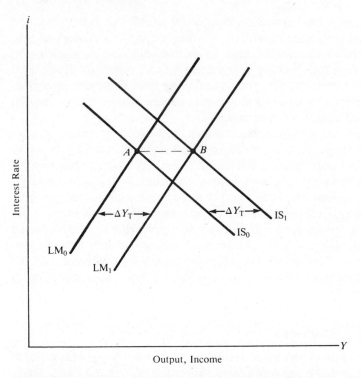

Figure 10.7 Coordination of monetary and fiscal policy

tary policy advocacy model assumes that the laissez-faire money market as-sumptions are valid, but rejects the assumptions that the economy, through price adjustments, can completely offset unemployment. It was demonstrated that the monetary policy advocacy assumptions (MP1–3) directly imply that a change in fiscal policy, or any autonomous change in spending, cannot have an effect on equilibrium income.

This result followed from the assumption that the only source of funds to transact an increase in government spending would be from lower private sec-tor spending. Hence, a fiscal expansion would result in raising the market in-terest rate until private sector spending declines exactly equal to the fiscal expansion occur. There would be no change in equilibrium income since the government expansion is completely offset by a private sector spending con-traction.

Keynes rejected these assumptions and, instead, argued that there was an alternative source of expansionary funds—private sector speculative balances. He claimed that unless interest rates were already high, a rise in the market in-terest rate would lower the speculative demand for money, releasing funds to finance the fiscal expansion. In this case, the existing money supply would be able to support an economic expansion. This was reflected in the derivation of an interest rate sensitive LM curve.

According to the Keynesian schedule, an interest rate insensitive LM schedule occurs only in the classical range. Outside of the classical range, fiscal policy is effective since it can draw additional funds from idle balances. Fiscal policy is completely effective if either the LM curve is perfectly elastic (liquidity trap region) or the IS curve is perfectly inelastic. In these two cases, monetary policy was shown to be ineffective.

If the IS curve is interest sensitive and cuts the LM curve in the intermediate range, then both monetary and fiscal policy have an effect on equilibrium income. The relative effect of each policy undertaken separately is dependent upon the slopes of the LM and IS curves.

The chapter ended by demonstrating that the monetary fiscal policy controversy is not very fundamental and really reflects a minor squabble between mainstream liberals. It is a minor squabble because, as was shown, it is possible to coordinate monetary and fiscal policy to meet economic objectives without determining the relative effectiveness of either policy. It is a squabble between mainstream liberals because by the very underlying assumptions of the model, laissez-faire (conservative), left-liberal, and marxian views are ignored. By assuming that government intervention is required and can be effective, the laissez-faire position is implicitly rejected.

By its choice of underlying assumptions, the Hicksian IS-LM framework was able to ignore left-liberal and radical viewpoints:

1. The IS-LM framework emphasizes the individualistic model of capital spending. Unlike either left-liberal or marxian investment models, the individualistic model implies that changes in capital spending reinforce equilibrating tendencies and are sensitive to money market conditions. Both left-liberal and marxian investment models ignore money market effects and instead imply that fluctuations of capital spending are the primary determinant of business cycles.

2. The IS-LM framework assumes that income distribution has no effect on aggregate spending. Hence, it can ignore the possibility that incomes policies are a necessary part of government intervention (left-liberal position).

This chapter briefly discussed that dropping assumptions MP2 and MP3 would have increased the interest rate sensitivity of the LM schedule, thus weakening the case for monetary policy and strengthening the case for fiscal policy. Chapter 11 will pursue these and other points which relate to the monetary-fiscal debate. This chapter also demonstrated how downward price flexibility can potentially compensate for any spending shortfall. Chapter 12 will indicate the underlying process by which price deflation could occur.

CHAPTER ELEVEN

MONETARY VERSUS FISCAL POLICY RECONSIDERED

The last chapter briefly highlighted the major issues in determining the effects of money variables on equilibrium income. It began by assuming that prices were not sufficiently downward flexible to warrant total reliance on private market mechanisms. It noted that as long as the demand for money and the money velocity were unchanged by interest rate changes, the money supply is the *only* determinant of equilibrium income. Hence, the monetary policy advocacy position was derived from a subset of the assumptions underlying the classical model. However, once it was assumed, through Keynes' speculative demand, that the demand for money could be interest elastic, it was shown that the relative effectiveness of monetary and fiscal policy was dependent upon the slopes of the IS and LM schedules. The chapter concluded by noting that as long as the money multiplier ($M_m = V$) and the simple income multiplier ($M_y = 1/1 - MPSP$) are known, then the coordination of monetary and fiscal policy can be used to reach given equilibrium income objectives even though the portion of the total effect attributable to either policy is unknown. This last result undercut the importance of the monetary-fiscal policy controversy.[1]

There are, however, some reasons for going into the issues surrounding the monetary-fiscal policy controversy. First, while ideally it can be argued that monetary and fiscal policy can be effectively coordinated, there is currently no mechanism to easily accomplish this. At present, monetary policy is administered by the Federal Reserve Board, while fiscal policy is administered by the actions of Congress. Besides the difference of opinion between these two groups, we have found a potentially large difference in timing. Whereas

---

1. Paul Davidson claims that the essential aspect of Keynes' monetary theory was that speculative demand was highly erratic rather than a stable function of the interest rate. If it is a stable function of the interest rate, then V is also a stable function of the interest rate; i.e., at any interest rate V is known. However, if speculative demand is erratic, then V will be erratic and the money multiplier will be erratic.

the Federal Reserve actions are continuous, the Congressional process is a slow bureaucratized and factionalized undertaking. Therefore, it is understandable why on a theoretical level the controversy can be dismissed, but on a practical level it cannot. It is also understandable why those economists who believe monetary policy is highly effective continue to urge *reliance* on monetary policy.

Second, while both policies can be used to change the level of equilibrium spending, they may have different effects on subcategories. Specifically, monetary policy may increase capital spending more and household spending less than would an equally effective tax cut. Also, though the level of total spending could be the same, they may have different effects on the level of employment and the distribution of income. For these reasons, this chapter will detail the debate within the economics profession over the relative effectiveness of monetary and fiscal policy.

11.1 DEVELOPMENTS IN THE DEMAND FOR MONEY

Extensions of the Keynesian Speculative Demand

Keynes argued that the demand for money should include a speculative component that is interest rate sensitive. Through this vehicle, Keynes was able to argue that the demand for money was interest rate sensitive. One criticism of Keynes' speculative motive contended that the assumption of a *normal rate* was not meaningful. In general, most investors would consider the current interest rate the best estimate of the future interest rate, so that consols would always be chosen and no speculative demand would exist. Moreover, the simple version of the speculative demand described in Chapter 10 implied that each individual would have all his wealth in either consols or cash, whereas most studies find that individuals keep some money in each.

James Tobin[2] has demonstrated that with a slight variation the assumption of a normal interest rate can be eliminated and that individuals will adjust their portfolios incrementally between consols and cash as the interest rate varies. Tobin, responding to the first criticism, assumed that investors expect the interest rate to remain the same. Accordingly, expected income increases by the interest earned on the consols. For example, suppose that the interest rate is 10% and the individual investor has income of $100 to allocate between consols and idle cash. For each $1 of consols purchased, his expected income increases by $0.10. While the marginal income from a purchase of an additional unit of consols is constant (in this example at 10¢), the marginal benefits in satisfaction (MB in Figure 11.1a) to the investor is decreasing. This occurs since, according to the law of diminishing marginal utility, as income increases its value lessens.

2. James Tobin, "Liquidity Preference as Behavior Towards Risk," *Review of Economic Studies* 25 (Feb. 1958): 65–86.

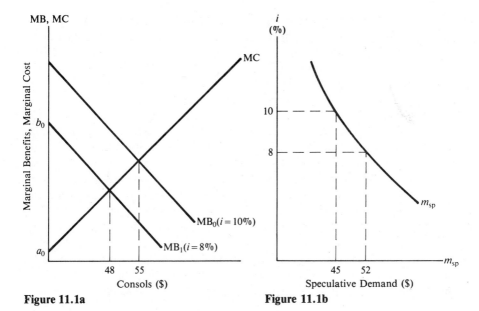

Figure 11.1a   **Figure 11.1b**

Figure 11.1   Household financial asset distribution

Tobin assumed that individual investors are risk averters. That is, if given a choice between a fixed amount of money with certainty or an *expected* value of the same amount, the investor would always choose the fixed amount.[3] The logic behind this assumption of risk aversion is also the law of diminishing marginal utility. It indicates that the potential gains from the possibility of receiving more than the fixed amount are valued less than the potential losses of receiving less than the fixed amount.

---

3. For example, suppose an individual is offered the following choices: (a) receive $100, or (b) pick from two envelopes—one containing $50 and the other $150. Option (b) has the same expected money as option (a) since there is a 50% probability of receiving $50 and a 50% probability of receiving $150; i.e., expected money, $E_b = \frac{1}{2}(50) + \frac{1}{2}(150) = 100$. This does not necessarily mean that the individual would consider the two options to be equivalent. While both options have the same expected money, option (b) has variability and, hence, risk associated with its choice. Suppose that our individual's preference function is subject to the law of diminishing marginal utility—each additional unit of money is worth less and less. For example, suppose that the first additional $50 is worth 80 units of satisfaction; the second $50 is worth 70 additional units; and the third $50 is worth only 50 units of additional satisfaction. In this case, option (a) would be valued at 150 additional units of satisfaction $(80 + 70)$. Option (b) would be valued at 80 if $50 was selected and at 200 $(80 + 70 + 50)$ if $150 was selected. Therefore, the expected *value* of option (b), $E_v = \frac{1}{2}(80) + \frac{1}{2}(200) = 140$. This individual would, therefore, wish to avoid the variability and choose option (a). This indicates that if an individual's preference function is subject to the law of diminishing utility, then this individual would be a "risk averter."

Returning to the decision of how many consols to purchase, the assumption of risk aversion implies that the purchase of consols involves a cost due to risk. With each additional consol more of one's income is subject to variability and hence, the risk increases. Following the law of diminishing marginal utility, we can assume that the purchase of additional consols increases risk at an increasing rate so that the marginal cost of each additional consol is increasing (MC in Figure 11.1a).[4]

The individual would buy additional consols as long as the marginal benefits (value of additional expected interest payments) outweighed the cost of bearing additional risk. According to Figure 11.1a, the individual investor would allocate $55 to consols since after this point the value of additional interest payments was less than the cost of the additional risk. Therefore, when $i = 10\%$, $45 would be allocated to idle balances (Figure 11.1b).

The next step in Tobin's analysis was to determine the effect on an individual's decision if the market rate of interest changed. Suppose that the market interest rate fell to 8%. According to Tobin, since each consol would now earn less interest, the additional value of purchasing consols would decline. This is represented by the shift to the left of the marginal benefit schedule

---

4. Suppose that an investor has $100 to allocate between a consol and cash. Suppose that he can buy consols in $20 lots. Let us assume that each consol has a 50% probability of being worth $10 when sold, and a 50% probability of being worth $30 when sold. Therefore, while the consol has no expected capital gains or losses when sold, it does entail risk. Suppose our investor's preference function is indicated below:

Income	50	60	70	80	90	100	110	120	130	140	150
Satisfaction	400	470	530	580	620	650	675	695	710	723	735
Marginal Utility		70	60	50	40	30	25	20	15	13	12

As the marginal utility row indicates, the preference function is subject to the law of diminishing marginal utility.

Suppose that the investor chose no consols. His income would be maintained at $100 and its value would be 650. However, if the investor bought one consol—keeping $80 in idle balances—his income would be $90 if the consol sold at its low value, or $110 if it sold at its high value. He therefore has a 50% probability of 620 and a 50% probability of 675, or an expected value, $E_1 = \frac{1}{2}(620) + \frac{1}{2}(675) = 647\frac{1}{2}$. The investor would therefore associate the purchase of the first consol with $650-647\frac{1}{2} = 2\frac{1}{2}$ units *cost*.

Suppose that the investor decided to purchase a second consol—only keeping $60 in idle balances. Since the $40 of consols has a 50% probability of being worth $20, and 50% probability of being worth $60, the investor's income would be either worth $80 or $120, depending upon the sale price of the consols. His expected value would be $E = \frac{1}{2}(580) + \frac{1}{2}(695) = 637\frac{1}{2}$. Therefore, the purchase of a second consol lowers his expected value of income by 10, from $647\frac{1}{2}$ to $637\frac{1}{2}$. Using the same procedure, the expected value of income declines to 620 with the purchase of a third consol; to $596\frac{1}{2}$ with the purchase of a fourth consol; and to $567\frac{1}{2}$ with the purchase of a fifth consol. Therefore, the marginal cost of each consol purchased rises; $17\frac{1}{2}$ for the 3rd; $23\frac{1}{2}$ for the 4th; and 29 for the 5th.

(from MB_0 to MB_1 in Figure 11.1a). At a lower interest rate the cost of bearing risk should not be substantially effected.[5] Therefore, with a decline in the marginal benefits uncompensated by a decline in the cost of bearing risk, the purchases of consols would decline. By inference, the demand for idle balances would increase to $52 as the interest rate declined to 8%.

Through this approach, Tobin was able to maintain the inverse pattern between speculative demand for money and the interest rate without making some assumption concerning a normal rate of interest (Figure 11.1b). Also, his model explained adjustments in portfolios of investors who placed some of their assets in both consols and idle balances.[6]

Interest Sensitive Transaction Demand[7]

In recent years, most mainstream economists have discarded Keynes' speculative demand for money as being the most significant reason for the interest sensitivity of money demand. They claim that with many shortterm financial instruments available, it is no longer necessary to hold idle balances if the objective is to avoid risk.[8] Instead, they have developed an alternative explanation of why the demand for money is interest rate sensitive. This currently dominant approach suggests that money demand for transaction purposes is interest sensitive.

Let us assume that the only demand for money is for transaction purposes, and that each individual is aware of the actual timing of his income and his required payments. Specifically, let us assume that an individual is paid $900 once each month and has a spending stream of $30 per day. Assuming 30 days in each month, our individual has no savings.

If the individual chose to keep all his funds in his checking account then, as Figure 11.2a indicates, his average daily balance would be $450. This average balance is his transaction demand for money. Instead, suppose the individual chose to place only $450 in his checking account on the first day of the month and place the other $450 in an interest-bearing asset. Given the spending stream, the individual's checking account would be depleted at the end of the 15th day of the month. At that point, he must transfer the other

---

5. It is possible that at a different interest rate the slope of the MC schedule could change.

6. Of course it is still possible for some individuals to keep all their wealth in either cash or consols. For example, if an investor was such a risk averter that his MC schedule is above b_0 (Figure 11.1a), then he will hold all his funds in cash if the interest rate is below 8%.

7. W. J. Baumol, "The Transactions Demand for Cash . . . ," *Quarterly Journal of Economics* 66 (Nov. 1952): 545–556.

8. Risk occurs only when you must sell a bond before its maturity date. As long as you can wait 90 days, you have no risk associated with the purchase of a 90-day Treasury bill.

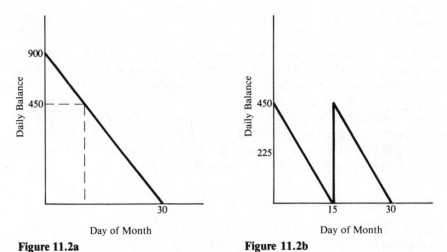

Figure 11.2a   Figure 11.2b

Figure 11.2   Daily checking account balances

$450 from the interest-bearing account to the checking account. This alternative allows the individual to have $450 earning interest for 15 days, or 6675 dollar-days.[9] As Figure 11.2b indicates, this alternative results in an average checking account balance and, hence, transactions demand of $225 per day.

Suppose he chooses to keep only $300 in his checking account and $600 in an interest-bearing account. He would only have enough funds in the checking account to transact 10 days of spending. On the 11th day he could again place $300 in his checking account by reducing the funds in his interest-bearing account. On the 21st day he would have to transfer the remaining interest-bearing funds to his checking account. If this procedure were followed, the individual would have had $600 in an interest-bearing account for 10 days, and $300 in an interest-bearing account for another 10 days. This is equivalent to 9000 dollar-days. Also, his average daily checking account balance would have been $150.

In general, as the number of transfers increases, the additional dollar-days of interest increase at a decreasing rate. This is shown in Table 11.1. For example, the 3rd transfer only increases the number of dollar-days of interest by 1125.[10] Therefore, for any given rate of interest, the marginal benefits to the investor from additional transfers decreases. If the transfers entail a cost,

---

9. Banks pay a specific interest on daily balances in savings accounts. Therefore, the total interest paid is the daily interest rate times the sum of the daily balances. In our example, our investor has an interest-bearing account balance of $450 for the first 15 days. The sum of the daily balances, $450(15) = 6750$, represents the equivalent funds on deposit for one day, or what is termed the number of *dollar-days of interest*.

10. $675(7\frac{1}{2}) + 450(7\frac{1}{2}) + 225(7\frac{1}{2}) + 0(7\frac{1}{2}) = 10,125.$

Table 11.1

Number of transfers (1)	Amount of each transfer ($) (2)	Average balance ($) (2)	Interval between transfer (days) (3)	Dollar-days of interest (4)	Addtnl dollar days (5)	Addtnl interest $r = .02$ (cents) (6)	Addtnl interest $r = .06$ (cents) (7)
1	450	225.0	15.0	6000	6000	120.0	360.0
2	300	150.0	10.0	9000	3000	60.0	180.0
3	225	112.5	7.5	10125	1125	22.5	67.5
4	180	90.0	6.0	10800	675	13.5	40.5
5	150	75.0	5.0	11250	450	9.0	27.0

Interest rates are cents/day for each $1 on deposit.

then at some point the additional benefits are no longer larger than the additional cost—making more transfers unprofitable. For example, if the cost of each transfer was 30¢ then, with an interest rate of 0.02¢/day on each $1, only two transfers per month are profitable. The 3rd monthly transfer would only increase interest payments by 22.5¢ which does not cover the cost of the transfer. In this case, the investor would have an average daily checking account balance and, hence, transaction demand of $150.

To illustrate the effect of an interest rate change on the transaction demand for money, let us suppose that the interest rate rose to 0.06¢/day. According to Table 11.1, the investor could now profitably make four transactions per month, thus reducing his transaction demand for money to $90. This demonstrates that there is an inverse relationship between the market interest rate and the transaction demand for money.

The Expansion of Use of Money Substitutes

We have so far defined the money supply as the demand deposits (checking accounts) of commercial banks. When monetary policy is discussed it usually means an attempt by the government to control the size of these demand deposits. Developments in recent years have questioned the assumption that control of commercial bank checking accounts controls the sum of funds available to transact business.[11]

During the last few years there has been an extensive expansion of alternative forms of payment. For example, credit cards have made it possible for individuals to borrow funds for transactions without receiving a formal loan, which would be identified by a demand deposit. Most important, the expanded use of savings account funds as vehicles for direct payment has allowed banks

---

11. N. Kaldor, "The New Monetarism," *Lloyds Bank Review* (July 1970): 1–17.

and businesses to circumvent any restrictions on demand deposits. The expansion of NOW account funds from less than $200 million in 1974 to over $2 billion by 1977 is the clearest example of this. The increasing use of savings account funds as a substitute for checking accounts in commercial banks is also reflected with the expansion of deposits in savings accounts by state and local governments and businesses. The total deposits in savings accounts of these groups in 1975 was less than $500 million, but by the end of 1976 it was close to $10 billion.[12]

These alternatives can be added to the use of commercial paper as a substitute means of payment as methods by which monetary policy can be circumvented. For example, suppose the government desires to limit transactions by reducing the money supply. This would decrease the funds available in commercial banks to make formal loans. However, firms and households, when faced with this contraction, can turn to the alternative forms. Hence, the government's policy, rather than restricting transactions, has just shifted the medium of payment.

One could argue that the government monetary objectives should encompass control over these alternative forms of transactions. However, at this time, this would be technically impractical. The Federal Reserve has enough trouble controlling the sum of demand deposits of commercial banks. To control the size of activities of savings banks or credit cards and overdraft privileges of customers at commercial banks could not easily be accomplished. Besides, any attempt by the Federal Reserve to control these alternative forms would probably only lead to the development of still more alternative forms of near money. Indeed, this has led many leading macroeconomics to argue that unless monetary policy had specific changes in interest rates as an objective, it cannot have predictable effects on real production.

Interest Sensitive Transaction Demand and the LM Schedule

We have seen how the demand for money can be considered interest rate sensitive even if we ignore the speculative motive. The transaction demand may be interest rate sensitive since it is plausible that with higher interest rates individuals will conserve their transaction demand by shifting more funds into interest-bearing accounts and/or using alternative forms for payment. Figure 11.3 illustrates the effect of this transaction demand on the LM schedule.

In Quadrant I we have no speculative motive. Therefore, all of the money supply must be absorbed by transaction demand in order to establish equilibrium in the money market. Recall that if the transaction demand was solely determined by the level of spending, such as schedule m_t^0, then the LM schedule would be LM_0, which is perfectly interest rate inelastic. However, suppose the

---

12. S. M. Goldfeld, "The Case of the Missing Money," *Brookings Papers* (1976): 720–721.

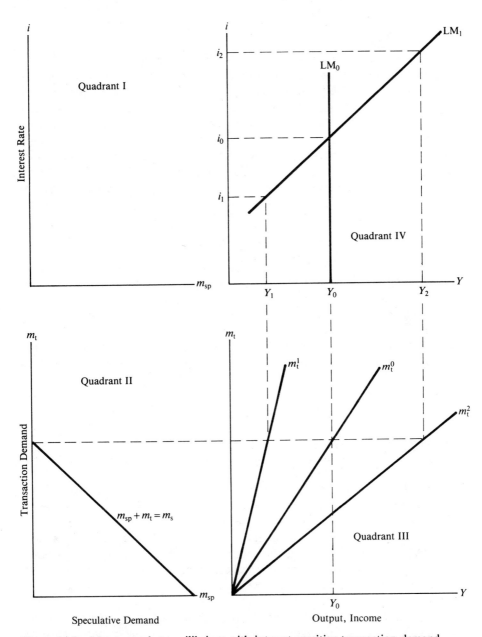

Figure 11.3   Money market equilibrium with interest sensitive transaction demand

m_t^0 is only the transaction demand schedule when the market interest rate is i_0. If the market interest rate declines to i_1, then at each level of Y transaction demand would be greater since it would no longer be as profitable to either make as many transfers between savings accounts and checking accounts and/or to use money substitutes. This is reflected in the shifting of the money demand schedule to m_t^1. Given m_t^1, equilibrium Y would only be Y_1.

On the other hand, suppose that the interest rate rose to i_2. According to the previous analysis, individuals would find it financially worthwhile to make more transfers between interest-bearing and checking accounts, thus reducing their transaction demand for money. Similarly, some individuals would now find it financially worthwhile to shift more of their transactions to money substitutes. Therefore, at each level of Y the transaction demand for money would be reduced. This is reflected by a shift of the money demand schedule to m_t^2 and the equilibrium income to Y_2. This indicates that the LM schedule becomes interest rate sensitive if the transaction demand for money is interest rate sensitive (LM_1 in Quadrant IV).

11.2 DEVELOPMENTS IN THE SUPPLY OF MONEY

Recall that one of the underlying assumptions in Chapter 10 was that the money supply was not influenced by the interest rate. The money supply was assumed to be determined by two factors: (1) the cash (reserves) held by banks, and (2) the reserve requirement. This view is correct only if banks are always desiring to be completely loaned up (making all the loans they are legally allowed). If we look closely at the decision-making process of the banking community, it is not at all obvious that banks would be willing to completely loan up at all times.

The Banking Firm Theory

A banking decision should be analyzed as any firm decision by comparing the marginal cost to the marginal revenues from each additional dollar loaned. Figure 11.4a depicts the marginal schedule for a typical banking firm. The MR schedule indicates that at the going market interest rate the firm believes that it can make any amount of loans desired. One marginal cost component of the banking firm is the transactions costs which are fixed per dollar loaned, represented by MC_t. The other component, represented by the marginal risk schedule, MC_r, is upward sloping, indicating that each additional dollar loaned entails higher risk.[13] Together they indicate that the marginal cost schedule, MC, is upward sloping. Given these factors, each typical firm makes loans equal to I_0.

Assuming a given number of identical firms, we can construct the industry supply curve, SS' in Figure 11.4b. Combining with the demand curve for dollars loaned, DD', we obtain the equilibrium dollars loaned and the interest rate on loans. Only if the money supply allows loans less than the equilibrium quantity, L_0, can government monetary policy be effective. For example, if the money supply allowed L_1 in loans, then the banking system would have excess

---

13. Due to less secure loans or diminishing marginal utility argument.

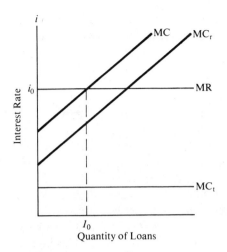

Figure 11.4a   Individual bank

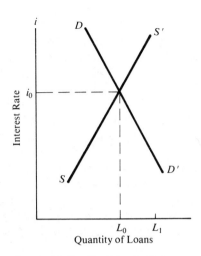

Figure 11.4b   Banking industry

reserves. In this case, changes in the money supply would only be reflected in changes in the excess reserves. There would be no change in the supply of loans.[14]

Similar results can be obtained if we assume a monopolistic rather than a competitive banking industry structure. This seems relevant, given the information on the concentration of commercial banking funds and the fact that many areas have limited competition between banks. If monopoly elements existed, each banking firm's marginal revenue schedule would be downward sloping. Suppose that the demand curve was generally interest rate inelastic. A monopoly bank facing such a demand curve would be discouraged from attempting to attract additional borrowing since it is better to make existing loans at the current interest rate than a larger volume of loans at the necessary lower interest rate. In this case, regardless of the marginal cost of making loans, there would be a limitation on the volume of loans, made by a monopoly bank. As in the competitive banking firm model, this indicates that there are natural limitations on the volume of banking loans independent of government restrictions.

This analysis is particularly relevant during deep recessions when the risk of default is substantial and many banks begin to have sizable excess reserve. In general, the more widespread excess reserves, the less responsive the bank

---

14. This analysis indicates that whenever excess reserves exist for an *individual* bank, monetary policy is ineffective. However, if we drop the assumption that all banks in the industry have identical cost and benefit schedules, then at any point in time it is possible to have some banks with excess reserves and others completely loaned up. Hence, some banks may be effected by monetary policy while others may not. Therefore, the implication is that the more widespread excess reserves are, the less effective is monetary policy. Since excess reserves are more widespread during recessions, this indicates that during recessions monetary policy is less effective.

loan policy is to monetary policy. If all banks had excess reserves, then monetary policy would be ineffective as only the size of each bank's excess reserves would be affected by monetary policy.

Banking Speculation and the Supply of Money

The previous analysis assumed that the risk of default was substantial, and that it eventually results in the limitation of banking loans, possibly before the legal maximum is reached. However, suppose that the risk of default is insignificant. In this case, the only direct marginal cost of a loan would be the constant administrative cost. As long as this cost is below the market interest rate, then it would seem that the banks would make all legally allowable loans.

However, there still might be some reason to hold excess reserves. Banks are not only interested in profits, but in earning *maximum* profits. Suppose that the interest rate is 5% while the transaction costs total to 4%. This implies that the firm can expect to earn 1% on the total volume of loans it makes. But what if the bank had waited a few weeks and the interest rate rose to 6%? The banking firm could then have made loans on which its earning would have doubled to 2% of the volume. This implies that for *speculative* purposes, banks may decide to hold onto excess reserves. Specifically, according to the Keynesian speculative motive, if banks believe the interest rate is going to rise, they would restrict the current loans made in expectation of even greater profits in the future.

The Tobin framework, which generalized the Keynesian speculative motive, becomes completely applicable to the loan decisions of banks. The bank must weigh the expected profits on additional loans against the increased variability of income (profits) by making these loans. A decline in the market interest rate lowers the additional profits from loans and, hence, some existing loans no longer cover the risk from income variability. Therefore, at lower interest rates, the banking system will shift resources from loans to free (excess) reserves.

Positive Relationship Between the Interest Rate and Money Supply

Both of these models imply that normally there is a positive relationship between the interest rate and the money supply. The banking firm theory contends that when the economy contracts, the demand for loans declines, thereby lowering bank profitability, and hence, the supply of loans. In this case, the decline in the interest rate is accompanied by a decline in the money supply. The speculative theory contends that when the interest rate declines, banks shift funds to excess reserves in anticipation of speculative gains if the interest rate subsequently rises.

The inclusion of an interest sensitive money supply into the macroeconomic model increases the interest rate elasticity of the LM schedule. This is

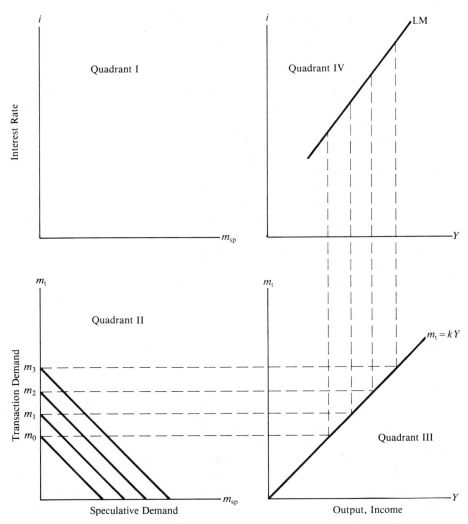

Figure 11.5 Money market equilibrium with interest sensitive money supply

shown in Figure 11.5. Quadrant I is left blank because no speculative demand is assumed. Quadrant III assumes that transaction demand is only a function of the level of income. We know that if the money supply was constant and insensitive to the interest rate, then the LM schedule would be perfectly interest rate inelastic. For example, if the money supply were m_0, then the LM schedule would be LM_0. However, according to the previous analysis, the actual money supply increases with increases in the interest rate. For example, the money supply is m_0 at interest rate i_0, but m_1 at interest rate i_1, m_2 at interest rate i_2, and m_3 at interest rate i_3. In this case, the LM schedule, LM_1, is interest elastic.

The Money Supply and International Capital Movements

The discussion so far has involved the use of cash reserves by the banking system. It was shown that only if the banking system has an excess demand for loans, is the monetary expansion effective at changing the number of loans and the shortterm interest rate. However, inclusion of foreign adjustments further weakens the ability of government monetary policy to change banking decisions. For example, suppose that the banking system was completely loaned up and the government attempted to limit the supply of funds. The government would sell bonds drawing cash out of the private sector. This would result in less cash and, hence, less loans by the banking system. If we include the foreign sector, we must account for the adjustments they would make to the changing situation in the United States. On the one hand, the restrictive monetary policy would raise U.S. interest rates relative to foreign interest rates. Therefore, some U.S. citizens would no longer find it as profitable to continue purchasing foreign financial securities. Hence, they would transfer their funds back to domestic instruments which would increase the amount of cash in domestic circulation. Similarly, some foreigners would now look favorably on investments in U.S. financial instruments and would shift part of the foreign dollar reserves to the United States. This indicates that at least part of the monetary-induced private cash decline would be offset by the natural movement of funds from abroad into U.S. financial markets. On the other hand, U.S. banks are now more able to borrow from foreign banking interests. If the demand warrants, U.S. banks could further offset Federal Reserve objectives by simply replacing cash reserves used to purchase government bonds with borrowed foreign funds.

A further ramification of the effect of shifting U.S. funds held abroad in response to changes in domestic interest rates is that monetary policy may have a stronger influence on balance-of-payments than on domestic production. That is, if foreign funds can substantially offset Federal Reserve objectives, monetary policy would not have a substantial effect on domestic production. However, the induced transfer of funds directly affects the U.S. balance-of-payments. The preceding analysis indicates that if the Federal Reserve undertakes a monetary contraction, its policies are offset by shifting of funds from abroad to U.S. financial instruments. The shifting of funds improves the U.S. balance-of-payments.

On the other hand, if the Federal Reserve undertook a monetary expansion, the primary effect would be to worsen the U.S. balance-of-payments. A monetary expansion would lower domestic interest rates creating a shift of funds abroad. Supply outflows would offset the government's attempt to increase the domestic money supply. Since the actual money supply and domestic interest rate would be little changed, domestic production would not be substantially affected. However, the resulting outflow of funds would worsen the U.S. balance-of-payments picture.

This analysis indicates that if we ignore the subsequent effects of changes in the balance-of-payments on the domestic economy, the banking system can substantially offset the objectives of the Federal Reserve.[15]

11.3 SPENDING AND THE INTEREST RATE

Investment

So far we have been assuming that one interest rate exists. In reality there are at least two important interest rates—the shortterm and the longterm. Capital spending projects are usually longterm with substantial losses to corporations if they are abandoned.[16] The relevant comparison for a firm is, therefore, between the longterm interest rate and the projected net revenues of the investment project. For example, suppose a current investment project that has an income stream over a 20-year period is only profitable when the interest rate is below 10% a year. Suppose that the shortterm interest rate is used by the firm as the relevant interest rate. Let us assume that the firm decision is based on the shortterm interest rate, which is currently 8%. The firm would borrow the funds in the shortterm market to finance the project. Now suppose that the shortterm rate rises the following year to 15%. Our investor is forced to pay higher interest rates on the borrowed funds when the shortterm loan must be refinanced. Since the firm has already bought the capital goods—plant and equipment—which cannot be resold without a substantial loss, the firm is now locked into a losing operation if in subsequent years the shortterm rate remains above 10%. If instead, the firm had used the longterm interest rate as the relevant measure, this problem would be avoided. Only when the longterm interest rate falls below 10% would the firm borrow by floating a 20-year bond. In so doing, the risk of being forced to refinance the capital spending at a higher interest rate is avoided.

The distinction between shortterm and longterm interest rates is critical for two reasons. First, monetary policy affects the shortterm rate. Its effect on longterm rates is dependent upon the interaction between the two rates. If a decline (increase) in the shortterm rate would induce a comparable decline (increase) in the longterm rate, then monetary policy would have a predictable outcome on the longterm interest rate. However, the effect of changes in the shortterm rate on the longterm rate is lagged and volatile. In this case, the out-

---

15. There will be secondary effects depending upon whether currency is regulated by fixed or flexible exchange rates. Under restrictive assumptions, if exchange rates are flexible, the inflow of funds (by raising the value of the dollar) would reduce U.S. exports. In this case, the attempt by monetary policy to restrict spending would still be effective.

16. If capital goods are highly specialized and have heavy transportation costs (when moved to an alternative location), then they will have substantially reduced value when resold.

come of monetary policy on longterm rates is neither rapid nor highly predictable.[17] If real spending is influenced by the longterm interest rate, this implies that monetary policy would have a highly unpredictable effect on equilibrium income.

Second, it is generally accepted that the interest elasticity of the transactions demand for money depends upon which interest rate the model includes. Specifically, most studies find that the transaction demand has a *small* elasticity with respect to *shortterm* rates and a *large* elasticity with respect to *longterm* rates. Figure 11.6 illustrates the importance of this distinction by specifying two LM curves, $LM_0(i_S)$ and $LM_0(i_L)$, which relate money market equilibrium to shortterm and longterm interest rates, respectively. $LM_0(i_S)$ is steeper than $LM_0(i_L)$ if we assume that the money demand is more elastic with respect to the longterm than the shortterm interest rate.

The IS curves in the diagram, IS_0 and IS_1, both relate equilibrium spending to the longterm interest rate. In this case, the *correct* effect of a fiscal

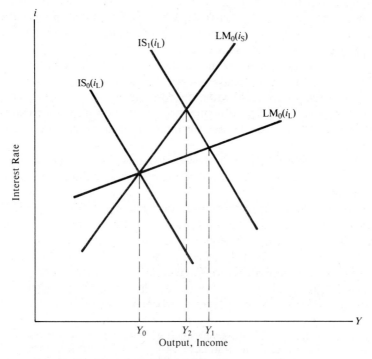

Figure 11.6   Effectiveness of fiscal policy with respect to changes in the shortterm and longterm interest rate

17. For a recent study which argues that the response of the longterm interest rate to changes in shortterm rates is rapid and predictable, see Frederic S. Mishkin, "Efficient-Markets Theory: Implications for Monetary Policy," *Brookings Papers* (1978): 707–752.

stimulus, which shifts the IS curve from IS_0 to IS_1, would be to increase equilibrium income from Y_0 to Y_1. If market conditions in the money market were incorrectly specified by the shortterm interest rate, $LM_0(i_S)$, then we would have underestimated the economic effect of the fiscal stimulus. In that case, we would have predicted an expansion to only Y_2—the intersection of IS_1 and $LM_0(i_S)$. Benjamin Friedman finds that when the longterm interest rate is used, fiscal policy is very powerful while monetary policy has only a weak effect on equilibrium income.[18]

Households Spending

Chapter 6 noted that, according to the Life Cycle Hypothesis (LCH), lowering the interest rate induces household spending because at lower interest rates:

1. The value of wealth increases, thereby stimulating current household spending.

2. The rate of return on financial investments declines, making investments in durable goods more advantageous.

Chapter 9 (Figure 9.5) indicated that its inclusion increases the interest rate sensitivity of the IS curve, increasing the effectiveness of monetary policy and weakening the effectiveness of fiscal policy. Some economists believe that even if the other criticisms of the monetary policy advocacy position are valid (interest sensitive demand and supply of money, interest insensitive capital spending), household spending is so interest sensitive that this factor alone is sufficient to tip the balance in favor of monetary policy.[19] Since this viewpoint has become so influential, it is important to evaluate it more closely.

Wealth effects on consumer spending Chapter 6 suggested that household consumption was directly related to the value of household wealth. If the value of wealth increases, then household lifetime income increases. Part of this increased lifetime income would then go to additional current consumption. According to this viewpoint, the government could stimulate current consumption by lowering interest rates. Lower interest rates would cause the price of stocks and bonds to rise. Households would take part of this increased wealth in the form of increased current consumption. Similarly, the government could stimulate current savings by raising interest rates. Higher interest rates would depress stock and bond prices. In response to a decline in wealth, households would cut back their current consumption plans.

---

18. Benjamin J. Friedman, "Crowding Out or Crowding In? Economic Consequences of Financing Government Deficits," *Brookings Papers* (1978): 593–641.

19. This is the position taken by F. Glahe, *Macroeconomics* (New York: Harcourt Brace, 1973), pp. 274–5.

If the only effect of interest rate changes on household lifetime income is wealth, then the above analysis is correct. However, there is another, often more important, effect that changing interest rates has on lifetime income —the future earning power of savings. In particular, lower interest rates, by lowering the earnings of future savings, have a negative effect on lifetime earnings. A numerical example will illustrate this effect. Let us assume that a household has an objective of attaining a retirement fund of $200,000 by saving an equal amount yearly for 20 years. In order to eliminate the wealth effect of interest rate changes, let us assume that no savings has occurred. If the interest rate is 10%, the household could fulfill its retirement fund objective by saving $5000 yearly.[20] However, with an interest rate of 8.33%, in order to compensate for the lower earnings of investment funds, the household would have to save $5455 yearly in order to fulfull its retirement fund objective.[21] Thus, if there are no wealth effects, a lowering of the interest rate would induce households to *increase* yearly savings in order to fulfill their retirement fund objective.

This indicates that only if the increase in wealth is more than the decline in future earning power of savings, would households reduce their yearly savings when interest rates decline. For households that have already accumulated a substantial portion of their retirement fund, the wealth effect would be substantial. The loss of future earnings would not be so great. Thus, these households would benefit from the lowering of interest rates, and increase their present consumption. The effects would be entirely different for those households who have only recently begun to accumulate their retirement fund. For these households, the wealth effect is small compared to the loss of future earning power of savings. For these households, a decline in interest rates would result in an increase in yearly savings!

This demonstrates that depending upon the distribution of households between those who are close to fulfilling their retirement fund and those who have recently begun to accumulate their retirement fund, the effects of interest rate changes on *aggregate* consumption could go either way. Therefore, there is no theoretical basis for the contention that due to the effect of interest rate changes on wealth, there is an inverse relationship between present consumer spending and the interest rate.[22]

---

20. If we ignore compounded interest, when an amount X is added each year to savings at an interest rate r, at the end of p years total interest payments $R = (rp/2)pX$, and total financial assets $A = pX + R = (1 + rp/2)(pX)$. In our example, with $r = 0.1$, $p = 20$, and $X = \$5,000$, $R = \$100,000$ and $A = \$200,000$.

21. Here, $A = \$200,000$, $r = 8.33\% = 1/12$, $p = 20$. If $A = (1 + rp/2)(pX)$ then $X = A/p(1 + rp/2) = \$5455$.

22. For further discussion of this point, see Martin Feldstein, "The Rate of Return, Taxation, and Personal Savings," *Economic Journal* 88 (Sept. 1978): 482–87.

Interest rate effects on investment portfolio So far we have assumed that financial assets are the only form a household's retirement fund takes. According to conservatives, households can invest their wealth in both financial and physical assets. The investments in physical assets are composed of durable goods, such as housing. Conservatives contend that a change in the interest rate influences the distribution of a household's wealth between these two assets. Specifically, conservatives contend that an interest rate rise would induce households to increase the share of wealth composed of financial assets. This would seem to imply that an interest rate increase would induce households to increase savings (financial investments) at the expense of additional purchases of durable goods (physical investments).

From this analysis, it would seem as if there must be an inverse relationship between consumption and the market interest rate. A numerical example, however, will demonstrate that this relationship does not necessarily hold. Let us begin by assuming that with a 10% interest rate, our typical household decides to allocate $5000 yearly to both financial investments and purchases of durable goods. Ignoring compounding interest, inflation, and the depreciation of durable goods, this allocation would provide our household with a $300,000 retirement fund at the end of 20 years—$200,000 of financial assets and $100,000 of physical assets. Now suppose that before our household has begun its allocation strategy (so that we can ignore wealth effects), the interest rate rises to 12.5%. In this case, lifetime household income would rise because of the increased earning power of savings. We would expect that this would be reflected in a decision to *increase* the retirement fund so that some of the additional lifetime income is shifted to the retirement years. Also, since financial investments have become more attractive, the household would increase the share of retirement funds held in financial assets above 66.7%.

Martin Feldstein has shown that savings would increase in response to an interest rate rise only if there is a *significant* increase in the desired retirement fund.[23] A numerical example will demonstrate that with a small increase in desired retirement fund, households could still increase their share of retirement funds held in financial assets by lowering their savings and increasing their current consumption. Specifically, suppose in response to the interest rate rise our household decides to increase its retirement fund objective to $318,000. This objective could be accomplished by *raising* yearly household purchases of durable goods by $100 (to $5100), *raising* household purchases of nondurable goods by $100; and *lowering* yearly savings by $200 (to $4800). At the end of 20 years, our household's financial assets would be worth $216,000 and durable goods would be valued at $102,000. Thus, despite lowering yearly savings due to the higher interest rate, the value of financial assets increased sufficiently so that the share of retirement fund held in this form increased to

---

23. Ibid.

$216/318 = 68.0\%$. This indicates that theoretical arguments are not sufficient to prove that there is a positive relationship between household savings and the interest rate.[24]

11.4 EMPIRICAL EVIDENCE

This chapter has developed in more detail the theories which reflect on the interest elasticity of the supply and demand for money and the interest elasticity of business and household spending. Numerous statistical studies have been done to measure the size of each of these four elasticities. From our previous experience with econometric results, we should not expect to resolve conflicting views on the basis of statistical findings.[25] However, there is still some use in presenting some of these results.

Almost all studies have found a significant interest sensitive demand for money. This is particularly true when the longterm interest rate is used.[26] One dramatic illustration of the difference the choice of interest rates makes is found by comparing the results from Stephen Goldfeld's study with Michael Hamburger's study. Goldfeld uses the shortterm interest rate and finds an elasticity of only -0.067. However, Hamburger, using the longterm interest rate, finds the interest elasticity of money demand to be -0.673.[27] Thus, one's perception of the interest sensitivity of the demand for money is dependent upon one's choice of interest rates rather than the quality of the statistical work.

There are a number of studies which indicate that the supply of money is sensitive to the interest rate.[28] This verifies the Keynesian contention that banks will adjust their amount of loans to interest rate changes independent of federal monetary policy instruments. Most Keynesians would argue that these studies underestimate the *potential* interest rate sensitivity of the money supply. They claim that the federal government is aware that the banking community can significantly circumvent monetary policy. Rather than allow this circumvention to occur, which might create major disorganization in the fi-

---

24. This is particularly true when Friedman's conception of permanent income is used. Friedman assumes that permanent income is equal to the future earnings on existing wealth $(Y_p = iW)$. In this case, interest rate induced changes in wealth would have no effect on permanent income and, hence, no effect on household spending.

25. Recall in Chapter 8 the wide range of estimates of the predicted effect of a $1 billion fiscal stimulus.

26. Friedman, "Crowding Out or Crowding In?"

27. Stephen M. Goldfeld, "The Demand for Money Revisited," *Brookings Papers* (1973): 577–638; Michael J. Hamburger, "Behavior of the Money Stock: Is There a Puzzle?" *Journal of Monetary Economics* (July 1977): 265–88.

28. See Robert H. Rasche, "A Review of Empirical Studies of the Money Supply Mechanism," *Review of The Federal Reserve of St. Louis* (July 1972): 11–19.

nancial community, the federal government *accommodates* money supply requirements. Since the banking community is never called upon to resort to its ability to circumvent monetary policy, statistical studies are never able to measure this ability. Indeed, most Keynesians contend that because the federal government is so committed to a policy of accommodation, it is foolish to try to separate the economic effects of monetary and fiscal policy.[29]

Most studies seem to find that certain types of capital spending are sensitive to the longterm interest rate,[30] and that the longterm rate eventually reacts in the same direction as the shortterm rate.[31] Therefore, after a sufficient lag, monetary policy can be effective at changing capital spending. Very few studies, however, have found that this interest sensitivity is sufficient to make monetary policy more effective than fiscal policy.[32]

As already mentioned, there are recent findings that allege a very powerful influence of monetary policy on household spending. Two mechanisms have been proposed: (1) interest rates by affecting the value of household wealth are able to influence household spending decisions, and (2) interest rates influence the distribution of household wealth between financial and physical assets. These hypothesized mechanisms have been measured by determining the statistical relationship between wealth and household spending and the relationship between household spending and the interest rate.

Studies by Franco Modigliani and Frederick Mishkin have found a significant correlation between the value of corporate stocks and the amount of household spending.[33] Since theory does not provide a clear explanation for this relationship, these results have not been widely accepted as verification of the thesis that changes in the value of wealth *cause* changes in household spending. Specifically, it has been argued that this correlation occurs because a third variable—household confidence—influences both stock prices and household spending.[34]

---

29. See Chapter 19 for further discussion of the theory that monetary policy is accommodating.

30. Michael Evans, *Macroeconomic Activity* (New York: Harper & Row, 1970), pp. 433-34; and Friedman, "Crowding Out or Crowding In?" p. 604.

31. Evans, *Macroeconomic Activity,* pp. 191-92.

32. For one study which contends that investment is determined by a shortterm interest rate and finds monetary policy more powerful than fiscal policy, see Robert E. Hall, "Investment, Interest Rates, and the Effects of Stabilization Policy," *Brookings Papers* 1 (1977): 61-103.

33. Franco Modigliani, "Monetary Policy and Consumption: Linkages via Interest Rate and Wealth Effects in the FMP Model," *Consumer Spending and Monetary Policy: The Linkages* (Federal Reserve Bank of Boston, 1971): 9-84; Frederic S. Mishkin, "What Depressed the Consumer?" *Brookings Papers* 1 (1977): 123-64.

34. This explanation and the following example come from Robert J. Gordon, "Discussant," *Brookings Papers* 1 (1977): 165-68.

Imagine the following example. Currently, 1% of all households plan to buy a new car this month, 1% the next month, and so on. Now imagine the nation is shocked by an unexpected event. Instantaneously, the stock market incorporates the news and declines; simultaneously, spending plans are revised downward, so that in each successive month only 0.9% of all households plan to buy a new car. There would be a strong correlation between stock market prices and household spending on durable goods, but the relationship is not one of cause and effect. Both the stock market and household spending reacted to a third variable—the national event. For this reason many economists reject the contention that monetary policy can have a significant effect on household spending through its influence on the value of household wealth.

Studies have also looked directly at the relationship between the interest rate and household savings and spending decisions. A 1976 study by Michael Boskin found that the interest rate had a significant influence on household savings.[35] Specifically, it found that raising the interest rate by one percentage point (say, from 5% to 6%) would raise the national savings rate by one percentage point (say, from 7% to 8%). Thus, if this study is accepted, monetary policy would have a powerful effect on the national spending behavior of households. However, not surprisingly, this study has been subject to substantial criticism. Phillip Howrey and Saul Hyman find that Boskin's results are sensitive to the measure of savings and interest rate used, as well as the years studied.[36] In their own study, they find that the interest rate has no significant effect on savings for a wide variety of measures of savings and interest rates.[37] Therefore, they regard Boskin's finding of a statistically significant relationship between savings and the interest rate as faulty, and believe it should be disregarded.[38]

So far we have been discussing the relative effects of monetary and fiscal policy on production. Michael Evans notes, however, that there are additional factors which should discourage government reliance on monetary policy. First, whereas a tax cut will immediately raise aggregate spending, monetary policy takes more than a year to affect the economy. Monetary policy only slowly affects the longterm interest rate, and then there is a delay until capital investment plans are actually implemented. Therefore, fiscal policy can be more effective in the shortrun than monetary policy. Second, and much more important, are the effects of each on income distribution and employment. Evans contends that monetary policy, while it expands production, results in a

---

35. Michael Boskin, "Taxation, Savings, and the Rate of Interest," *Journal of Political Economy* 86 (Apr. 1978, pt. 2): S3–S27.

36. E. Phillip Howrey and Saul H. Hymans, "The Measurement and Determinant of Loanable-Fund Savings," *Brookings Papers* 3 (1978): 666.

37. Ibid., p. 672.

38. Boskin vehemently rejected the criticisms made by Howrey and Hymans. For his response, see Michael Boskin, "Discussant," *Brookings Papers* 3 (1978): 694–97.

redistribution of income in favor of wealth holders and causes a decline in employment.[39] On the one hand, if the induced capital spending went for expansion of productive capacity, this investment leads to overcapacity which reduces GNP and, hence, employment in the future. On the other hand, if the capital expansion results in a substitution of capital for labor, the implications are again not encouraging for labor. Evans estimates that for these reasons, the overall effect of a monetary expansion on employment is *negative*. He notes that corporate earnings would continue to grow, for owing to the weakening of their bargain power, labor cannot get a full share of increased production. Hence, monetary policy can expand output and corporate earnings while increasing unemployment.

11.5 CONCLUSION

This chapter completes the inquiry into the United States version of Keynes' macroeconomics model. It traced some of the post-World War II developments of mainstream macroeconomics. The evidence seems to weigh heavily against the monetary policy advocacy position. During the last thirty years, most studies have found that the demand for money is significantly interest rate sensitive. Not only has Keynes' speculative motive been used to explain these findings, but also the effect that interest rate changes have on the allocation of funds between checking accounts and interest-bearing accounts and the allocation of payment between money and money substitutes (near money). Similarly, there has been an increased interest in the interest sensitivity of the money supply. It has been found that the size of excess reserves of the banking system is sensitive to the interest rate. Moreover, with the increased international mobility of financial assets, it was demonstrated how monetary policy can be completely offset by international dollar movements. For these reasons the effects of monetary policy on shortterm interest rates may not always be significant.

The second aspect of the transmission mechanism—the effect of interest rate changes on real spending—was explored. We found that capital spending is influenced by the longterm rather than by the shortterm interest rate. Also, studies have indicated that the transaction demand for money is much more sensitive to movements in the longterm interest rate than to movements in the shortterm rate. Therefore, the LM curve, when the longterm interest rate is used, is substantially more interest elastic than when the shortterm rate is used. This indicates that if the longterm interest rate is the appropriate measure when evaluating the effects of government macro-policies, fiscal policy would be quite effective while monetary policy would be quite ineffective.

---

39. Evans, *Macroeconomic Activity,* pp. 578–79.

Monetary policy advocates have shifted their attention in recent years to the effects of interest rate changes on household spending decisions. Two channels of monetary policy were identified, neither of which seems to be empirically and/or theoretically sound. It is possible that as interest rates on financial assets change, households shift funds from financial assets to the purchase of household durables. However, there is little evidence that this relationship is of significance. As to the alleged transmission of interest rate changes through effects on the value of stocks onto household spending, it has been found both theoretically and empirically wanting. Theoretically, only when wealth changes are greater than the changes in future earnings on savings, should households adjust their present spending inversely to interest rate changes. Empirically, the correlation between household spending and stock prices is not considered convincing. Rather, stock prices and household spending both react to consumer confidence—not to each other.

Finally, even when monetary policy was shown to have some effect on the economy, it was found to be undesirable. Specifically, it was found that an expansion of the money supply can increase production, but at the expense of employment and household income. This occurred because the principal component of the economic expansion was labor-saving capital investment. At lower interest rates, firms are induced to replace labor with capital. While the initial expansion of employment in the capital goods sector outweighs the contract of employment in the consumer goods industries, eventually the reverse is true. Not only does labor employment eventually decline, but due to the weakening of labor bargaining power, labor's share of income declines. Hence, monetary policy, rather than serving the "national interest," favors capital against labor. It is an example of how class conflicts, rather than "national interest," may dictate government economic decisions.

CHAPTER TWELVE

PRICE FLEXIBILITY AND A SELF-CORRECTING ECONOMY

In previous chapters the laissez-faire model has been presented. Advocates claim that no government intervention is required because of the self-correcting mechanisms present in the private sector. Moreover, even if the private sector could not completely correct for unemployment, it should still be relied upon since government intervention is considered unpredictable and destabilizing by laissez-faire advocates. Chapter 10 noted that for a laissez-faire economy to be completely self-correcting, downward price flexibility is necessary. This chapter will demonstrate that a perfectly competitive and smoothly adjusting market system is necessary for downward price flexibility. This chapter will also demonstrate that if labor market impediments exist, then downward price flexibility is not sufficient to guarantee full employment production. Finally, it will indicate how price effects, which adjust the value of household wealth, could affect real spending directly, thus strengthening the laissez-faire viewpoint.

12.1 THE LAISSEZ-FAIRE MODEL

Price adjustment affect both the supply of and demand for production. This section will develop aggregate supply and aggregate demand curves from the laissez-faire perspective. They will indicate that if labor markets and output markets are competitive, price declines will guarantee full employment.

Labor Markets and Aggregate Supply

Laissez-faire advocates assume that the labor market is sufficiently competitive so that each firm must hire according to the value of productivity of each worker. The value of labor, if output markets are competitive, equals the price of output times the increase production resulting from an additional unit of labor. Marginal productivity theory requires more than the assumption that capitalists can measure each workers' productivity, and that this is the sole criterion for determining the workers' value.[1] Marginal productivity theory makes these additional assumptions:

D1—Capitalists decide how much labor to hire at the given market wage rate.

This assumption implies that individual capitalists have no control over the wage rate; that they are "wage takers" just as in the output market a competitive firm is a "price taker." If individual firms have no control over the wage rate, then it is impossible for them to gain from not hiring a worker with sufficient productivity. It would make no sense for an individual capitalist to try to maintain a reserve army of the unemployed.

D2—Each firm is assumed to have a fixed stock of capital so that the only production decision is how much labor to hire at the market wage rate.

This assumption implies that the price of substitutes, such as machines, has no effect on the demand for labor.

Under these assumptions, at any money wage rate, w, regardless of current employment conditions or the cost of alternative inputs, each firm hires all labor whose value is at least equal to the wage rate. At equilibrium, the money wage rate just equals the value of production of the last worker.

$$w = pX_n$$

where

$$X_n = \text{output of the last worker}$$

If we divide both sides by the price level

$$w/p = X_n$$

This states that given the *real* wage rate, w/p, firms hire until the physical production of the last worker, X_n, just equals the real wage rate.

This explains how *each* firm determines its demand for labor. It does not explain how many firms exist. If we assume that competitive industries exist, then the number of firms in each industry will be determined by market demand for the output of each industry. Hence, the *aggregate* demand for labor is dependent upon *aggregate* spending.[2] For example, if aggregate spending declines, then the number of firms in each industry would decrease. Each firm would continue to have the same output and demand for labor. However, the

---

1. Capitalists could, of course, have other objectives, such as race or sex discrimination. We will ignore these possibilities.

2. This assumes that industry adjustments to deviations from normal profits are incorporated into labor market decisions. Only if labor market adjustments are quite rapid, so that longterm industry adjustments can be ignored, is it possible to consider the aggregate demand for labor to be independent of aggregate spending.

aggregate demand for labor would be reduced. This would be reflected by a shift of the aggregate demand curve for labor.

D3—It is assumed that throughout the adjustment process the aggregate demand curve for labor is based upon full employment spending.[3]

According to these assumptions, the aggregate demand curve for labor is determined solely by the physical productivity of labor and does not shift during an adjustment process. At real wage, w_0^* (Figure 12.1), firms can profitably hire L_0 workers. If the real wage declines to w_1^*, firms expand their employment by hiring those additional workers whose productivity was less than w_0^* but at least as large as w_1^*. Employment expands to L_1.

On the supply side we must identify the motivations of workers. Conservative economists make two assumptions:

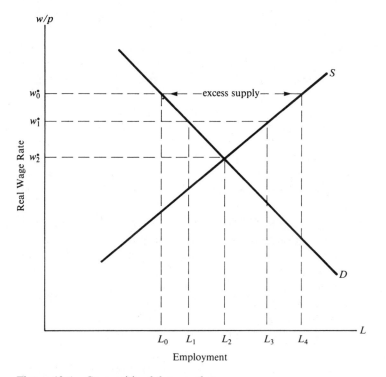

Figure 12.1   Competitive labor market

---

3. A somewhat equivalent assumption is to assume that each firm uses all of its total revenues on production, regardless of current *spending* and prices. This assumes that each firm would absorb any deviation from current spending in inventory changes.

S1—Workers' wage decisions are based solely on their individual choice between income, work, and leisure. These decisions are unchanged by employment conditions.

This assumption implies that even if unemployment occurs, individual workers do not change the amount of labor they would be willing to supply at each wage rate. If this is the case, then bargaining power has no effect on the wages that workers are willing to work for.[4]

S2—Workers are only interested in the purchasing power of their wages. Therefore, they are only interested in the real wage rate offered. If money wage rates and prices declined by the same amount, each household would not change the labor they would be willing to supply.

This assumption implies that workers are not subject to money illusion. Money illusion implies that workers are far more conscious of changes in money wages than prices. If this were the case, then when money wage rates and prices decline by the same amount, workers being more sensitive to money wages, would consider this to be a decline in payment for labor supplied. In response, they would lower the amount of labor they would be willing to supply.

Under these two assumptions, the labor supply curve SS ' in Figure 12.1 is a stable function of the real wage rate. If the real wage rate was w_0^*, the aggregate demand for labor would be less than the desired supply. When more workers are willing to work at the *market* real wage rate than are being hired, we have *involuntary* unemployment. If the real wage rate happened to be w_2^*, then no involuntary unemployment would exist and the market would be in equilibrium.

If the labor market is well working, then adjustments should occur to quickly eliminate any disequilibrium situation. For example, if we begin with real wage rate w_0^*, the excess supply will result in a decline in the market real wage rate. A real wage rate decline to w_1^* would increase employers' labor demand since some less productive workers can now be profitably hired. It also reduces the supply since some workers are no longer willing to work at the market rate. They would rather be *voluntarily* unemployed. For both these reasons, involuntary unemployment is reduced. This process continues until the real wage rate is lowered to w_2^*.

Suppose aggregate spending declined from its full employment level. This would result in a price level decline as producers would face an excess supply

---

4. For theoretical and empirical studies which contend that unemployment rates and bargaining power affect wage rates, see Michael Evans, *Macroeconomic Activity* (New York: Harper & Row, 1970), pp. 263–67.

of output. According to D3, this would not affect the aggregate demand curve for labor. If the money wage rate remained constant, real wages would increase and involuntary unemployment would result. However, if the money wage rate declined so as to maintain the initial real wage rate, w_2^*, full employment equilibrium in the labor market could be maintained.

DEFINITION **The aggregate supply curve depicts the quantity of total production which would be supplied at each price level.**

According to the laissez-faire model, equilibrium in the labor market always occurs, regardless of the price level. Any lowering of the price level would momentarily raise the real wage rate above its equilibrium value. However, excess supply would cause the money wage rate to decline until equilibrium is reestablished. Similarly, a price level rise would generate a compensating rise in the money wage rate. Therefore, the aggregate supply schedule (AgS in Figure 12.2) would always be at full production, regardless of the price level.

Aggregate Demand Curve

DEFINITION **The aggregate demand curve depicts the level of equilibrium spending which occurs at each price level, holding constant monetary and real factors.**

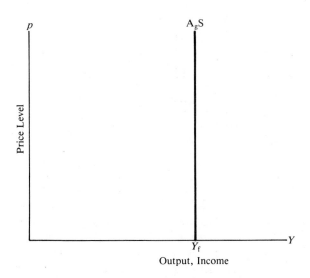

Figure 12.2   Aggregate supply with competitive markets

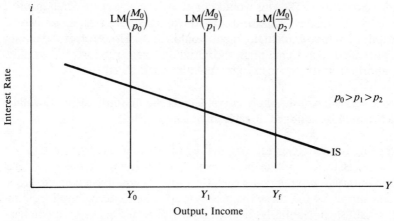

Figure 12.3a   Equilibrium income in monetary policy advocacy model

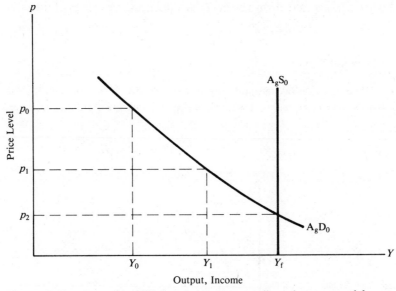

Figure 12.3b   General equilibrium in monetary policy advocacy model

According to the laissez-faire model, equilibrium spending is determined by the real money supply, M_s/p. Figure 12.3a indicates, given $M_s = M_0$ and $p = p_0$, that equilibrium spending equals Y_0, regardless of the spending schedules (regardless of the position of the IS curve). In this model, as the price level changes, holding the nominal money supply constant at M_0, equilibrium spending changes. As we change the price level we can trace out the aggregate demand curve AgD_0 in Figure 12.3b. It indicates that at $p = p_2$, equilibrium spending is Y_f. Since the laissez-faire advocates also assume a perfectly adjusting labor market, the aggregate supply curve is AgS_0. Therefore, downward price flexibility is sufficient to guarantee full employment production will be sustained.

12.2 MAINSTREAM LIBERAL MODELS OF PRICE ADJUSTMENTS

Mainstream liberals believe that output markets are competitive so that price levels would decline at less than full employment. However, they also believe that there are barriers to competitive adjustments in the labor market. Next we will analyze the implication of these mainstream liberal views on the ability of downward price flexibility to generate full employment production.

Aggregate Supply Curve

Mainstream liberals contend that there are institutional factors which limit the ability of money wage rates to decline when the price level declines. It is argued that corporations desiring a stable workforce no longer lower wage rates when contractions occur. These firms fear that such actions would result in the loss of their most valuable skilled workers, who could not be rehired when the subsequent expansions occur. Hence, even if workers are willing to accept money wage rate reductions, management (especially in the larger corporations) would inhibit such actions.[5]

However, it is not necessarily true that workers would accept money wage rate cuts in response to price level declines. They may suffer from money illusion and only be interested in money wages, not real wages. More likely, they would only adjust their *expectations of future prices* slowly to price level declines. Since they negotiate multi-year contracts, workers are concerned with the future price levels, and would base their decisions on expectations rather than current price levels. Because they only adjust their price expectations slowly, they would not lower their money wage demands significantly in response to a price level decline unless it continues for a substantial period of time.[6]

These arguments imply that it is unlikely that most firms would encourage a money wage rate reduction, or that most workers would quickly accept such a reduction when the price level is lowered. For these reasons, mainstream liberals contend that it is best to assume that money wage rates are inflexible downward over extended periods of time.

Suppose that the current money wage rate, w_0, is the minimum amount workers are willing to accept. At the current price level, p_0, the labor supply

---

5. See Arthur Okun, "The Great Stagflation Swamp," *Challenge* 20 (Nov./Dec. 1977): 6.

6. See R. J. Gordon, *Macroeconomics* (Boston: Little, Brown, 1978), Chapter 7 for a fuller treatment of the wage expectations hypothesis.

curve, $S(p_0)$ in Figure 12.4a, is horizontal at the real wage rate w_0/p_0, up until the full employment level L_f. After L_f, firms must raise money wage rates to induce new entrants into the labor force. Given labor demand curve D and labor supply curve $S(p_0)$, equilibrium in the labor market occurs at L_f, which is reflected in full employment production Y_f (Figure 12.4b).

At any higher price level, excess labor demand appears and the money wage rate rises proportionally. Therefore, at any $p>p_0$, adjustments in the labor market continue to sustain full employment production. However, suppose the price level declined to $p_1<p_0$. Since money wage rates do not decline

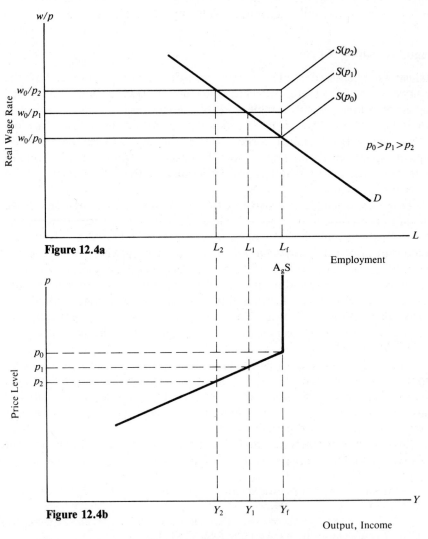

Figure 12.4a

Figure 12.4b

Figure 12.4   Aggregate supply curve with fixed money wage rate

the real wage, minimum rate is raised to w_0/p_1, reflected in labor supply schedule $S(p_1)$. At this price level, labor market equilibrium occurs at L_1 and this reflects real production Y_1. If the price level declines to p_2, the labor supply schedule shifts to $S(p_2)$, employment to L_2, and real production to Y_2.

This process indicates that with inflexible money wage rates, lowering the price level would also lower the level of production. Hence, below the current price level, the aggregate supply schedule, as depicted in Figure 12.4b, is upward sloping.

Aggregate Demand Curve

Most mainstream liberals believe that the LM curve is interest rate sensitive, therefore, they believe both monetary and fiscal variables affect the aggregate demand curve. Let us begin with nominal money supply M_0 and equilibrium goods market schedule IS_0 and trace out the aggregate demand schedule (Figure 12.5a).

At price level p_0, equilibrium spending would be Y_0. Only when prices fell to p_2 would equilibrium full employment spending be generated. Therefore, given M_0 and IS_0, the aggregate demand curve would be AgD_0 (Figure 12.5b). Aggregate supply curve AgS indicates that downward price flexibility is not sufficient to generate full employment. In this case, the price level decline would terminate at p_1, where aggregate supply equals aggregate demand.

Given aggregate supply schedule AgS, it is possible for either monetary or fiscal policy to generate full employment spending at p_0, the lowest price level at which aggregate supply would be at Y_f. For example, given IS_0, LM_1 in Figure 12.5a indicates that full employment spending would be generated at real money supply M_0/p_2. If a money expansion was initiated so that the new money supply $M_1 = M_0(p_0/p_2)$, then full employment spending would occur at price level p_0. Similarly, if fiscal policy shifted the goods market equilibrium schedule to IS_1, full employment spending would occur with M_0 and price level p_0. In either case, the aggregate demand schedule is shifted to the right so as to intersect the AgS schedule at Y_f and p_0.[7]

12.3 CRITICISMS OF THE DEFLATION PROCESS

The process by which increases in the real money supply, acting through interest rate changes, generates an economic expansion is called the Keynes Effect. Both laissez-faire advocates and mainstream liberals content that through the Keynes Effect, full employment spending can be generated by a large enough deflation. They only disagree as to whether or not full employment would be supplied at the deflated price level.

---

7. The new aggregate demand schedule (labeled AgD_1) would differ for each of the policies. However, since both policies would shift the schedule to pass through (Y_f, p_0), the diagram only shows one such schedule.

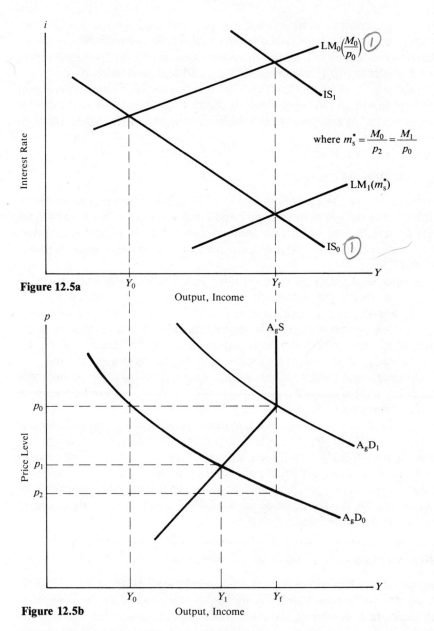

Figure 12.5a

Figure 12.5b

Figure 12.5 General equilibrium with fixed money wage rate

One criticism of this view, attributed to left-economists, is that in certain situations the Keynes Effect is not sufficient to generate full employment spending, regardless of how much deflation occurs. These situations—an interest rate inelastic spending schedule and an effective liquidity trap—are the situations that Keynes claimed existed during severe contractions; just the situations in which neither monetary policy nor deflation could be effective. In the view of many of Keynes' collaborators, these situations, not the Keynes Effect, are the essence of his *General Theory*. These collaborators, known now as the Cambridge Group, believe that emphasis on the Keynes Effect, embedded in the Hicksian IS–LM framework, is really a bastardization of Keynes' own work because it emphasizes the efficacy of private market mechanisms.[8] Therefore, this criticism should be considered the Keynesian criticism of the deflation process.

Left-economists reject the possibility of a significant deflation occurring in the United States. Instead, they contend that lower money wage rates result in higher profit margins rather than lower prices. This redistribution reduces equilibrium spending and, hence, intensifies the contraction. We will now detail the Keynesian and left criticisms of the deflation process.

Keynesian Criticism

Keynes claimed that during contractions, spending is not very sensitive to the interest rate and, therefore, the Keynes Effect is too weak to be relied upon. Suppose the goods market equilibrium schedule is represented by IS_0 (Figure 12.6a). It indicates that there is no positive interest rate at which full employment spending occurs. It implies that factors other than the interest rate determine capital investment. The aggregate demand curve, resulting from IS_0 and nominal money supply M_0, is depicted in Figure 12.6b. Even if the labor market was perfectly competitive, so that full employment production would be supplied at any price level, the economy would have persistent unemployment. Only fiscal policy, by shifting out the IS curve, is capable of generating full employment in this situation.

A second situation in which the Keynes Effect is insufficient to generate full employment is when the liquidity trap does not allow the interest rate to decline sufficiently. Suppose the goods market equilibrium schedule is represented by IS_0 (Figure 12.7a). It indicates that if the interest rate could be lowered to r_0, full employment spending would occur. However, the LM schedules indicate that a liquidity trap exists at r_1, which is greater than r_0. Therefore, regardless of how much price deflation increases the real money supply, it will be absorbed in idle balances at r_1. The maximum spending that a deflation would generate is Y_1 (Figure 12.7b).

The Pigou Effect

It would seem as if there are certain situations in which deflation would not solve the problems of unemployment. However, even in the two situations in which the Keynes Effect is too weak, it is possible for deflation to generate full

---

8. For a fuller discussion of the concept of bastard Keynesian, see Paul Davidson, *Money and the Real World,* (London: MacMillan, 1973), Chapter 1.

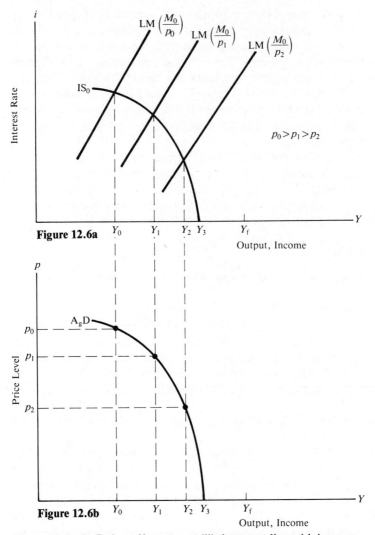

Figure 12.6a

Figure 12.6b

Figure 12.6 Deflation effects on equilibrium spending with interest rate inelastic spending schedule

employment spending. A. C. Pigou claimed that the price level directly affects spending by changing the purchasing power of money held by households. Like the LCH, Pigou claimed that household spending is significantly affected by the real value (purchasing power) of financial assets held. Deflation, by causing interest rates to decline, increases the value of financial assets held and, therefore, induces additional consumption. This is part of the Keynes Effect. However, a deflation increases the value of financial assets, even when the interest rate is unchanged.

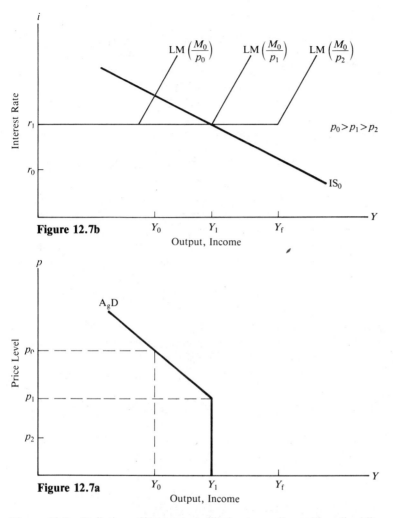

Figure 12.7b

Figure 12.7a

Figure 12.7 Deflation effects on equilibrium spending with a liquidity trap

Suppose a household, desiring a retirement fund of $100,000, began saving $3,000 per year twenty years ago. Let us assume that due to a contraction there is a price deflation of 30%. When this occurs, our household's $60,000 has almost the purchasing power of its $100,000 objective. It is therefore reasonable to assume that this household would reduce its savings rate independent of current income. This would shift the IS curve to the right. In this way, a deflation, by acting directly on the value of financial assets, can shift out the IS curve and potentially generate full employment spending despite a weak Keynes Effect.

Left Criticisms

Most left-liberals and all radicals believe that money wage rates are strongly influenced by the size of the reserve army of the unemployed. In this case, an economic contraction would result in a lowering of money wage demands. Many left economists also believe that market forces are strong enough to lower money wage rates, especially with 80% of the United States labor-force nonunionized.

Suppose we have two labor markets—one which is unionized with money wage rates negotiated in multi-year contracts, and the other is nonunionized where competitive forces dictate shortrun adjustable money wage rates. Let the current price level equal p_0 and the money wage rate in the unionized sector equal w_0. Suppose that full employment initially exists in both sectors—L_0^u in the unionized sector (Figure 12.8a), and L_0^c in the nonunionized sector (Figure 12.8b).

Assume a deflation to p_1 occurs. In the unionized sector, where money wage rates are inflexible downward, the supply curve shifts upward from S_0^u to S_1^u, resulting in lower employment L_1^u and lower production. However, suppose that the excess supply of workers in the unionized sector, $L_0^u - L_1^u$, decide to seek employment in the competitive sector, and as unemployed workers are not subject to money illusion. As a result of this movement, the competitive labor supply curve shifts from S_0^c to S_1^c, and the unionized labor supply curve from S_1^u to S_2^u. In the unionized sector, full employment is reestablished at the higher real wage rate w_0/p_1, while full employment occurs in the nonunionized sector at w_2/p_1. In this case, deflation shifts the labor force toward the nonunionized sector and increases the real wage rate differential between the two labor sectors.

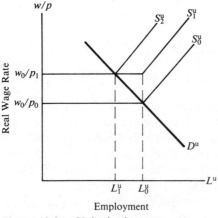

Figure 12.8a Unionized sector

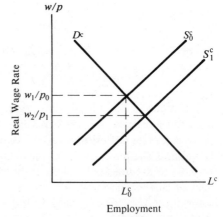

Figure 12.8b Competitive sector

This analysis indicates that as long as some significant section of the labor market is competitive, full employment results through the adjustment of workers from one labor market sector to another. This process is not very rapid. It requires workers to not only change the type of job they expect, but to also relocate where necessary. During the 1970s, this process required shifting employment from the unionized Northeast and Midwest to the nonunionized South; from unionized government employment to nonunionized white collar employment in private industry.

While some lowering of prices may occur in a severe contraction, left-liberals claim the monopoly structure of industry makes the deflation quite mild. Post-World War II data indicates, in fact, that a majority of the less competitive industries and an increasing percentage of the more competitive industries *raise their profit margins during contractions.*[9] The process of rising profit margins during contractions was also found by Kalecki during the Great Depression.[10] Therefore, regardless of the movement of money wage rates, left-economists claim that there is no reason to expect a sizable deflation to occur during an economic contraction.

Income Shares Redistribution

The previous analysis indicates that according to left-economists lower money wage rates would be absorbed in higher profit margins rather than lower prices. This indicates that *if each firm could maintain its sales,* total profits would be higher. However, Chapter 7 indicated that this redistribution would only intensify the contraction, possibly generating a Paradox of Profits.

Let us assume that with IS_0 and M_0, the current price level is p_0. Figure 12.9 indicates that equilibrium income is Y_0. If prices were downward flexible, then p_1 would be sufficient to generate full employment spending. Due to the monopoly structure of industry, left economists claim that prices would only decrease to p_2, and because of the redistribution of income away from wage-earners, the IS curve shifts to IS_1. In this case, the expansionary effects of the meager price deflation are more than offset by the negative effect the process has on aggregate consumption.

12.4 CONCLUSION

This chapter developed aggregate supply and aggregate demand schedules to more fully explain the effects of price level changes on equilibrium spending. Aggregate demand schedules depict the relationship between the price level

---

9. H. M. Wachtel and P. D. Adelsheim, "How Recessions Feed Inflation: Price Markups in a Concentrated Economy," *Challenge* 20 (Sept./Oct. 1977): 6–13.

10. Michal Kalecki, "Cost and Prices," *Selected Essays* (Cambridge, U.K.: Cambridge Press, 1971), especially pp. 50–51.

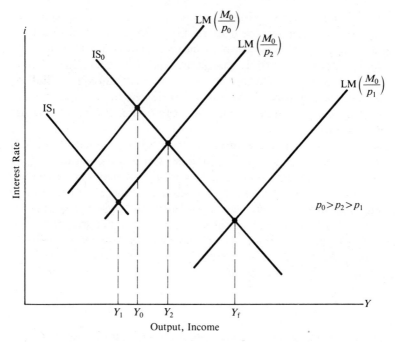

Figure 12.9   Equilibrium income with changes in bargaining power

and equilibrium aggregate spending, while the aggregate supply schedule depicts the relationship between the price level and the total production that businesses are willing to undertake. In the laissez-faire model, because money wage rates are downward flexible in competitive labor markets, full employment production would occur at any price level. If output markets are also competitive, then downward prices would occur at less than full employment spending. Since downward prices increase the real money supply, interest rate declines would result until full employment spending is generated. This is called the Keynes Effect. This deflationary process completed the laissez-faire viewpoint. The complete laissez-faire viewpoint is:

1. Due to the PIH, the M_y is small.

2. Due to the LCH and interest sensitive investment, the M_y^* is even smaller.

3. Government intervention is uncertain and potentially destabilizing.

4. Price flexibility further reduces equilibrium income changes in a laissez-faire economy.

Mainstream liberals do not believe that the deflation process is capable of generating full employment. They claim that because of the inability to reduce money wage rates, production declines during the deflation process and general equilibrium occurs at less than full employment.

Keynes directly attacked the notion that a deflationary process was capable of generating full employment. He emphasized the structural and institutional limitations of the Keynes Effect. First, factors other than the interest rate were considered the principle determinants of capital spending so that the MEI schedule was considered to be interest rate insensitive. Second, Keynes believed that banks would not lower interest rates below some minimum rate. In response, laissez-faire advocates have argued that the deflation process could increase real spending directly by raising the value of wealth. This is called the Pigou or Real Balance Effect.

Left-economists reject the view that a substantial deflation is possible in today's economy. They claim that because of the uncompetitiveness of modern industry, regardless of changes in money wage rates, price levels will not decline significantly during economic contractions. Hence, deflation cannot stimulate the economy and indeed, as the Paradox of Profits (Chapter 8) indicated, declining money wage rates can have a destabilizing effect on the economy.

CHAPTER THIRTEEN

STRUCTURALIST MODELS
OF CAPITAL SPENDING

The individualistic theory of capital spending stresses the wide discretion of firms. It assumes that external funding is always possible so that internal funds (profits) are not an important factor. It assumes that the economy is only subject to short cyclical fluctuations, so that capital spending projects having long gestation periods are not very sensitive to current sales. Whatever the merits of this viewpoint, it totally ignores the effects of technology. Left-liberals, while ignoring the funding problem, and hence the role of profits on capital spending decisions,[1] do emphasize the critical role of technology in determining the timing and rate of capital spending. We will call these models of investment *structuralist* because they emphasize the structural properties of technology.

The three most emphasized properties of technology are: (1) there is a lack of choice among productive technologies available; (2) capital goods are often bulky resulting in uneven timing of production; and (3) capital goods are highly specialized so that once installed on one activity, they are not easily transferable. This chapter will detail three distinct structuralist theories of investment, each emphasizing one of these properties. It will be demonstrated that none of these theories result in capital spending adjustments reinforcing equilibrium tendencies. Instead they imply *predictable* cyclical behavior for the economy. They will characterize the private market economy as being subject to a "boom then bust" process rather than smoothly equilibrating. They also identify longterm trends, which can result in prolonged periods of prosperity and long periods of depression.

13.1 ACCELERATION MODEL

The most widely known structuralist theory of capital spending is the accelerator model. It begins by assuming that there is only one feasible method of pro-

---

1. Throughout this chapter, we will ignore the possibility that external funding may not be available and/or that demands are not profitable.

ducing output which requires a fixed amount of capital per dollar output.[2] In this case, the stock of capital desired would be proportional to the level of aggregate demand. Then at any point in time, $K_0 = \alpha(Y_0)$, where K_0 is the initial desired stock of capital and α the technically determined capital-output ratio which relates the desired stock of capital to the level of output.

If we assume an unchanging capital-output ratio, then the required stock of capital will change in successive periods only with changes in output. Suppose in the next period output rose to Y_1. The required capital to produce the new output would be αY_1 so that the change in capital stock required $K_1 - K_0 = \Delta K = \alpha(K_1) - \alpha(Y_0) = \alpha(Y_1 - Y_0) = \alpha(\Delta Y)$. Recall that net investment (I_n) was defined as the *change* in the capital stock, $I_n = \Delta K$. Therefore, according to the accelerator model,

$$I_n = \alpha(\Delta Y)$$

Gross investment consists of both net investment and replacement investment (I_r). The accelerator model makes some simplifying assumptions concerning replacement investment. First, it is assumed that current replacement requirements are based on capital goods bought a long time ago. If we assume that the current capital stock was bought in a constant fashion many years ago, and that they all have the same useful life, then the replacement investment required would be constant, R. Therefore the investment schedule of the accelerator model is

$$I = I_n + I_r = \alpha(\Delta Y) + R$$

where α and R are technically determined constants.

Effect of Monetary Factors

It should be immediately apparent that monetary factors will have little impact upon the level of capital spending. The individualistic model identifies three areas in which lower interest rates would induce more capital spending and higher interest rates would discourage capital spending. The first area is that of automation. When a firm has two alternative techniques, its choice is dictated by the relative costs of each technique. Since the interest rate has a significant effect on the full price for capital, it is argued that a lower interest rate would encourage the choice of the more capital-intensive technique, while the higher interest rate would encourage the choice of the least capital-intensive technique.

For example, suppose that two different production processes are available. Process I requires 3 machines and 60 hours of labor to produce each unit of output. Production Process II requires 4 machines and 30 hours of labor.

---

2. More specifically, it assumes a fixed ratio between output and required capital inputs, and ignores price changes.

Suppose that the price of labor remains constant at $3 per hour. If the full cost of each machine is greater than $90, then Process I is cost effective. If the full cost of each machine is less than $90, then Process II becomes cost effective.[3] Hence, if the full cost of the machine falls, the firm would shift from Process I to Process II, which increases capital investment. However, by assuming a single fixed process, no such choice is available. The same technique would be used regardless of changes in the relative costs of the inputs.

A second area in which the interest rate was thought to affect the level of capital spending was through the timing of replacement. It was suggested that if the interest rate is lowered, then it might be cost effective to have early replacement of older equipment. Table 13.1 specifies alternative estimations of the productivity of a unit of capital equipment according to its age. Suppose column 2 represents the actual productivity measure. The cost of the equipment would effect the timing of replacement. As the cost of replacement is lowered, it becomes profitable for earlier replacement.[4] Since the interest rate

Table 13.1
Variation in productivity of capital goods with age

Age at beginning of production period (1)	Value of each machine's productivity ($)	
	Actual (2)	Accelerator assumption (3)
1	100	100
2	100	100
3	100	100
4	95	100
5	90	100
6	80	100
7	65	100
8	45	100
9	20	100
10	0	0

---

3. For Production Process I: unit cost $(UC_I) = 3p_M + 60p_L$ and for Production Process II: unit cost $(UC_{II}) = 4p_M + 30p_L$ where p_L = price of unit of labor and p_M = price of unit of machine. If $p_L = 3$, then $UC_{II} - UC_I = 4p_M + 30(3) - [3p_M + 60(3)] = p_M - 90$.
Therefore, $UC_{II} - UC_I \gtreqless 0$ if $p_M \gtreqless 90$.

4. For example, suppose that the cost per period to replace each machine is $40. According to column 2, each machine should be replaced at the beginning of the 7th year.

is one of the major determinants of the full cost of equipment, changes in the rate would affect the timing of replacement. However, according to the accelerator model (column 3), the productive ability of capital equipment does not decline continuously. The equipment maintains its original productive capacity until it wears out instantaneously at the end of its last productive year. In this case, the cost of equipment cannot affect the timing of replacement.

The only area in which the interest rate could affect the level of capital spending according to the accelerator model would be new ventures. It still remains possible that at lower interest rates some new ventures become profitable. However, this area cannot be longterm significant, since at a given level of total spending, if new ventures are profitable they must take sales away from existing activities. If sales are taken away from existing activities, then subsequent capital spending contractions would offset the capital expansion on new ventures.

Policy Implications

Suppose that the government is choosing between a purchase of two different type goods, such as welfare services and airplanes. Our past analysis would seem to indicate that both of these purchases would result in the same autonomous change in spending and, hence, the same eventual change in equilibrium income. However, suppose that the capital-output ratio was higher in the airline industry than in the production of welfare services. If this were true, then government spending on airplanes would stimulate more capital spending than an equal increase in social welfare service spending.

Similarly, suppose the government has a choice between giving a tax cut to two different groups of households, Group P and Group R, each having the same MPC but spending the additional income on different types of goods. For example, Group P would spend the additional income on food, while Group R would spend it on durable goods (cars, washing machines). If durable goods have a higher capital-output ratio than food production, then the tax cut to Group R would have a greater expansionary effect on the economy.

During the 1960s, the population of Florida increased by 300,000 each year. Part of this migration was construction workers who anticipated expanding employment possibilities in a growing area. But does a positive growth rate alone *expand* construction employment possibilities? According to the accelerator model, capital spending, such as construction, is dependent upon the change in aggregate income. Therefore, if the growth rate is constant, so will be the level of capital investment.

In our example, if a new home for every 3 people is required, then the effect of the constant growth of population each year by 300,000 would be to create a *constant* yearly demand for 100,000 new homes. Once the number of construction workers sufficient to build these 100,000 new homes per year have migrated to Florida, then the maintenance of the population growth is required just to maintain the employment opportunity for the existing construction force. A constant growth rate is required to maintain existing construction employment.

Let us now assume that the growth rate in Florida is halved; only 150,000 per year migration rate. In this case, the number of new homes required would decline to 50,000. If the number of new homes is halved, then half of the workforce would be laid off. Here, we find that despite continued growth there are massive layoffs. This results because construction employment is dependent upon the change in economic conditions, not the absolute level.

Workings of the Accelerator[5]

Let us trace the period-by-period economic process. Suppose that the economy has been at $Y=200$ for a number of periods (Table 13.2). If $\alpha=3$, then the desired capital each period equals 600. If this capital was bought at constant intervals and has a useful life of 20 years, then in each period 5% of the capital stock wears out, so that $I_r=(0.05)600=30$.

We begin the process with the economy at equilibrium $Y=200$ for the first two periods. In each of these periods the only capital spending is to replace the worn out capital. When, in $t+2$, the economy expands to $Y=205$, the desired capital stock expands to 615. Since only 570 is available at the beginning of the production period, the firm must purchase 45 of capital goods; 30 for replacement, and 15 of net investment. The capital expansion (30 to 45) accelerates the upturn so that in $t+3$, the economy expands by 15 to $Y=220$. As a result, required gross investment increases 75. In $t+4$, the economy expands by 10, to $Y=230$. Since the change in Y is less than the previous period, the amount of gross investment declines (75 to 60). With declining investment, we would expect the increase in Y to be less than 10 in the following period. If the increase in $t+5$ is only 6, to $Y=236$, then required capital spending declines to 48. The economy continues to expand as the laid-off capital goods workers find jobs in the still expanding consumer goods industries. However, the expansion is dampened still further. In $t+6$, the economy only expands by 4,

---

5. The numbers in Table 13.2 were chosen for illustrative purposes and do not correspond to a specific model. An accelerator model would be represented by:

$$C_t=a+bY_{t-1}, \ I_t=\alpha(Y_t-Y_{t-1})+d, \ Y_{t+1}=C_t+I_t$$

For a given value of the MPC, economic movements depend upon the size of the accelerator term (α):

- For very small values of α, the accelerator is so weak, compared to the multiplier process, that equilibrium tendencies dominate and no fluctuations occur.
- For larger values of α the accelerator is sufficiently strong to create self-generating cycles, as in Table 13.2, but these cycles become progressively smaller. Equilibrium tendencies are still dominant.
- For still larger values of α, specifically $\alpha>1$, the accelerator is dominant so that fluctuations become explosive.

Table 13.2
Workings of the accelerator

Period	Output	Required capital stock	Capital stock available at beginning of period	Gross investment	Net investment	Replacement investment
t	200	600	570	30	0	30
$t+1$	200	600	570	30	0	30
$t+2$	205	615	570	45	15	30
$t+3$	220	660	585	75	45	30
$t+4$	230	690	630	60	30	30
$t+5$	236	708	660	48	18	30
$t+6$	240	720	678	42	12	30
$t+7$	240	720	690	30	0	30
$t+8$	233	699	690	9	-21	30
$t+9$	220	660	669	0	-30	30
$t+10$	210	630	639	0	-30	30
$t+11$	202	606	609	0	-30	30
$t+12$	195	585	579	6	-24	30
$t+13$	192	576	555	21	-9	30
$t+14$	192	576	546	30	0	30
$t+15$	195	585	546	39	9	30

causing required capital spending to contract still further. This time, the still expanding consumer goods industries are just able to absorb the newly laid-off capital goods workers so that in the next period $(t+7)$, production remains constant at $Y=240$. However, since production remains constant, the only capital spending required is replacement investment of 30. Thus, capital spending continues to decline, and this time, since consumer spending is unchanged, there is a decline in aggregate spending to $Y=233$.

The decline in aggregate demand in $t+8$ not only induces further declines in household spending (the multiplier effect), but also further declines in capital spending. In $t+8$, only part of the worn out capital needs be replaced, hence, capital spending declines to 9, and accelerates the downturn. In $t+9$, the economy contracts by 13 to $Y=220$. At this point, there is an excess of capital so there is no need to have any replacement investment. Gross investment declines to 0. In $t+10$, the economy declines by 10 to $Y=210$, so again no capital spending is required. The economy continues to have an excess of 9 in capital.

With capital spending remaining constant at 0, the multiplier indicates that the continued declines will become smaller. In $t+11$, the economy only declines by 8 to $Y=202$. Now the declines are less than the rate at which the capital equipment wears out, so the excess capacity diminishes from 9 to 3. In the following period ($t+12$), the capital stock has worn out sufficiently, therefore, some replacement investment is now required. Since this represents a capital expansion, from 0 in $t+11$ to 6 in $t+12$, the declines in consumer spending are partially offset. The economic contraction is reduced so that in $t+13$ the economy only contracts by 3 to $Y=192$. Again, there is an expansion in required capital spending as 21 of the worn out capital must be replaced. This further expansion of capital spending is now able to completely offset the decline in consumer spending so that in $t+14$ the economy remains stationary at $Y=192$. However, if production remains constant, the entire worn out capital (30) must be replaced. Thus, capital spending continues to expand, and since there are no longer contractions in consumer spending, the overall economy begins to expand.

Investment Theories and Economic Fluctuations

So far, we have isolated three factors which systematically effect capital spending: the market interest rate, the level of Y, and the change in Y. It is certainly possible to build models which incorporate all three factors. The most widely known example is the Jorgenson investment models.[6] However, in almost all models, one factor dominates the investment behavior. In Jorgenson's models, the shortterm interest rate is emphasized while the accelerator is lagged and small. Therefore, it is important to identify the ramifications of investment models where each of the three factors is emphasized. For this purpose, we will assume that there are three distinct theories: $I(i)$, $I(Y)$, and $I(\Delta Y)$.

Economic Expansion

Let us look at how each of these previous theories predicted changes in capital spending in response to an economic upturn. If $I=f_1(Y)$, during an economic upturn capital spending would increase, further increasing the expansion. While the expansion is increased by induced capital spending, these fluctuations in I do not create conditions to set off a downturn. When the economy peaks, so does capital spending. Therefore, both capital spending and the overall economy become stationary at the same time.

If instead, $I=f_2(i)$, then as the economy expands, interest rates rise and capital spending contracts. In this case, fluctuations in capital spending

---

6. Jorgenson's early work is "Capital Theory and Investment Behavior," *AER* 53 (May 1963): 247–57. For a complete biography, see his "Economic Studies of Investment Behavior: A Survey," *Journal of Economic Literature* 9 (Dec. 1971): 1111–47.

dampen rather than accelerate the expansion. The actual multipler effect is reduced. However, the contractions of capital spending diminish as the economy peaks. At the peak, money market equilibrium terminates interest rate changes and, hence, terminates capital spending declines. Therefore, capital spending bottoms and the overall economy peaks at the new equilibrium value.

These two previous theories have substantial differences. $I = f_1(Y)$ implies that capital spending *increases throughout the expansion,* thus increasing the actual multiplier effect. $I = f_2(i)$ implies that capital spending *decreases throughout the expansion,* thus decreasing the actual multiplier effect. According to both theories, capital spending fluctuations diminish as fluctuations in the overall economy diminish. Therefore, both theories imply that equilibrating tendencies are present in the economy.

The accelerator theory, $I = f_3(\Delta Y)$, differs from both of these previous theories in the following respects:

1. Whereas both previous theories have capital spending changing in *one* direction, the accelerator theory has capital spending both increasing and decreasing during the expansion. Therefore, according to the accelerator theory, capital spending fluctuations both increase the expansion (during the early phase) and dampen the expansion (during the later phase).

2. Whereas both previous theories implied that the fluctuations in capital spending would diminish as the economy peaked, according to the accelerator theory, capital spending continues to decrease at the peak of the economy. Therefore, declines in capital spending make it impossible for the economy to equilibrate at the higher level. As sales peak, capital spending declines force the economy to begin a contraction.

Economic Contraction

Once the economy begins to contract, according to $I = f_1(Y)$, capital spending will also begin to decline, accelerating the downturn. However, as the economy begins to bottom so does capital spending. Eventually, they both bottom at the new equilibrium. According to $I = f_2(i)$, as the economy begins to contract, interest rates begin to fall, thus stimulating additional capital spending. Throughout the contraction, interest rate declines induce capital spending increases, thus dampening the multiplier effect. As the economy bottoms, interest rate declines terminate. Therefore, capital spending peaks and the overall economy bottoms at the new equilibrium level.

As during an expansion, these two previous theories have differences. $I = f_1(Y)$ implies that capital spending *decreases throughout the contraction,* thus increasing the actual multiplier effect. $I = f_2(i)$ implies that capital spending *increases throughout the contraction,* thus reducing the actual multiplier effect. In both theories, however, capital spending fluctuations diminish as fluctuations in the overall economy diminish. They imply equilibrating tendencies are present in the economy.

The accelerator theory differs from both of these previous theories in the following respects:

1. Whereas both previous theories have capital spending changing in *one* direction, the accelerator theory has capital spending both decreasing and increasing during the contraction. Therefore, according to the accelerator theory, capital spending fluctuations accelerate the early downturn and then dampen the latter contractions.

2. Whereas both previous theories implied that capital spending fluctuations terminate when the economy bottoms, according to the accelerator theory, capital spending is expanding so that it is impossible for the economy to equilibrate at this lower level. As sales bottom, capital spending increases force the economy to expand.

These comparisons are summarized in Table 13.3. They indicate that models which emphasize the accelerator will have different results from models which emphasize either of the other two factors. Accelerator-dominated investment models would predict cyclical fluctuations, while other models would predict equilibrating tendencies.

Table 13.3
Changes in capital spending according to alternative theories

Investment theory	Stage of Aggregate Spending Fluctuation					
	Early Expansion	Late Expansion	Peak	Early Contraction	Late Contraction	Trough
$I = f_1(Y)$	+	+	0	−	−	0
$I = f_2(i)$	−	−	0	+	+	0
$I = f_3(\Delta Y)$	+	−	−	−	+	+

Generalized Explanation of Economic Fluctuations

It is possible for the accelerator process to self-generate cyclical fluctuations in aggregate spending. Indeed, a simple accelerator model of the economy—$C = bY + a$, $I = \alpha(\Delta Y) + R$—will generate a continuous cyclical pattern when traced through the period-by-period adjustment process, for reasonable values of the parameters. Sir John Hicks developed a general explanation of how the accelerator can be responsible for cyclical patterns in aggregate spending.[7]

---

7. J. R. Hicks, *A Contribution to the Theory of the Trade Cycle* (London: Oxford University Press, 1950).

According to Hicks, the simple accelerator model was incomplete because it did not incorporate the concept of growth of the economy into the analysis. To incorporate growth, Hicks assumed that there was a constantly growing laborforce. In this case, full employment production would be capable of growing at the rate of growth of the labor force. This growth rate of potential full employment production is reflected in the rising PP′ schedule in Figure 13.1.

Hicks separated capital spending into two components: induced investment and autonomous investment. Induced investment was the required capital spending to meet production requirements. Hicks assumed that induced investment was represented by the accelerator model, $I = \alpha(\Delta Y) + R$. Autonomous investment (I_a), according to Hicks, was generated by longterm factors, and increased yearly independent of current spending. Schedule AA′ represents the growth rate of autonomous investment. If the economy had no induced investment, then it would grow along at the rate of the autonomous increase in capital spending. This is represented by schedule FF′. From the diagram it should be clear that the economy must always lie between the full employment "ceiling" (PP′) and the zero induced investment "floor" (FF′).

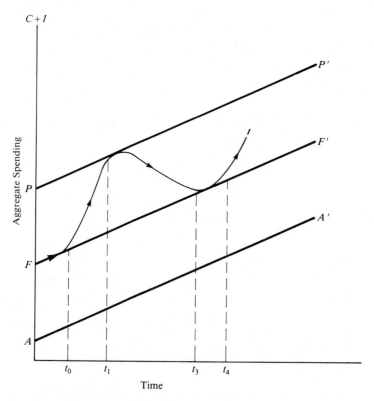

Figure 13.1 The Hicksian theory of the cycle

Hicks explained why the accelerator model of induced investment would result in the economy self-generating movements from the floor to the ceiling and back to the floor.

Suppose the economy was in the midst of a long depression so that induced investment was zero. According to the Hicks model, there would still be some growth since autonomous investment is still growing. Eventually, some replacement investment would be required so that induced investment eventually rises (in t_0). Hicks then assumed that, once it begins to expand, the economy grows until it approaches the full employment ceiling. His rationale was that the accelerator influence on induced investment was powerful enough to offset any slackening of the growth of household demand. During the expansion, the growth rate is faster than the growth rate of the labor force. However, once the full employment ceiling is reached (in t_1), the growth rate of the economy cannot exceed the growth rate of the labor force. But this means that induced investment must decline, resulting in an economic contraction. Consequently, induced investment declines to zero, and the economy slumps. In t_3, the economy has reached the floor. It will then continue to grow at the floor until replacement investment is required. At that point (t_4), a new expansionary phase will begin.

13.2 KONDRATIEFF CYCLES

The simple Hicksian Accelerator model assumed that autonomous investment—capital spending independent of aggregate spending—grew at a constant rate. If we assume that technological innovation is the most important determinant of autonomous investment, then the simple Hicksian model assumes that technological innovation grows at a constant rate. Kondratieff models are attempts to incorporate the structural properties of technological innovation in order to explain *fluctuations* in the rate of change of autonomous investment.[8]

Bulkiness of Capital Goods

Capital goods, such as plant facilities and production infrastructure (roads, lighting, water supply), cannot be efficiently built at less than some minimum size. Due to this, capital goods will not be purchased in a direct period-by-period response to changes in sales.

For example, suppose a firm's output needs are growing at 10% per year. It would be optimal to increase plant size by 10% per year. However, due to technology, it would be tremendously cheaper to build a new plant (which would double capacity) every ten years rather than increase capacity 10% each year.

---

8. Nikolai D. Kondratieff, "The Long Waves in Economic Life," *Review of Economic Statistics* 17 (Nov. 1935): 105–115.

A second effect of the bulkiness of capital goods is that the production time necessary to build the new plant would be a number of years. This increases the inability of investment to respond on a continuous basis to changes in demand.

Suppose we assume that plant planning and construction takes 6 years. One possible decision for the firm could be to begin construction of a new plant in year 2 and have it completed by the end of year 7.

In this case, the firm would not have optimal capacity utilization at all times. It should be noted that the optimal utilization rate for most firms is far less than 100% of capacity. If we consider 100% to be $(24)(7) = 168$ hours per week, then the highest the overall capacity utilization rate has been in the last twenty years was 23.8%.[9] Therefore, the firm has a substantial amount of flexibility.

For a number of years, before the new plant is operational, the firm would be producing above its optimal utilization rate. This would be reflected in overtime, extra shifts, greater use of subcontracting, and a build up of backlog orders. Once the new plant is operational, there will be a period of suboptimal utilization. This sequence would repeat itself every ten years as long as demand continues to grow at 10% per year.

The pattern described in Figure 13.2 might seem to contradict the assumption concerning induced investment of the simple accelerator model. Recall that induced investment was supposed to reflect an instantaneous adjustment of the economy to changes in aggregate spending. Specifically, it assumed that if the growth rate of sales (aggregate spending) was constant, then induced investment would be constant each year. There is not necessarily a contradiction.

It is possible for *total* investment to be constant when the growth rate of sales is constant while *each firm's* investment is cyclical. For example, assume that there are ten firms in the industry, all of the same size, each having a 10% increase in sales each year. Suppose, due to bulkiness, each firm has a cyclical capital spending path, as depicted in Figure 13.2. If each firm decided to start to build its new plant in the same year (year 2, year 12, etc.), then the industry's capital spending outlay would magnify the cyclical pattern of the individual firm. However, it is certainly possible that firms could begin construction in different years. If each of the ten firms started construction in a different year (Firm A in year 1, year 11, etc.; Firm B in year 2, year 12, etc.; Firm C in year 3, year 13, etc.; . . . Firm J in year 10, year 20, etc.), then the industry's capital spending would be constant. In every year there would be essentially one plant being built.

Therefore, despite bulkiness, it is possible for the total investment to respond in a continuous fashion if the cyclical patterns of firms are sufficiently

9. M. F. Foss, "The Utilization of Capital Equipment: Postwar Compared with Prewar," *Survey of Current Business* 43 (June 1963): 8-16.

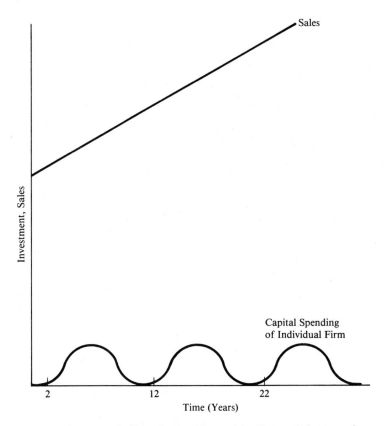

Figure 13.2   Investment pattern of firm with constant sales growth

unsynchronized. This is probably a reasonable assumption for normal investment related to sales expansion. The Kondratieff models, however, assume
that it is not a reasonable assumption for capital spending due to technological
innovations.

Combining the Accelerator and Kondratieff Processes

In the Hicksian accelerator model, autonomous investment was assumed to
grow at a constant rate. According to the Kondratieff model, technological
innovations in key industries tend to clump around important discontinuous
discoveries. The clumping in the key industries also resulted in the clumping of
capital spending in dependent industries. Therefore, the Kondratieff model
implies that autonomous investment would follow a cyclical pattern, with the
upturns determined by the initial technological discovery. Schedule AA ' (in
Figure 13.3) indicates the pattern of autonomous capital spending according to
the Kondratieff model. It indicates that in years t_1, t_2, and t_3, there were important technological discoveries in key industries.

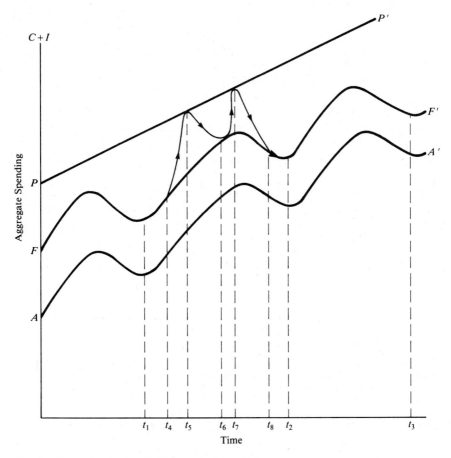

Figure 13.3 The Kondratieff theory of the cycle

If there were no induced investment, then the income path of the economy would be dictated by the path of autonomous investment. Let FF' represent this path. Suppose we are at the bottom of an economic contraction so that the economy is moving along the floor. Eventually, at t_4, firms require some replacement investment, setting off an expansion upward. According to the Hicksian accelerator, the growth would be great enough for the economy to reach its full employment ceiling (PP'). As before, according to the accelerator, at the ceiling the growth rate of the economy must slow down, resulting in a decline in induced investment.

The contraction begins at t_5 and continues until the floor is reached (at t_6). This first cycle had a limited downturn since autonomous investment was at the upturn of its cycle. Therefore, the excess capital is quickly worn off, replacement investment begins, and an economic expansion rises to the full employment ceiling at t_7. Again, the growth rate declines, lowering the level of induced investment and a contraction begins. This time the contraction is severe. It is severe because the economy is now on the downside of the autonomous investment cycle. The declines in autonomous investment accelerate even further the contraction. At t_8, the floor is reached. However, due to the continued declines in autonomous investment, the economy continues to decline. In this case, it may be quite a long time before firms have worn off their excess capital, hence, it would be a long time before replacement investment is required.

The combination of the accelerator and Kondratieff explanations of fluctuations in capital spending is, therefore, capable of explaining why the economy has historically had continuous cycles of varying lengths, and why every once in a while the contraction is severe. The accelerator explains the continuous cycles, while the Kondratieff model explains the periodically severe depressions.

Kondratieff Cycles and the Transportation Industry

The preceding analysis assumes that autonomous investment followed a cyclical pattern, and that this cycle was independent of movements in other sectors of the economy (the fluctuations were completely determined by technological factors). The underlying rationale for these fluctuations was that technological discoveries affect in a discontinuous fashion some "key" industry. According to the most popular version of the Kondratieff model, it is the transportation industry that is the key industry.[10]

According to this version, at discontinuous points in time, new modes of transportation are discovered. Due to the bulkiness of new transportation systems and their tremendous efficiencies, it is rational to build large systems immediately—even though large excess capacities would be created. When these systems are built, they are necessarily followed by long periods of minimal transportation investment. Moreover, transportation systems stimulate investment and production in dependent industries, thus intensifying the cyclical pattern. These transportation cycles appear to be about fifty years from peak to peak.

The first cycle, which peaked in the decade after the War of 1812, can be explained by the massive investment in harbor and canal development. During this period, all of the Middle Atlantic states attempted to reach the growing markets of the Midwest through the canals. Moreover, cities along the Ohio and Mississippi Rivers extensively developed their harbor facilities to support the growing trade. By the 1830s, much of this investment had occurred and transportation investment declined. Only after the Civil War, with the building of the national railroad system, did transportation investment grow substantially. Again, competition (now between railroad barons rather than states) stimulated a railroad system which far outpaced current needs. By the

10. This analysis follows Michael Zevin, "Political Economy of the American Empire, 1974," *Radical Perspectives on the Economic Crisis of Monopoly Capital* (New York: Union for Radical Political Economics, 1975), pp. 131-37.

1890s, railroad development could go no further and transportation investment dramatically declined. The third great wave of transportation investment occurred after the First World War. By then, the automobile had become a technically feasible means of mass transportation. During the 1920s, massive investment occurred as the automobile industry built up its productive capacity and the states built up their road systems. By the 1930s, productive capacities and road systems were sufficiently expanding, therefore, capital investment in these areas sharply declined. The suburbanization process of the post-Korean War period induced the last great wave of transportation investment. During the succeeding decade, the Interstate Highway system and two-car families were a direct result of the suburbanization process. Now with the completion of the new highway system and the great expansion of per capita automobile ownership ended, a strong decline in transportation investment can be predicted according to this Kondratieff theory.

Alternative Explanation of Autonomous Investment

The Kondratieff model attempts to explain the fluctuations in autonomous investment by emphasizing the key role of transportation technology. It explains, from a structuralist viewpoint, the causes of large scale contractions and stagnation. Its structuralist viewpoint is emphasized by its assumption that technological considerations are the sole determinant of the *timing* and *size* of technological innovation.

The timing and size of technological innovation has been explained from an individualistic perspective. According to this viewpoint, these changes are due to the psychological motivation of decision-makers. The most widely known variant of this viewpoint is the work of Joseph Schumpeter.

Schumpeter made a distinction between an innovation and an invention. Technological discoveries, the product of the work of scientists and engineers, can be assumed to occur at a continuous rate. It is unlikely that we would find periods of great bursts of inventions and then periods of limited bursts of inventions.[11] Schumpeter, however, argued that the adoption of these inventions by innovators does not follow a continuous pattern. He believed that businessmen were inherently risk-averters, unwilling to gamble on a new untried process. Therefore, only under favorable conditions could we expect innovations to be undertaken. This makes some sense when we realize that often the conversion to a new process can be very costly and the firm always has the option to continue to use the still-productive older equipment. Accord-

---

11. If inventions were positively correlated with funds expended on research, and these funds were positively correlated with the rate of change of the economy, then the rate of inventions would be a function of the change in the economy. Schumpeter, however, viewed inventions from a very individualistic perspective and, therefore, assumed that they occurred independent of funding and, hence, independent of economic conditions.

ing to the major thrust of Schumpeter's work, expectations were determined by how favorable the future is expected to be.

During a downturn, decision-makers are pessimistic and decline to make use of inventions that continue to be discovered. As the contraction continues, a stockpile of innovations builds up. At some point, the economy begins to bottom out and decision-makers begin to turn optimistic concerning the future. At this point, some decision-makers will begin to innovate, bringing about an expansion. The expansion is further stimulated as the imitators (those decision-makers who follow) —also begin to innovate. As each successful innovator is followed by numerous imitators, the economy is spiralled upward.

The continued growth of autonomous investment cannot be maintained. At some point, the stockpile of discoveries is exhausted and the number of imitators declines. Hence, the growth rate of the economy must begin to decline. However, as the growth rate declines, expectations of future growth are dampened. With the decline in expectations of future growth, pessimism among innovators sets in. Autonomous investment declines still further as some inventions begin to be stockpiled. This creates the conditions for an actual contraction, which diminishes business confidence still further. Once more, autonomous investment is reduced, and the economy must begin to bottom before business confidence is sufficient to begin the next expansion.

Schumpeter's model emphasizes how the cyclical fluctuations of autonomous investment are due to the changing psychological motivations of decision-makers. As described, this psychological motivation is determined by the *rate of change* of the economy. His model of autonomous investment can be represented by

$$I_a = c_a(\Delta Y)$$

where

I_a = amount of autonomous investment

c_a = size of response of innovative investment to changes in Y

Notice that this model of autonomous investment has the same exact form of the accelerator model of induced investment. Schumpeter would argue that the fluctuations in induced investment (I) follows structurally-determined factors, while the fluctuations in autonomous investment (I_a) follow from psychological factors. Since they both respond to the rate of change of Y, they occur simultaneously, reinforcing the effects of each other. A full Schumpeterian model of the economy would be:

$$C = bY + a_1$$
$$I = \alpha(\Delta Y) + a_2$$
$$I_a = c_a(\Delta Y) + a_3$$
$$I_t = I + I_a = (\alpha + c_a)(\Delta Y) + (a_2 + a_3)$$

where

I_t = total investment

a_1, a_2, a_3 are constants

α = capital-output ratio

As this full model indicates, autonomous investment fluctuations, because they are perfectly synchronized with the fluctuations of induced investment, increase the size of all cyclical behavior uniformly. Unlike the Kondratieff model, where the fluctuations of autonomous investment are independent of other fluctuations, it is unable to systematically explain why some cycles are larger than others. Therefore, not only does the Kondratieff model rely on a different explanation of the cyclical behavior of autonomous investment than the Schumpeterian theory, but it also is more compatible with the actual fluctuations of the economy—some small and others large.

Marxist Perspective

The marxist perspective argues that the size of the innovative investment is dictated by profit-seeking competitive market forces rather than technical efficiency or psychological factors. For example, when canal technology became efficient during the 1820s, rather than rational expansion of its use, states competed for markets and overproduced canals. Similarly, after the Civil War when it became technically feasible to develop a national railroad system, competition between industrial tycoons led to an inefficient overproduction of railroads. In each of these cases it can be argued that there would have been a more rationally balanced growth of transportation systems if planned from a national perspective rather than by private profit-seeking individualism. If we look at the surburbanization process from this perspective, there are numerous examples of overproduction which could be cited. One of the more apparent has been the overproduction of suburban shopping centers in many metropolitan areas. In this case, national merchandise chains, in an attempt to increase their market shares, overexpanded the number of stores. This has resulted, during 1975 and 1976, in the closing of many branches, consolidations, and some bankruptcies.

More generally, marxists would argue that inventions and innovations are central factors in industrial economies. According to this marxist perspective, new means of production are periodically discovered which, while able to lower unit cost, are not yet feasible to innovate. They are not feasible because firms have already invested in new plants using the older technology, and without an increase in demand, there is no need for expanded capacity. However, suppose that one firm (Firm A) decides to innovate. If no other firm innovates, then Firm A could increase its *market* share since its costs would be lower than its competitors. In this case, each remaining firm, not wanting to risk losing its market share, is forced to innovate. The problem is that *all* firms cannot increase their market shares. Therefore, when all firms innovate, excess capacity is created.

If all firms in the industry could collude with each other they would avoid overinvestment. They could agree not to innovate unless *total* demand dictated it. Under this agreement, firms could only expand when the overall market expanded, and not at the expense of existing firms. This agreement restricts competition between firms by holding market shares constant. However, in a competitive environment, these agreements (called *cartel* agreements) are impractical if not illegal. It only takes one firm, attempting to increase its market share at the expense of its competitors, to innovate and the cartel would break down. This viewpoint will be developed in subsequent chapters.

13.3 GALBRAITH'S THEORY OF CAPITAL SPENDING

The individualistic viewpoint suggested that changes in the rate of investment in new ventures are determined by changes in the market interest rate. Structuralist theories, such as Galbraith's,[12] contend that new venture investments are more sensitive to technologically-related changes in risk than to changes in the initial capital costs. According to Galbraith, technological innovations have become increased capital-intensive. An example of the increasing capital-intensity of production is illustrated in Table 13.4.

Table 13.4
Textile industry

Production costs, 1970					Production costs, 1920			
Unit cost	Total cost	Capital cost	Labor cost	Output	Labor cost	Capital cost	Total cost	Unit cost
11.00	1100	1000	100	100	300	200	500	5.00
6.00	1200	1000	200	200	600	200	800	4.00
4.33	1300	1000	300	300	900	200	1100	3.66
3.50	1400	1000	400	400	1200	200	1400	3.50
3.00	1500	1000	500	500	1500	200	1700	3.40
2.67	1600	1000	600	600	1800	200	2000	3.33
2.43	1700	1000	700	700	2100	200	2300	3.29

According to the hypothetical figures, textile production in 1920 used relatively little capital (200) compared to textile production in 1970 (1000). As long as production is at a high enough level (greater than 400 units), it is cheaper (lower unit cost) to produce with the capital-intensive process than with the older labor-intensive process. For example, if the firm sold 600 units, using the 1920 production process, its unit cost would be $3.33, and its capital costs represent only 10% of total production costs. If it used the 1970 production process, the same 600 units could be produced at a unit cost of $2.67, and its capital costs would represent 62.5% of total production costs.

12. J. K. Galbraith, *The New Industrial State* (New York: Houghton Mifflin, 1969).

Galbraith claims that this increasing reliance on capital investment (greater percentage of costs being capital costs) makes the firm's profits more sensitive to changes in market demand. In the past, when firms had little *fixed* capital costs, a decline in demand would result in massive layoffs. Declines in revenue would be substantially offset by declines in labor costs, resulting in only mild declines in profits. Today, however, much of the declines in demand must be absorbed by firms since they cannot layoff much labor and cannot stop paying their fixed costs of machinery.

This can be readily shown if we convert the cost data of Table 13.4 to profit data. Table 13.5 indicates the profits of the firm, depending upon the production process used and the quantity sold, assuming that the selling price is $4 per unit.

Table 13.5
Textile firm profits if selling price is $4.

Quantity sold	Total revenue	Total cost (1920 technology)	Profits	Total cost (1970 technology)	Profits
100	400	500	− 100	1100	− 700
200	800	800	0	1200	− 400
300	1200	1100	100	1300	− 100
400	1600	1400	200	1400	200
500	2000	1700	300	1500	500
600	2400	2000	400	1600	800
700	2800	2300	500	1700	1100

If sales were 500, then it would be most profitable to use 1970 technology. In this case, the firm would make 500. However, what if sales fell to 300? Using 1970 technology, where most of the firm's cost are fixed capital, the firm would lose money. On the other hand, if the firm had used 1920 technology, then while profits at sales of 500 would be lower (300), the firm would be less sensitive to fluctuations. If sales fell to 300, the firm could lay-off a substantial number of workers and still make a profit. This can be shown in Figure 13.4.

Galbraith argues that the result of this technological-induced increase in demand sensitivity makes firms increasingly reluctant to invest in new product development. He claims that without increased government investment incentives and/or demand guarantees, capital investment will stagnate. Indeed, he has used this theory to explain the secular stagnation of investment during the 1965–75 period.

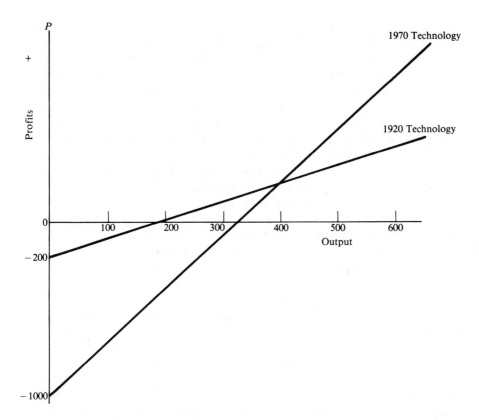

Figure 13.4   The output-profit relationship

Criticisms of Galbraith's Investment Theory

Galbraith claims that technical innovations have increased the capital (fixed) cost requirements of production relative to labor (variable) costs. Plant and equipment once bought for a specific purpose are not easily adaptable to other uses. Therefore, producers have become less flexible in their ability to adjust to changes in consumer demand.

According to Galbraith, this makes capital investments, especially in new products and new markets, more risky than 50 years ago, and results in the secular stagnation of capital investment. However, many economists who agree with Galbraith that capital investment has become more risky do not agree with his *explanation* and/or his *prognosis.*

For example, Joan Robinson has drawn a different set of conclusions from the same observations. Robinson is also concerned with the inflexibility of capital equipment; "the fact that individual items of the capital stock cannot be costlessly transformed into one another, but exist in particular forms, embodying particular techniques, reflecting the superceded expectations of the past.''[13]

Robinson contends that this inflexibility of capital weakens the ability of producers to make *rational* investment decisions—decisions based upon expected cost and revenue calculations. Instead, psychological motivation would play an increasingly important role in decision-making. Earlier, we found that when innovative investment was determined by psychological factors, it was subject to accelerator-type fluctuations. Similarly, this Robinsonian theory, which claims that *all* investment decisions reflect psychological factors, may also result in self-generating fluctuations. Hence, from this perspective, increasing capital intensification reinforces accelerator-type fluctuations rather than any stagnation tendencies.

Galbraith claims that structural factors explain the increasing riskiness of capital spending. However, it is possible to argue that the decline of capital spending is due to the increased volatility of consumer demand rather than the increased inflexibility of capital goods. This alternative view has been most identified with the work of George Katona.

According to Katona, during the last thirty years the fastest growing component of spending has been consumer spending on durable goods. By 1973, consumer spending on durable goods, after discounting for inflation, rose to $5\frac{1}{2}$ times its 1946 level. In contrast, the increase in business capital spending was only threefold. According to Katona, consumer spending on durable goods is dependent upon both the ability to pay (income) and the willingness to buy (rate of confidence or optimism). To emphasize the importance of sentiment rather than objective need, Katona distinguishes between business saturation and consumer saturation. Businesses are considered saturated with capital goods when firms have a large capacity relative to current needs. However, "saturation with automobiles and other durable goods cannot be defined in terms of the quantity of goods held, because wants for second cars, second television sets, or second homes may arise when people are optimistic and confident. Consumers feel saturated not when they have many possessions but when they are pessimistic and uncertain about the future."[14]

Katona, therefore, would claim that any secular stagnation in capital spending has resulted from the larger share of income allocated to consumer durables. As household income has increased, greater consumer spending fluctuations have occurred. This may have created increasing risk for producers *independent* of their capital flexibility. So instead of structural factors creating increased risk for producers, it has been argued that the cause has been the increasing importance of household psychological attitudes.

---

13. Joan Robinson, *The Accumulation of Capital* (London: MacMillan, 1956).

14. George Katona and Burkhard Strumpel, "Consumer Investment Versus Business Investment," in *The Challenge of Economics*, Myron Sharpe, ed. (New York: Random House, 1977), p. 73.

Katona's major thesis, however, is not that the unreliability of consumer purchases has caused secular stagnation of capital spending. Instead, Katona and his associates at the University of Michigan Survey Research Center contend that fluctuations in consumer sentiment have been the decisive factor in accurately predicting economic turning points. Katona believes that the "important role of consumers' discretionary expenditures in originating cyclical changes and their dependence on attitudes and expectations have made it possible to predict major cyclical swings by monitoring consumer sentiment."[15] In support of this contention, Katona offers the results from past recessions (Figure 13.5), in which downturns in consumer sentiment, as measured by the index developed at the Survey Research Center, have preceded the beginnings of economic recessions; while upturns in the consumer sentiment index have preceded economic recoveries.

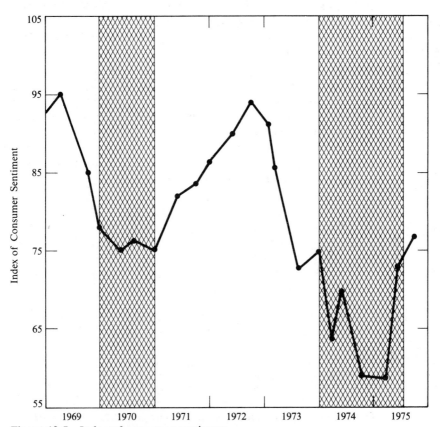

Figure 13.5   Index of consumer sentiment

Index computed by Survey Research Center, University of Michigan.
Index = 100 in February 1966. Shaded portions indicate recessions.

---

15. Ibid., p. 74.

Suppose that consumer sentiment was fully determined by economic indicators and that the importance of these indicators was unchanged. In this case, fluctuations in the purchase of consumer durables would still be determined solely by economic factors, with psychological factors reflecting only the mechanism through which these changes are manifested. For example, suppose that consumer sentiment was directly dependent upon the current change in the level of Y. According to this formulation, the demand for consumer durables

$$C_d = c_d(\Delta Y)$$

where

$$c_d = \text{given constant}$$

Notice that this response of households is analogous to the Schumpeterian theory of induced investment. In both cases, an economic slowdown creates pessimism and a decline in spending.

Katona's view is a variation on this model. He desires to give a more independent role to psychological factors. Katona and associates contend that consumer sentiment cannot be fully explained by economic factors. They cite factors, such as confidence in government, as examples of determinants of consumer sentiment not directly related to economic indicators. They argue that even if economic factors enter into the determination of consumer sentiment, they may be "perceived differently under different circumstances (for example the same stimulus may be seen differently when it occurs a second time) and therefore may provoke different emotions and reactions. Expectations are not merely a projection of recent trends but are influenced by current perceptions and news received."[16]

Therefore, according to Katona: (1) c_d would not be constant, but have a different size depending upon the specific historical circumstances; and (2) the relationship could not explain all the variation in durable goods purchases because it ignores noneconomic factors.[17]

13.4 CONCLUSION

This chapter has indicated a number of alternative models of capital spending that rely on structuralist properties. These theories all minimize monetary

16. Eva Mueller, "Ten Years of Consumer Attitude Surveys . . . ," *Journal of the American Statistical Association* 58 (Dec. 1963): 901–902; quoted in and critically evaluated in M. K. Evans, *Macroeconomic Activity* (New York: Harper & Row, 1970), p. 463.

17. It is possible to generate a consumer durables accelerator without relying on subjective factors. Specifically, assume that the *stock* of durable goods (C_K) is a fixed proportion of one's income; i.e., $C_K = kY$. If this proportion is always constant, then $\Delta C_K = k(\Delta Y)$. If we ignore replacement, then $\Delta C_K = C_d$ so that $C_d = k(\Delta Y)$. For a detailed presentation of this model, see R. J. Gordon, *Macroeconomics* (Boston: Little Brown, 1978), pp. 384–6.

influences on capital spending decisions. The accelerator model assumes that at any point in time, there is only one technology that can be chosen. Therefore, changes in the market interest rate will have little influence upon the rate of automation—capital-labor substitution. The accelerator model assumes capital goods maintain their initial productive value throughout their entire useful life. In this case, changes in the rate of interest cannot influence the speed of replacement. Both Galbraith's and Kondratieff's theories contended that technology, not the interest rate, is the most important determinant of capital investments in new ventures. Therefore, whereas conservatives suggest that changes in the market interest rate significantly influence capital decisions regarding automation, the speed of replacement of older equipment, and the likelihood of investments in new ventures, structuralist theories reject each of these contentions.

All three structuralist theories presented in this chapter—the accelerator, Galbraithian, and Kondratieff models—are compatible with each other. They all indicate that capital spending decisions are quite inflexible; that technological factors dictate the fluctuations in capital spending; and that these fluctuations must continue to reoccur. Therefore, they all imply that government economic planning rather than ad hoc discretionary actions are required if the economy is to avoid serious economic problems.

The chapter also indicates that some theorists, while agreeing that there are cyclical forces present in a private market economy, disagree as to the origins of these forces. We found that Schumpeter's theory contended that psychological factors rather than the timing of discoveries of key technologies determined the cyclical behavior of autonomous investment. Similarly, George Katona has argued that changes in consumer sentiment determine the fluctuations of household spending on durable goods and, hence, the fluctuation of capital spending in durable goods industries. These models indicate that psychological rather than structural factors can explain recurring cyclical tendencies in the U.S. economy.

Conservatives contend that the major fluctuations of capital spending are unpredictable. As developed in Chapter 9, conservatives believe that those fluctuations which are predictable are determined by changes in the market rate of interest. According to this viewpoint, these adjustments have a stabilizing effect on the economy. (See Table 13.6.)

Mainstream liberals also contend that the major fluctuations of capital spending are unpredictable. However, they are less likely to believe that predictable changes in capital spending have a stabilizing effect on the economy. Instead, most believe that, to a limited degree, psychological and structural forces accelerate fluctuations and occasionally are the initiators of cyclical behavior in aggregate spending. Specifically, some mainstream liberals support Katona's thesis that psychological factors influence household spending decisions, which in turn influence capital spending plans. Other mainstream liberals believe that while the accelerator model does not dominantly explain

Table 13.6
Alternative investment theories

Political outlook	Primary explanation	Secondary explanation
Conservative	Unpredictable shocks	Stabilizing effects due to monetary influences.
Mainstream liberal	Unpredictable shocks	Psychologically-induced fluctuations due to changes in consumer sentiment
		Selective accelerator-induced fluctuations in capital spending
Left-liberal	General accelerator-induced fluctuations in capital spending	Psychologically-induced responses to new inventions
		Fluctuations due to discontinuous discoveries in key industries
Radical	Overinvestment cycles due to intraindustry struggle over market shares	General accelerator-induced fluctuations in capital spending

fluctuations in major components of capital investment, it does explain fluctuations in some areas, most notably planned changes in inventories. For these mainstream liberals, predictable inventory cycles, determined by structural factors, are considered to have a significant influence on the size of economic fluctuations.[18]

It is important to remember that mainstream liberals do not believe that these destabilizing effects dominate the private market adjustment process. They only believe that they are significant enough to warrant government stabilization policies. These policies consist mainly of automatic stabilizing programs with some ad hoc discretionary policies when required. However, since mainstream liberals consider the economy to have sufficiently strong tendencies towards equilibrium and only limited endogenous disequilibrating tendencies, no planning is required.

---

18. Let I_{pi} = planned investment in inventories and I_K = stock of inventories. Suppose that the stock of inventories is always equal to a fixed proportion of total sales; i.e., $I_K = k(Y)$. Then $\Delta I_K = k(\Delta Y)$. But since $\Delta I_K = I_{pi}$, then $I_{pi} = k(\Delta Y)$, which is an accelerator function.

Left-liberals favor various combinations of the structuralist theories presented in this chapter. In general, all variations place primary emphasis on the accelerator model. There is some disagreement over the causes of fluctuations in autonomous investment among left-liberals. Some favor the Kondratieff model, which emphasizes the discontinuity of new discoveries in key industries. Along with Kondratieff cycles, some have attempted to identify other long waves of capital spending fluctuations, such as Kuznets cycles, which depend upon the durability and indivisibility of capital goods. Others such as Schumpeter and Robinson, while emphasizing structural factors, also believe psychological factors play an important role. This group is unified in their belief that capital spending fluctuations are predictable, and if unchecked, will create serious economic problems.

We have yet to fully develop a marxian theory of capital spending. However, it was indicated that the marxian theory will emphasize the tendency towards overinvestment (capital expansion at a faster rate than the growth that household demand warrants) inherent in an unplanned competitive capitalist society. Before proceeding to detail marxian macroeconomic theories, however, it will be useful to complete structuralist economic theories. In the next chapter, we will more fully discuss growth theories from the structuralist perspective.

CHAPTER FOURTEEN

ECONOMIC GROWTH

Structuralist theories of investment emphasize the direct relationship between capital spending and productive capacity. If capital spending has predictable effects upon productive capacity, then one must immediately view capital spending as having a dual aspect. On the one hand, additional capital spending, through the income multiplier process, expands aggregate demand. On the other hand, since it creates additional capacity, it increases the potential supply of output. Within this framework, sufficient aggregate spending to generate full employment in one period may create a capital imbalance (divergence between potential supply and aggregate demand) in future periods. That is, if the maintenance of full employment in one period creates deficient (excess) productive capacity for future periods, then disequilibrium situations would be generated.

In Chapter 13, some of the structuralist implications for growth were indicated. This chapter will further detail the structuralist theories of growth. We will begin by demonstrating that given society's propensity to save and the capital requirements of production, there will be a unique growth rate of capital spending which would sustain balanced growth—continuous full utilization of resources. It will be argued, according to the structuralist assumptions, that it is unlikely that balanced growth would occur and that private market disequilibrium adjustments only worsen the imbalance.

This chapter will also apply the structuralist growth model in order to explain chronic problems of developing and developed countries. In each case, their problems will be related to the technical requirements for balanced growth. For each set of countries, policy proposals to rectify these imbalances will be derived from the technical considerations developed in the early part of this chapter.

Structuralist growth models are emphasized by left-liberals. We will outline criticisms of the structuralist growth model made by the other outlooks. Both conservatives and mainstream liberals contend that production techniques can be sufficiently flexible to adapt to fluctuations in capital spending and savings decisions. Therefore, while an adjustment process might be necessary, these outlooks believe that balanced growth should be expected. Radicals side with left-liberals in their belief that it is unlikely for a capitalist economy to sustain the requirements for balanced growth. However, radicals differ with left-liberals as to the sources of the tendency towards imbalance and the corrective measures necessary to restore balanced growth.

14.1 BALANCED GROWTH REQUIREMENTS

In Chapter 13, the dual aspect of capital spending was implied by both the Hicksian accelerator and Kondratieff models. In both these models, there was a divergence between the aggregate demand induced by capital spending and the growth rate of productive capacity (aggregate supply). In the Hicksian model, when the full employment ceiling is reached, productive capacity expansions cannot keep pace with the growth rate of aggregate demand. However, when firms adjust downward their capital investment plans, they cause a contraction in aggregate demand sufficient to induce the economy to contract. In the Kondratieff model, it was assumed that the supply of transportation capacity grows faster than the demand for it.

In order to discuss the implications of the divergence of the growth rate of aggregate demand and aggregate supply resulting from a capital spending expansion, let us first inquire into the technical possibility of balanced growth. That is, let us first indicate if it is possible for an economy to grow in a balanced manner, where the growth of capital spending results in an equal growth of both the demand for goods and the capacity to produce them.

According to the structuralist viewpoint,[1] there is a fixed relationship between aggregate demand and capital stock requirements. Let us assume that each unit of aggregate demand requires α units of capital; i.e., $K/Y = \alpha$. Rearranging terms, this indicates that $Y = (1/\alpha)K$. Since we are assuming that this capital stock requirement is fixed, $\Delta Y = (1/\alpha)\Delta K$. However, since $\Delta K = I_n$, the increase in the potential supply of output, ΔY_s, due to the capital spending expansion is

$$\Delta Y_s = (1/\alpha)(\Delta K) = (1/\alpha)(I_n)$$

---

1. The two major structuralist models of growth are found in E. Domar, "Capital Expansion, Rate of Growth and Employment," *Econometrica* 14 (Apr. 1946): 137–47; and R. F. Harrod, "An Essay in Dynamic Theory," *Economic Journal* 49 (Mar. 1939): 14–33. The principal difference is that the Domar model, which is followed in this chapter, makes no assumption concerning the determinants of actual investment, while the Harrod model assumes that investment is determined by the accelerator principle. A more complete structuralist model, which explicitly assumes that the savings rate is dependent upon the distribution of income between wages and profits, is found in N. Kaldor, "Alternative Theories of Distribution," *Review of Economic Studies* 23 (1955–56): 80–95.

At the same time, the capital spending expansion is also changing the equilibrium level of aggregate demand through the multiplier process. Specifically, the change in equilibrium aggregate demand

$$\Delta Z_d = (M_y)(\Delta I) = (1/s)(\Delta I)$$

where

$$s = \text{MPS}$$

Note that this assumes that either we can ignore monetary factors or monetary policy is coordinated with economic growth. Let us assume replacement investment is zero so that $I_n = I$. Combining the two effects of capital spending

$$\frac{\Delta Z_d}{\Delta Y_s} = \frac{(1/s)\Delta I}{(1/\alpha)I} = (\alpha/s)(\Delta I/I)$$

This indicates that balanced growth $(\Delta Z_d = \Delta Y_s)$ can occur only if $(\Delta I/I) = s/\alpha$. We, of course, have yet to explain why firms would undertake the balanced growth rate of capital spending, s/α. However, since full utilization of productive capacity occurs when firms undertake this growth rate of capital spending, it would be warranted. Indeed, s/α is called the warranted growth rate of capital spending for just this reason.[2]

Numerical Example

Suppose that $\alpha = 0.5$ and that $C = 0.9Y(s = 0.1)$. The situation is illustrated in Figure 14.1, where it is assumed that the economy is initially at equilibrium, with full utilization of capacity, at $Y = 1000$. The economy is at equilibrium at $Y = 1000$, since $C = 900$, $I = 100$. For full utilization of capacity to occur at $Y = 1000$, then the initial capital stock, $K_0 = (\alpha)Y = (0.5)1000 = 500$.

In the following period, the capital stock grows to $K_1 = 600$ so that full utilization of capacity $Y_1 = 1200$. Since at $Y_1 = 1200$ $C = (0.9)Y = (0.9)1200 = 1080$, equilibrium could occur only if $I_1 = 120$. In the following period, the new capital stock, $K_2 = 720$, results in a further increase in productive capacity to $Y_2 = 1440$. Since $C = (0.9)1440 = 1296$, there must be $I_2 = 144$ for full capacity output to be bought. This indicates that balanced growth of capacity is possible if capital spending increased by 20% each period, from 100 to 120 to 144. Therefore, 20% would be the warranted rate of growth of capital spending. We could have obtained this value by using the formula already derived for the warranted growth rate of capital spending, $s/\alpha = .1/.5 = 0.2$.

Labor Requirements

Our analysis has assumed that each unit of output requires a fixed amount of capital, α. There is no ability to substitute between productive inputs, such as

---

2. The concept of "warranted growth rate" was developed by R. F. Harrod, *Toward a Dynamic Economics* (New York: St. Martin's, 1948), p. 82.

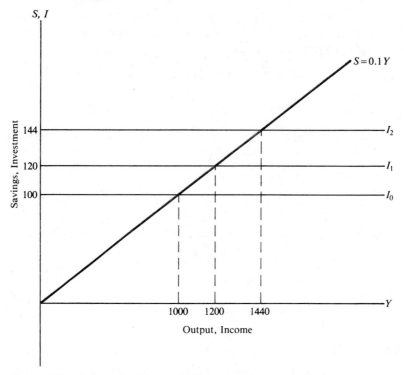

Figure 14.1 Balanced growth with fixed capital-output ratio

labor for capital. Therefore, no matter how much other resources are available, without an increase in the capital stock, production cannot expand. At the same time, the underlying production process assumes that other inputs, such as labor and energy, also have fixed requirements in production. Let us assume that for each unit of aggregate demand, the unit labor requirement $l_0 = \frac{1}{5}$, the unit capital requirement $\alpha = \frac{2}{5}$, and the unit energy requirement $e_0 = \frac{1}{3}$. Suppose that society has 100 units of labor (L), 200 units of capital (K), and 150 units of energy (E). Given the input requirements, society would have enough capital and labor to produce 500 units of aggregate demand, but only enough energy to produce 450 units. Since no substitution of inputs is possible, total production would be 450 with unused labor and capital.

In general, the fixed input requirement production function we have been describing is represented by

$$Y_s = \min (L/l_0, K/\alpha, E/e_0)$$

This production function indicates that the maximum supply of production (Y_s) is equal to the minimum amount which could be produced by each of the inputs, where L/l_0, K/α, and E/e_0 represent the maximum amount which could be produced by labor, capital, and energy, respectively. It now becomes clear that our previous assumption that $Y_s = (1/\alpha)K$ holds only in the special case where there is a sufficient supply of the other necessary inputs.

Let us continue to ignore the possibility of insufficient supplies of energy, but include the possibility of a labor constraint. With a fixed proportions production function, which includes both capital and labor requirements, the capital stock would grow at its warranted rate only if sufficient labor was available. Let us assume that the growth rate of the labor force, $\Delta L/L = n$, is a culturally-determined constant. Suppose that the growth rate of the labor force is slower than the warranted growth rate of capital; i.e., $n < s/\alpha$. Sooner or later, labor scarcity will occur. At that point (full employment of labor), though firms could continue to invest at the warranted rate, the growth rate of real production would only be at the lower rate of labor force growth. Productive capacity would outpace its ability to be utilized. Household money demand would be sufficient, but because of labor scarcity, it would only fuel inflation and excess capacity.

On the other hand, suppose that the labor supply is growing at a faster rate than the warranted growth rate of capital; i.e., $n > s/\alpha$. If the economy had begun its expansion with an excess capacity, then it would be possible to absorb the faster growing labor supply for awhile—though we might wonder why firms would continue to expand capacity with the existence of excess capacity. However, even if firms invest at the warranted rate, sooner or later excess capacity would be eliminated. At that point, capital spending expansions at the warranted rate would not be sufficient to absorb the new entrants into the labor force. Unemployment would grow even though full utilization of productive capacity is continuously maintained.

In summary, if $n < s/\alpha$, then excess productive capacity and inflation occurs if firms attempt to invest at the warranted rate. On the other hand, if $n > s/\alpha$, then labor unemployment would occur when capital spending equaled its warranted rate. Therefore, continuous full employment of both labor and capital is possible only if the growth of the labor force equals the warranted rate of growth of capital spending; i.e., $n = s/\alpha$.

The Anarchy of Production Revisited

According to the left-liberals, each of the three parameters (n, s, α) that determine the balanced growth condition is independently determined. The growth rate of the labor force is culturally determined; the savings rate is determined by the distribution of income; and the capital stock requirement is determined by technology. Therefore, it is unlikely that $n = s/\alpha$, so it is unlikely that continuous growth, with full utilization of labor and capital, would occur in an unplanned economy. Moreover, it will be demonstrated that in an unplanned economy market decisions would accentuate problems resulting from a lack of balanced growth.

Recall that for the full utilization of capital to occur, changes in aggregate demand must equal changes in aggregate supply; i.e., $\Delta Z_d / \Delta Y_s = 1$. We found that the actual ratio of the change in aggregate demand to the change in aggregate supply is given by

$$\Delta Z_d / \Delta Y_s = \alpha / s (\Delta I / I)$$

The actual ratio schedule is illustrated in Figure 14.2. Since it is upward-sloping, it indicates that aggregate demand fluctuates more than aggregate supply in response to a change in capital spending. Therefore, if capital spending grows at a faster rate than s/α, like W_1, then excess demand would exist. If capital spending grows at a slower rate than s/α like W_2, then excess capacity would exist.

Let us assume that firms adjust their capital spending decisions as follows: if excess capacity exists, they lower the growth rate of capital spending; if excess demand exists, they raise the growth rate of capital spending. We can now analyze the adjustment process if the economy is not growing at its balanced growth rate; i.e., $n \neq s/\alpha$.

When $n > s/\alpha$ if firms invest at the warranted rate, unemployment of labor occurs. Suppose that in order to correct this problem, capital spending is increased to correspond to the growth rate of the labor force. Figure 14.2 indicates that any attempt to expand the capital stock at a rate faster than s/α creates an excess demand for goods. According to our assumed decision-making process, when excess demand exists, firms will increase their rate of capital spending. However, as Figure 14.2 indicates, the more the rate of capital spending is increased above its warranted rate, the more excess demand is created. Therefore, once firms begin to invest above the warranted rate, they will create greater and greater excess demand through their individual decisions. This can only cause higher and higher rates of inflation.

Suppose that $n < s/\alpha$. In this case, if firms invest at the warranted rate, eventually labor could not be found to compliment the expanding productive facilities. What if firms decide to lower their actual rate of capital spending below the warranted rate? Figure 14.2 indicates that this would create excess capacity since the decline in aggregate demand would be greater than the decline in aggregate supply. However, if excess capacity exists, each firm would further decrease their growth rate of capital spending. Therefore, once firms begin to invest below the warranted rate, they will continually adjust downward their future capital spending plans as more and more excess capacity occurs.

The structuralist growth model implies that an unplanned economy will be subject to volatile adustments. Since it is unlikely that the growth rate of the labor force will balance the warranted growth rate of capital spending, either labor or capital is in a state of disequilibrium. Even a slight disequilibrium would cause destabilizing adjustments of individual firms—either producing

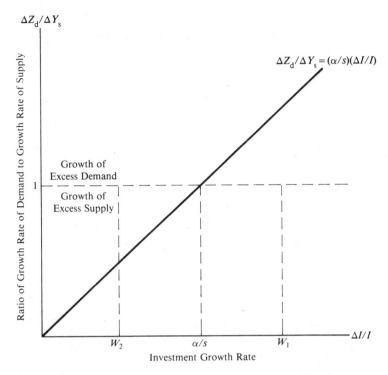

Figure 14.2   Balanced growth requirement and the razor's edge

runaway inflation or a collapse of capital spending. In each case, the destabilizing adjustments are made because firms only take into account the effects of investment decisions on aggregate supply—their ability to produce. They ignore the effects that their investment decisions will have on aggregate demand. Since the effects on aggregate demand are more powerful than the effects on aggregate supply, their decisions lead to the opposite results—attempts to decrease excess demand only increase excess demand, while attempts to decrease excess capacity only increase excess capacity.

This is another example of the anarchy of capitalist production. Recall in Chapter 7 we found that each individual firm took into account the effects of wage cutting on its profits, while underestimating its effects on aggregate demand. By underestimating the effects on aggregate demand, firms believed that wage cuts would raise their profits. However, when the full effect on aggregate demand of wage cuts occurred, in certain situations (Paradox of Profits case) profits declined. In these situations, using wage cuts in an attempt to raise profits resulted in the opposite outcome—lower equilibrium profits.

In both cases, firms made decisions which led to the opposite outcomes because in an unplanned economy it is impossible for individual firms to fully incorporate the effects of their decisions on aggregate demand. They only incorporate the effects of their decisions on the costs of production and the available productive capacity. In each case, it was the unexpected effects of their decisions on aggregate demand that caused the opposite outcome to occur. Therefore, government incomes policies are needed to prevent firms from undertaking destabilizing wage-cutting tendencies. And, government planning of capital spending is required to prevent firms from undertaking destabilizing investment decisions. Only a central planning board is able to fully account for the effects of individual business decisions on aggregate demand.

14.2 APPLICATIONS

In order to have a clearer understanding of the policy implications of the structuralist growth model, let us apply this theory to a number of situations.

Growth in Lesser-Developed Countries

It is often argued that the problem in lesser-developed countries is that the growth rate of population outpaces the growth rate of production. Often, these countries experience high rates of inflation in addition to their slow rates of growth and high unemployment. Let us use the structuralist model of growth to explain this situation.

Lesser-developed countries, due to their poverty, tend to have low private savings rates. Having a low savings rate, the warranted growth rate of capital spending is low. With a high population growth rate, it would seem that these countries are typified by $n > s/\alpha$.[3] As the previous section demonstrated, in this situation if firms invested at the warranted growth rate, the economy would not grow fast enough to absorb all new labor force entrants. Furthermore, any attempts to expand the capital stock at a faster rate would cause inflation since aggregate demand increases would outpace the capacity to produce. Therefore, the structuralist growth model can explain the simultaneous occurrence of high unemployment, inflation, and slow rates of growth.

If it is impossible to solve the problems of slow growth rates in lesser-developed countries through capital spending expansions at rates greater than the warranted rate, then another alternative is to raise the warranted rate. The warranted rate is directly related to the savings rate and inversely related to the capital-output ratio. A society's warranted growth rate could, therefore, be increased by either raising the savings rate and/or by lowering the capital-output ratio. Let us continue to assume that the capital-output ratio is technically

---

3. Note that there can be a distinction between the rate of growth of population and rate of growth of the laborforce.

determined and fixed over the planning period so that we will limit our inquiry to raising the savings rate.

Before we proceed any further, it is important to understand that our interest in raising the savings rate has nothing to do with society's desires to shift present to future consumption. Our objective is to raise the growth rate so that the increasing labor force entrants can be fully absorbed by the economy. Moreover, unlike the Paradox of Thrift (Profits) model, more savings (profits) are not harmful to the economy because in this model all additional savings is offset by additional capital spending.

According to the structuralist viewpoint, the savings rate is determined by the distribution of income between wages and profits. The more income going to profits, the higher the savings rate. Therefore, one method of increasing the warranted growth rate would be to shift income from wages to profits—to worsen the income inequality of the economy. This can be considered a "trickle-down" theory of growth since it proposes that the poor give money to the rich so that someday the induced growth would raise the income of the poor.

For these reasons, many economists have argued that we should expect worsening inequality to accompany growth in the early stages of development. For example, Simon Kuznets hypothesized that during the first thirty to fifty years, a country embarking upon the growth process is likely to worsen rather than improve the distribution of income.[4] The problem with this solution is that it asks the poor to give up some of the little income they have for the possibility of higher growth rates in the future. Moreover, by giving up control over accumulation to the wealthy, this policy increases political and social inequalities.

This anti-egalitarian strategy is, of course, only one method by which an economy could increase its savings rate. Historically, the major alternative method has been through socialist revolution and the adoption of central planning. According to socialist theories, it is possible to dramatically increase the warranted growth rate without having an accompanying increase in inequality. The socialist method is to eliminate the discretionary spending of the upper-income groups and to equalize the utilization of scarce household goods by making more use of collective ownership.[5] It is not surprising, therefore, why poorer groups within lesser-developed countries, faced with the structuralist-type or socialist-type models of growth, choose the latter method.

---

4. Simon Kuznets, "Economic Growth and Income Inequality," *American Economic Review* 45 (Mar. 1955): 1–28. A recent opposing view, which argues that high economic growth rates without worsening income inequality occurred in Brazil, is found in Gary S. Fields, "Who Benefits from Economic Development?" *American Economics Review* 67 (Sept. 1977): 570–582.

5. For example, a socialist society would require more collective use of consumer durable goods. This obviously results in personal inconveniences, but enables greater utilization of scarce goods.

Advanced Capitalist Societies

In most advanced capitalist societies there is a high private savings rate and a low rate of population growth. Hence, there is a significant likelihood that the rate of growth of the labor force is lower than the warranted growth rate of capital spending. In these cases, due to the lack of growth of the labor force, the actual growth rate will fall below the warranted growth rate. The Hicksian accelerator model explicitly reflects such a situation. Therefore, let us restate the Hicksian accelerator model in the context of the balanced growth requirements elaborated in this chapter.

According to the Hicksian accelerator model, once an economy moves off its floor it will grow at an accelerated rate. The growth rate becomes rapid enough to absorb not only new entrants into the labor force but also those who are unemployed. In the language of this chapter, we would say that the warranted growth rate of capital spending is above the growth rate of the population. Therefore, once firms begin to invest at the warranted rate, unemployed labor is absorbed into the production process.

The economy grows at its warranted rate until the full employment ceiling is reached. Then, the economy could continue to grow only at the lower growth rate of the labor force. Hicks assumed that firms realize this and cut back the growth rate of capital spending. However, now capital spending is below its warranted rate. Therefore, the growth of demand is no longer sufficient to buy full capacity production. With excess capacity, individual firms will cut back their capital spending even further. Thus, the adjustment process accelerates the economy downward as each cutback in capital spending creates more excess capacity.

If it is impossible to solve the problem of cyclical behavior in advanced capitalist countries through adjustments of the capital spending growth rate, then either changes in the warranted growth rate or in the growth rate of the labor force is necessary. Increasing labor force growth rates in advanced capitalist countries has historically been associated with drawing new entrants into the labor force—women, children, rural migrants, or immigrants. This certainly is the alternative chosen by capitalists who wish to maintain their high rate of warranted growth. On the other hand, if income were redistributed from profits to wages, thus lowering the savings and warranted growth rates, balanced growth could be sustained. This, of course, would be considered an inferior solution by capitalists.

This foregoing analysis can provide a framework within which the early twentieth century in the United States can be interpreted. During this period, extreme income inequality dictated a high savings rate and, hence, a high warranted growth rate. To maintain this growth rate, which was greater than the growth rate of the native urban population, capitalists championed the open door to immigration view. On the other hand, workers demanded a redistribution of income and restrictions on immigration. According to the structuralist growth model, *either* of these policies would be capable of moving the economy along a balanced growth path.

In 1924, with the passage of the Immigration Restriction Act, extensive immigration ended. During the period 1925–29, the growth rate of capital spending adapted to the lower rate of growth of the labor force.[6] However, the inequality in income distribution remained[7] so that now the growth rate of capital spending was below its warranted rate. The growth rate of aggregate demand was no longer sufficient to buy full capacity production. Excess capacity began to grow, and when each individual capitalist adjusted, it caused a collapse of further capital spending and economic growth. Hence, according to this view, the Great Depression was caused when the restriction on immigration lowered the rate of growth of the labor force and there was no compensating decline in the warranted growth rate.

14.3 ALTERNATIVE VIEWS OF GROWTH

The earlier sections of this chapter developed the structuralist model of economic growth. It indicated that all of the requirements for balanced growth, with continuous full utilization of both labor and capital, were extremely unlikely in an unplanned economy. In particular, since it assumed a fixed proportions technology, disequilibrium in labor and/or capital markets must occur and disequilibrium decisions by firms would have a destabilizing effect. This model reflects the left-liberal viewpoint. In response to these implications, each of the other philosophical viewpoints has developed alternative models of growth.

Conservative Model of Economic Growth

The conservative growth models build on the laissez-faire model of the economy. Recall that the laissez-faire model assumed there was substantial choice available to producers as to production techniques. Moreover, since the labor market was rapidly adjusting, any amount of labor would be absorbed into the production process. This viewpoint is described as the putty-putty model of capital since it implicitly assumes that both new and old capital are completely malleable (like putty) inputs—they can adapt to any size labor force. Therefore, the laissez-faire model begins by assuming that regardless of the growth

---

6. According to the estimates of J. A. Swanson and S. H. Williamson in "Estimates of National Product . . . ," *Explorations in Economic History* 10 (Fall 1972), investment expenditures on plant and equipment rose continuously from 1921–26 and then levelled off.

7. Robert Keller, "Monopoly Capital and the Great Depression," *Review of Radical Political Economy* 7 (Winter 1975) documents the claim that the share of income going to profits actually rose slightly during the period 1923–29.

rate of new entrants into the labor force, the wage rate will rapidly adjust, and the capital stock will fully adapt, so that all labor is fully utilized in production.

The next step in the conservative model of economic growth is to indicate how full production will always be bought. As previously indicated, according to the laissez-faire model, regardless of the amount of capital spending of firms, regardless of full employment supply, the rate of interest will adjust until full employment savings just equals the amount of capital spending undertaken. If capital spending is initially lower than what would be required for the purchase of full employment production, the interest rate will decline. The decline in the interest rate would induce households to shift part of their savings to the purchase of consumer durables and firms to automate. This process continues until aggregate demand is sufficient to purchase full employment production. This process is assumed to be completed before firms contemplate changing their capital spending decisions in response to changing sales. Therefore, before firms could undertake destabilizing disequilibrium adjustments, such as lowering their capital spending plans when faced with excess capacity, the market adjusts so that full utilization of their current plant facilities occurs.

The conservative growth model is, therefore, able to ignore the two major constraints on growth that are highlighted in the structuralist model. By assuming completely malleable capital and a rapidly adjusting labor market, full employment of labor is guaranteed. Next, by assuming rapid adjustment of spending to changes in the market interest rate, the conservative model guarantees that full capacity supply will always be bought so that capital and labor are always fully utilized. Moreover, since the adjustments are so rapid, there is no time nor need for firms to adjust their capital spending plans to any disequilibrium situation. Hence, the destabilizing capital spending adjustment process posited by the structuralist model can be ignored.

Let us demonstrate the way the economic process would appear in the world of the conservative growth model. We will begin with an initial capital stock, K_0, and labor force, L_0. Let us assume that in the initial period the economy was at full employment and full utilization of all available capital stock. Suppose that in the initial period capital spending equalled I_0. Therefore, we begin the next period with capital stock $K_1 = K_0 + I_0$.

Let us pick any change in the labor force, ΔL_1, to occur in period t_1. According to the structuralist model, only if $\Delta L_1 / L_0 = \Delta K_1 / K_0 = I_0 / K_0$ could full utilization of both capital and labor occur. However, in the laissez-faire model, capital is completely malleable and wage rates adjust so that K_1 and $L_1 = L_0 + \Delta L_1$ are fully utilized in production, regardless of the relationship between $\Delta L_1 / L_0$ and $\Delta K_1 / K_0$.

Suppose that the resulting output from K_1 and L_1 is Y_1. We would still have disequilibrium if aggregate demand would not buy all of full employment production (aggregate supply). It is certainly possible that household savings would just equal current capital spending (I_1) at full employment production. However, suppose that I_1 is less than full employment savings, sY_1. According to the structuralist theory, the average savings rate, s, is determined by income distribution. Moreover, as Chapter 7 indicated, if a disequilibrium occurs, capitalists would attempt to lower wages to increase profits, which would raise the savings rate and destabilize the economy even more. That is, if $I_1 < sY_1$, according to the structuralist viewpoint, capitalists would attempt to raise profits which would raise the savings rate to $s' > s$. However, by raising the savings rate, the gap between capital spending and full employment savings is widened.

The individualistic model ignores the effects of income distribution on savings. Instead, it assumes that financial savings is determined by the market interest rate. If $I_1 < sY_1$, the market interest rate would decline. According to the conservative model a lower interest rate would induce households to shift financial savings to purchases of durable goods. Therefore, the average savings rate would decline to s'' so that $I_1 = s''(Y_1)$. Regardless of the growth rate of the labor force or growth rate of capital spending chosen, market adjustments will guarantee full utilization of all resources.[8]

In the structuralist growth model, capital spending, the labor force, and total production must all grow at the same rate for full utilization of resources to occur. However, under the assumptions of the conservative model, any combination of growth rates of labor and capital and the resulting growth rate of total production can be compatible with full utilization of resources. Under special assumptions, the growth rates do tend to equalize but this is of secondary importance. See Appendix for details.

Mainstream Liberal Growth Theories

The mainstream liberal growth model takes a middle position between the structuralist and purely individualistic (conservative) models of technology. The structuralist model assumes a clay-clay technology where capital, both old and new, is required in fixed proportions. The conservative model assumes a putty-putty technology where both old and new capital can be adapted to virtually any size labor force. The mainstream liberal model assumes a putty-clay technology where old capital has fixed requirements but new capital can be adapted to fluctuations in the labor force.[9]

---

8. The earliest presentations of the individualistic (neo-classical) growth model are found in Robert M. Solow, "A Contribution to the Theory of Economic Growth," *Quarterly Journal of Economics* 70 (Feb. 1956): 65–94; and T. W. Swan, "Economic Growth and Capital Accumulation, *Economic Record* (Nov. 1956): 334–361.

9. For a further elaboration on the putty-clay theory of investment, see Edmund S. Phelps, "The New View of Investment: A Neoclassical Analysis," *Quarterly Journal of Economics* 76 (Nov. 1962): 548–567.

According to the mainstream liberal viewpoint, the ability to adjust the production process to absorb fluctuations in the labor force is limited to adjustments of new investment. Therefore, unlike the conservative model which assumes complete flexibility and instantaneous adjustment of the production process to absorb any growth of the labor force, the mainstream liberal model assumes that significant structural constraints (fixed old capital stock) exist so that this adjustment process is limited. Specifically, the labor force cannot be absorbed *until* capital spending decisions are adjusted to reflect the new supply of labor relative to the existing capital stock. Therefore, unlike the conservative model, disequilibrium in the labor market and disequilibrium capital spending decisions occur.

In general, mainstream liberals believe that the disequilibrium adjustment process in the labor market and firms' investment decisions have a stabilizing effect on the economy. Structuralists, however, believe they are destabilizing. First, mainstream liberals assume that since new capital stock is malleable it can adjust to absorb fluctuations in the labor force growth rate. Next, they believe that capital spending adjustments to disequilibrium are determined more by the changes in interest rates than the existence of excess capacity. Therefore, whereas structuralists believe that capital spending will be lowered with the appearance of unbought capacity production, thus destabilizing the economy, mainstream liberals contend that the declining interest rate will cause capital spending to increase. Finally, while mainstream liberals do not believe the conservative contention that savings rates will adjust downward to the falling interest rate, neither do they believe the structuralist contention that the disequilibrium process would increase profits and savings rates. Thus, according to the mainstream liberal model, while some disequilibrium adjustments are required, they tend to stabilize rather than destabilize the economy.

Marxian Growth Theories

Marxists agree with left-liberals that capital spending must grow at a specific rate for balanced growth to be sustained. In fact, Marx's reproduction schemes, just as the structuralist growth models, demonstrate that as long as the growth of capital is at its warranted rate, balanced economic growth is sustainable. The specific rate in Marx, just as with the structuralist model, is determined by the distribution of income and the capital-output ratio.

Marx, like left-liberals, specified the warranted rate in order to demonstrate the impossibility of balanced growth within a private market capitalist economy. Marx claimed that predictable changes in the parameters determining the warranted growth rate would cause it to diverge from the actual growth rate of capital spending. These changes had their origins in the capitalist production process. Therefore, even if it would happen that the actual capital spending growth rate equalled its warranted rate, Marx claimed that capitalist forces would create an imbalance. This imbalance would make continued growth impossible until certain adjustments occurred. This adjustment process *required* the bankruptcy of a sufficient number of capitalists and the lowering of the real wage rate in order to restore profitability. Then it would be possible for capitalism to begin a new expansionary phase.

The structuralist model assumes that the two parameters (s and α) which determine the warranted growth of investment are fixed and independent of market forces. Marxists, on the other hand, believe that they are influenced by market forces and attempt to emphasize movements in these parameters. For this reason, marxist theories identify the market-induced divergence of the actual and warranted growth rates of capital spending as the source of imbalance, but structuralists tend to neglect this possibility. Instead, structuralists emphasize that even if capital spending grows at its warranted rate, balanced growth would be impossible because of the further structural requirement of maintaining equality with the growth rate of the laborforce.

The disequilibrium adjustment process differs between structuralist and marxist models. The structuralist model identifies destabilizing tendencies due to the anarchy of production—the inability of individual producers to take into account the effects of their capital spending decisions on the demand for their production. If this were the case, government economic planning would be in the interest of both capitalists and workers since it would increase the efficiency of capital spending decisions. The destabilizing tendencies within the marxian framework cannot be overcome through some consensus government intervention. For example, if the bankruptcy of some firms is required to reduce the capital-output ratio, then any government intervention on behalf of these failing firms would only prolong the crisis. However, if the government promotes the bankruptcy of these firms, thus speeding up the adjustment process, it will not find a consensus support for this type of intervention. Moreover, whereas the structuralist disequilibrium adjustment process implies that it would be impossible for the economy to eventually reestablish conditions for balanced growth, most marxian crisis theories believe that market forces will eventually create the conditions for a new expansionary period.

14.4 CONCLUSION

This chapter has detailed the structuralist growth model, applied it to specific problems, and outlined criticisms of the model made by the other outlooks. The structuralist model assumes that there is a direct relationship between capital spending and productive capacity. Therefore, unless an economy purchases investment goods in a specific proportion to total purchases, capacity imbalances will occur in the future. When a labor condition was added, it became extremely unlikely that an unplanned economy could fulfill all the necessary requirements for balanced growth.

The model also indicated that disequilibrium adjustments in an unplanned economy will worsen imbalances. This occurs because in an unplanned economy producers can only take into account the effects that their decisions have on their supply. They cannot take into account the effects of their decisions on aggregate demand. This was also true in the Paradox of Profits case in Chapter 7, when wage-cutting decisions could not take into account their full effect on sales (demand). In both cases, because business decisions have a greater effect on demand than on their supply or cost, the situation is only worsened. These problems are due to the "anarchy of production," which can only be avoided by extensive government planning. The government, through incomes policies, could guarantee that the Paradox of Profits case does not occur and, through capital investment planning, could guarantee that destabilizing responses to capital imbalances are avoided.

The structuralist model was applied to the experience of developing and developed countries. It was suggested that in developing countries $n > s/\alpha$, while in developed countries $n < s/\alpha$. The structuralist growth model predicts that there would be tendencies to high unemployment and low growth rates in developing countries with inflation if they attempt to raise capital spending. It was then shown that the encouragement of income inequality or a socialist transformation are alternative methods of eliminating imbalances and raising growth rates.

It was shown that the Hicksian accelerator model was really an example of imbalance when $n < s/\alpha$. In this situation, tendencies towards alternating periods of excess capacity and high growth rates would be predicted. In order to eliminate imbalances in the developed economies, either high rates of labor force growth or lower savings rates are required. This framework was able to explain the economic growth pattern for the thirty years prior to the Great Depression.

The final section of this chapter indicated that neither conservative nor mainstream liberal economists expect growth imbalances to occur. Conservatives believe that capital can be reshaped to be used with any amount of labor. Moreover, since labor and capital markets are assumed to adjust rapidly to equilibrium, there will be no need for firms to readjust their future spending decisions because of momentary imbalances. Mainstream liberals are somewhat more guarded than conservatives in their belief that equilibrating adjustments will rapidly occur. They believe that the production process cannot immediately adapt to fluctuations in the labor supply. However, they regard the possibility of destabilizing disequilibrium adjustments as small.

Marxists agreed with left-liberals that growth requirements add to the problems faced by an unplanned economy. It strengthens their contentions that an unplanned economy is an inherently volatile and unstable system. Marxists contend that it is capitalist market forces, rather than purely structuralist problems, which create these imbalances. These marxist theories contend that even if there was a momentary fulfilling of the requirements for balanced growth, forces endogenous to the capitalist production process would tend to undermine its continuation. Therefore, marxists contend that not even government intervention can avoid the problems of imbalance.

APPENDIX

NEO-CLASSICAL GROWTH MODEL

As has already been indicated, regardless of the values of the parameters, growth with full utilization of all inputs will always occur in the neo-classical world. Therefore, the growth rates of the capital stock, laborforce, or production do not have to be the same. However, Figure 14A.1 is helpful in indicating under what conditions these growth rates will tend to equalize. The horizontal

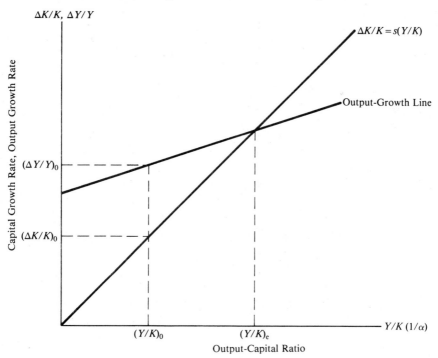

Figure 14A.1 Balanced growth with variable capital-output ratio

axis indicates different values of the output-capital ratio, which is the inverse of the capital-labor ratio. Holding the savings rate constant, there is a positive relationship between the growth rate of production, $\Delta Y/Y$, and the output-capital ratio. The relationship has a positive intercept because independent of the output-capital ratio, income will grow due to growth of the laborforce and its slope is less than the savings rate.[1]

Since full employment savings is absorbed by capital spending, which equals the change in the capital stock, $sY = I = \Delta K$ or $sY = \Delta K$. Dividing both sides by K, $sY/K = \Delta K/K$. This shows that the growth rate of the capital stock is proportional to the output-capital ratio.

We are now ready to explain adjustments in the capital-output ratio necessary to maintain full utilization of all resources. Suppose that the current output-capital ratio is $(Y/K)_0$. Figure 14.A1 indicates that full utilization requires the growth of output to be greater than the growth rate of the capital stock. However, if $(\Delta Y/Y)_0 > (\Delta K/K)_0$, then the output-capital ratio must increase. This increase will continue as long as $(\Delta Y/Y) > (\Delta K/K)$. Eventually, at $(Y/K)_e$, both growth rates are equal and no further adjustment in the output-capital ratio is necessary. This indicates that in the longrun, the growth rate of the capital stock will equal the growth rate of output. If the production function is subject to constant returns to scale, then this value will also equal the growth rate of the laborforce.

---

1. Suppose aggregate production $Y = AK^c L^{1-c}$. In this formulation, A is a constant reflecting technology and $0 < c < 1$. The growth of output

$$\Delta Y = (\partial Y/\partial K)\Delta K + (\partial Y/\partial L)\Delta L$$
$$\Delta Y = c(Y/K)\Delta K + (1 - c)(Y/L)\Delta L$$

Dividing through by Y

$$\Delta Y/Y = c(\Delta K/K) + (1 - c)(\Delta L/L) = c(\Delta K/K) + (1 - c)n$$

Since the neoclassical model assumes that all savings is invested, $I = \Delta K = sY$, so that

$$\Delta Y/Y = cs(Y/K) + (1 - c)n$$

As long as the rate of growth of the laborforce is greater than zero the equation has a positive intercept. Also, since $c < 1$, the slope, which equals cs, is less than the savings rate. Finally, the aggregate production function is subject to the law of diminishing marginal returns as long as $c < 1$.

CHAPTER FIFTEEN

THE MARXIAN CONCEPTION OF COMPETITION

These next four chapters will develop marxian macro-models. All marxian macro-models imply that continuous full employment growth is impossible in a capitalist society. Central to this view is the marxian contention that capitalism requires a reserve army of unemployed workers in order to maintain the necessary hierarchical relations and the rate of profit. However, Marx claimed that besides the normal unemployment, capitalism would be subject to periodic crises during which unemployment would be greatly expanded. One prominent cause of these crises, according to Marx, was the destructive effect of capitalist competition. Since capitalist competition is so important to the marxian theory of economic crises, it is important to detail its distinguishing features. This is the purpose of this chapter. It will be shown that apart from its implications for the possibility of continuous growth, capitalist competition reduces the potentials for human liberation and rewarding occupations.

The first section of this chapter will develop Marx's conception of human liberation. Whereas conservative economists consider human freedom and competition inseparable, Marx considered them to be in conflict. Examples of racial discrimination and agricultural production are used to highlight the distinctions between the marxian and conservative views on the interrelationship between competition and human freedom.

Next, the underlying assumptions of the marxian model of competition will be detailed. It will be shown that the neo-classical competitive model results from the adoption of a number of restrictive assumptions concerning the nature of technological innovations and access to financial markets.

This chapter will also develop the marxian contention that competitive forces and the profit motive reduce the rewarding nature of work, making work alienating. The last section will outline the marxian criticisms of the mainstream contentions that work processes are determined by technical considerations, differences in native ability, and the choice of goods that households desire.

15.1 HUMAN LIBERATION[1]

Marx considered the purpose of political economy to aid in the realization of human freedom. For Marx, human freedom is a condition in which each individual is able to develop his or her personal capabilities in both material and intellectual activity. The limits of human freedom are not merely technical (inability to control nature); they are also socio-political. Only when man has complete control over the fruits of his labor can human freedom be unconstrained.

For Marx, human freedom is a social rather than individual concept since production is always a social activity. As he put it, "Whenever we speak of production, then, what is meant is always production at a definite stage of social development—production by social individuals."[2] Labor is social, not merely because production is accomplished by the interdependent activities of numerous individuals, but because man's intellectual facilities can develop only in a society. Marx, therefore, rejects any analysis which views man as an individual, such as the individualistic conception of man as an individual utility maximizer.

The quest by man for human freedom develops through various stages. In each stage, the oppression by one class over another restricted the freedom of the underclass to develop, and with it the ability of society to progress. Therefore, by the reaction of man against class oppression, society is liberated and able to continue its development. In each stage, then, there is a beginning period of *progress,* in which new structures are developed to enable man to gain increasing control over nature in pursuit of his needs. However, each stage prior to socialism continues to have class oppression. It takes different forms and is composed of a specific set of economic relations. This economic structure, Marx maintained, is "the real foundation on which arises a legal and political superstructure and to which corresponds definite forms of social consciousness. The mode of production of material life conditions the general process of social, political, and intellectual life."[3]

Eventually, the *progressive* period of the new stage passes and the *decaying* period of class oppression emerges. At that point, the decadent and parasitic aspects become dominant. Only when the underclass rebels and a process of change to the next stage occurs can human development be continued.

The current stage is capitalism. In its early competitive period, capitalism was able to expand man's ability to subject nature to its needs on a scale never

---

1. Much of the organization of the first part of this section follows M. C. Howard and J. E. King, *The Political Economy of Marx* (New York: Longman, 1975), pp. 2–7.

2. Karl Marx, *Grundrisse* (Harmondsworth: Penguin, 1973), p. 85.

3. Karl Marx, *A Contribution to the Critique of Political Economy,* Maurice Dobb, ed. (London: Lawrence & Wishart, 1971), p. 20.

before imagined. As Marx noted, capitalism created "more massive and more colossal productive forces than have all preceding generations together. . . . What earlier century had even a presentiment that such productive forces slumbered in the lap of social labor?"[4]

However, capitalism is far from the ideal world, for it still is a class society. Therefore, the control of the productive forces would not be in accordance with man's developing needs. They would be in accordance with the needs of the oppressing class—profits. As long as capitalism remained competitive the productive forces were expanded, increasing the potential of society. However, once capitalism passed into its monopoly period, even this vitality of capitalism disappeared. Therefore, according to marxists, we are currently in the age of decaying parasitic capitalism—an age where its decadence is typified by the legitimation of a drug-sex culture and the breakdown of social organizations. In production, its parasitic nature emerged with the replacement of the competitive entrepreneur by the monopoly finance capitalist.

The distinctions between the marxian concept of human freedom and the mainstream conception are profound. The mainstream view conceives of human freedom as independent of one's situation. Moreover, the conception identifies freedom in individual terms rather than class terms. The marxian response to this alternative conception is predictable. As the standard economics textbook in the Soviet Union during the 1930s states, "There is nothing more disgusting than the hypocrisy of the bourgeoisie who asserts the 'equality' of rich and poor, the well-fed and the hungry, the drone and the over-worked laborer. In reality the bony hand of hunger drives the worker into bondage to the capitalist more effectively than the severest legislation."[5]

Individualistic Conception of History

Marx's concept of history and the struggle for human liberation is distinctly at odds with the individualistic view. The individualistic view is most clearly presented in Milton Friedman's work, *Capitalism and Freedom.* For Friedman, human liberation is always constrained by government intervention, since government intervention must necessarily impose its will on each individual in society. According to Friedman, the free market increases human freedom by reducing "the range of issues which must be decided through political means."[6] In essence, Friedman is arguing that the free market, by removing

---

4. Karl Marx, *Selected Works*, vol. I (Moscow: Progress Publishers, 1969–70), p. 113.

5. A. Leontiev, *Political Economy* (New York: International Publishers, 1935), p. 104.

6. Milton Friedman, *Capitalism and Freedom* (Chicago: University of Chicago, 1962), p. 15.

political motives from economic decision-making, achieves not only economic freedom but also personal political freedom as well.

Friedman emphasizes how capitalism, with its concern for productive efficiency, has given more individual freedom to oppressed groups than any previous economic system. He claims, "It is a striking historical fact that the development of capitalism has been accompanied by a major reduction in the extent to which particular religious, racial, or social groups have operated under special handicaps in their economic activities."[7]

Since Friedman considers free markets to be inseparable from the attainment of human freedom, he suggests that "underlying most arguments against the free market is a lack of belief in freedom itself."[8] Given this viewpoint, Friedman considers it to be a paradox that it is "minority groups that have frequently furnished the most vocal and most numerous advocates of fundamental alterations in a capitalist society."[9]

As we have seen, beginning with Chapter 2, criticisms of a capitalist society do not necessarily reflect a paradox. These criticisms can be derived from an alternative conception of the workings of capitalist market mechanisms. Whereas Friedman emphasizes freedom of choice, marxists emphasize the concentration of ownership of capital as the distinguishing feature of capitalism. However, the distinction between the individualistic and marxian conceptions of capitalism are even deeper than this. Marxists contend that the economic efficiency imposed by free market mechanism is itself an obstacle to human freedom. Therefore, marxists would argue that even if capital was initially evenly distributed, the market would progressively restrict the freedom of the majority. The relationship of economic efficiency and human freedom can be analyzed in terms of differing views on government agricultural policies and the relationship between competition and racial discrimination.

Agricultural Policies

The conflict between these differing conceptions of human freedom is no more graphically illustrated than by the assessments each has of agricultural policies. Agriculture is typified by sizable economies of scale. That is, unit production cost decreases with size since only with size can specialized mechanization be effectively used.

In the United States this has meant that over the last one hundred years the number of farms has decreased while the average size has increased. Moreover, as long as size differentials exist, there will be a continued decline in the number of farms. In 1969, the agricultural census indicated that the smallest

---

7. Ibid., p. 110.

8. Ibid., p. 15.

9. Ibid., p. 111.

50% of fulltime farms produced less than 10% of the value of total farm sales, while the largest 2.7% produced 34% of total farm sales.[10] It is, therefore, predictable that small farmers will continue to be replaced by fewer and fewer large farms as long as the free market is allowed to operate.

This predictable process is accelerated by natural disasters, such as crop failures due to adverse weather conditions, since it is the small farmer who has little reserves and cannot wait for better crops in succeeding years. It is accelerated by the normal operations of banks, which are reluctant to loan funds to marginal operations. By favoring the well-established farm over the smaller marginal farm, banking policies increase the cost differential between the two. Finally, cyclical economic fluctuations, which adversely affect agricultural prices during the downturns, also accelerate the failure rate of small farms. For these reasons, besides the continuous downward trend in the number of farms, there have been periods of acceleration. During the 1890s, adverse banking policies together with an economic depression drove small farmers to bankruptcy. During the 1930s, adverse weather conditions together with another depression again accelerated the rate of farm failures. During the 1970s, another economic downturn has lowered prices of agricultural products, endangering the survival of small farms again.

From the mainstream view of human freedom this is a natural process of free competition. The fact that it is predictable that a few large farms will remain while the majority will go bankrupt is not an infringement on human freedom. According to this viewpoint, restrictions on human freedom only occur when there is some conscious intervention to restrict freedom of choice—for example, if the government only legally allowed specific farmers to purchase farm equipment. Since no legal restriction exists and all farmers have the freedom to choose, bankruptcies have no bearing on the degree of human freedom.[11]

As might be expected, this view of human freedom is not accepted by the small farmer. He is not interested in the freedom to become a farm laborer or industrial proletariat. He desires survival at farming, and the "free" market won't accomplish this. During the 1890s, an agrarian populist movement demanded cheap credit through the massive expansion of silver-backed money. During the 1930s, tenant farmer organizations demanded government-backed loans to prevent bankruptcies. During the 1970s, farm organizations engaged in nationwide strike activities, demanding government price support at higher levels. During this entire period, the objective of the smaller farmer has been to have the federal government keep farm prices sufficiently high so that he cannot be driven out of business by the efficiency of the large farms.

10. U.S. Bureau of Census, *Census of Agriculture, 1969,* vol II, Chapter 7, quoted in Lloyd Mercer, "American Farm Problem," *Economics of Pressing Social Problems,* L. Phillips and H. Votey, eds. (Chicago: Rand-McNally, 1977), p. 39.
11. This is the position taken by Mercer, "American Farm Problems."

Under pressure from the agricultural community, the federal government has had a policy of limited price supports which has slowed the process of concentration. However, the side effects of this policy have been to (1) keep prices to consumers higher than they would have been under "free" competition; (2) limit output in order to keep prices high; and (3) disproportionately subsidize large farmers since the price subsidy is proportional to sales. Indeed, it is for these reasons that the individualistic economists contend that government farm policy is responsible for restrictions on human freedom.

This example has attempted to demonstrate that the concept of human freedom cannot be easily abstracted from an individual's economic class when uneven development is present. If one is a rich farmer, then the market system preserves his freedom. However, if one is a small poor peasant farmer, then the market system suppresses freedom.

Competitive Forces and Discrimination

According to Friedman, competitive forces have been responsible for the decline of discriminatory practices. It is argued that when an employer discriminates by not hiring the most qualified worker, he reduces productive efficiency. An employer who does not fear his competition may choose to do so—he may be willing to trade productive efficiency to indulge in his discriminatory attitudes. However, if competition is fierce, no employer can afford to sacrifice productive efficiency to indulge in personal tastes. Under competition, high-cost producers will be driven out of the industry. Therefore, under the whip of competition, each capitalist is forced to refrain from acting on his personal tastes when making employment decisions.

Radicals agree with Friedman that *employment* discrimination is unprofitable and, hence, will be weeded out by competitive forces. However, radicals contend that employment discrimination is only one form that labor market discrimination takes. The more prevalent form is *wage* discrimination—hiring disadvantaged workers at a superexploited wage.[12] Beginning with Marx, radicals have claimed that competition increases the superexploitation of disadvantaged workers.

As the agricultural example indicated, technology, characterized by economies of scale, creates uneven development within industries. The larger firms are able to build on their technological advantages until the majority of smaller producers are driven to bankruptcy. The smaller producers are not unaware of this process. There are a number of actions they undertake to try to forestall bankruptcy. One strategy recently developed by Galbraith is to

---

12. For a more detailed discussion of the distinction between employment and wage discrimination, see R. Cherry, "Economic Theories of Racism," *Problems in Political Economy*, D. Gordon, ed. (Lexington, Mass.: Heath, 1977), pp. 170–182.

increase the level of self-exploitation.[13] The owner and his family overwork themselves in order to compensate for their technological deficiencies. The typical example today is the family grocery store which maintains solvency in the face of competition from the large supermarkets by remaining open for long hours and using children as employees.

Self-exploitation may typify the reaction of small-scale service firms to competition. However, superexploitation of workers is considered by radicals to be typical of the response of small-scale manufacturing firms. Marx discussed the effect of uneven development on the situation of disadvantaged workers when he analyzed competition between the factory system (large-scale production) and domestic industry (small-scale production). The domestic industry consisted of producers who set up small production facilities in rural areas, often in the basement of residential structures. These producers sought out women, children, and others made destitute by continued unemployment. Marx considered these workers to be the most exploited. According to Marx, "because domestic industry must always compete with either the factory system, or with manufacturing in the same branch of production . . . [it] robs the workman of the conditions most essential to his labor, of space, light, and ventilation."[14]

Marx, however, did not believe that in the longrun superexploitation could fully compensate for the technological disadvantage of the small-scale producer. Eventually, "The cheapening of labor-power, by sheer abuse of the labor of women and children, by sheer robbery of every normal condition requisite for working and living, and by the sheer brutality of overwork and nightwork, meets at last with natural obstacles that cannot be overstepped."[15] At this point, bankruptcy cannot be avoided, and with it, the reduction of both competition and the superexploitation of the disadvantaged. Therefore, for Marx, the *elimination of competition* from small-scale producers was a principal reason for the decline in discrimination.

During the 1970s, the major example of this destructive aspect of competition, according to radicals, is the situation of small-scale clothing firms in

---

13. The self-exploitation of small scale producers was reflected in the situation of nonslave-owning ("small") farmers prior to the Civil War. These farmers, who were the majority group in the Old South, had to compete with the Plantation. The small farmer had to sell his produce at the same price as the Plantation. The only way this could be done was for the small farmer and his family to work and live like slaves. Indeed, some historians have found evidence that the economic well-being of plantation slaves was actually superior to that of the small farmer during this period. For a discussion of how poor whites were adversely affected by slavery, see Sarah Elbert, "Good Times on the Cross: A Marxian Review," *Review of Radical Political Economy* 7 (Fall 1975): 58–60.

14. Karl Marx, *Capital*, vol I (New York: International Pub., 1967), p. 462.

15. Ibid., p. 470.

large urban areas. These firms, under increasing competitive pressure, have reverted back to sweatshop conditions, increasingly relying on undocumented workers for labor. Often, facilities are makeshift operations, unsafe, and unhealthy. But as Marx points out, these actions are necessary for survival, and not the result of greed. So once again, fierce competition has required small-scale firms to intensify the exploitation of the most disadvantaged workers.

15.2 MARXIAN CONCEPT OF COMPETITION

At the time Marx began writing, there was already a large anti-capitalist pro-socialist movement. This movement was morally opposed to capitalist market mechanisms. It was repelled by the exploitative nature of the market for labor, highlighted by the ability of idle rich to live in royal splendor by employing six-year-old children for 70 hours per week at starvation wages.[16] In Marx's opinion, this movement, while well-intentioned, was doomed to failure because it lacked a correct understanding of the capitalist system. While members of this movement were acutely aware of the existence of exploitation, they had a limited understanding of its source. The main purpose of Marx's economic writings was to correct these mistakes.

Marx's concept of capitalist competition is probably one of the most important breakthroughs of his analysis. Nonmarxian theories of competition emphasize that problems in capitalism exist when competition is absent. Marx was well aware that a lack of competition would result in exploitative relationships. However, he emphasized that the very nature of competition is destructive. As indicated, the marxian concept of uneven development makes predictable the bankruptcy of the majority of small property owners as well as the superexploitation of disadvantaged workers. Marx also considered competitive forces to have a thoroughly dehumanizing effect on man. Finally, as the next chapter will show, it was competitive economic forces that were responsible for the periodical and unavoidable economic crises. Because of this central role that Marx's theory of competition played in his analysis, it will be useful to fully elaborate the distinctions between marxian and nonmarxian theories of competition.

Distinguishing Features

In the traditional nonmarxian (neo-classical) competitive model, all firms are assumed to be able to sell any output they desire at the current market price. Since its expected sales are independent of its competitors, each firm makes its

---

16. It has come to be called the utopian socialist movement. It is most identified with the socialist collectives, such as one founded by Robert Owens (the Owenites), which were forerunners of the original Israeli Kibbutz experiments.

decision on choice of inputs independent of its competition. It is further assumed that each firm would choose the same set of inputs to produce the same level of output. Hence, each firm would have the same supply response to market conditions. Changes in industry supply would occur only when the number of firms in the industry changed or when the cost structure of all firms changed simultaneously. In the neo-classical model, since all firms always have the identical supply curve, they will always have the identical share of the market.

By assuming that no intra-industry differences exist, the neo-classical model ignores the possibility that market shares could change as a result of different production decisions of competing firms. This is in sharp contrast with the marxian competitive model which emphasizes the role of changing market shares. Therefore, we should detail the basis for the neo-classical assumption of identical market shares.

The neo-classical assumption can be logically derived from a set of underlying assumptions concerning the nature of competitive markets:

C1—**Each producer has perfect knowledge of technology available.**

C2—**All input markets are competitive, enabling all producers to buy resources at the same price.**

C3—**There is no friction in the system. Producers can incorporate production changes instantaneously and the rate of interest on savings is exactly the same as the rate of interest for borrowing for all producers.**[17]

Given these three assumptions, there are only three situations in which two firms in the same industry would appear to have different cost structures.

Natural productive differentials There may be cases in which it is impossible to supply inputs of the same productive ability to all producers in a given industry. This will occur when productive ability is determined by the natural endowment of the resource. Examples are the differences in productive ability of agricultural land or professional basketball players. This may at first glance appear to dictate that the firm using the best natural resources (best land, best basketball player) would have a lower cost structure than its competing firms. However, in competitive markets for these inputs, rapid pricing adjustments would eliminate any cost differential. We would find that the more productive

---

17. The assumption of unconstrained access to debt instruments at the market rate of interest during economic contractions is critical to the conservative theories of permanent income hypothesis and interest-sensitive capital spending. The unconstrained access enables decision-makers to take a longrun viewpoint rather than being dominated by their immediate financial situation. This assumption reflects a middle-class conception of society in which decision-makers (households and firms) are only slightly inconvenienced by a shortrun downturn; where concerns over possible bankruptcies are virtually nonexistent.

land would be selling at a correspondingly higher price than other land. Similarly, the wage rate of the more naturally endowed ballplayer would be correspondingly higher than the less endowed players. Indeed, it is just this role of equalizing out production differentials which is used to highlight the concept of rents and "quasi-rents."[18]

Different objectives Another possible reason for cost differentials between firms is that they may have different objectives. Suppose that one firm in the industry is not a pure profit maximizer—it has some nonmonetary objectives. This firm may be interested in sales growth (independent of profits), social objectives, or in discriminating against hiring minority workers. If, however, any of these nonmonetary objectives conflict with the allocation necessary for least cost production, this firm would have higher costs than its profit maximizing competitors. In a competitive industry, each firm must be as efficient as possible in order to make the minimum necessary rate of return required to remain in the industry. Therefore, this nonprofit maximizing firm would eventually be forced out of the industry unless its customers and/or workers were willing to subsidize these nonmonetary objectives.

Unexpected gains or losses It is always possible that for some external reason one firm will have an unexpected gain or loss. For example, suppose that Firm A had a natural disaster while its competitor, Firm B, did not. Firm A would then be at an *initial disadvantage* to its competitor. According to the three underlying assumptions of the neo-classical model, this initial disadvantage would be quickly dissipated. In a short period of time, Firm A would again have an identical supply response to Firm B.

Suppose that a fire destroyed some inventory of Firm A so that its current profits were lower than the profits of Firm B. Due to the decline in profits, Firm A must borrow money the next period to meet its capital investment requirements. Firm B has just enough profits to fully internally fund its capital spending requirements. According to assumption C3, Firm A would be able to instantaneously receive the necessary credit at the market rate of interest. In the next period, according to assumptions C1 and C2, both firms would again have the same productive facilities at the same unit production cost. The only difference is that Firm A would have interest payments from the banking loan while Firm B would not.

It would, therefore, seem as if Firm B's total cost of production would be below Firm A's total cost. However, total cost, from an economic standpoint, must include each firm's opportunity costs—the profits which could have been made on alternative activities. Since Firm B had invested its profits while Firm

---

18. In economics, the term *rent* refers to payments to land above the minimum supply price (assumed to be zero). *Quasi-rents* refers to payments to labor above the supply price.

A used external funds, the opportunity cost of Firm B will be higher than Firm A's opportunity cost. Specifically, Firm B's opportunity cost will be higher by the opportunity cost on the additional internal funds used for investment purposes. According to assumption C3, Firm B could have placed these funds in a savings account and earned the market rate of interest. Therefore, if this represents the additional opportunity costs to Firm B, each firm will again have the same total cost. Whereas Firm A has interest payments, Firm B will have additional opportunity costs of the same amount. If each firm's total costs are identical, then so will their supply responses.

Marxian Competitive Model

Marx would agree that neither natural differences nor different objectives are the basis of divergent supply responses of competing firms. Marx believed that productive resources could be considered homogeneous and that the only objective of the firm was personal financial success.[19] Therefore, any differences between the neo-classical and the marxian models must result from how each model assumes firms respond to unexpected profits or losses. We have seen that the neo-classical model implies that any initial disadvantage would have no longterm effect on the competitive position of the affected firm. By contrast, according to the marxian model, any initial disadvantage can result in a cumulative disadvantage after successive periods.

Marx assumed that technological change was dominantly dependent upon access to capital funding. He rejected the neo-classical assumption concerning the banking system. He believed that uncertainty alone would discourage banks from committing funds to a firm already at an initial disadvantage. Hence, the firm with an initial disadvantage would have difficulty obtaining loans necessary to regain a competitive position. Second, capital innovation opportunities are continually available so that any firm with an initial advantage has the ability to more rapidly incorporate the latest innovations than its competitor. Since capital spending projects have long gestation periods, firms with initial advantages can maintain these advantages for a long time. Finally, technological innovations often require increased sales to become economically feasible. Hence, the firm with the initial disadvantage will not be able to grow fast enough to take advantage of many important technological innovations.

Under the marxian assumptions, any firm with an initial advantage would be able to add to that advantage in successive periods. Having larger profits, it could make investments in new technology, and in more research and development than its competitor. If it required some external funds, banks would be more willing to extend it the necessary credit than to its disadvantaged compe-

---

19. Marx assumed that different skill levels were solely due to prior investments in labor (school, training) and not to differences in native ability.

titor. With the greater efficiency, its sales expand more rapidly than its disadvantaged competitor. With size comes the ability to take advantage of even more technological innovations, expanding further its productive strength over its disadvantaged competitor. As the previous agriculture example indicated, the outcome of this process is the eventual bankruptcy of the firms at initial disadvantage.

15.3 ALIENATION AND CAPITALISM

One of the logical outcomes of competition is that work procedures are dictated by technical considerations rather than any humane considerations. The market compels each individual capitalist to produce at least cost, whatever his personal values. Therefore, he cannot pay decent wages as long as lower wages are possible. He can only organize production in the most efficient manner, regardless of the degree of dissatisfaction it entails. For example, the capitalist cannot air condition his plant only because without it working is extremely uncomfortable. He can air condition only if, by reducing the discomfort, workers increase their output sufficiently to financially compensate for the additional expenditures.

However alienated the owner becomes by this process, its major effect is on the situation of workers. What is critical is that, as a result of the market pressures, the worker is subordinated to the material objects he produces. There is a complete devaluation of the worker's humanity.

This dehumanization occurs because under capitalism each worker has no control over the fruits of his labor. He contracts at a wage and his output and conditions of employment are controlled by the capitalist. Indeed, the worker's labor service becomes just another commodity to be bought at the marketplace. Moreover, as already noted, the conditions of work are dictated by technical considerations. These considerations have continuously reduced the scope of the work routine—through extending the divisions of labor. The intellectual activities in shaping the work process are done by one worker while the actual physical activity is done by another worker. This intellectual-physical separation makes the industrial worker a mere appendage of the machine he operates.

Marx chooses a most grotesque example to illustrate how under the laws of capitalism there is no humanity but only service of the production process. He notes,

> The laborers in the mines in South America, whose daily task consists in bringing to the surface on their backs a load of metal weighing from 180 to 200 pounds, from a depth of 450 feet, live on bread and beans only; they themselves would prefer the bread alone for food, but their masters, who have found out that the men cannot work so hard on

bread, treat them like horses, and compel them to eat beans, which are relatively much richer in bone-earth (phosphate of lime) than bread.[20]

As a consequence, work becomes not a means of developing man's creativity, but a simple degrading activity undertaken out of necessity. The profit motive of competitive capitalism thus robs the worker of the properties which Marx felt separated man from other species—his ability to create from nature and reduce man to his animal activities. Marx expresses this as follows,

> *The worker, therefore, feels himself at home only during his leisure time whereas at work he feels homeless. His work is not a satisfaction of a need but only a means for satisfying other needs. Its alien character is clearly shown by the fact that as soon as there is no physical or other compulsion it is avoided like the plague . . . the worker feels himself to be freely active only in his animal functions—eating, drinking and procreating, and at most also in his dwelling and in personal adornment—while in his human functions he is reduced to an animal. The animal becomes human and the human animal.*[21]

Is Work Intrinsically Alienating?

As has been noted at numerous points, the conservative economist contends that market decisions are controlled by households so that if work is organized in a routinized dehumanized manner it must reflect the choice of workers. As Galbraith has noted, the imagery of choice implies that "if people are abused, it is because they choose self-abuse."[22] Mainstream liberals do not dwell on this characterization of the labor market. Instead, they contend that work by its very nature is alienating; that the primary objective of man is to maximize his enjoyment of leisure. Hence, the only objective for working is a means to earn money to increase one's enjoyment of leisure. This viewpoint can be found in works by Adam Smith. It continues to underly the neo-classical labor-supply models, where a trade-off is posited between work and leisure, where the only objective of work is to earn income. However, the most forceful presentation of this viewpoint can be found on commercial television. Beverage, travel, and sporting goods commercials constantly advertise that the objective in life is to get away from work and enjoy your leisure in the most hedonistic manner possible. The "good life" is to party, to indulge, to satiate oneself in material pleasures. Sporting events, particularly college football,

---

20. Ibid., p. 573n.

21. Karl Marx, *Early Writings,* T. Bottomore, ed. (London: Watts, 1963), p. 125.

22. J. K. Galbraith, *Economics and the Public Purpose* (Boston: Houghton Mifflin, 1973), p. 6.

emphasize that the well-rounded normal individual should invest his energies in the "drama" of witnessing the outcomes of his hometown's sports teams. Prime-time series are postured to give people excitement.

Marx believed that alienating work is a condition specific to class societies. He strongly criticized the view that work must reflect disutility. In response to Smith's presentation of this thesis, Marx writes,

> "Tranquility" appears as the adequate state, as identical with "freedom" and "happiness." It seems quite far from Smith's mind that the individual, "in his normal state of health, strength, activity, skill facility," also needs a normal portion of work, and of the suspension of tranquility. Certainly, labor obtains its measure from the outside, through the aim to be attained and the obstacles to be overcome in attaining it. But Smith has no inkling whatever that this overcoming of obstacles is in itself a liberating activity—and that, further, the external aims become stripped of the semblance of merely external natural urgencies, and become posited as aims which the individual himself posits—hence real freedom, whose action is, precisely labor. He is right, of course, that in its historic forms as slave labor, serf-labor, and wage labor, labor always appears as repulsive, always as external forced labor; and not labor, by contrast, as "freedom, and happiness."[23]

15.4 SPECIALIZATION AND CAPITALISM

Under capitalism, labor specialization is extensively used. Not only are productive activities broken into separately performed parts, but each worker specializes in each of the separate parts.

It is argued that the reason for the breakdown of production activities into their separately performed parts is that it speeds up the process. Less extraneous movements are required. The reason why each worker specializes in only one part of the production process is less clear. Usually, it is claimed that comparative advantage between individuals dictates individual specialization. For example, Samuelson, in illustrating the notion of comparative advantage, takes the case of the "best lawyer in town who is also the best typist."[24] Fortunately, he has a comparative advantage at law, so he will find it profitable to hire a secretary. After some severe criticism for the selection of such sexist stereotyping,[25] Samuelson resorts to an example in which women

---

23. Marx, *Grundrisse,* pp. 611–12.

24. Paul Samuelson, *Economics,* 7th ed. (New York: McGraw-Hill, 1967), p. 647.

25. Cheryl Payer, "The Lawyer's Typist: Variations on a Theme by Paul Samuelson," *Monthly Review* (Mar. 1974): 44–48.

"are three times as productive as men in welding, twice as productive in mining, and three-fourths as productive in distilling."[26]

The marxian outlook rejects any attempt to justify the degree of job segmentation and labor specialization as being required for technical efficiency reasons.

Specialization and Hierarchy

Marxists argue that while part of the reason for job segmentation is technical efficiency, under capitalism, a significant portion of job segmentation does not increase productive efficiency. Instead, job segmentation is chosen as a means of reducing the power of workers. Kathy Stone attempts to demonstrate this contention by analyzing the change in job classifications in the steel industry at the turn of the century.[27]

Between 1860 and 1890, steel production in the United States increased from 12,000 net tons to 4,800,000 net tons per year. During this period, occupations in the steel industry were divided into two groups—skilled workers who performed activities requiring training, and unskilled workers who performed the heavy manual labor. The usual procedure was for the skilled workers to directly hire the unskilled workers. In return for the use of the productive facilities, the skilled workers agreed to sell the steel produced to the owners at a specified rate, which varied with the market price for steel.

Under this procedure, the owner of the steel mill was a pure rentier. Once the tonnage rate was specified, he had no influence over the organization of production or the distribution of income among the individual workers. The skilled steel workers' union was the strongest workers' organization of its day since it directly controlled the entire work process. During the 1880s, with the expansion of production signalling the potential for profits, the owners desired a far greater share of the revenues from steel production than the negotiated rates with the skilled workers' union allowed. Moreover, foreign competition increased the need to institute cost-reducing technology. However, without the union's approval, the owners could not change work rules.

By 1893, the owners had had enough of unions. The strongest union lodge was at Andrew Carnegie's Homestead (Pennsylvania) Plant. He ordered the plant to be fenced in, platforms for sentinels constructed, housing inside for strikebreakers, and hired 300 Pinkertons. At that point, he closed down the plant, laid off the entire workforce, and announced they would henceforth operate nonunion. With the sheriff, state militia, and federal government siding with Carnegie, his planned destruction of the union was successful.

---

26. Paul Samuelson, *Economics,* 10th ed. (New York: McGraw-Hill, 1976), p. 859n.
27. Kathy Stone, "The Origins of Job Structures in the Steel Industry," *Review of Radical Political Economy* 6 (Summer 1974): 61–97.

Kathy Stone contends that with the defeat of the union, Carnegie and other owners set about to make sure a strong union would never again be possible. In order to reduce the potential power of the skilled workers, Carnegie reorganized production to eliminate the need for skilled work. Jobs previously done by skilled workers were either eliminated through mechanization or divided into separate activities. Without the requirement of a skilled workforce, Carnegie had little to fear—for now all workers could be easily interchanged.

Steve Marglin[28] claims that the experience in the steel industry can be generalized to all areas of manufacturing. He presents numerous examples to demonstrate that a principal objective of job segmentation was to reduce the power of skilled workers rather than to increase the technical efficiency of the process.

If it is true that a significant amount of job segmentation is due to the desire of capitalists to maintain power, then a great deal of segmentation could be eliminated without loss of efficiency. Instead, jobs could revert back to craft-activities and become less dehumanizing.

Specialization and Native Ability

As already noted, even if jobs should be performed in a segmented fashion it does not follow that each worker must be solely employed permanently at one segmented job. Marxists contend that with a breakdown of hierarchy on many jobs, intellectual and manual functions could be integrated. For example, with sufficient technical training, the same workers could both design and work on the production process. Jobs with purely routinized and dehumanizing characteristics could be rotated. By minimizing the amount of degrading labor performed by each individual and allowing all workers to participate in intellectual activity, labor can truly become a liberating experience.

Implicitly underlying mainstream contentions that specialization is required for technical reasons is the notion that native ability differences are substantial. Some, like McConnell, claim that few individuals have the native abilities to enter the high paying (intellectually-rewarding) professions.[29] Thomas Sowell contends that one reason for the lack of economic success of blacks is that they have large family sizes, and IQ studies have shown that "mental development tends to be greatest among small families."[30]

If IQ tests are accepted as measures of native ability, then it can easily be argued that substantial productivity losses would result from the integration of

28. Stephen A. Marglin, "What Do Bosses Do? The Origins and Functions of Hierarchy in Capitalist Production," *Review of Radical Political Economy* 6 (Summer 1974): 33-60.

29. Campbell McConnell, *Economics,* 5th ed. (New York: McGraw-Hill, 1972), pp. 559, 659.

30. Thomas Sowell, *Race and Economics* (New York: McKay, 1975), p. 137.

manual and intellectual labor. In turn, assumptions that this productivity loss is substantial implies that equality in the workplace is costly. Therefore, there is a substantial trade-off between "equity and efficiency."[31]

Marxists reject the notion of an "equity-efficiency trade-off." Instead, they suggest that the purpose of IQ tests has always been to legitimate hierarchy. If this marxist contention is correct, then a society would be able to have substantial integration of manual and intellectual functions without any loss of technical efficiency.

Specialization and Consumption

Under capitalism, market forces dictate resource allocation. Goods are produced in the marketplace as long as the marginal benefits (MB) are larger than the marginal costs (MC). Individualist economists emphasize that this approach demonstrates that we should not try to completely eliminate negative goods, such as pollution or dangerous alienating labor. They claim, as illustrated in Figure 15.1, that we should only eliminate these negative goods, up to the point at which the MB = MC. This is at quantity P^*. As the figure indicates, if society attempted to eliminate more of the negative goods, the additional benefits would not fully compensate for the additional cost. This implies that there is an optimal level of pollution, dangerous labor, rapes, etc.[32] The pure example often referred to by conservatives during the 1970s was the issue of mandatory airbags in cars. These airbags, at a cost of $200, would instantaneously inflate in the front section of the automobile when a specific level of contact occurred. It would reduce the amount of serious injuries from automobile accidents. The conservatives argue that it should be a matter of individual choice. Each car owner would weight the marginal benefits against the marginal cost to decide how much auto safety to buy. Presumably, for many the expected additional benefits would not outweigh the additional cost. Of course, if it happens that some are still killed from automobile accidents, it would still reflect the "optimum"—the additional benefits from reducing highway accidents (deaths) further would not outweigh the additional costs. Similarly, the personal decision to smoke cigarettes reflects the rational choice of individuals so that the death rate from cigarette-induced cancer is "optimal."

31. For mainstream discussions on the importance of the "equity-efficiency trade-off," see Paul Samuelson, *Economics,* 8th ed. (New York: McGraw-Hill, 1970), pp. 766–767. It is significant that Arthur Okun should make this the central point of his bicentennial article, "Equal Rights but Unequal Incomes," *New York Times,* July 4, 1976, pp. 98–104.

32. For a derivation of the "optimal" amount of pollution and crime, see H. Votey and L. Phillips, *Economic Analysis of Pressing Social Problems* (Chicago: Rand McNally, 1977); "Environmental Quality: A View from the Marketplace"; "The War on Crime: Prevention or Control."

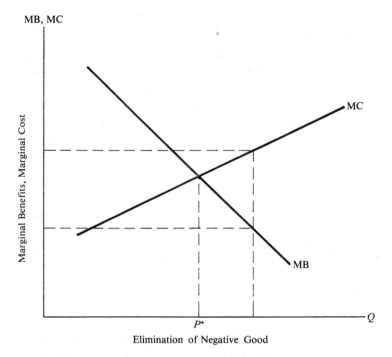

Elimination of Negative Good

Figure 15.1 The optimal level of a negative good

There is a certain internal logic in each of these examples that seems hard to refute. After all, aren't people rational? Isn't it their choice if they want to "buy" some potentially "negative goods"? As with most choice theory arguments, they make some sense when related to pure consumption issues. In each of these examples, both the benefits and costs were borne by the same individual.[33] However, once the context is changed to where the benefits and cost fall on different people, the benefit-cost framework loses much of its charm.

Suppose we take the example of the purchase of consumer goods which emanate "negative goods," not in their consumption as cigarettes, but to those who are necessary for its production. Here, the costs to the buyer are not the negative goods but only the payment necessary to induce others to bear these costs. If the buyers are wealthy and the laborers are poor, then the market will dictate a substantial production of both the consumer good and the negative good. Marx gives the example of lace manufacturing. He reported that a health survey found that one in eight women, mostly between the ages of 17 and 24, engaged in that occupation suffered from tuberculosis.[34] Was this "optimal"?

---

33. To the extent that parts of the costs of cigarette smoking are borne by the fetus of pregnant mothers, there are still external effects to the individual decision-maker.

34. Marx, *Capital*, vol I, p. 466.

John Kenneth Galbraith gives an interesting example of how the specialization of labor encourages the production of goods requiring "negative labor." He claims,

> *Beyond a certain point the possession and consumption of goods becomes burdensome unless the task associated therewith can be delegated. Thus the consumption of increasingly elaborate or exotic food is only rewarding if there is someone to prepare it. . . . So also with dress, vehicles, the lawn, sporting facilities and other consumer artifacts. If there are people to whom responsibility for administration can be delegated and who, in turn, can recruit and direct the required servant labor force, consumption has no limits. Otherwise the limits on consumption are severe.*[35]

Galbraith claims that the role of women thus became relegated to housewife, to becoming a "crypto-servant" class. He then goes on to argue how, by having women "specialize" in procuring, processing, and distributing consumer goods, men can maintain a high level of demand for such products. If, however, men had to labor rather than just pay for these goods, they would soon lose their taste for such delicacies. Since only the high-wage male profession can comfortably afford such an arrangement, Galbraith's model is another example of the ability of upper-income groups to take advantage of "specialization."[36]

In both the Marx and Galbraith examples, specialization in the context of an available low-wage workforce encourages the consumption of goods which require menial, degrading, and often physically harmful labor.

Specialization and Technological Innovation

Labor-saving technology was considered by Marx the most important way society could liberate man. Through mechanization, the most brutal and damaging labor could be eliminated. This is why he saw the factory system as a step forward from the manufacturing and domestic industries. Labor-saving technology first requires invention and then the ability to innovate. Both of these steps are hindered by capitalist-engendered job segmentation.

Under capitalism, the gains from the introduction of labor-saving technology accrue in the first instance to the firm in the form of higher profits and, at most, trickle down to the remaining workers and consumers. The workers who are eliminated have little benefits from the innovation. They face a period of unemployment, possibly require relocation, and the need to change

---

35. Galbraith, *Economics and the Public Purpose*, pp. 28–29.

36. Galbraith attempts to obscure the *class* nature of exploitation of housewives by making it seem that all husbands can shift degrading work to wives. However, most working class husbands must themselves perform degrading work for a living and/or must spend two hours per day commuting.

occupations. Not surprisingly, there is a pact among workers not to offer "productivity" suggestions to management and to resist any change in work rules which would facilitate innovation. The term "featherbedding" has come to refer to situations where labor has been able to maintain certain jobs even after they have been made superfluous by technological innovations.

The segmented worker, therefore, discourages the innovation that is necessary for the liberation of man. On the one hand, the existing job may be degrading, even dangerous. On the other hand, faced with unemployment, the worker chooses the existing job and fights against innovation. Two major examples of this paradox are the shipping and coal industries. In the shipping industry, containerization is capable of eliminating the most backbreaking work. However, longshoremen have been able to strike and retard the introduction of containerization. Similarly, coal miners have fought stripmining (which is many times safer than traditional mining) because it will eliminate a vast number of jobs.

If workers have no fear of unemployment and forced relocation, no paradox exists. Workers are free to use their energies to devise new labor-saving procedures. Since workers, through their on-the-job experience, are in the best position to discover innovative techniques, this freedom is capable of increasing the number of innovative techniques far above the number under capitalism. Moreover, there would be no reason for workers to fight against the adoption of labor-saving technology. The elimination of specialization, therefore, not only releases new energies attempting to reduce dehumanizing labor, but it also makes existing jobs less dehumanizing. These jobs no longer are purely physical labor since now workers, while performing these tasks, are encouraged to use their intellect to devise more efficient procedures.

15.5 CONCLUSION

This chapter has developed the marxian model of competition. Unlike the neo-classical model, the marxian model assumes that differences in firm size and speed of technological innovations play a critical explanatory role. Marx assumed that due to the risk-averting behavior of banks and the time lags associated with technological innovations, production cost differentials between competing firms tend to grow with time. Specifically, those firms which lag behind in technological innovation tend to have lower profits and less access to financial markets. In time, these weaker firms will be forced out of the industry. Hence, firms are forced to innovate as quickly as possible or risk bankruptcy.

When the concept of uneven development was applied to the examples of agriculture and racial discrimination, it was implied that competition intensifies restrictions on human liberation. In the case of agriculture, it makes it predictable that the majority of small farmers will go bankrupt, regardless of their efforts. Only those few farmers who can mechanize and expand at the expense of the many survive. Hence, small farmers, as well as marxists, have long fought *against* the workings of the free market. Small farmers have favored government support of artificially high prices. The equity and efficiency costs of this policy are great. Since large farms produce most of the market output, they will receive most of the subsidy. Since prices are higher, urban workers pay for the protection of the small farmer. Since small farms are maintained, technological innovations are not implemented as widely as possible. For these reasons, as well as ideological ones, marxists have chosen to collectivize agriculture.

Uneven development implies that with identical wage rates, smaller producers will have a higher unit production cost than the larger producer. To forestall bankruptcy, the small producers must engage in superexploitation of labor. They must take advantage of the least protected groups of workers (women and children in England's domestic industries of the 1850s and undocumented workers in the U.S. garment industry of the 1970s) as a last ditch attempt to forestall bankruptcy. Therefore, from the marxian, as well as the Galbraithian standpoint, the elimination of small scale competition will have a liberating effect on mankind.

The final part of this chapter developed the marxian contention that competition among capitalists and their need to control the labor process substantially influence the degree and allocation of degrading alienating labor. Marxists argue that:

1. The segmenting of jobs was influenced by the needs of capitalists to break the power of skilled workers.

2. The lack of rotation and integration of manual and intellectual activities, which rationalizes inequality, has no scientific basis.

3. The demand for degrading labor-using goods is influenced by the separation of production and consumption, due to capitalist hierarchy, rather than their intrinsic value.

It was also mentioned that Marx considered competitive forces to be responsible for the periodical economic crises. The next chapter will develop some marxian macro-models which demonstrate this last point.

CHAPTER SIXTEEN

MARXIAN CRISIS THEORY

In previous chapters we found that conservatives contend that a laissez-faire economy can sustain full employment; mainstream liberals contend that some government intervention is necessary to sustain full employment; and left-liberals contend that government economic planning is necessary to maintain full employment. Marx claimed that no government intervention could forestall periods of unemployment because of the contradictions inherent in the capitalist system. These contradictions stem from the irreconcilable conflicts which exist within a capitalist system—the conflict between capital and labor, and the conflict between competing capitalists. Chapter 15 has already indicated how competition can undermine the quality of life and, in fact, intensify the forces of discrimination and exploitation. This chapter will detail the basis for the marxian assertion that competitive forces make it inevitable that capitalist economies will experience extended periods of economic contraction.

The first section presents an overview of marxian crisis theory. It indicates the distinction made between an economic crisis and an economic recession. It also describes the characteristics of previous economic crises in the United States.

Next, the chapter will develop the marxian notion of the average profit rate. The average profit rate will be determined by two variables—the rate of exploitation and the organic composition of capital. Each of these terms and their underlying determinants will be discussed.

For Marx, the tendency for the average profit rate to decline was the most important manifestation of the contradictions of competitive capitalism. Two theories of the tendency will be developed. One theory highlights the effect of class struggle on the rate of exploitation. The other emphasizes how the inability of individual capitalists to coordinate their investment decisions (the anarchy of capitalist production) results in a tendency towards overinvestment. Thus, excess capacity rises and the rate of profit declines.

Marxists assert that economic contractions due to the falling rate of profit are more severe than those due to aggregate demand deficiencies. The basis of this assertion is discussed in the last section of this chapter. First, due to uneven development, bankruptcies will be incurred as weaker firms in each industry go under. Hence, the contraction has differential effects on capitalists and thus fragments their policy recommendations. Second, attempts to correct profit rate declines through wage rate adjustments intensifies the conflict between labor and capital. For these reasons, the lack of national interest becomes glaring during profit rate decline-induced contractions. This differs dramatically from contractions due to deficient demand. Finally, the possibility that bankruptcies and contractions are *necessary* will be discussed. In this event, government policies which protect the economy from bankruptcies would be counterproductive.

16.1 AN OVERVIEW OF MARXIAN CRISIS THEORY

The radical viewpoint argues that the problems of the 1970s are not the result of a series of unfortunate independent events—Watergate, the 1974 oil embargo, the 1970s food price inflation. Nor are they the result of the political ambitions of individuals, such as Nixon, Carter, or Reagan. These problems are the inevitable consequences of domestic and international contradictions within the world capitalist system. Moreover, this period is not just another recession in which adjustments to correct imbalances easily occur, thus preparing the way for the next expansion. Instead, radicals claim that this period is a *crisis* for capitalism.

Radicals claim that the distinction between recessions and crises is not quantitative; not a matter of the extent of unemployment or production contractions alone. Crises are distinguished by the universality of their effects. They are universal in two senses. First, their effects have never been confined to narrow economic dimensions—they have affected nearly every sphere of peoples' daily experience. Two spheres of daily life affected by crises have been the structure of government and social relationship within society. Second, crises ignore national boundaries, spreading throughout the capitalist economies. These generalizations can be illustrated with a comparison of the 1970s with two earlier periods of capitalist crisis, the 1890s and 1930s.[1]

Structure of Government

During the 1890s, the movement for municipal reform arose. This movement, claiming to reduce corruption, centralized government decision-making in municipal and county bodies rather than at the precinct or ward levels. "Better

---

1. For a broader discussion of the relationship of institutional changes to economic crises, see David M. Gordon, "Up and Down the Long Roller Coaster," in URPE, *U.S. Capitalism in Crisis,* pp. 22–34.

government'' was initiated by leading businessmen who desired a local government which would be responsive to corporate requirements rather than local community interests.[2]

During the 1930s crisis, the next major structural shift began—the movement for an activist federal government and the abandonment of states' rights (prerogatives). With the New Deal programs of unemployment benefits, social security, and public works programs, the Federal government began asserting its control of the national economy even when this conflicted with the objectives of individual state governments. This shift from states' rights to federal regulation extended over the next three decades, culminating with the Civil Rights legislation of the 1960s.

In the 1970s, radicals argued that the current crisis required a further restructuring of the government's role in the economy—the move to federal economic planning. John Kenneth Galbraith began promoting the necessity for federal economic planning to avert economic stagnation in the late 1960s. In 1974, leading liberal economists and corporate executives formed the ''Initiative Committee on Economic Planning,'' which was followed by planning recommendations from the Rockefeller-funded Trilateral Commission in 1976.[3] If the radical thesis is correct, then the 1980s will witness the beginning of economic planning by the federal government.

Social Restructuring

At a social level, the 1890s were identified with the rise of anti-egalitarian movements espousing racist ideologies. The anti-immigration movement began. It claimed that eastern and southern Europeans were inferior races who should not be allowed to immigrate to the United States.[4] These views legitimated violence against immigrant groups, especially when they were involved in union-organizing efforts. At the same time, the birth of the anti-black movement in the South began.[5] In 1895, the Supreme Court ruled that ''separate but equal'' was legal, setting the stage for Jim Crow (''whites-only'')

---

2. This thesis is found in Samuel Hays, ''Municipal Reform in the Progressive Era: Whose Class Interest?'' *Pacific Northwest Quarterly,* 55 (Oct. 1964): 157–69.

3. For a fuller discussion of the movement towards planning, see William Tabb, ''Domestic Economic Planning Under Carter: The Imprint of Trilateralism,'' in URPE, *U.S. Capitalism in Crisis,* pp. 275–82.

4. For a discussion of the extent of racist ideology within the economics profession, see Robert Cherry, ''Racial Thought and the Early Economics Profession,'' *Review of Social Economy* 34 (Oct. 1976): 147–62.

5. One of the most widely held myths is that anti-black movements became widespread with the ending of Reconstruction in 1876. However, it was not until the late 1890s that broad-based multi-racial unity was broken. For a discussion of this, see C. Vann Woodward, *The Strange Career of Jim Crow* (New York: Oxford University Press, 1974).

laws. Social Darwinist theories were popularized which claimed that blacks were at a lower stage of human evolution than whites. These movements developed during the next decades, reaching their pinnacle in the 1920s, when anti-immigration laws were passed and lynchings of blacks were publicly defended by Southern politicians.

With the 1930s crisis, the anti-egalitarian racist movement was undermined. The famous Scottsboro case, the multi-racial union-organizing drives of the CIO, and the March on Washington Movement for fair employment laws changed the direction of race relation and improved the economic position of all working people.[6] This rank-and-file movement extended over the next three decades.

The crisis of the 1970s, radicals argue, has dictated a corporate attack on egalitarian anti-racist policies. The decline in profit rates and the intensified international competition have left no room for liberal reforms. Instead, cutbacks in social spending are required. In order to justify these cutbacks, racist ideologies (Jensen's thesis of black genetic inferiority) and racial conflicts (school busing) have been promoted. Politicians such as Rizzo (Philadelphia) and Hicks (Boston) have attempted to organize movements to assert white people's rights. If the radical thesis is correct, this racist movement will continue to grow during the 1980s.

World Conflict

In each of these three periods, economic contractions have been experienced on an international scale. During the 1890s, the entire industrialized world had declining production, employment, and sales. Radicals suggest that the extension of foreign domination of less developed countries, which lowered raw material costs and opened new markets, was chosen as a solution to economic stagnation. The Spanish-American War, Boer War, and Boxer Rebellion (China) were all fought by advanced capitalist countries attempting to gain increased spheres of economic influence. Radicals argue that these imperialist ventures brought capitalist countries into conflict with each other over spheres of economic influence and eventually caused World War I.

During the 1930s, the world crisis again brought capitalist countries into conflict over world markets and spheres of economic influence. Tariff wars and protectionism grew. Japan, Germany, and Italy attempted to increase their spheres of economic influence at the expense of Anglo-American spheres of influence. Radicals argued that it was these conflicts which precipitated World War II.

---

6. For a discussion of the anti-racist movement of the 1930s, see Robert Cherry, "Economic Theories of Racism," in *Problems in Political Economy,* David M. Gordon, ed. (Lexington, Mass.: Heath, 1977), pp. 170–182.

The 1970s also brought a worldwide economic crisis. Low profit rates and capital investment stagnation characterized the entire capitalist world.[7] The common problems of production stagnation and excess capacity are leading to similar solutions. A *Fortune* article notes, "In the early 1930s, an epidemic of trade restrictions nearly strangled international trade, and thereby helped sink the world into the Great Depression. . . . [I]n 1977, rather suddenly, protectionism has once again become a dangerous presence in the world economy."[8] If the present period follows the pattern of the previous crisis periods, then the intensification of conflict can spill over into a world war.

Marxian crisis thesis, therefore, is important because it argues that certain policies (economic planning and anti-egalitarian racist actions) will be pursued during the 1980s with an increasing potential for military conflicts.

16.2 THE MARXIAN ECONOMIC MODEL[9]

The major objective of Marx's economic analysis was to explain the broad movements of the entire economy. In this regard, Marx and the other classical economists before him, most notably David Ricardo, were macroeconomists. Marx desired an analytical framework which would highlight the most distinguishing features of a capitalist economy:

1. Labor is a commodity which, like all others, is exchanged in the marketplace at its competitive value.

2. Industrial production is the dominant sector of the economy.

3. The distribution of income between wages and profits is the most important determinant of economic growth.

4. Rapid technological change is a central feature of industrial production.

5. The industrial reserve army is necessary for the maintenance of a capitalist society.

Marx considered the labor theory of value to be the appropriate analytical framework. The underlying assumption of the labor theory of value is that the value of all goods exchanged in the marketplace is completely determined by

---

7. For data on the manifestations of the crisis in the United States, see Rick Seltzer, "The Development of the Crisis in the United States," in URPE, *U.S. Capitalism in Crisis*, pp. 35–45.

8. *Fortune* (Nov. 1977): 103.

9. Much of this section follows the outline used in Paul Sweezy, *Theory of Capitalist Development* (New York: Oxford University Press, 1942), Chapters 3 and 4.

the socially necessary labor time required for its production. Let us see how Marx was able to measure all goods in terms of the labor time expended in production.

Abstract Labor

In order to compare the labor time expended to produce various goods, the labor units must be of the same quality. Therefore, Marx begins his analysis by defining a standard labor unit—abstract labor—which will serve as the measuring unit of labor time for all commodities.

Two problems must be surmounted if all production is to be measured in standardized units of abstract labor. First, since production techniques may vary between firms producing the same commodity, a "typical" firm must be chosen. It is the labor time expended in production by this typical firm that is used to determine the value of each commodity. In particular, Marx considered the *socially-necessary* labor time to be that required to produce "an article under the normal conditions of production, and with the average degree of skill and intensity prevalent at the time." Here, Marx decided to begin the analysis of the general laws of motion of capitalist societies by ignoring the differences that exist between firms in the same industry—what was called uneven development in the last chapter. As indicated there, the law of uneven development was a central feature of the dynamics of the capitalist system and will be incorporated at a later stage of the analysis.

Second, in order to measure labor time in standardized units, it is necessary to assume that labor more skilled than average ("abstract") must have a correspondingly great power of production. That is, a unit of a specific level of skill can be considered a fixed multiple of the standardized labor unit.

By assuming a specific skilled worker is equivalent to a *fixed* multiple of the standardized unit is to imply that the skilled worker is consistently more productive than the standardized unit, regardless of the occupation. This indicates that the possibility of an individual worker having an uncommon natural ability in a specific occupation is ignored. According to Sweezy, Marx felt that examples of selective skills would be minimal for the overwhelming number of activities performed by industrial labor. For these activities, general characteristics of strength and dexterity determine productivity so that "as a rule the superiority of the more skilled will manifest itself regardless of the line of production in which he may be engaged."[10]

It is clear when one discusses professional and artistic labor that substantial specialized skills exist. There are individuals who only have an above average productivity in one line of production—art, mathematics, football. However, since Marx was concerned with industrial production, he felt justified in ignoring these cases.

---

10. Ibid., p. 43.

If the difference in productivity between two workers is due to training, then it is assumed that this difference exactly reflects the labor time involved in the training. For example, suppose that the productive life of a skilled worker is 100,000 hours (10 hours per day, 250 days per year, for 40 years) and 20,000 hours were expended on his training. In this case, each unit of skilled labor must be equivalent to 1.2 units of the standardized unit of labor. This assumes that the capitalist class regulated training and would only allow workers to receive education if the increased productivity offsets the labor time expended on training. In our example, if the value of a skilled labor unit was only 1.1 units of standardized labor, it would have been more productive to only use standardized units and the capitalist class would not have invested in training.

Simple Commodity Production

The classical economists called the system in which workers owned the entire means of production *simple commodity production.* In such an economy it can easily be demonstrated that the forces of competition dictate that the exchange ratio between any two commodities (their relative price) would correspond exactly to their labor time ratio.

Suppose that the labor time necessary for killing and preparing beaver skins is exactly twice the time necessary to kill and prepare deer skins. In this case, the market price of beaver skins must be twice that of deer skins. If the price of beaver skins is less than twice the price of deer skins, it would be foolish for hunters to attempt to gather beaver skins. The hunters' time would be more profitably spent gathering deer skins. As they begin to switch from beaver to deer hunting, the price of beaver skins rises and the price of deer skins is lowered. Eventually, this price adjustment results in the price of beaver skins rising to become twice that of deer skins. At this point, there is no longer an incentive for hunters to switch away from beavers. Competition thus forces the price ratio to correspond to the labor time ratio between the two commodities.[11]

Commodity Production Under Capitalism

Capitalism is distinguished from simple commodity production by the different form of ownership of means of production. In simple commodity produc-

---

11. Marx was quite aware that unique and nonreproducible goods, such as art, would not sell at prices having any relationship to their value. However, Marx was concerned with the process of production of manufacturing, which he considered the central industries of capitalism. Therefore, the simplistic criticism of value theory, which uses examples of art objects to demonstrate that utility "preferences" determine price, distorts the purpose of value theory.

tion the worker owns the means of production, while in a capitalist society they are owned by the capitalist. This, according to Marx, profoundly affects the decision to produce.

Under simple commodity production, the worker produces commodities, sells them in the marketplace, and then buys other commodities. Marx designated this circuit as C-M-C. The value of commodities received (in labor time) would just equal the value of the commodities sold. Workers would produce in this situation because the commodities acquired are qualitatively different than those produced. The equality of trade implies that there is no accumulation of wealth through trade since no worker is able to increase the value of his assets.

Under capitalism, the capitalist dictates the amount of production. As a capitalist, he expends money to produce commodities which he then sells in the marketplace for money. Marx designated this circuit as M-C-M'. The distinction between M and the larger quantity M' occurs because the only reason a capitalist would produce is if the sum of the value of his sales (M') is larger than the money expended for its production (M). The difference between M and M' is the profits made by the capitalist. Marx called this difference surplus value. Note that, according to this formulation, profits are specific to a capitalist system since they are not required in a society of simple commodity production.

Labor and Labor Power

When the capitalist goes into the marketplace he must pay a certain sum to buy the worker's capacity to work, his labor power. For Marx, the value of labor power as with all other commodities, is determined by the necessary labor time required for its production. Marx assumed that the subsistence necessary to maintain and reproduce a laborer was culturally determined and fixed in the shortrun.

The assumption made by Marx that the wage paid for labor power is fixed at a subsistence level has been the subject of widespread misunderstanding.[12] Much of his analysis only required that two underlying assumptions concerning the subsistence wage hold:

1. The subsistence wage bundle is fixed independent of the productivity of the labor power.

---

12. In particular, the contention that Marx predicted that the standard of living of the working class would continually stagnate is not easy to substantiate, nor is it critical to much of Marx's analysis. Moreover, his law of the falling rate of profit, which was central to his analysis, requires that the standard of living of the working class rises. For a discussion of these issues, see M. C. Howard and J. E. King, *The Political Economy of Marx* (Burnt Mill, U. K.: Longman, 1975), pp. 132–135, 209.

2. The subsistence wage bundle is invariant with the specific labor activity; i.e., it is the same for all labor activities.

We might ask why wages don't have to be bid up to their productive level or respond to the desirability of specific occupations. For Marx, there was a simple answer. In normal times, the size of the industrial reserve army is sufficient to suppress all alternatives available to workers. A sufficient reserve army eliminates the need for firms to compete for scarce labor, and eliminates the ability of workers to easily shift to other firms or occupations. Thus, wages do not have to respond to the productivity of individual workers. The reserve army is also sufficient to suppress any preferences for jobs among workers. Workers must take available jobs in order to exist, thus, firms are not required to pay any premium for undesirable occupations.

In normal times two factors insure the maintenance of a sufficient reserve army. Most important, Marx assumed that there were always groups within the population who were incompletely absorbed into the labor force. In his time they were dominantly composed of agricultural workers who were migrating to urban centers. Today, it is argued that the secondary workforce comprises the incompletely utilized labor force. This group, which is disproportionately nonwhite and nonmale, provides a reservoir of labor, sufficient in normal times to enable employers to maintain existing wage rates when expanding. Rather than being forced to raise wages to attract scarce labor, employers are able to draw more secondary workers into the permanent workforce at the existing wage.[13]

The second mechanism operating is the continuous innovation of labor-saving technology. Automation is usually sufficient to keep the growth of labor demand low enough so that the attraction of secondary workers at existing wages is sufficient to meet production requirements.

Once a fixed amount of money is chosen as the subsistence wage it could then be converted into a bundle of commodities. In turn, this subsistence bundle could then be reduced to the labor time necessary for its production. We could then calculate the hours of labor that are required each day to produce the subsistence bundle paid to each worker for his labor power.

Given current levels of productivity, suppose that it would require 8 hours each day to produce the subsistence bundle. If workers only labored 8 hours each day then there would be no surplus value. The revenues that a capitalist would receive from his sales must be entirely used up to pay each worker his subsistence wage. However, if the worker labored 12 hours each day, surplus value would be created. The worker would labor 8 hours each day to produce his own subsistence and labor 4 hours each day to produce goods for the capitalist.

---

13. This position is discussed in Chapter 2 and developed in Michael Piore, "Alternative Views on the Relationship of Unemployment and Inflation," *Challenge* 21 (May/June 1978).

Marxian Rate of Exploitation

Marx defined the rate of exploitation as the ratio of the hours worked for the capitalist (s) to the hours worked to produce the subsistence bundle (v). He believed that due to labor mobility the rate of exploitation s/v would be the same for all industries. Therefore, the average rate of exploitation for the economy as a whole, $S/V = s/v$. There are three factors which can independently influence the rate of exploitation: the size of the subsistence bundle, the length of the working day, and the level of labor productivity.

If any of these three factors change, the rate of exploitation will also change. For example, increased mechanization increases the productivity of labor. The subsistence bundle can now be produced in less time. If the length of the working day is also unchanged, then the effect of increased labor productivity is to reduce V and increase S. The rate of exploitation would also increase if the length of the working day were to increase, holding labor productivity and the subsistence bundle constant. In this case, workers would labor additional hours for the capitalist. Finally, suppose the subsistence bundle was increased, holding constant the length of the working day and labor productivity. In this case, the time necessary to produce the subsistence bundle rises. Hence, V increases and S declines so that S/V declines.

The Components of Value

There are three components that determine the necessary labor time required for the production of each commodity. We have seen that the labor time expended by workers hired directly by capitalists can be divided into two components. The labor time necessary for the production of the workers' subsistence bundle is the sum the capitalist must pay the worker, and is called variable capital. The rest of the time that the worker labors, which becomes the capitalists' profit, is called surplus value.

Each capitalist does not produce through the purchase of direct labor alone. He also purchases capital equipment. During each period of the production process, the machinery depreciates. The capitalist also must use raw materials and intermediary goods. The sum of the labor time required for the production of the worn out machinery and the used up raw materials and intermediary goods is called constant capital.

The total value of production of any firm, therefore, is $c + v + s$ where c, v, and s represent the constant capital, variable capital, and surplus value of the firm, calculated in labor-time. For the economy as a whole, the total value of production is $C + V + S$ where C, V, and S, are the sum over all firms of constant capital, variable capital, and surplus value.

Organic Composition of Capital

Marx believed that the ratio of constant capital to variable capital had an extremely important influence on the capitalist process. It indicates the ratio of expenditures the capitalists must make on finished goods (equipment, raw materials, and intermediary goods) to their expenditures on direct labor. This ratio, C/V, is called the organic composition of capital.[14]

The Rate of Profit

For each production period, capitalists receive the difference between the selling price (P) and their expenditures for production $(C + V)$. If all goods sell at their value, then $P = C + V + S$ and total profits would just equal total surplus value (S). Capitalists, however, are not primarily interested in the size of profits but in the size of the profit rate—the ratio of profits to total capital outlay. Marx assumed for simplicity that the rate of profit

$$\pi = \frac{S}{C + V}$$

As already noted, this formulation assumes that the total selling price of production just equals the total labor value of production. However, this formulation makes some further assumptions. For Marx to directly identify surplus value with profits, he assumed that no part of it had to be paid to landlords in the form of rent. In general, Marx believed that the division of surplus value between rent, interest, and direct capitalist profits was of secondary importance. Therefore, until he undertook a more detailed discussion of profits in the third volume of *Capital,* Marx ignored this issue.

Marx also made certain assumptions in order to simplify the denominator of the profit rate formula. Specifically, the denominator of his formula represents the capital used up in each production period—the finished goods (C) and the subsistence bundle for workers (V). This is a *flow* per production period of goods. The usual procedure, however, is to relate profits to the *stock* of capital outlay. The stock of capital is composed of the stock of capital equipment necessary for production, as well as the monetary advances required to hire direct labor and receive the raw materials and intermediary goods used in production. Only if capital goods have a useful life of one production period and if all finished goods and direct labor must be paid for in advance will the stock of capital outlay just equal the flow of capital used up in production. These of course are not realistic assumptions. Capital goods last more than one production period, and monetary advances are usually less than the value of direct labor and raw materials used up in production. However, the adoption of more realistic assumptions will not change the factors that influence the rate of profit.[15]

---

14. Sometimes the organic composition of capital is defined as the ratio of the *stock* of capital to the amount of variable capital. This alternative definition would not change any of our results.

15. Suppose we assume each production period is one year and only capital equipment and direct labor are used in production. Let C' equal the stock of capital

(cont'd)

In order to highlight the factors that directly affect the rate of profit, Marx divided both the numerator and denominator of the profit rate formula by V,

$$\pi = \frac{S}{C+V} = \frac{S/V}{C+V/V} = \frac{S/V}{C/V+1}$$

This indicates that the rate of profit is directly related to the rate of exploitation and inversely related to the organic composition of capital.

The Deviation of Prices From Labor Values

One of the major issues concerning the accuracy of Marx's formulation of the profit rate is that it was based upon the assumption that individual prices just equal their labor values. This enabled him to equate surplus value with profits in each industry and, therefore, in the aggregate. Marx, however, was well aware that it was necessary for individual prices to deviate from their values in a competitive capitalist economy. Table 16.1 was constructed with the assumption that the rate of exploitation was the same in each industry. If each

Table 16.1
Profit rates in industries with different organic compositions of capital but the same rate of exploitation $(S/V = 1)$

Industry	c	v	s	$c+v$	$s/(c+v)$
I	100	50	50	150	0.33
II	200	50	50	250	0.20
III	300	50	50	350	0.14

necessary for production and V' equal the wage fund advanced to workers at the beginning of the production period. The profit rate would then be $\pi = S/(C'+V')$. Now let us assume that the average capital equipment lasts n years and that the wage fund advanced at the beginning of the production period is m times the total wage bill. Under these assumptions $C' = nC$ and $V' = mV$. Substituting into the profit formula,

$$\pi = \frac{S}{(nC+mV)} = \frac{S/V}{nC/V} + m.$$

If m and n are exogenously determined, then the rate of profit is directly related to the rate of exploitation, and inversely related to the organic composition of capital. This also holds in the special case where $m = n = 1$, which is the basis of the simplified marxian profit rate formula.

industry sells its production at its labor values, then its profit rate will be equal to $s/(c+v)$. Table 16.1 assumes that the organic composition of capital varies between industries. Under this assumption, the last column indicates that there will be different profit rates in each industry. In particular, Industry I, which has the smallest organic composition of capital, has the highest profit rate. Industry III, which has the highest organic composition of capital, has the lowest profit rate.[16]

In a competitive economy, these results are unstable. Capitalists would begin moving into Industry I (high profit industries), increasing the supply of production and, hence, lowering its price below its labor value. Similarly, capitalists would shift out of Industry III (low profit industries), lowering supply and, hence, raising its price above its labor value. This adjustment process must continue until the profit rate in all industries is equalized.

Marx attempted to demonstrate that the adjustment process would continue to maintain equality between aggregate market sales and aggregate labor values, even though values and market prices deviated in individual industries.[17] While his solution was incorrect, others have shown that a proper solution to the problem of transforming labor values into market prices would continue to find that the rate of profit was directly related to the rate of exploitation, and inversely related to the organic composition of capital.[18]

16.3 MARXIAN THEORIES OF THE SHORT CYCLE

Marx implicitly divided his crises theories into explanations of short cycles and long cycles (waves). Figure 16.1 illustrates the distinction between short cycles and long waves. Short cycles are shown peaking at A, B, C, . . . , J. They represent what has been commonly called business cycles. However, as the dashed-line connecting all these peaks indicates, there is an underlying long wave, which peaks at D and bottoms at H. The marxian distinction between short and long cycles was also found among structuralist models. Specifically,

---

16. Joan Robinson, *An Essay on Marxian Economics* (New York: MacMillan, 1966), pp. 15–17, argues that it could be possible for commodities to sell at their values, with a uniform rate of profit between industries, if the rate of exploitation varied directly with the organic composition of capital. For example, if the rate of exploitation was 0.6, 1.0, and 1.4 in industries I, II, and III, respectively, then the surplus value in Table 16.1 would be 30, 50, and 70 for the three industries, respectively. In this case, each industry would have a profit rate equal to 0.20. Marx, however, did not believe there was any basis for expecting that there would be a systematic relationship between the rate of exploitation and the organic composition of capital.

17. For a discussion of Marx's attempt as well as a full treatment of the transformation problem, see Howard and King, *Political Economy of Marx,* pp. 106–108, 143–149.

18. A. Medio, "Profits and Surplus-Value . . ." in *A Critique of Economic Theory,* E. Hunt and J. Schwartz, eds. (Baltimore: Penguin, 1972), pp. 339–40.

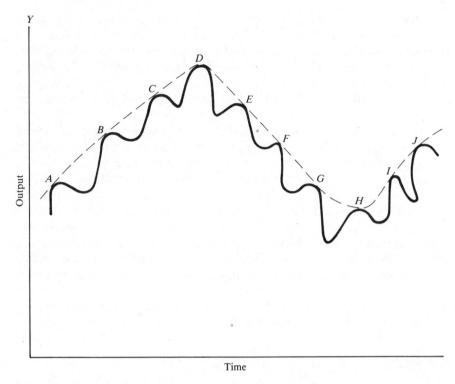

Figure 16.1 Relationship of long and short cycles

the Hicksian accelerator model was clearly a short cycle model, while the Kondratieff model was clearly an explanation of long waves.

Marx spent most of his energies on explanations of long waves. His falling rate of profit thesis was primarily directed to this purpose. However, Marx was well aware that capitalism was subject to short cycles, and his theory of uneven development implies certain theories of the short cycle. This section will outline two such theories—the class struggle and overinvestment theories.

Both of these theories build on the marxian theory of profits. Recall that the average rate of profit was directly related to the rate of exploitation, S/V, and inversely related to the organic composition of capital, C/V. The class struggle theory claims that at full employment there will be a tendency for S/V to decline without a compensating change in C/V. Therefore, the rate of profit would decline. The overinvestment theory claims that intra-industry competitive forces will generate tendencies to building productive capacity at a faster rate than the growth of sales. Hence, idle capacity or, equivalently, a rise in C/V will occur without a compensating increase in S/V. Again, the result will be a decline in the average rate of profit.

It is often mistakenly assumed that Marx had a breakdown theory of capitalism. According to this breakdown theory, Marx allegedly claimed that capitalism would collapse because of its inability to provide longterm economic growth and rising living standards. On the contrary, Marx believed that capitalism, because it was the first organization of society that was able to harness the productive potentials of technology, would be characterized by unparalleled material growth. Though he tended to believe that in its early stages of growth labor's share of income would decrease, he never questioned that the real wage rate would rise in the longrun. His subsistence wage rate is culturally, not physiologically, determined. He held the real wage rate constant only in the shortrun when he wanted to demonstrate that *independent* of wage rate changes capitalism would be periodically subject to a falling rate of profit.

Marx's crisis theories are meant to indicate that it is impossible for capitalism to sustain *balanced* growth. He believed that inherent contradictions in the growth process would force periodic contractions to occur, and that at times these contractions would attain crisis proportion. According to Marx, these contractions discipline the growth process by eliminating excesses—real wage rate or investment growth rates beyond the levels that could maintain economic and political stability. Economic contractions, by reducing employment, lower the growth rate of real wages, and by causing bankruptcies, reduce excess industrial capacity. Eventually, the economy is reorganized to begin another expansion. Thus, the marxian class struggle and overinvestment theories are an integral part of the overall capitalist growth process.

Class Struggle Business Cycle

The reserve army thesis implies that the level of unemployment dictates the relative bargaining power of labor and capital. When unemployment is high, labor is weak and capital is in a strong bargaining position. However, when unemployment is low, labor is in a stronger bargaining position than capital. The reserve army thesis underlies the political business cycle theory first popularized in the 1940s by Michal Kalecki. At the time, mainstream economists were beginning to assume that governments were willing and able to maintain full employment through the use of fiscal policies. Kalecki argued that the needs of capitalists for a reserve army of unemployed to maintain social and political discipline of the working class would undermine any government attempts to maintain full employment.

Kalecki believed that monopoly capitalists would pass along wage increases as price increases. Therefore, only the smaller capitalists and the rentier class would have direct economic reasons for government intervention. He suggested that socio-political motives of the large capitalists and the economic interest of the smaller capitalists would lead to their unity in pressuring a termination of government expansionary policies.[19]

19. Michal Kalecki, *Selected Essays on the Dynamics of Capitalist Societies* (New York: Cambridge University Press, 1971), pp. 140–41.

Kalecki's theory emphasized socio-political motives rather than direct economic motives. During the 1970s, marxists began to argue that economic as well as other motives underly the requirement of maintaining a reserve army. This viewpoint, most identified with the work of Ray Boddy and Jim Crotty,[20] argues that Kalecki underestimated the negative effect that sustained full employment would have on profits. They contend that there is still enough competition that the majority of large firms are unable to simply pass wage demands along to consumers as price increases. Boddy and Crotty, therefore, believe that when the economy reaches full employment, the profit-wage (P/W) ratio would begin to decline. In turn, to the extent that the rate of exploitation (S/V) is positively correlated with the P/W ratio, they conclude that the rate of profit would decline with sustained full employment. Figure 16.2 summarizes the experience of the P/W ratio during the period 1952–72. In each of the four business cycles during this period, the P/W ratio began to decline during the second half of the expansionary phase—just when the economy began to approach full employment. This strongly supports the Boddy-Crotty contention that full employment results in a corporate profit squeeze.

It should be noted that mainstream liberals reject this thesis. According to Arthur Okun,

> *The U.S. labor market does not resemble the Marxist model in which employers point to a long line of applicants ("the reserve army of unemployed") and tell their current workers to take a wage cut or find themselves replaced. Employers have investments in a trained, reliable, and loyal work force. . . . In a few areas, where jobs have high turnover and thus employers and employees have little stake in lasting relationships, wages do respond sensitively to the level of unemployment. But, in most areas, personnel policies are sensibly geared to the long run.[21]*

Marxian Theories of Overinvestment

Even if the level of unemployment had no effect on the rate of exploitation (S/V), competitive forces could still cause a decline in average profit rates. The marxian theory of competition emphasizes the struggle between firms over market shares. Marx assumed that a major objective of each firm was to more quickly innovate new technology than its competitors. In so doing they could increase their market share by being able to undersell their competitors. Firms could then justify capital spending, not because of a growing market nor because it would lower unit cost on existing sales, but because it offered the

20. Ray Boddy and Jim Crotty, "Class Conflict and Macro-Policy: The Political Business Cycle," *Review of Radical Political Economy* 7 (Spring 1975): 1–19.

21. Arthur Okun, "The Great Stagflation Swamp," *Challenge* 20 (Nov./Dec. 1977): 8.

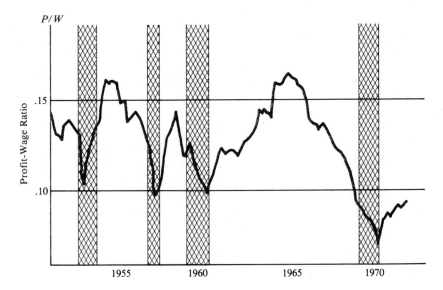

Figure 16.2   The profit-wage ratio

Shaded areas represent periods of business recession. Profits are measured by profits after taxes for nonfinancial corporations. Wages are measured by total compensation in non-financial corporations.

potential to attract sales away from its competitors. Moreover, uncertainty may lead firms to invest out of the fear that they may fall behind competitors in technical sophistication. Therefore, each firm will have a tendency to invest more than is warranted from either a cost or industry sales standpoint.

The prisoners' dilemma framework is an excellent device to highlight the tendencies towards overinvestment in competitive industries.[22] Let us assume for simplicity that the industry is composed of two identically-sized firms. Later we will introduce the implications when firms are of unequal size (uneven development). Now suppose that a new capital-using technology is discovered that has a lower unit production cost than the existing facilities. Each firm is aware of the new technology and is financially capable of implementation. Marx assumed that this type of discovery was typical of technology. These discoveries would often occur soon after the completion of new facilities.[23] Since the just-completed facilities would be fully capable of meet-

22. If prisoners' dilemma framework not covered previously, refer to the appendix to Chapter 7.

23. The speed with which technological progress occurs, according to Marx, is reflected in the following passage: "The inanimate machinery not only wears out and depreciates day to day, but a great part of it becomes so quickly super-annu-ated, by constant technical progress, that it can be replaced with advantage by new machinery after a few months." *Capital,* vol. I (New York: International Pub, 1973), p. 576.

ing productive needs for a long time, each firm has a decision concerning when it would be *profitable* to build the more efficient facilities.

Let us assume that abandonment of the existing facilities in favor of the installation of the more efficient technology would be unprofitable at existing sales levels. This implies that without a change in market shares, each firm should wait until there is an increase in *market* sales before installation of the new technology. If sales would not increase significantly during the construction period, then both firms would have higher profits by delaying construction than if they both immediately began investing in the new facilities.

This situation is depicted in Table 16.2. Both firms have initial sales of 100 and profits (in parentheses) of 20, which will continue if neither builds the new facilities. If *both* firms invest in the new facilities, then market demand only increases slightly (to 220 divided equally) so that due to excess capacity each firm's profits decline to 10.

Table 16.2
Investment decisions of competing firms[24]

Firm B   *Firm A*

	Invest	Do Not Invest
Invest	110 (10) / 110 (10)	50 (2) / 150 (40)
Do Not Invest	150 (40) / 50 (2)	100 (20) / 100 (20)

The dilemma results because of the effects when only one firm invests in the new technology. The firm that invests will be able to undersell its competitor and thus gain a larger market share. For example, the sales of the firm that invests rise to 150 while the other firm's sales drop to 50. With this redistribution of market shares, the investing firm's profits increase to 40 while the drop in sales reduces the other firm's profits to 2.

This indicates that though investing will probably result in lower profits, as other firms will also invest, not investing runs the risk of a loss of market share and even smaller profits. If firms cannot quickly recoup their market

---

24. The numbers indicate the outcomes depending upon the independent choices made by each firm. There are four possible outcomes: both invest, both don't invest, Firm A invests alone, or Firm B invests alone. For each of the four possible outcomes, the numbers in the upper-right hand triangle indicate the outcome for Firm A. The numbers in the lower-left hand triangle indicate the outcome for Firm B.

shares, the longterm penalties for making the wrong decision are substantial. On the other hand, by investing there is the possibility of increasing market shares and profits if competitors do not also invest. Therefore, each firm will be forced to invest and the outcome will be excess capacity (a rise in the C/V ratio) and, hence, a decline in the rate of profit.

The analysis becomes complicated with the introduction of uneven development. Such an industry would be characterized by a significant number of smaller firms, which had neither the technical nor financial ability to implement the new technological discoveries. Now when the larger firms invest in the new technology they will have lower costs than the smaller firms, and through a sales effort, they will be able to increase their market shares. These smaller firms will not be able to stand the strain and will be forced out of business. In this case, the entire burden of the industry overinvestment falls on the small firms which are driven to the brink of bankruptcy.

Some writers, such as Steindl, believe that as long as the larger firms are not adversely affected, no economic problems will result.[25] He contends that the excess capital in the industry will disappear with the bankruptcy of the small firms. Steindl assumes that the capital stock of the bankrupt firm will remain idle, becoming totally depreciated. Excess industry capacity is thus eliminated so that there will be no adverse effects on future industry investment decisions. This ignores the possibility of larger firms taking over the bankrupt firms as an alternative to future capital spending. Moreover, Steindl assumes that a sufficient number of smaller firms will go bankrupt so that the profit rate of the innovative firms will not deteriorate. This is not always true. It is quite likely that at times the effects of innovations will be the creation of excess capacity in large firms only partially offset by bankruptcies of smaller firms.

Marx emphasized this tendency towards overinvestment in his discussion of the cotton trade.[26] In its early stages of development, Marx, like Steindl, believed that technological innovations will drive so many small firms bankrupt that the profit rate of the innovative firms would actually rise. However, when the industry matures, continuous investment in new technologies results in overproduction. When this occurred in the cotton trade, Marx argued that the industry intensified its search for new markets. One area was the foreign market, where the dumping of cotton goods destroyed indigenous handicraft

25. J. Steindl, *Maturity and Stagnation in American Capitalism* (Oxford: Basil Blackwell, 1952), pp. 42–43.

26. Karl Marx, *Capital,* vol. I (New York: International Pub, 1973), p. 453:

The enormous power, inherent in the factory system . . . begets feverish production, followed by over-filling of the markets, whereupon contraction of the markets brings on crippling of production. . . . Except in periods of prosperity, there rages between the capitalists the most furious combat for the share of each in the market. . . . Besides the rivalry that this struggle begets in power, and of new methods of production, there also comes a time . . . when a forcible reduction of wages . . . is attempted.

industries around the world. Thus, domestic competitive forces spill over into the struggle for foreign markets.

Some economists, working in the left-liberal tradition, also identify over-investment as a major cause of the economic difficulties of the 1970s. However, rather than intensified competition, these economists emphasize volatile attitudes towards risk-taking as the principal explanatory factor. Like Keynes, they claim that due to decentralization of decision-making, uncertainty makes it impossible for individual firms to rationally determine investment plans. Instead, these plans are determined by general attitudes towards risk-taking. These economists suggest that for most firms, attitudes in the early post-World War II period were shaped by the Depression. "The habits of mind developed during the terrible experiences of those years kept our business leaders from throwing caution to the wind and from forgetting the realities of risk."[27]

The result was a cautious investment policy, believed to be the principal explanation for the high levels of economic growth during this period. However, by the 1960s, the corporate leadership had passed to individuals who had no memories of the Depression. "This naturally led to much more carefree attitudes towards risk. Indeed the new breed were convinced that it was they who moved the world . . . when in fact the absolutely necessary precondition for their achievement was the sense of caution and care that the older generation had carried forward from the depression era."[28] These economists suggest that this changing attitude was responsible for the "overbuilding of capacity, excessive risk-taking, and burgeoning debt leverage."[29]

Worldwide Steel Production

The worldwide steel industry is an example of the inherent problems of over-investment. Japan is pre-eminent among large steel producers worldwide. It continually innovates with the most advanced technologies. However, as the previous analysis indicates, it can maintain capital utilization and profit rates only if it can increase its share of the market. In order to accomplish this, it must aggressively attempt to expand its foreign sales. This is possible if the capacity of other nations to produce steel does not grow as fast as world demand. However, under the whip of competition, other countries, such as the United States, also increase their steel production capacity by technological innovations. As a result, even when growth in demand expands there is worldwide overcapacity. For Japan to increase its share of the market it must take away sales from other countries. The effects of Japanese sales efforts were felt

27. Peter L. Bernstein, "Is the System Still Working?" *Challenge* 21 (Sep./Oct. 1978): 22.

28. Ibid., p. 23.

29. Ibid.

most strongly by American steel companies and their workers when world demand stagnated in the mid-1970s. These companies experienced large profit losses and were forced to lay off large numbers of workers. Calls for protection against the "dumping of Japanese steel on U.S. markets" were heard, and some form of tariff barrier and/or import controls were legislated.

The outcome of this situation is predictable. With overinvestment in steel *some* firms (countries) must experience a fall in the rate of profit. If legislation limits the penetration of the U.S. market by Japanese steel, most of the slump will be on the Japanese steel industry while continued penetration will shift part of the slump onto U.S. steel producers.[30]

16.4 THE FALLING RATE OF PROFIT AND ECONOMIC CRISES

The two Marxian models developed earlier in this chapter suggest that competitive forces tend to lower the rate of profit. On the one hand, competition between capitalists and workers over the distribution of income results in a declining profit rate as full employment is approached. On the other hand, competition between capitalists over market shares can result in overinvestment by all producers in an industry. In the next chapter these theories will be used to explain the economic events of the 1970s. However, before applying them to a specific historical situation, there are a number of general properties which should be developed.

Marxian Models and Aggregate Demand

In all previous macroeconomic models, aggregate demand was the critical determinant of economic well-being. Whether conservative, mainstream liberal, or structuralist, they all implied that an economic contraction occurs *because* of deficient aggregate demand. In sharp contradiction, both the overinvestment and class struggle models posit a declining profit rate, independent of changes in aggregate demand. Indeed, one of the central objectives of Marx was to demonstrate that capitalism would experience economic crises independent of effective demand considerations.

Marx was well aware that income could be in such imbalance that workers would have limited purchasing power and capitalists could become reluctant to increase capital spending. However, Marx believed that deficient demand would not create fundamental problems for capitalist societies. In particular, Marx felt that competitive forces would make it unlikely that deficient capital

---

30. According to the *New York Times* (May 24, 1979; p. D1), there will be a falling rate of profit and increased concentration in the cement industry during the 1980s. Investments of upwards of $100 million by individual firms are required in order to incorporate new energy-saving technology. Due to uneven development, these investments will result in a reduction of the number of firms in the cement industry from fifty to fifteen. This is another example of the problems of overinvestment.

investment could continue for very long. Beginning in the 1930s, some economists, working within the marxian tradition, began to suggest that with the declining of competition, deficient capital spending was increasingly possible. Hence, problems of deficient demand could now be serious. This neo-marxian thesis has provided a vehicle to develop more fully the underconsumptionist strains which have always been part of the marxian tradition. Chapter 18 will detail these neo-marxian models of underconsumption, as well as alternative marxian interpretations of the effects of monopolies on the economic process.

Marxian Short Cycles Versus Long Waves

Both the class struggle and overinvestment theories are present in Marx's writings. He identified them as factors to explain the periodic short cycles in economic activity. Marx did not pursue these theories, but instead developed his long wave theory of the rising organic composition of capital. According to Marx, technology tended to be capital-using. Hence, the c/v ratio would rise, not because of excess capacity but due to the nature of technology. This technological tendency would be reinforced by wage pressures. Specifically, when growth enables workers to bid up wages high enough to threaten the profit rate, capitalists increase their rate of automation. Indeed, Marx tended to emphasize that capitalists overcome rising wages by automation rather than contractions and, therefore, was highly critical of contemporary attempts to explain the falling rate of profit by the rise in wages.[31] While automation enables capitalists to forestall declines in the rate of exploitation (s/v), it does not resolve problems for capitalists. Since it raises the organic composition of capital, c/v, the rate of exploitation *must rise* or the rate of profit would decline. Marx assumed that automation would increase the rate of exploitation, but not by enough to offset the rise in the c/v ratio. Therefore, firms only shift the source of the rate of profit decline from a wage-induced decline in s/v to an automation-induced rise in c/v.

Marx underplayed the importance of overinvestment as a cause of the rising c/v ratio. Marx realized that, to some extent, the overinvestment problem could be resolved through increases in aggregate demand. As the economy grows—either naturally or by artificial (government) stimuli—excess capacity could be decreased, thus lowering c/v. Also, as older plants depreciate, excess capacity would be reduced. These two factors would tend to weaken the severity of the problems created by overinvestment.

---

31. Marx illustrates this point in *Capital,* vol I, p. 638 as follows:

    Between 1849 and 1859, a rise of wages. . . took place in the English agricultural districts. . . . Everywhere the farmers were howling. . . . What did the farmers do now? . . . They introduced more machinery, and in a moment the labourers were redundant again in a proportion satisfactory even to the farmers.

In contrast, the marxian long wave theory is a much stronger theory of crises. The rise in c/v is not due to excess capacity, but rather to a shift to a more capital-using technology. Since plants are operating at full capacity, changes in sales, either through government stimuli, market growth, or bankruptcies of weaker firms, will not help reverse the profit decline. Moreover, the overinvestment theory can only hold for specific industries and/or sectors, while the long wave theory can be generalized to all industries.

While these reasons explain Marx's preference for the long wave theory, it would be a mistake to ignore the overinvestment short cycle theory. First, though specific increases in spending could offset excess capacity, it would require government fiscal policy to be directed at this problem. In effect, it would require the government to guarantee sales, regardless of the investment decisions of industries. This is certainly possible, but it is unlikely to become a consistent policy. Second, it is true that eventually the depreciation of facilities eliminates excess capacity. However, this may take substantial time. Third, the seriousness of the damage from overinvestment is dependent upon the speed at which weaker firms go bankrupt. If bankruptcies occur rapidly, the adverse effects are isolated. Surviving firms are only mildly affected by overinvestment since they quickly absorb the market shares of the bankrupt firms. However, if weaker firms are able to survive for any length of time, large firms which have capitalized face periods of excess capacity and declining profits. In this case, the damage from overinvestment is more widespread. Not only do weaker firms eventually go bankrupt, but many larger firms are brought to the brink of bankruptcy.

Marx did not believe that bankruptcies would occur quickly enough to totally contain the damages from overinvestment. However, he did believe that they would occur rapidly enough to prevent such widespread damage that serious crises would be created. It can be argued that for a variety of reasons the trend has been for firms to be able to survive longer in the face of continuous economic losses. Due to increased diversification, some firms can now use profits from other activities to sustain losing products; due to increased banking involvements external loans are more likely, especially if there are already financial obligations; and it is more likely today that failing firms can obtain direct government subsidies. Therefore, it can be argued that overinvestment now creates more serious problems than at the time Marx wrote.

Similarly, Marx underplayed the class struggle theory because of his preference for the long wave theory. However, Marx overstated the speed by which automation could replace militant labor and, hence, underestimated the effects of rising wages on profitability. Marx wrote when technological innovation was rapid and workers were unorganized. This implied that capitalists could rapidly innovate new labor-saving technology. In the second half of the twentieth century, the ability of capitalists is substantially constrained. Technological innovations are bulky and require long lead time before implementation. Also, unions have the ability to retard the introduction of technology. Therefore, capitalists cannot simply order a labor-saving machine in response to wage demands, making it more likely that lay-offs and economic contractions will be required.[32]

For these reasons, it is possible to explain severe economic disruptions with reliance on *only* marxian short cycle theories. As should be clear, the marxian long wave theory reinforces the tendency for the rate of profit to decline, and reinforces the contention that increases in aggregate demand cannot resolve the resulting problems. The marxian long wave theory is the most criticized aspect of Marx's economic theories. Therefore, one advantage in separating his long wave theory from his short cycle theories is that we can, at this point, avoid dealing with the most controversial aspect of his economic work. It enables us to proceed with a marxian analysis of the economic performance during the 1970s, regardless of the correctness of his long wave theory. This is important since there has been a tendency within the economics profession to disregard *all* marxian falling rate of profit theories because of criticisms of his long wave theory.

The Falling Rate of Profit and Economic Crises

Even if the marxian short cycle models are correct, it is not immediately clear why a profit rate decline *must* result in an economic crisis. Certainly *subjective* factors could discourage further capital expansions. Capitalists could *fear* that the decline will continue and, in anticipation, contract capital spending. However, as long as capitalists are making profits it would seem that the decision to end the expansion is *a matter of choice and not necessity.*[33] Keynes, for example, believed that it was certainly possible for capitalists to adjust to a lower rate of profit. He said, "It is not necessary . . . that the game [production] should be played for such high stakes [profits] as at present. Much lower stakes will serve the purpose equally well, as soon as the players are accustomed to them."[34] Hence, Keynes believed that "enlightened capitalists" of the Okun variety, would not precipitate an economic contraction because of a decline in the profit rate.

---

32. There is some empirical evidence that labor-saving technology is mainly innovated during the contraction and early stages of the expansion rather than at the peak of the boom, as Marx implies. See Ray Boddy and Michael Gort, "The Substitution of Capital for Capital," *Review of Economics and Statistics* (May 1971): 179–188.

33. A recent paper which makes a distinction between a purely subjective basis for capitalist expectations and an objective basis is David Laibman, "Marxian Profit Cycle: A Macromodel," *Eastern Economic Journal* (forthcoming).

34. John M. Keynes, *The General Theory* (New York: MacMillan, 1936), p. 374.

Left at this point, it would seem that debate over the prediction of an economic contraction revolves around which psychological motivation dominates capitalists. Are they the enlightened capitalists of the Okun/Keynes variety or are they the shortsighted greedy capitalists of the Boddy/Crotty/Kalecki variety? However, one important factor has been neglected—the fact that capitalist production is characterized by uneven development.

Uneven development implies that not all firms earn the average rate of profit. The stronger (generally larger) firms in each industry earn higher than the average profit rate, while the weaker (generally smaller) firms earn less than the average profit rate. When the *average* profit rate is high, all firms can make sufficient profits to maintain solvency. However, as the average profit rate declines, the weaker firms in each industry begin to experience *losses*. Weak firms that are losing money begin to find it impossible to obtain external funds to maintain solvency. Hence, a decline in the average profit rate will create the conditions for bankruptcies.

If, as has been argued, weaker firms survive for some time, then a broader grouping of firms is brought to the brink of bankruptcy. It is the actions of this broad grouping that causes economic crises. Their actions are not based upon psychological motivation—their actions have nothing to do with becoming accustomed to the "rules of the game." These firms are forced to act because of *objective* conditions.

The weakest firms, which eventually go bankrupt, have a relatively small direct effect on economic conditions. They tend to undertake little capital spending, even during prosperous times, and often tend to mainly purchase used obsolete capital goods. Therefore, their bankruptcies have little effect on the level of capital spending. The major direct effect of their bankruptcy is the unemployment created by the resulting lay-offs.

The second group of firms affected are "intermediate" firms. While many experience profit rate declines that bring them close to bankruptcy, they usually have sufficient resourcefulness to survive. However, actions taken to survive have damaging effects on the economy. In general, these intermediate firms will become reluctant to undertake long term capital projects. Instead, they will consolidate by contracting less profitable areas of the company. They will strive for liquidity by placing funds in short term assets until the danger of bankruptcy passes. Though they are aware that by sacrificing these long term projects and company diversification they risk weakening their position in the future, they must first guarantee short term survival. All of these actions result in a capital spending decline and some direct lay-offs.

The larger, more prosperous firms will also cut back on their expansionary capital spending for objective reasons. New alternative activities rather than subjective pessimism are responsible for these cutbacks. With declining profit rates resulting in near bankruptcies, these larger firms can choose to buy up or take over failing corporations rather than undertaking internal capital spending. This becomes an especially attractive alternative when it is possible to buy up cheaply an intermediate firm that is facing bankruptcy. It enables prosperous firms to diversify by purchasing existing companies in other industries.

The instability created by the falling rate of profit also adversely affects the financial community. Many firms, especially intermediate firms that are at the brink of bankruptcy, have large outstanding financial obligations. This creates a dilemma for members of the financial community. If they refuse further loans, bankruptcies will make it unlikely that past financial obligations will be met. These losses will be absorbed by members of the financial community. If these losses are large enough and held by a few financial firms, it might cause these firms to also go bankrupt. On the other hand, continued loans to these faltering firms cannot guarantee survival. If they still go bankrupt, then the losses to the financial community are even larger and the risk of banking failures increases. This indicates that bankruptcies in the sphere of production creates losses for members of the financial community. If these losses are substantial, then the prospect of banking failures increases. These prospects force the banking community to retrench. Funds will be denied to all but the most sound firms (AAA-rated), regardless of the interest rate the other firms are willing to pay. Therefore, the striving for liquidity in the financial community (excess reserves) creates further contractions of capital spending.

Economic Crises and Government Intervention

Since the falling rate of profit is not a result of deficient demand, Keynesian spending policies will be ineffective. Indeed, marxists would argue that it is necessary for the economy to experience a contraction before a period of rapid growth is possible. Without bankruptcies and the resulting unemployment, the wage-induced profit squeeze would continue, and industries with overinvestment will continue to have excess capacity.

This indicates that bankruptcies are a *necessary* part of the adjustment process. First, by creating some unemployment, it enables capitalists to lower real wages (raise s/v ratio). Second, in industries with excess capacity, bankruptcies enable the surviving firms to expand their sales, thus lowering the c/v ratio. Finally, bankruptcies reduce the value of the capital stock by *destroying* capital. Capital values are destroyed when either the bankrupt firm's capital stock is abandoned or sold at a fraction of its productive value.

One of the major implications of this viewpoint is that government support for failing firms may keep the economy from experiencing a sharp contraction, but it also keeps it from being able to begin a period of rapid expansion. Another implication is that the government will attempt to lower real wages and shift income to capitalists. This can be in the form of either legislation on taxes and subsidies or labor legislation. Finally, it should be clear that the falling rate of profit intensifies the conflict between capitalists. Each group of capitalists will attempt to shift as much as possible of the bankruptcies onto the other capitalists. This implies that each capitalist grouping will attempt to control government economic policies in order to shift the adjustment to other groups.

The falling rate of profit thesis is critical to Marx because it demonstrates that capitalism cannot be reformed. If there is a tendency for the rate of profit to decline independent of aggregate demand, then no amount of planning can stop the economy from experiencing contractions which can be resolved only through increased exploitation of the working class and cannibalism among capitalists. If, instead, economic contractions are due to deficient demand, as the marxian underconsumptionist models imply, then government reforms can be effective. Not surprisingly, left-liberals who claim sympathy with the works of Marx emphasize the underconsumptionist theories and sharply attack the falling rate of profit theories.

16.5 CONCLUSION

This chapter has developed the marxian contention that competitive forces make it impossible for a private market economy to maintain full employment. Marxists contend that a decline in the rate of profit precipitates the contraction. While Marx emphasized his long wave theory, this chapter chose to present the less controversial class conflict and overinvestment theories. We found that these marxian theories did not require that (1) the subsistence wage be fixed in the longrun, and (2) individual prices equal their individual marxian labor values. Instead, all that was required was that wages adjust slowly and that the sum of market values of production equal the sum of their labor values. Under these assumptions, it was shown that the average rate of profit was directly related to the rate of exploitation, and inversely related to the organic composition of capital.

The marxian class conflict model contends that at full employment the rate of exploitation is lowered. The overinvestment theory suggests that competitive forces create tendencies towards overinvestment and, hence, a rising organic composition of capital. A decline in the rate of profit precipitates an economic contraction because of the uneven development within each industry. As the average rate of profit declines, weaker firms begin to face bankruptcy while other firms must contract capital spending plans due to liquidity requirements. Hence, the contraction is determined by objective factors rather than subjective expectations. The contraction is due to the survival needs of corporations rather than their greed.

Since the contraction was due to a decline in the rate of profit independent of aggregate demand, neither monetary nor fiscal policies can effectively offset this decline. Indeed, if the cause is full employment wage demands, any attempt by the government to maintain full employment would only worsen the situation for capitalists. Similarly, if the cause was overinvestment, then any attempt by the government to keep the weaker firms from failing will only put off the necessary industry reorganization. In fact, the very nature of the crisis dictates that unemployment and bankruptcies are necessary prerequisites for any further expansions, and not the result of "mistakes," as mainstream liberals claim.

CHAPTER SEVENTEEN

RADICAL INTERPRETATION OF ECONOMIC EVENTS DURING THE 1970s

Chapter 16 developed the theoretical foundations of the major marxian theories of economic fluctuations. Whereas Marx emphasized long waves determined by changes in the organic composition of capital (average capital-labor ratio), Chapter 16 emphasized short cycle theories determined by class struggle and the anarchy of capital investment decisions. It was also indicated that these short cycles could be transformed into full-blown economic crises, given certain historical circumstances. These latter views have been the basis of most radical analyses of U.S. economic events during the 1970s. One such analysis will be presented in this chapter.

Since those marxian theories presented in Chapter 16 emphasize the critical role of a profit rate decline, any analysis must first demonstrate that in fact the profit rate did decline during 1965–74. This chapter presents mainstream studies of the U.S. corporate profit rate during this period. They indicate a declining profit rate but also present different explanations than radicals for the decline.

This chapter describes the response of the capitalist class to these declines and its effect on government policies, and speculates on political and economic strategies that could dominate the 1980s. It argues that food inflation, the energy crisis, Watergate, and the revival of racist theories are all the result of the economic crisis. The radical analysis concludes that, in an attempt to solve the crisis, the state will increasingly move towards planning.

17.1 DECLINE OF THE U.S. CORPORATE PROFIT RATE

The 1970s was an unexpected period for mainstream economists. Keynesians had just announced the "obsolescence of the business cycle" when unemployment and inflation reached their highest levels since the 1930s, and the recovery was rather weak and slow moving. Despite the inability of traditional explanations to satisfactorily account for economic changes, mainstream economists as *theorists* continue to reject the view that the rate of profit was a determinant of these economic changes. However, mainstream economists as policymakers did, in fact, place significant importance on changes in the rate of profit. Between 1970–77, the Brookings Institute published four articles on the declining profit rate. The article, written by Harvard economists Martin Feldstein and Lawrence Summers, was fittingly titled, "Is There a Falling Rate of Profit?"[1]

One of the measures of the profit rate, developed by Feldstein and Summers, is illustrated in Figure 17.1. It indicates that except for a strong profit rate upsurge during the early 1960s, there has been a rather consistent decline in the profit rate during 1950–75. The decline was especially dramatic during 1965–74, in which the profit rate fell from 13.7% to 6.3%.

The explanations given for this decline vary among members of the Brookings staff. In 1974, William Nordhaus suggested that the profit rate tended to decline throughout the entire post-World War II period and was a result of the increasing confidence of capitalists.[2] According to Nordhaus, since World War II, capitalists, believing that government intervention will offset any major contractions, do not perceive capital spending projects to be as risky as during previous periods. Hence, they are willing to invest in capital projects with lower expected rates of return.

The Feldstein/Summers explanation differs somewhat. In their more detailed analysis of the data, they find that except for the most recent period, 1970–76, fluctuations in the profit rate can be explained by fluctuations in aggregate demand. Therefore, they believe that only in the most recent period has there been a profit rate decline *independent* of aggregate demand. Feldstein and Summers offer two reasons for the falling rate of profit during the 1970s. First, they suggest that exogenous factors—wage and price controls of 1971–73 and the 1974 oil embargoes—caused a shift in the rate of profit. Second, they claim that capitalists perceived their profits to be higher than they actually were due to an *accounting illusion*. During the early 1970s, profits appeared to be rising when profits on inventories were included. These inventory profits were illusionary because they would be absorbed by firms when they must replace inventories. However, Feldstein and Summers claim that capitalists did not realize this and set prices lower than they would otherwise have.[3]

---

1. Martin Feldstein and Lawrence Summers, "Is There a Falling Rate of Profit?" *Brookings Papers* (1977): 211–227.

2. William Nordhaus, "The Falling Rate of Profit," *Brookings Papers* (1974): 169–208.

3. Here, Feldstein and Summers refer to the effect of inflation on inventory evaluation profits when FIFO (First-In-First-Out) is used. Under this method, the "profits" are completely dissipated when inventories are replaced. This is similar to the profits that individuals make on the rising price of houses. A rise in housing prices from $20,000 to $50,000 gives sellers a profit of $30,000. However, this profit is usually absorbed by the corresponding rise in price of the next house bought.

Figure 17.1 Rate of profit for U.S. corporations, 1948–1976

Profit rate is for all nonfinancial corporations. Profits include earnings and interest paid before taxes. The profit rate relates profits net of depreciation to the net capital stock. For a more detailed discussion of the measure, see Martin Feldstein and Lawrence Summers, "Is There a Falling Rate of Profit?" *Brookings Papers* 1 (1977).

What is interesting about the explanations given by Feldstein/Summers and Nordhaus is their attempts to derive an individualistic explanation—profits are lower because capitalists choose them to be lower. According to Nordhaus, capitalists' perceptions concerning risk explained their choice while, according to Feldstein and Summers, it was their perception about accounting profits which led them to choose lower profits. Galbraith must find Nordhaus' explanation particularly humorous since the major thesis of the *New Industrial State* was that capitalists strive for government intervention because of the increased risk of capital spending. The Feldstein/Summers choice theory explanation also runs counter to the left liberal-radical viewpoint, which assumes that capitalists were well aware of the accounting methods used to compute profits. Radicals have also consistently argued that wage and price controls, as well as the energy crisis, were symptoms, not exogenous causes of economic decline during the 1970s.

Of particular interest are some of the comments made of the Feldstein/Summers paper by other members of the Brookings staff. Michael Wachter felt that combining manufacturing and nonmanufacturing industries underestimates the sharpness of the declining profit rate. He "suspected that a disaggregation might show a significant decline for manufacturing in the 1970s."[4] Stanford economist Pentti Kouri (without giving Marx as his source) also believed that Feldstein and Summers had underestimated the importance of, and given mistaken explanations for, the decline in the rate of profit. According to Kouri, "declining rates of return to capital had been experienced in other countries, and [there] attributed to increasing competition in international commodity markets, [and] decreasing competition in labor markets . . ."[5]

The explanations given by Kouri flow directly from the theories presented in Chapter 16. According to the overinvestment theory, worldwide excess capacity in steel and autos has resulted in increased international competition. According to the class struggle theory, full employment lessens competition among workers and enables them to win higher real wages.

Radical Interpretation of Falling Rate of Profit

Radicals argue that the decline in the rate of profit reflects deep-seated problems for U.S. capitalism. During the 1960s, imbalances occurred which would not allow the U.S. economy to sustain full employment. During the mid-1960s, full employment created conditions favorable to wage increases. Workers could afford to be "uppity" since many jobs were available. Capitalists were unwilling to risk strikes because it would have been difficult to make up lost production. At the same time, foreign competition, fueled by excess capacity in key manufacturing areas, increased markedly. Foreign competition made it difficult for domestic firms to pass wage increases along to consumers so that profit margins were lowered. Hence, as Figure 16.2 indicated, the P/W ratio declined.

At the same time that full employment was squeezing profits, national and international imbalances created overcapacity in important sectors. As already discussed, growing competition in the steel industry created worldwide excess capacity *despite* growing demand. It is also likely that similar conditions began to appear in worldwide automobile production. Within the United States the suburbanization process, together with increasing competition, led service industries to overexpand the number of branches and the number of suburban shopping centers. Also, in some stagnating cities, such as New York, there was an overproduction of new office facilities.

Capitalists, faced with a declining profit rate, were severely constrained by the environment created by the anti-war and Civil Rights movements. These movements made it very difficult to avoid maintaining full employment and expanding government spending on social services. These factors worsened the situation. The government, rather than shifting funds to corporate profits,

4. Michael Wachter, "Discussion," *Brookings Papers* (1977): 228.
5. Pentti Kouri, "Discussion," *Brookings Papers* (1977): 228.

was forced to shift funds to workers in the form of social spending on health, education, and welfare. Instead of providing funds for capital expansion, $100 billion was used to pay for the war in Viet Nam.

According to Marx, capitalists should have responded by accelerating the substitution of capital for labor. However, as already indicated, in the modern capitalist society it is not possible to implement this strategy quickly. Moreover, the cost of automation, together with the decline in profits, would have required corporations to substantially increase their level of external financing of capital spending. Many firms were reluctant to immediately expand their external financing and, hence, chose to postpone capital spending.

Some radicals have argued that, given these constraints, the major short-run alternative chosen was to increase surplus value through the intensification of labor—by trying to speed up the pace of production in order to get more output from workers in any given hour of labor.[6] They argue that this speed up was reflected in the dramatic increase in the industrial accident rate during this period. Between 1926 and 1960 there was a continuous decline in the industrial accident rate in manufacturing. However, during the late 1960s this rate increased from 12.8 accidents per million employee-hours in 1965 to 14.8 accidents in 1969.[7]

Before accepting at face value the radical explanation for the sudden and significant increase in the industrial accident rate, it should be pointed out that there are other possible explanations. From the individualistic perspective, one could argue that the economic expansion resulted in producers employing many unqualified workers, especially minority workers who lacked the proper behavioral requirements. These workers were more accident prone, thus raising the accident rate. Structuralists, on the other hand, would identify technical and institutional factors. They would argue that most of the capital stock in the manufacturing sector was built during and prior to World War II. Due to a variety of factors, these facilities, which were becoming outmoded and unsafe, were not sufficiently replaced during the 1960s. Moreover, full employment also increased the length of the average work week (more overtime). The accident rate is higher when workers work longer hours. Hence, the age of plants and the length of the workweek, rather than profit-induced speed-up, were the factors responsible for the dramatic rise in the manufacturing accident rate.

By the late 1960s, not only was the proportion of income going to wages rising, but so was the proportion going to government social and military spending. The profit rate decline had predictable effects. Weaker firms were

---

6. This contention is fully developed by David Gordon, "Capital Vs. Labor: The Current Crisis in the Sphere of Production," in *Mainstream Reading and Radical Critiques,* David Mermelstein, ed. (New York: Random House, 1976), pp. 362–72.

7. This dramatic change in trend holds for virtually all subgroups of manufacturing. Specifically, the industrial accident rate rose for 19 of the 20 subgroups during the 1960s. See Robert Cherry, "Class Struggle and the Nature of the Workingclass," *Review of Radical Political Economy* 5 (Summer 1973): 56, table V.

brought to the brink of bankruptcy. Big and intermediate firms were thus able to buy up these bankrupt firms at bargain prices. This was particularly advantageous to strong firms that desired to enter new industries. Rather than having to set up a new firm, they could take over an established firm that was experiencing financial problems. Hence, the merger movement appeared.

The merger movement, together with the recession of 1970, might have been sufficient to rejuvenate the profit rate if the only problem had been full employment wage demands. However, the international dimension made the situation too serious to overcome so easily. Not only did continued worldwide investment in durable goods industries continue to create overcapacity, but because of the profit problems in the United States, domestic corporations fell further and further behind in technical superiority in some areas and began losing their technical superiority in other areas. Therefore, it was not enough to arrest the profit rate decline. It was necessary to substantially increase the funds available for capital investment.

17.2 CORPORATE STRATEGIES
TO CORRECT THE PROFIT RATE DECLINE

Corporations undertook a number of strategies to combat the lack of international competitiveness of domestic production. The earliest strategy was to shift an increasing percentage of production overseas to take advantage of cheaper sources of labor. Firms began moving their production to the Far East and Latin America.[8] A second strategy was to reluctantly finance capital spending through external funding. Figure 17.2 indicates the pattern of internal financing of capital spending. From 1961–65, internal financing was consistently more than 80%. With the declining profit rate, corporations were not able to continue to expand capital spending without increased external financing. When corporations realized this in 1966, they held back capital spending. In 1967, capital spending *declined* for the first time since the 1958 slump. This enabled the corporations to continue momentarily to maintain an 80% internal funding ratio. However, given the pressures of foreign competition, domestic industries could ill afford to avoid capital spending. Therefore, they reluctantly began to externally fund an increasing proportion of their spending. By 1969, the ratio had plummeted to 73.5%. This, together with the rising bankruptcies and mergers, caused another momentary decline of capital spending in 1970. However, since then, the needs for innovation outweighed the desires for liquidity so that capital spending has continued to expand with the internal funding ratio averaging 75%.

---

8. Among the fifteen leading exporting countries to the United States are Hong Kong, South Korea, Mexico, and Taiwan. For further discussion of the rise of overseas capital investment by U.S. firms in search of cheap labor, see R. Fernandez, "The Border Industrial Program on the U.S.-Mexico Border," *Review of Radical Political Economy* 5 (Spring 1973): 37–52.

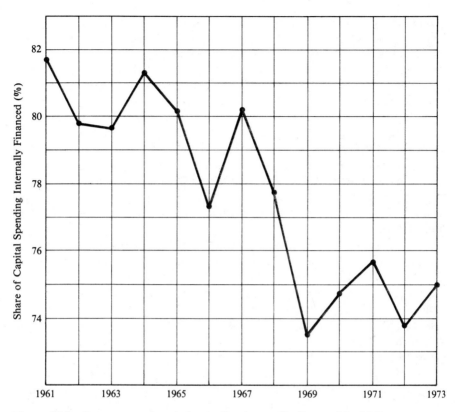

Figure 17.2   Percentage of capital spending internally financed by U.S. corporations, 1961–1973

Percentage internally financed equals cash flow divided by gross domestic investment, where cash flow equals capital consumption allowance plus undistributed profits.

Financial Instability

This strategy created difficulties for both corporate management and financial institutions. Management feared the ever increasing involvement of the banking community in corporate decisions. The banking community, by providing increased external financing, became increasingly vulnerable to corporate bankruptcies.[9] Indeed, as the bankruptcy of corporations such as W. T. Grant continued, some banks began to experience financial difficulties themselves—including the bankruptcy of a number of fairly large banks.[10]

---

9. One measure of the rise of corporate vulnerability was the decline in the corporate liquidity ratio (the ratio of ready cash to total liabilities) from 29% in 1965 to 17% by 1974.

10. The seriousness of the banking situation is discussed in Paul Sweezy, "Banks: Skating on Thin Ice," *Monthly Review* (Feb. 1975).

By 1974, the financial community was unwilling to accept more risk. They began withholding funds from all but their best customers. They were unwilling to continue to underwrite weakened corporations, such as Lockhead, without federal guarantees. They also began to shift funds away from noncorporate areas—municipal bonds and the housing market—in order to provide funds to beleaguered corporations.

This scenerio is also able to explain what appeared to be unusual actions by the Federal Reserve during 1974–75. Traditional theory claims that monetary constraint is necessary in order to eliminate inflation. However, despite record inflation levels, the Federal Reserve liberally increased the money supply during much of this period. The reason was quite simple. With so many corporations in financial difficulty, a drastic tightening of the money supply would have caused extensive bankruptcies in both the manufacturing and financial sectors.[11]

The most important strategy was to reverse the shift in the distribution of national income. Many liberals have claimed that the funds used for the war in Viet Nam could have been more effectively used to improve the productive facilities of domestic industry. While the United States was spending money on bombs, Japan was spending money building the most sophisticated productive facilities. Seymour Melman, in particular, has argued that the economic problems of the 1970s could have been avoided if we had spent our money on new plants rather than bombs.[12]

Radicals contend that this liberal view ignores the realities of the time. Many capitalists, whether rightly or wrongly, believed that to give up Southeast Asia would begin the decline of the American sphere of influence. Moreover, within the capitalist class there were certain sections that directly benefitted from war production—the new firms of the Sun Belt. Therefore, on reflection, while it would have been better for the vitality of the U.S. capitalist system to have not fought the war, it was neither apparent at the time nor reflected the interests of all groups of capitalists.

Radicals contend that with the continued decline of the economic vitality of domestic corporations, more economic interventions may be necessary. Therefore, funds for capital expansion cannot now be taken away from the military. For this reason, radicals contend that both the conservative Ford and

---

11. Mainstream economist Edward Kane noted this problem in his review of the 1974 Federal Reserve Report. Kane said, "Large banks' aggressive acceptance of greater interest rate and default risks has effectively backed the Fed into a corner and underscored the potential conflict between the Fed's duty to fight inflation and its responsibility to maintain confidence in the liquidity and integrity of private financial institutions." E. J. Kane, "All For the Best: The Federal Reserve Board's 60th Annual Report," *American Economics Review* 64 (Dec. 1974): 849.

12. Seymour Melman, *The War Economy in the United States* (New York: St. Martins, 1971), pp. 155–157; 122–133, and especially 5–7.

liberal Carter administrations have forcefully argued for increased military spending.

If the capitalist class desires more military spending to shore up the declining empire, and more profits to rejuvenate the capital base, it must severely attack both the personal income of workers and the government spending on social services. In order to accomplish this reduction, the capitalist class began to promote racist themes. In order to create the view that social spending was a waste of money, that the poor were undeserving, racist ideas of Edward Banfield and Arthur Jensen were actively promoted. Jensen[13] claimed that compensatory programs were doomed to fail because the black population was genetically inferior and intelligence was genetically determined. Banfield[14] claimed that the poor were undeserving and had no legitimate reasons for rebelling against their situation. These ideas helped convince many whites that massive cutbacks in social spending were justified. However, as the analysis implies, these cutbacks were not going to increase the share of income going to working people. Instead, these cutbacks helped reduce the share of government services financed by taxes on corporations.[15]

Nixon and Corporate Strategies

Radicals contend that Nixon's personal ambitions, as well as his choice of allies, worsened the situation. Nixon, because of his desire to win reelection, refused to allow the economic recession of 1970 to continue long enough to reverse the trends in wage demands and social spending. Moreover, Nixon allied himself with the newer capitalists of the Sun Belt, who benefitted from continued full employment. Much of the financial security of this group required continued growth. Therefore, while a recession would be helpful to the vitality of the capitalist class as a whole, it would not have been beneficial to these capitalists. Radicals have argued, as discussed in Chapter 3, that it was Nixon's unreliability, rather than his handling of Watergate, that forced the Eastern Establishment, through their control of the media, to unseat him.

---

13. Arthur Jensen makes these claims in "How Much Can We Boost IQ and Scholastic Achievement?" *Harvard Education Review* (1969). For a thorough critique of Jensen's assertions, see Allan Chase, *The Legacy of Malthus* (New York: Knopf, 1975), Chapter 21.

14. Edward Banfield, *The Unheavenly City Revisited* (Boston: Little, Brown and Co., 1974), claims that ghetto rebellions were caused by the latent sex drives of young black males, and likens them to "rampages for pillage and plunder." For a critique of the Banfield view, see Chase, *Legacy of Malthus,* Chapter 22.

15. Corporate tax receipts as a percentage of total federal tax receipts fell dramatically during the 1970s. In every year between 1958-67, this ratio was between 21.0% and 23.0%. During 1970-76, it was never higher than 17.0% and was as low as 13.8% in 1975.

Defensive Adjustments

As should be clear, the radical analysis indicates that by 1970 the capitalist system required restructuring before a new stage of expansion could begin. Since this restructuring would take some time, U.S. capitalists were forced to react defensively, especially in the area of foreign trade. As the competitive position of the United States deteriorated, imports had to be increasingly paid for through the export of agricultural produce. Between 1970 and 1977, food exports rose from $7 billion to over $25 billion annually.[16] The effect of agricultural exports, while alleviating somewhat the balance of payments difficulties, deteriorated the distribution of income. It shifted income to agricultural capitalists rather than to industrial capitalists. While much of this was at the expense of household income, part of it indirectly hurt the capitalists' attempts to shift income from workers to industrial corporate profits.[17]

Foreign competition had made it difficult for many domestic firms to raise prices during the late 1960s. One way to reduce foreign competition is to devaluate the dollar. The first devaluations occurred in 1971, enabling some corporations to raise prices without fear of losing additional sales to foreign competitors.[18] Again, in 1977, over the protest of other industrialized countries, the United States allowed the value of the dollar to decline by over 20%. This enabled many weak domestic firms to push back the competition of foreign producers, especially in automobiles and steel. These devaluations necessarily increase the cost of imports, especially Middle East oil. Therefore, the attempts to shore up the sales of domestic firms by devaluation were responsible for the dramatic rise in the price of oil, not the 1973 Six-Day War.

What should be clear from this analysis is that radicals contend that food inflation and energy price increases are not a series of unfortunate unpredictable accidents, but are a direct result of the decline of competitiveness of the domestic manufacturing sector, together with worldwide overinvestment in the 1960s. Moreover, this analysis indicates why the U.S. economy experienced simultaneously high inflation and high unemployment. They are both the result of the falling rate of profit.

---

16. For the radical analysis, see URPE/PEA National Food Collective, "The Capitalist System: A Framework for Understanding Food Inflation," in *Economics: Mainstream Readings,* David Mermelstein, ed. (New York: Random House, 1976).

17. Unions with cost of living clauses recouped part of the inflation while food inflation resulted in a rapid expansion of the government Food Stamp Program.

18. Suppose a German-made Volkswagen costs 16,000 marks to make. If the exchange rate is $1 = 4 marks, then Americans only need $4000 to buy a Volkswagen. However, suppose the dollar devaluates so that $1 = 3 marks. Now the same Volkswagen must sell at $5333 in the United States. Devaluation, by making foreign goods more expensive, allows domestic corporations to raise prices.

Corporate Strategies for the 1980s

By 1977, the spectre of massive bankruptcies had abated. The financial position of both corporations and banks had improved and the profit rate began to rise. As has already been indicated, the strength of the recovery was weakened by a number of factors. Portions of the decline in national income going to household income and social services instead went to (1) profits of agricultural capitalists; (2) necessary increases in military spending; and (3) balance of payment obligations for Middle East oil. All of these factors weakened the shift of income to industrial corporate profits.

The economic expansion of the late 1970s was weakened by other factors as well. Most important was the continued disunity within the capitalist class. As has already been indicated, bankruptcies eliminated the most backward firms and allowed the remaining firms to begin an expansion. However, because of Nixon's policies and the fear of banking failures, the federal government has given support to many failing firms. One subsidy that was given was the 10% investment tax credit. This enabled all firms to receive government tax credits totaling 10% of the value of capital spending. The Carter administration, despite extensive corporate pressure, decided not to increase this across-the-board subsidy. Similarly, the Carter administration has been reluctant to give financial assistance to urban areas where the productive facilities are technically inefficient. Instead, it has attempted to be more selective in the form of corporate subsidies given. In this way, corporate profits will be increased to the more efficient firms rather than providing a crutch for weaker firms to survive on.

Radicals contend that the necessary restructuring will force the capitalist class to increasingly rely upon state planning. As discussed in Chapter 3, Carter's energy plan reflected this need. While "new" money capitalists were able to forestall Carter's program, it is likely that the 1980s will witness another attempt by "old" money forces to institute some form of state planning.

A second part of the corporate strategy for the 1980s is how to continue to contain the black population. Given the crisis of capitalism, with continued declines of social spending and standards of living, the situation of innercity minority groups *must* continue to deteriorate. The Presidential Commission on Civil Disorder and Terrorism indicated that in many ways the situation in innercities was worse in 1977 than in 1967. They believed that more rebellions were inevitable. The corporate strategy to minimize the extent of these rebellions has been to cultivate the support of the black professional class. Carter supported the use of racial preference for medical schools. He appointed Andrew Young as Ambassador to the United Nations. In New York City, Mayor Koch appointed members of the minority community to visible posts in the city administration. Jesse Jackson was even warmly received by the

Republican Party when he demanded that more black Republicans be given administrative positions in the party's bureaucracy. It is hoped that by winning enough black professionals and "leaders" to the system, they will, in turn, be able to forestall ghetto rebellions.

Reducing the Size of the Industrial Reserve Army

The attempt to institute state planning, under the control of "old" money forces, and the attempt to placate the minority community by giving visible posts to minority leaders is also required to fulfill another objective—the reduction of the size of the industrial reserve army. The effects of these political policies on the size of the industrial reserve army can be best understood by looking at recent history.

The rise of fascism The reserve army is required because within parliamentary democracies labor must voluntarily enter into labor contracts. If labor is particularly anti-capitalist, then these contracts would reflect a high degree of class conflict. Militant strikes would be the normal process by which settlements would be reached. In this context, a great deal of unemployment would be periodically required to weaken the backbone of labor. This situation was typical of the early periods of industrialization in the United States and Western Europe.

The Soviet socialist revolution had a profound effect on the workings of the capitalist system. It demonstrated to workers that capitalism was only *one* possible organization of an economy. This created increased problems for capitalists. On the one hand, by maintaining high levels of unemployment, they risked radicalization of workers who would look towards socialist revolution. On the other hand, if unemployment was kept low, militant workers would undermine profits—the very foundation of capitalism. During the 1930s, capitalist economies could no longer maintain stability through its traditional method of using the industrial reserve army to discipline labor without risking socialist revolutions. In response, the weaker capitalist economies moved towards fascism. Not only Italy and Germany, but the entire continent of Europe was ruled by fascist governments by 1939. Only Great Britain and Sweden could be considered to have retained parliamentary democracy. Kalecki, in his work on the political business cycle, was the first major economist to emphasize the role of fascism in allowing capitalist economies to function at high levels of employment without fear of having profits eroded. He said,

> One of the important functions of fascism, as typified by the Nazi system, was to remove the capitalist objections to full employment.
> . . . "discipline in the factories" and "political stability" under full

employment are maintained by the "new order," which ranges from suppression of the trade unions to the concentration camp. Political pressure replaces the economic pressure of unemployment.[19]

Labor-business alliance After World War II, capitalists in North America and most of Western Europe adopted another tactic in order to reduce the minimum necessary reserve army. In these countries, especially the United States, West Germany, and Scandinavia, capitalists solidified their alliance with noncommunist trade union leaders. The basis of the alliance was that labor would refrain from initiating militant and political strikes which endangered profitability and/or political stability. In return, capitalists would guarantee economic growth and historically lower levels of unemployment for the heavily unionized sectors.

Radicals contend that it was this alliance, rather than Keynesian economics per se, which was responsible for the dramatically lower unemployment rates experienced by Western democracies during the quarter of a century after World War II. The principal effect of Keynesian economics was to reduce the excessive fluctuations of a decentralized capitalist economy. It enabled capitalists to fulfill their part of the alliance. However, according to the radical thesis, the implementation of Keynesian policies would not have been possible without the agreement of labor to limit its demands. In a somewhat more complicated manner, capitalists were able to make a similar agreement with the French and Italian Communist Parties.

Breakdown of the labor-business alliance Radicals contend that certain forces began to put pressure on the labor-business alliance during the mid-1960s. Uneven development among world powers created increasing competition over shares of world markets. The world competition was particularly intensified by the entry of the Soviet Union into the fight for markets, and the transition of lesser powers (Iran and Brazil) from neo-colonies into semi-independent economic forces. This forced capitalists in each country to begin to break their commitments to continued high employment growth.

Not only did world events create problems for growth, so did internal developments. In the United States, the alliance was cemented between the "old" money capitalists of the Northeast and white labor aristocracy. During the 1960s, the Civil Rights movement and the rise of "new" money capitalists in the Sun Belt created problems for the old alliance. Formerly, disenfranchised groups wanted a bigger share of the economic pie.

These disenfranchised groups strained the alliance in a number of ways. Old money forces could no longer guarantee that benefits would continue to

---

19. Michal Kalecki, *Selective Essays on the Dynamics of the Capitalist Economy* (Cambridge, U.K.: Cambridge University Press, 1971), p. 141.

improve for organized labor because of their declining ability to dictate government policy. For example, in 1978, old money was willing to allow unionization to be expanded through revisions of the National Labor Relations Act. However, it did not pass Congress because of the rising influence of the new money grouping. Also, traditional labor leaders increasingly have lost the ability to guarantee that labor will be held in check. Younger workers, and especially minority workers, who had never benefitted from the labor-capital alliance, increasingly were engaged in strike activities against the desires of traditional labor leaders.

Radicals contend that with the breakdown of the labor-business alliance, capitalists had little choice but to continue high levels of unemployment and direct federal intervention into the labor process during the late 1970s. These policies were necessary in order to maintain stability and profitability. However, if state planning can reassert the predominance of old money, and if the incorporation of black leaders can reduce the disruption caused by disenfranchised minorities, then the labor-business alliance could reemerge. In this case, capitalism could lower the size of the industrial reserve army.

17.3 CONCLUSION

The radical interpretation gives a gloomy forecast for the near future. It suggests that the restructuring will be painful for low and middle-income households. One implication of the radical view is that the Democratic and Republican Parties are not capable of being vehicles for progressive change during this period since these parties are committed to existing power relations and dominated by corporate money and capitalist ideology. The trade union hierarchy, which is also committed to existing relationships and a capitalist ideology, is unlikely to take the necessary actions. Instead, this period requires the growth of left parties and rank-and-file organizations.

CHAPTER EIGHTEEN

NEO-MARXIAN UNDERCONSUMPTIONIST MODELS

Chapter 16 indicated that the major thrust of Marx's economic theories was to demonstrate that independent of aggregate demand, there is a tendency towards a falling rate of profit in capitalist societies. Prior to Marx, social critics of capitalism contended that because capitalists saved rather than consumed there would be a tendency towards deficient *consumer* demand in capitalist societies. This theory, which considered the source of economic crises to be the lack of consumer demand, has been called the underconsumptionist viewpoint. Marx, through his reproduction schemes, demonstrated that regardless of the level of capitalist savings, balanced growth with full utilization of capital was possible.

Just as the structuralist growth theories, Marx's reproduction schemes indicated that there were special conditions required for balanced growth—conditions which were unlikely to be met in an unplanned capitalist economy.[1] Many of Marx's followers therefore interpreted the reproduction schemes as a *verification* of the underconsumptionist view and often presented it as the primary contradiction of capitalism. Indeed, today there is an important school of marxian thought which continues to place primary emphasis on the tendencies towards underconsumption in capitalist societies.[2] This chapter will discuss the history of underconsumptionism in radical thought.

---

1. From Chapter 14, for full utilization of capital, $(\Delta I/I) = s/\alpha$ where s equals propensity to save and α equals K/Y. For full utilization of both capital and labor, $n = s/\alpha$ where n equals rate of growth of population. According to structuralists, n, s, and α are independently determined by institutional, cultural, and technical factors so that balanced growth is impossible in an unplanned economy.

2. For a detailed discussion of the history of underconsumption theories, see Michael Bleaney, *Underconsumptionist Theories* (New York: International Pub, 1976).

18.1 HISTORY OF UNDERCONSUMPTIONIST THEORIES[3]

One specific problem voiced since the beginning of the epoch of capitalism results from the effects of income distribution on aggregate consumption. The early classical economists assumed that workers, owing to their subsistence income, only consumed, while capitalists having discretionary income could save. Therefore, any shift of income from wages to profits would necessarily lower consumer demand. Moreover, if capitalists took their savings and bought capital goods, productive capacity grows while at the same time consumer demand is falling. In this case, accumulation was thought to widen the gap between productive capacity and effective demand. As this gap became apparent, capitalists in the consumer goods industries would be forced to cut back production, precipitating an economic crisis. Since the crisis was a result of a lack of consumer demand, these views were labeled as underconsumptionist.

Early underconsumptionists claimed that *too much* capital accumulation would cause a crisis. They would begin by assuming that the economy was growing at a "sustainable" rate. They would then assume that capitalists cut back their consumption and invest the amount saved in additional productive capacity. Thus, while investment expands productive capacity, the net cutback in consumer demand results in underutilization of even the capacity which had existed before. "Too much savings" had led to the slump.

Conservative and Radical Underconsumptionist Theories

The first major economist to clearly enunciate the underconsumptionist view was Thomas Malthus during the 1820s. Malthus argued that it is the demand for consumer goods that regulates production. He believed that the pressures of competition under capitalism forced each industrialist to cut back consumption, both his own and his workers, in order to accumulate as fast and as much as possible. Hence, capitalist competition resulted in a widening gap between capacity in the consumer goods industries and effective demand.

Malthus argued against solving the problem by redistributing income to workers. He felt that it was necessary to keep the working class in poverty because raising incomes would only cause the working class to lose their willingness to work and lead to a dangerous increase in population. His solution was to abandon industrialization and return to an agricultural-based economy. Malthus reasoned that the agricultural aristocracy had little concern for productive accumulation. They were quite content to extract rent from

---

3. This follows the discussion in Anwar Shaikh, "An Introduction to the History of Crisis Theories," in URPE, *U.S. Capitalism in Crisis* (New York: 1978), pp. 219–240.

peasants and spend it on opulent consumption. According to Malthus, it was this opulent consumption which enabled the economy to maintain production. Excessive savings was avoided. For these reasons, the consumption of the feudal aristocracy kept not only aggregate demand and productive capacity balanced but kept the social fabric of the nation in equilibrium as well.

In the hands of Malthus, underconsumptionist theories were used as a reactionary apologetic for the parasitism of the feudal class, but in the hands of Simonde de Sismondi, they were the basis of a radical criticism of capitalism. Sismondi was a contemporary of Malthus who also saw a tendency towards underconsumption in capitalist societies. Once again, we find the argument that the level of consumption regulates overall production so that production can grow only as fast as consumption grows. But capitalism restricts the consumption of the masses by keeping them in poverty so that demand grows more slowly than the productive capacity of the consumer goods industries. Moreover, as capitalism develops, income distribution becomes more and more unequal so that underconsumption gets worse as capitalism matures.

Unlike Malthus, Sismondi was a radical who was deeply impressed by the suffering of the peasants and workers under capitalism. In his time, he stood at the head of what Marx called petty-bourgeois socialism, which struggled against the cruelty and destruction engendered by capitalism, and sought to reform it so as to ameliorate these conditions. Sismondi himself championed radical changes in income distribution in favor of peasants and workers, and looked to the state to carry out these and other economic reforms.

Marx's Reproduction Schemes

Marx was sympathetic to the radical underconsumptionists like Sismondi. He agreed with their moral criticisms of capitalism based upon its tendency to greater income inequality. However, Marx believed that they made crucial errors which undermined their criticisms. In particular, Marx believed that income inequality in and of itself would not cause a gap between productive capacity and effective demand. In order to demonstrate that balanced growth was possible in a capitalist society at any rate of savings, Marx developed his reproduction schemes.

In these schemes, Marx divided production into two sectors: Sector I produced capital goods while Sector II produced consumer goods.[4] Each sector's output is divided between capital replacement costs (C), labor costs (V), and

---

4. In more sophisticated models, Marx also included a luxury goods sector. For a detailed analysis of reproduction schemes, see M. C. Howard and J. E. King, *The Political Economy of Marx* (New York: Longman, 1975), Chapter 6.

profits (S).[5] In his simplest reproduction schemes, the following assumptions are made:

R1—The ratio of capital replacement costs to labor costs, C/V, was assumed to be the same in both sectors.

R2—The ratio of profits to labor costs, S/V, was assumed to be the same in both sectors.

R3—Workers spend all their income on consumer goods.

R4—It is assumed that capitalists in both sectors have the same MPC out of profits and that all savings goes to capital spending in the same sector.

R5—All capital goods wear out in one production period so that capital replacement costs equal the capital stock, and the new capital stock equals the production of capital goods.[6]

In order for balanced growth to occur, the demand for goods must equal full capacity production in each sector. Let us look at the consumer goods sector (Sector II) and determine the necessary condition for balanced growth.

The value of full capacity output in the consumer goods industry is $C_2 + V_2 + S_2$. The demand for consumer goods is composed of four quantities; demand by (1) workers in the capital goods sector, equal to V_1; (2) capitalists in the capital goods sector, equal to bS_1; (3) workers in the consumer goods sector, equal to V_2; and (4) capitalists in the consumer goods sector, equal to bS_2. Therefore, for equilibrium in Sector II:

$$(V_1 + V_2) + b(S_1 + S_2) = C_2 + V_2 + S_2$$

This equilibrium condition can be transformed by incorporating assumptions R1 and R2. According to R1, $C_1/V_1 = C_2/V_2$ and according to R2, $S_1/V_1 = S_2/V_2$.[7] This implies that $C_1/C_2 = V_1/V_2 = S_1/S_2 = \bar{r}$, where $\bar{r}$ is some constant. Marx called $\bar{r}$ the "proportionality" constant. It indicates the ratio of the productive capacity of the capital goods industry to the productive capacity of the consumer goods industry. Substituting for V_1 and S_1,

$$(\bar{r}V_2 + V_2) + b(\bar{r}S_2 + S_2) = C_2 + V_2 + S_2$$
$$(1 + \bar{r})(V_2 + bS_2) = C_2 + V_2 + S_2$$

5. Chapter 16 indicated that if C/V is the same in each industry, then market prices equal marxian values in each industry. Therefore, in the simple reproduction scheme presented, the variables are equivalent to their marxian concepts: S = surplus value, C = constant capital, V = variable capital, C/V = organic composition of capital, and S/V = rate of exploitation.

6. Note that this is the opposite extreme of the structuralist growth models. There, it was assumed that capital lasts forever so that *no* replacement capital costs occur.

7. If $S_1/V_1 = S_2/V_2$, then $S_1/S_2 = V_1/V_2$. If $C_1/V_1 = C_2/V_2$, then $C_1/C_2 = V_1/V_2$. Therefore, $C_1/C_2 = S_1/S_2 = V_1/V_2$.

If we divide both sides by V_2

$$(1+\bar{r})\left(1+b\frac{S_2}{V_2}\right)=\frac{C_2}{V_2}+1+\frac{S_2}{V_2}$$

Solving for b,

$$b=\frac{\dfrac{C}{V}+\dfrac{S}{V}-\bar{r}}{\dfrac{S}{V}(1+\bar{r})}$$

This equilibrium condition indicates that given the distribution of productive capacity $(\bar{r})$, the capital-labor ratio (C/V), and the profit-labor ratio (S/V), there is only one value for the MPC out of profits for which balanced growth will occur. If the MPC is larger, then excess demand for consumer goods exists, while if the MPC is smaller, excess supply of consumer goods exists. This demonstrates the conditions under which underconsumption could occur in capitalist societies.

However, this equilibrium condition also indicates that given C/V and S/V, there exists a proportionality constant, $\bar{r}$, which will generate balanced growth for any MPC. Hence, while underconsumption is possible, it is not a necessary outcome, regardless of the MPC out of profits.

These results are illustrated in Figure 18.1 when $C/V=4$ and $S/V=1$. Under these conditions, if the MPC out of profits equals 0.5, balanced growth would occur if $\bar{r}=3$.[8] If the MPC out of profits should decline to 0.33, Figure 18.1 and the Appendix indicate that this would create an excess supply of consumer goods. If firms would respond by shifting out of the consumer goods industry, the proportionality constant would increase. Figure 18.1 and the Appendix to this chapter indicate that if the proportionality constant rises to 3.5, balanced growth would be reestablished.

Monopoly and the Disproportionality Problems

Just as the structuralist growth model of Chapter 14, the marxian reproduction schemes demonstrate that only under special conditions will balanced growth occur.[9] They both indicate that without planning it is unlikely that these conditions will be met. Since nineteenth century capitalism was totally unplanned, many of Marx's followers interpreted his reproduction schemes as

---

8. $b=(5-\bar{r})/(1+\bar{r})$ if $C/V=4$ and $S/V=1$. Therefore, $b=(5-3)/(1+3)=2/4=0.5$ if $\bar{r}=3$.

9. In reproduction schemes, rate of growth equals $(1-b)S/C$. In structuralist models, rate of growth equals s/α. However, since $s=$ Savings$/Y$ and $\alpha=K/Y$, $s/\alpha=$ (Savings)$/K$. But in the simple reproduction scheme $(1-b)S=$ Savings and $C=K$ so that both models give the same balanced growth rate.

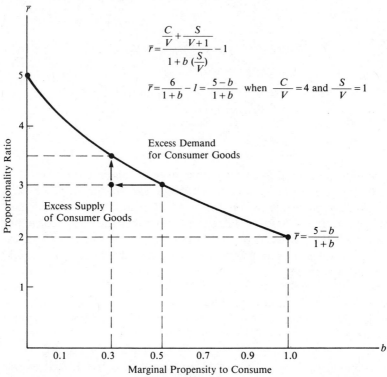

Figure 18.1   Balanced growth requirements

proof that capitalism was subject to severe imbalances. By the twentieth century, it was usually considered *the* marxian theory of crises.[10]

With the emergence of monopoly capital, a split within the marxist movement occurred. One group of marxists, including Karl Kautsky and Rudolph Hilferding, claimed that with the growth of monopoly power there is an end to the blind forces of the market.[11] Capitalism is able to organize itself, competition disappears, anarchy of production is eliminated, crises become a thing of the past, and a planned, conscious organization predominates. They claimed that trusts and cartels grow into planned socialist economies so that revolu-

---

10. This is usually explained by the fact that Marx's falling rate of profit thesis, which was in Volume II of *Capital,* was not published until 20 years after Volume I. Also, the falling rate of profit was a longterm tendency which was not meant to explain the periodic business cycles.

11. Rudolf Hilferding, *Finance Capital* (Vienna: 1910) and Karl Kautsky, *National State, Imperialist State and the Union of States* (Nuremberg: 1915). The widespread agreement within the radical group that the disproportionality problem was the central problem of capitalism is typified by A. Leontiev, *Political Economy* (New York: International Pub, 1935), which was the standard textbook in the Soviet Union during the 1930s.

tions are unnecessary. This group of marxists reasoned that since capitalism has "reformed itself," it need not be destroyed. Instead, they urged marxists to work within the system to speed its transformation into a planned society. They, therefore, severed relationships with those who preached revolution and became the initiators of Western European Social Democratic Parties.

The other group of marxists, which included Lenin and Rosa Luxemburg, rejected the Kautsky-Hilferding thesis. They argued that monopoly power ". . . does not eliminate [free competition], but exists alongside it and hovers over it, as it were, and, as a result, gives rise to a number of very acute antagonisms, frictions and conflicts."[12]

This revolutionary group claimed that competition intensifies in the monopoly phase of capitalism. It intensifies because formerly, under free competition, many separate capitalists fought one another. Now, powerful unions of capitalists enter the fight—group against group. The fierceness of the struggle is usually identified in two ways. First, it is argued that these groups within each country struggle for political power, for predominance in government institutions. A current example of this is said to be the struggle between the Sun Belt (new money) corporate grouping, centered in energy, electronics, and agribusiness, and the (old money) Eastern Establishment, centered in finance and durable goods manufacturing. Second, it is argued that national groupings struggle against each other for control over world markets. Japanese interests, West German interests, and U.S. interests are in fierce competition with the Soviet Union for control over world markets.

Lenin claimed that the laws of uneven development made it impossible for conflicting groups to ever eliminate fierce competition. He noted that planning would require market shares for firms and industries to be fixed. Only in this way could growth be balanced with each firm's and each industry's growth rate identical. However, the structure of each market is always composed of weaker declining firms and rising stronger firms; of growing industries and declining industries. Therefore, planning will be in the self-interest of the declining firms and industries, but against the self-interest of the rising firms (industries). In this situation, it is impossible for the competing groups to agree on the market shares for each. Again, the situation in the United States is instructive. During the 1970s, the Rockefeller-funded Trilateral Commission recommended extensive planning presumably to revitalize the declining Northeast productive base.[13] However, the rising Sun Belt concerns, as exemplified by the energy conflict, have been adamant in their opposition to any government planning.

---

12. V. I. Lenin, *Imperialism* (New York: International Pub, 1939), p. 88.

13. For a discussion of the Trilateral Commission's support of planning, see Samuel Bowles, "The Trilateral Commission . . . ," and William Tabb, "Domestic Economic Policies Under Carter: The Imprint of Trilateralism," in URPE, *U.S. Capitalism in Crisis* (New York: 1978).

Lenin argued that it was impossible for nation-based interest groups to avoid conflict. He assumed that each nation's profit-labor ratio was historically determined and not subject to rapid adjustment. Differences between national savings rates would therefore exist and could not be easily eliminated. Both the marxian reproduction schemes and the structuralist growth model indicate that the higher the savings rate, the higher is the balanced growth rate. This indicates that to meet internal requirements for balanced growth, countries must grow at different rates. However, if countries must grow at different rates, then they must have different rates of growth of foreign trade and raw material utilization. Countries with higher savings rates would, therefore, require an increasing share of world trade and raw material markets. This would require slower-growing countries to give up portions of their spheres of economic influence (markets and raw material supplies). Lenin argued that no capitalist country would voluntarily shift its markets and raw material sources to its rivals. He believed that redistribution of spheres of economic influence occur only after *wars*.

Even if the heavily industrialized countries could agree on a trade formula, this agreement presupposes that no developing countries can upset the balance of economic power. However, as the cases of the Soviet Union or China or Iran demonstrate, there are always developing countries able to be transformed into industrialized nations. These new industrialized nations are no longer markets for the heavily industrialized powers but instead become competitors. As these newly-transformed nations begin to successfully compete for their own spheres of economic influence, the agreements between the industrialized powers break down. A new division of the world must occur.

The Leninist analysis indicates that during the 1980s a substantial redivision of the world must take place to reflect the faster growth rates of the Soviet Union and Japan compared to the United States. In particular, the Soviet Union seems to desire increasing markets for its manufactured goods and sources of raw materials. This creates the strong possibility of military conflict over these spheres of economic influence.

18.2 BARAN AND SWEEZY: CONTEMPORARY UNDERCONSUMPTIONISTS

As the marxian view indicates, without planning, continuous balanced growth is impossible. The recent work of Paul Baran and Paul Sweezy attempts to demonstrate that these imbalances will be underconsumptionist (rather than overconsumptionist).[14] Moreover, Baran and Sweezy claim that the actions of capitalists will intensify problems of underconsumption. Therefore, they claim that capitalism will tend towards deep stagnation with no endogenous means of rectifying the situation. The effects of monopoly on the *reduction of competitive forces* are critical to their explanation for these tendencies. However, they reject the notion that monopoly power ushers in the possibility of plan-

---

14. *Monopoly Capital* (New York: Monthly Review, 1966).

ning. In this way, their views on the effect of monopoly power are distinct from both the Leninist position and the Kautsky-Hilferding position.

Monopoly Power and Income Distribution

Baran and Sweezy claim that the growth of monopoly power has created a continuous shift in *potential* income between production workers and capitalists.[15] Monopoly power, they contend, has enabled capitalists to gain disproportionately from technological progress since workers are not strong enough to win sufficient wage increases, and because no competitive pressures exist which would require capitalists to pass the savings onto consumers. Therefore, if sales, as measured by capacity utilization, remain constant, then profit rates rise over time. Baran and Sweezy illustrate this point by referring to the "profit schedule" of U.S. Steel (Figure 18.2), which indicates a shift upward of its profit rate at each level of capacity utilization. For example, according to the 1920–55 profit schedule, if capacity utilization was 90%, the profit rate would be 6%, but according to the 1955–60 schedule, it would be 9%.

This thesis was originally formulated by Michal Kalecki who claimed that with a given cost of production, market price would vary in direct relationship with the degree of monopoly in the industry.[16] Since Baran and Sweezy believe that there is a continuous increase in monopoly power, they argue that the divergence between production costs and market prices (the mark-up) has been rising continuously. Therefore, the U.S. Steel profit schedule is considered a glaring example of a general phenomenon.

During the 1970s, there were a number of attempts to verify the Kalecki hypothesis. First, data indicates that the degree of monopoly is increasing.[17] Second, data indicates that the share of total manufacturing assets held by the 200 largest manufacturing firms is increasing.[18] Next, there is evidence to sup-

---

15. As Chapter 7 indicated, a shift of income from wages to profits only raises *actual* profits if *Y* is unchanged. Depending upon other assumptions of the model, actual profits may or may not increase from a redistributional shift. If profits have no effect on capital spending and the MPC out of wages equals one, then actual profits are unchanged by a redistributional shift (Paradox of Profits). Baran and Sweezy make neither assumption.

16. Michal Kalecki, "Costs and Prices," in *Selected Essays,* M. Kalecki, ed. (Cambridge, U.K.: Cambridge University Press, 1971), especially pp. 48–49.

17. H. M. Wachtel and P. D. Adelsheim, "How Recession Feeds Inflation: Price Markups in a Concentrated Economy," *Challenge* 20 (Sept./Oct. 1977). Table 4 on p. 12 indicates that, especially among low concentration industries, the concentration ratio (% of industry sales by 4 largest firms) is rising.

18. The percentage of all manufacturing assets held by the 100 largest corporations increased from 38% to 48% between 1950 and 1970. For the 200 largest corporations, it increased from 48% to 58% during that period. For discussion, see Richard Edwards et al., *The Capitalist System* (Englewood Cliffs, N.J.: Prentice-Hall, 1978), pp. 131–134.

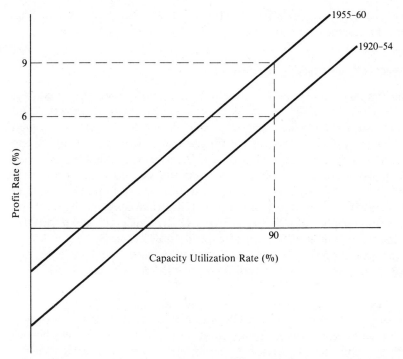

Figure 18.2 U.S. Steel Corporation: Relationship between capacity utilization and profit rates, 1920–60

port the contention that there is a positive correlation between the degree of monopoly and profits.[19] Also, downward pricing during periods of falling demand are less prevalent than in the past.[20]

These pieces of data have been interpreted to mean that competitive pressures on pricing are weaker than in the past, so that profit margins grow larger in relationship to production costs. If we now redefine V as production costs, this viewpoint claims that S/V steadily increases.

Changes in the MPC Out of Profits

Baran and Sweezy assume that the rate of consumption out of profits is directly related to the percentage profits distributed to households as dividends. They assume that increases in profits are not immediately passed on to stockholders in the form of dividends. According to Baran and Sweezy, this lagged structure of dividend pay-out implies that, with a continuous increase

---

19. Ibid., pp. 140–144, especially Figure 4-G and Table 4-C.

20. Wachtel and Adelsheim, "How Recession Feeds Inflation," p. 9, tables 1 and 2.

in profits, the share of profits going to dividends declines.[21] Hence, they believe that the MPC out of profits declines as monopoly power increases.

Stability of the Capital-Labor (C/V) Ratio

According to traditional marxian thought, technology was capital-biased so that there would be a continuous increase in the C/V ratio. Moreover, class struggle would indicate that this process is periodically accelerated by the replacement of militant labor by machinery. Baran and Sweezy reject these contentions. They argue that monopoly power has enabled capitalists to pass along any money wage demands to consumers as price increases, so that the full-employment profit squeeze is no longer a possibility. If capitalists can off-set wage demands by price increases, then they have no reason to resort to labor-saving technology. Second, Baran and Sweezy argue that the capital-bias of technology was only dominant in the early stages of capitalism—when new technology replaced men with machines. In mature capitalism, technology replaces machines with better machines so that there is no compelling reason to believe the C/V ratio should continually rise.[22] Sweezy attempts to support this contention by referring to a study by Joseph Gilman. Gilman found that C/V rose until 1919, leveled off in the 1920s, and continuously declined starting in the mid-1930s. Between 1923 and 1952, Gilman found that C/V fell from 4.2 to 3.6. For these reasons, Baran and Sweezy assume that C/V has probably been quite stable throughout the period of monopoly capitalism.[23]

Balanced Growth Requirements

Earlier we found that balanced growth is possible only if

$$\bar{r} = \frac{\dfrac{C}{V} + \dfrac{S}{V} + 1}{1 + b\dfrac{S}{V}} - 1$$

---

21. While the Baran/Sweezy contention may be true, their explanation that dividend increases lag profit rises is not sufficient. For example, let $D(t) = mP(t-x)$, where $D(t)$ are dividends in time t, $P(t-x)$ are profits x time periods prior, and $0 < m < 1$. Suppose that the economy is growing at a constant continuous growth rate, g, so that $P(t) = P(O)(e^{gt})$ where $P(O)$ = initial level of profits. In this case, $D(t) = P(O)(e^{g(t-x)})$ so that

$$\frac{D(t)}{P(t)} = \frac{mP(O)\,(e^{g(t-x)})}{P(O)\,(e^{gt})} = m(e^{-xg}),$$

which is a *constant*.

22. See Paul Sweezy, "Some Problems in the Theory of Capital Accumulation," *Monthly Review* 26 (May 1974): 38–56.

23. A more recent study, Victor Perlo, "Capital-Output Ratios in Manufacturing," *Quarterly Review of Economics and Business* 8 (Autumn 1966): 29–42, finds that capital-output ratios have continued to increase since World War II.

We also found that Baran and Sweezy assert that with the growth of monopoly, S/V rises, b declines, and C/V is unchanged. This implies that equilibrium $\bar{r}$ rises over time. Therefore, Baran and Sweezy assert that the share of production going for capital goods must increase if underconsumption is to be avoided.

This can be illustrated. Let us assume that initially $C/V = c_0$, $S/V = s_0$ so that $B(c_0, s_0)$ in Figure 18.3 represents the balanced growth schedule. If we begin with MPC $= b_0$, then balanced growth requires $\bar{r} = r_0$. According to Baran and Sweezy, if S/V rises to s_1, the equilibrium schedule shifts to $B'(c_0, s_1)$ which indicates that (b_0, r_0) is now a combination of deficient demand (underconsumption).[24] This is further aggravated if the MPC declines to b_1. Only if the proportionality constant increases can balanced growth be maintained.

Monopoly Capitalism and Capital Spending

Figure 18.3 indicated that balanced growth requires that an increasing share of production must be shifted to capital goods. The next step of the Baran/Sweezy thesis is to claim that monopoly power *retards* capital spending. The theoretical foundation for their contention is the work of Josef Steindl.[25]

According to Steindl, when capitalism is in its competitive stage, each firm must invest as fast and as much as possible in order to gain a technical advantage over its competitors. This process results in rapid technological innovation by the stronger firms, which drives the weaker firms out of business. The problem of overcapacity is avoided by the failure of the weaker firms and the destruction of their obsolete equipment. This has been described as "The Process of Creative Destruction."[26]

Steindl claims that within monopoly industries, each firm no longer acts under the compulsion of competitive pressures. The remaining firms all realize the futility of trying to outpace each other. They realize that it will be impossible to drive competitors out. Hence, the only effect of accelerated capital spending would be industry-wide excess capacity and lower profits for all firms. Therefore, in monopoly industries, when a new cost-saving technology

---

24. The balanced growth schedule shifts upward and to the right only for $b < 1/(1 + [C/V])$. At higher MPCs out of profits, the consumption by capitalists in the capital goods industry more than offsets the savings by capitalists in the consumer goods industry. We will assume that these lower values of b are the relevant values. Moreover, in more complicated reproduction schemes, the general situation is that raising S/V also raises equilibrium $\bar{r}$ for any MPC out of profits.

25. Josef Steindl, *Maturity and Stagnation in American Capitalism* (Oxford: Basil Blackwell, 1952), especially Part I, Section V, pp. 40–55.

26. This was the description given to this process by Joseph Schumpeter, *Capitalism, Socialism, and Democracy* (New York: Harper Torchbook, 1962) title of Chapter 7.

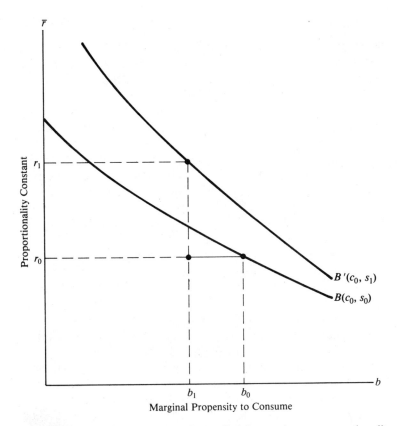

Figure 18.3 Effect of increase in profit-labor ratio on proportionality requirement

is invented, it is much more slowly innovated than when the industry was competitive. This enables each firm to extend the useful life of outmoded equipment and facilities.

Baran and Sweezy support this hypothesis that the diffusion of innovations is retarded under monopoly capitalism by referring to the McGraw-Hill 1958 capital survey which indicated that despite very rapid changes in technology "less than one-third of [U.S. capital] is modern."[27] Baran and Sweezy also found that the growth in capital investment during the 1950s did not grow as fast as expenditures on research and development. They conclude, "Under monopoly capitalism there is no necessary correlation, as there is in a competitive system, between the rate of technological progress and the volume of investment outlets."[28]

---

27. Dexter M. Keezer et al., *New Forces in American Business,* (New York: McGraw-Hill, 1958), p. 23, quoted in Baran and Sweezy, p. 96.

28. Baran and Sweezy, p. 97.

Irrational Consumption

The foregoing analysis implies that in mature capitalist societies there is a chronic and increasing problem of deficient consumer demand, not offset by growing investment demand. This stagnationist view differs dramatically from the orthodox marxian view of crises and self-generating recoveries. Moreover, in the orthodox marxian models, problems are precipitated by a declining rate of profit. In the Baran/Sweezy model, they are precipitated by a rising rate of profit.

Baran and Sweezy contend that only epoch-making inventions and the growth of irrational consumption has enabled the United States to avoid permanent stagnation.[29] Irrational consumptions are categories designated by Baran and Sweezy as having no social value—expenditures which would cease to occur under socialism. The major components of irrational consumption are expenditures on the "sales effort" and military expenditures.

The sales effort reflects the expenditures on advertising, product differentiation, and planned obsolescence necessary for the profitability of the monopoly corporation. Baran and Sweezy believe all of these expenditures increase with the growth of monopoly capitalism. In no respect is this contention different than the Naderites and Galbraithians who also see increasing waste in expenditures on consumer advertising and "product design." However, unlike left-liberals, who believe that these expenditures come at the expense of socially meaningful production, Baran and Sweezy contend that without these expenditures only increased unemployment would be produced. Therefore, these wasteful expenditures serve a *functional* role by absorbing the corporate surplus profits. Like Malthus, but from a different perspective, Baran and Sweezy contend that capitalism *requires* conspicuous wasteful consumption.

Similarly, they consider the growth of military spending wasteful but necessary for the maintenance of balanced growth. Indeed, advocates of this perspective usually claim that military spending is the most important vehicle for the absorption of capitalist surplus. In support of the view that military spending is necessary for jobs, advocates have claimed that the percentage of the labor force who either are unemployed or engaged in military production was virtually constant between 1930 and 1970. Hence, all variations in military expenditures were inversely related to variations in the unemployment rate during this 40-year period.

Evaluation of the Baran/Sweezy Model

The Baran/Sweezy model takes the disproportionality problem one step further than previous theorists. It explains why disproportionality problems

---

29. In Chapter 8, Baran and Sweezy argue that by 1900 the stagnationist tendency was so strong that only World War I saved the U.S. economy from a severe depression.

are underconsumptionist and why they will tend to become more serious with time. Moreover, the model indicates what factors have, up until the 1970s, forestalled a permanent period of stagnation. While there are some technical errors in their assertions their thesis is logically derived. Criticisms of it must, therefore, be directed to a number of underlying assumptions made. Orthodox marxists, in particular, have been extremely critical of a number of these underlying assumptions:

Baran/Sweezy concept of monopoly Throughout their work, Baran and Sweezy take a middle position on the economic effects of monopoly. On the one hand, they maintain that there is fierce competition between monopolists when they discuss the tendency of capitalists to introduce cost-reducing technologies. On the other hand, it must be controlled enough to eliminate destructive competition (overinvestment) and enable capitalists to fully pass along wage increases to consumers.

Baran and Sweezy may be correct in specific shortrun situations. However, it is extremely unlikely that this middle position can reflect the situation over longer periods of time. For all their efforts to imply that these characteristics have been occurring since the turn of the twentieth century, almost all of their evidence is from the 1952–62 period. From this period, they present data on the obsolescence of machinery, the rising ratio of invention to innovation, the shifting upward of the profit schedule in the steel industry, and the general lagging of capital spending. One can accept their thesis as correct during this period, but not accept it as a general condition in monopoly capitalist societies.

This is especially true since the 1952–62 period was quite unusual if not unique. During this period, the lack of foreign competition, owing to the destruction of productive facilities everywhere in the industrialized world except the United States, gave domestic capitalists a brief respite from competitive pressures. Moreover, the total destruction of left-wing influence in the trade union movement made it increasingly possible for capitalists to temporarily raise the rate of exploitation, independent of mechanization (changes in C/V).[30] Unless Baran and Sweezy assume that the existence of a docile workforce and limited foreign competition are permanent features of U.S. capitalism, no generalizations can be made from their evidence.

The necessity of irrational consumption The Baran/Sweezy thesis is that government spending is necessary, and it must be increasing as a percentage of

---

30. The major result of the anti-communist crusade after World War II was that communists, who had leadership of between one-half and one-quarter of the membership of trade unions, were expelled and the government installed alternative leadership. Also, constitutions of unions were changed to give the national officers more control over locals. The result was a more pro-capitalist, more conservative, less militant trade union leadership.

GNP if capitalism is to avoid underconsumptionist stagnation. This thesis in and of itself does not represent a damaging attack on capitalism. Indeed, Keynes came to the same exact conclusion. Keynes said, "[The underconsumptionist] schools of thought are, as guides to practical policy, undoubtedly in the right. . . . For it is unlikely that full employment can be maintained whatever we may do about investment, with the existing propensity to consume."[31] However, Keynes was confident that government intervention with social spending could counteract any stagnationist tendencies.

Baran and Sweezy reject this left-liberal thesis by claiming that "*given the power structure of United States monopoly* capitalism, the increase in [social welfare] spending had about reached its outer limits by 1939."[32] They give three examples to support this contention. First, they claim that much social spending is financed locally through the property tax, which immediately creates antagonisms between upper middle-class taxpayers who do not benefit from social spending and the low income beneficiaries. This conflict results in a limit to the property tax and, hence, limit to social spending. Second, they claim that public housing projects would significantly conflict with real estate interests (savings banks and slum landlords). This conflict occurs because the growth of decent public housing would dramatically lower the value of slum housing, hurting slum landlords and the banks that hold mortgages on the real estate. Third, Baran and Sweezy claim that social spending on medical services is limited because of the opposition from the medical profession. Hence, because government social spending programs will be opposed by upper middle-income taxpayers, slum landlords, savings banks, and doctors, the government is "forced" to spend on military goods, which are in the "national interest."

Events since the writing of *Monopoly Capital* have cast serious doubts on each of these examples. States have shifted from property tax to income taxes to finance local spending. Medicare and medicaid have become a financial bonanza for the medical profession. Urban renewal projects have reshaped slum areas enabling real estate interests to reap speculative profits on the sale of slum housing. However, the most glaring problem with the concrete examples given by Baran and Sweezy is that in each case the opposition comes from *small entrepreneurs, small bankers, and better paid workers,* rather than sections of monopoly capital. Baran and Sweezy rely on stereotypes of a reactionary middle class, rather than explaining the relationship of the structure of monopoly capital to limitations on social spending. Indeed, as already stated, orthodox marxists and left-liberals argue that significant sections of monopoly capital desire state planning. Left-liberals, such as Galbraith, contend that

---

31. J. M. Keynes, *The General Theory* (London: MacMillan, 1936), p. 325.
32. Baran and Sweezy, p. 161.

monopoly corporations desire government planning to eliminate risk and uncertainty associated with capital investments. Orthodox marxists contend that planning can help revitalize corporations associated with the Rockefeller interests. Therefore, Baran and Sweezy's assertion that the limits of government social spending were reached by 1939 because of the potential conflict between private sales and government social projects is totally unfounded.

18.3 CONCLUSION

Underconsumptionist models developed still further the macroeconomic implications of income distribution begun in Chapter 7. There, it was demonstrated that if capital spending is independent of profits, any shift of income from wages to profits would lower equilibrium income. Chapter 14 indicated that even if savings would be offset by capital spending, there *could* still be an imbalance between productive capacity and aggregate demand. In this chapter, the underconsumptionist model of Baran and Sweezy claims there *will* be a widening imbalance between productive capacity and aggregate demand because of the monopoly power of large corporations.

The implications of the marxian underconsumptionist model dramatically differs from the orthodox marxian theories presented in Chapter 16. According to the former, problems occur when profits are too high and there are no endogenous mechanisms that can overcome the economy's tendencies to stagnate. According to the latter, problems occur when profits are too low, but that endogenous forces will eventually create conditions necessary for a new expansion. The differences are reflected in each perception of the economic effects of military spending during the late 1960s. According to the underconsumptionist view, this spending stimulated the economy, thereby helping it avoid stagnating. According to the orthodox marxian view, the military spending worsened the falling profit rate and, hence, intensified the economic crisis.

The Baran/Sweezy model is internally logical and, therefore, cannot be dismissed on theoretical grounds. Indeed, there has been too little research done to evaluate it on the basis of concrete evidence. However, some observations seem warranted. First, while the model seems consistent with data from the 1950s, this was too special a period to be used to generalize from. Second, some of the auxiliary assumptions, such as the assertion that military expenditures and other forms of wasteful expenditures are the only forms that government absorption can take, are less defendable than the core assumptions—assumptions concerning incentives to invest and income shares. In particular, the hypothesis that there has been a decline in the tendency to invest under monopoly capitalism is one possible explanation for events during the 1970s. Despite rising profit rates and a relatively docile working class, corporate investment lagged behind the economic expansion during 1976–78.

APPENDIX

MARXIAN REPRODUCTION MODEL

The first section of Chapter 18 indicated that for every MPC out of profits, there exists a proportionality constant, $\overline{r}$, at which balanced growth would occur. Table 18A.1 details the marxian reproduction model. As in Chapter 18, let us assume that $C/V=4$ and $S/V=1$. In Model I, $\overline{r}=3$ and the MPC out of profits equals 0.5. In period 1, the capital stock in Sector I and Sector II equals 6000 and 2000, respectively. Given $C/V=4$ and $S/V=1$, wages (and profits) equal 1500 and 500 in Sector I and Sector II, respectively. Since it is assumed that all capital wears out each period, the replacement costs are 6000 and 2000 in Sectors I and II, respectively. Therefore, the total value of production in Sectors I and II are 9000 and 3000, respectively.

Worker demand is 2000, 1500 by workers in the capital goods industry and 500 by workers in the consumer goods industry. Since $b=0.5$, capitalists spend 1000 on consumer goods, 750 by capitalists in the capital goods industry and 250 by capitalists in the consumer goods industry. Therefore, total demand in Sector II equals 3000, which is full capacity production. Similarly, the demand by capitalists for capital goods, $C+(1-b)S$, just equals full capacity production (9000).

In period 2, the capital stocks, which equal the capital purchases by each sector in period 1, are 6750 and 2250 in Sectors I and II, respectively. Each Sector has grown by 12.5%. Once more, with $b=0.5$, demand will just equal full capacity production. As long as $b=0.5$ and capitalists continue to only invest in their own sector, balanced growth at 12.5% per period will continue.

What if capitalists reduced their MPC to 0.33? Model II in Table 18A.1 indicates that with $\overline{r}=3$, growth would not be balanced. Specifically, the demand for consumer goods would only be 2666.67. This is a case of underconsumption. However, this does not mean that $b=0.33$ is too low a consumption rate. As Figure 18.1 indicates, there is some proportionality constant

Table 18A.1
Numerical examples of Marx's model of reproduction with $C/V = 4$ and $S/V = 1$

Period	Sector	Replacement investment (C)	Wage bill (V)	Profits (S)	Total value of production (C + V + S)	Worker demand for consumer goods (V)	Capitalist demand for consumer goods (bS)	Total demand for consumer goods (V + bS)	Capitalist demand for capital goods (C + [1 − b]S)
[Model I] $\bar{r} = 3$ and $b = 0.5$									
1	I	6000	1500	1500	9000	1500	750	2250	6750
	II	2000	500	500	3000	500	250	750	2250
								3000	9000
2	I	6750	1687.5	1687.5	10,125	1687.5	843.75	2531.25	7593.75
	II	2250	562.5	562.5	3375	562.5	281.25	843.75	2531.25
								3375.00	10,125.00
[Model II] $\bar{r} = 3$ and $b = 0.33$									
1	I	6000	1500	1500	9000	1500	500	2000	7000
	II	2000	500	500	3000	500	166.67	666.67	2333.33
								2666.67	9333.33
2	I	7000	1750	1750	10,500	1750	583.33	2333.33	8166.67
	II	2333	583.3	583.3	3500	583.3	291.67	875.00	2625.00
								3208.33	10,791.67

[Model III] $\bar{r} = 3.5$ and $b = 0.33$

1	I	7000	1750	1750	10,500	1750	583.33	2333.33	8166.67
	II	2000	500	500	3000	500	166.67	666.67	2333.33
								3000.00	10,500.00
2	I	8167	2041.67	2041.67	12,250	2041.67	680.53	2722.22	9527.78
	II	2333	583.33	583.33	3500	583.33	194.44	779.78	2722.22
								3500.00	12,250.00

for which any value of b will generate balanced growth. If the proportionality constant was raised to 3.5, then $b = 0.33$ would produce balanced growth. This is demonstrated in Model III of Table 18A.1, where the initial capital stock in the capital goods industry is $3\frac{1}{2}$ times as large as the initial capital stock in the consumer goods industry (7000 to 2000).

CHAPTER NINETEEN

THEORIES OF INFLATION

Up until now we have been preoccupied with understanding the reasons for fluctuations of real income—especially why real income is not always sufficient to generate full employment. Even when price changes were included, the objective was to determine the effects that price changes would have on real income rather than to determine the causes of those price level changes.

The emphasis on theories of income determination over theories of inflation reflects the general assessment of priorities generated by the Keynesian Revolution. Following the experience of the 1930s and the views of Keynes, most economists believed that the central problem of private market economies was unemployment. Inflation was considered of secondary importance because (1) only in exceptional periods did industrialized countries experience sustained high levels of inflation; (2) inflation was associated with full employment prosperity; and (3) inflation had little effect on real production and only minor distributional effects.

Since the late 1960s, industrialized market economies have been experiencing persistent high inflation rates. Increasingly, the economics profession has begun to consider problems of inflation as important as problems of insufficient demand. This chapter develops the principal theories of inflation which have attempted to explain the most recent period. Chapter 20 will discuss the costs of inflation and the effectiveness of incomes policies, such as wage-price controls, in limiting inflation.

Chapter 12 developed aggregate supply and demand schedules in order to analyze the effects of price changes on real income. This chapter will use these schedules to develop the mainstream explanations of inflation. Here, the basis for the monetarist thesis that the growth rate of the money supply is the principal determinant of the inflation rate is introduced.

This chapter also develops the principal alternative theory—the left-liberal view that changes in the money wage rate are the dominant determinant of the inflation rate. The Phillips Curve analysis, which postulates that there is an inverse relationship between unemployment and inflation rates, is introduced.

The last section presents the radical and mainstream critiques of the left liberal view. For entirely different reasons, both groups argue that the principal left-liberal finding (that unemployment could be permanently reduced if higher inflation rates are maintained) is incorrect. Both radical and mainstream economists contend that there is a minimum unemployment rate below which a market economy cannot permanently remain. The dramatically different implications of the radical and mainstream critiques will be discussed.

19.1 AGGREGATE SCHEDULES AND THE GENERAL PRICE LEVEL

Under competitive assumptions, there exists aggregate supply and aggregate demand schedules which determine the general price level and equilibrium output. The aggregate supply schedule is the relationship between the total amount of goods and services that producers are willing to supply and the general price level. The aggregate demand schedule indicates the relationship between equilibrium spending and the general price level. The equilibrium price level is assumed to be the general price level at which aggregate supply equals aggregate demand.

Aggregate Supply Schedule

The aggregate supply schedule was constructed in Chapter 12 under various sets of assumptions.[1] Both conservatives and mainstream liberals assume that since output markets are competitive, the demand for labor is determined by the marginal productivity of labor. Moreover, it was assumed that the demand curve for labor is downward sloping because of the law of diminishing returns.

Conservatives assumed that workers are only concerned about the real wage rate and make labor market decisions independent of employment conditions (the unemployment rate). These assumptions are necessary to guarantee that the supply curve of labor is upward sloping and independent of the demand for labor.

Under these assumptions, there exists an equilibrium real wage rate at which full employment is attained. At this level of production the natural rate of unemployment prevails. If, for any reason, the price level rises so that the real wage rate decreases, market conditions would raise the money wage rate until the real wage rate returns to its full employment equilibrium level.[2] Similarly, if the price level declines so that the real wage rate rises, market conditions would lower the money wage rate until the real wage rate returns to its

---

1. See assumptions D1–3 and S1–2 in Chapter 12.

2. For example, let equilibrium real wage rate, $w/p = 10$, with $w = 10$ and $p = 1.0$. If the price level rises by 10% to $p' = 1.1$, then momentarily the real wage rate, $w/p' = 10/1.1 = 9.1$, is *below* its equilibrium level of 10. This creates an excess demand for labor, raising the money wage rate. The money wage rate would continue to rise until $w' = 11$, so that the real wage rate, w'/p', returns to its equilibrium value of 10.

full employment equilibrium level. Therefore, regardless of the price level, money wage rates would adjust so that full employment is maintained. This is reflected in the aggregate supply schedule AgS* in Figure 19.1a, where, regardless of the price level, aggregate production is at full employment output Y_f.

Mainstream liberals also assume that labor market decisions by workers are made independent of the unemployment rate (the demand for labor) and that competitive conditions in the labor market prevent money wage rates from rising at less than full employment. However, they reject the notion that workers are only concerned with the real wage rate. Instead, mainstream liberals claim that workers suffer from "money illusion" and, because of institutional constraints (longterm contracts), it is impossible to lower the money wage rate regardless of the existence of excess labor supply. Hence, if the price level declines, it would not be offset by a compensating decline in the money wage rate. Since the labor process is assumed to be subject to the law of diminishing returns, a rising real wage rate will force firms to lay off workers. Therefore, a decline in the price level would result in a decreased aggregate supply. This is reflected in the aggregate supply schedule AgS** in Figure 19.1b.

Mainstream Demand Theories of Inflation

Chapter 12 indicated that a price level decline can stimulate equilibrium real spending. Specifically, with a constant nominal money supply (M_s), a price level decline increases the real money supply (M_s/p). A rise in M_s/p, assuming

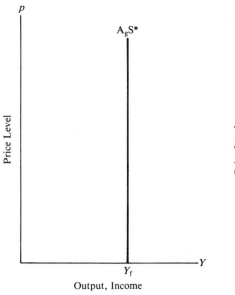

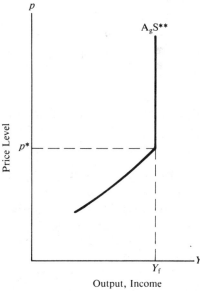

Figure 19.1a Fixed money wage rate   **Figure 19.1b** Flexible money wage rate

no change in the demand for money, would induce interest rates to decline as lending institutions attempt to attract more borrowing. In turn, the interest rate decline would induce according to mainstream economists, increased real spending by businesses and possibly households. Firms would now find some additional capital investment profitable and households might substitute durable goods for financial investments (savings). Thus, through its effects on the money market, the economy would expand as a result of a price level decline.

If, instead, the price level would rise, there would be a decline in equilibrium real income. Higher prices lower M_s/p, creating excess money demand, which induce interest rates to rise. Higher interest rates discourage capital spending and household durable goods purchases, thereby lowering equilibrium real income.

This analysis indicates that the aggregate demand schedule is downward sloping. Suppose that we begin with aggregate demand schedule AgD_0 (Figure 19.2). Since conservatives assume that the aggregate supply schedule would be depicted by AgS, general equilibrium would occur at p_0 with full employment production (Y_f).

At a given price level, either monetary or fiscal policy is capable of changing equilibrium real spending. For example, due to either a monetary or fiscal stimulus, equilibrium real spending would increase at each price level.[3] In this case, the aggregate demand schedule would shift from AgD_0 to AgD_1. Without a change in prices, there would be an expansion of equilibrium spending from Y_f to Y_1. Conservatives contend that this could occur for only a brief period of time. Since Y_1 is above full employment production, conservatives contend that shortages of labor and production would induce prices and wage rates to rise. A rising price level lowers M_s/p, raises interest rates, and discourages private sector spending. This economic decline, reflected by a movement upward along AgD_1, continues until private sector spending declines totally offset the initial stimulus—until the price level has risen to p_1 and equilibrium spending returns to Y_f.

This exercise indicates that under laissez-faire labor market assumptions, a fiscal and/or monetary stimulus causes a price level rise. Also, it indicates that any federal stimulus would have no effect on equilibrium real income since market adjustments would "crowd out" the equivalent amount of private sector spending.

The mainstream liberal viewpoint differs from the conservative viewpoint. Due to money illusion and/or institutional constraints in the labor market, money wage rates are inflexible downward. Hence, at low price levels, real wage rates are too high for full employment production to occur. Thus, it is possible for a general equilibrium to occur at less than full employment. This is illustrated in Figure 19.3 where the market clearing price p_0 is below the full employment production price p^*.

---

3. Refer to Chapter 12.

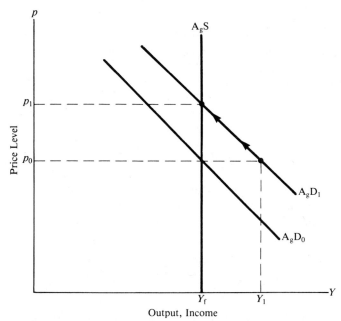

Figure 19.2   Effects of a government stimulus, when completely adjusting labor markets is assumed

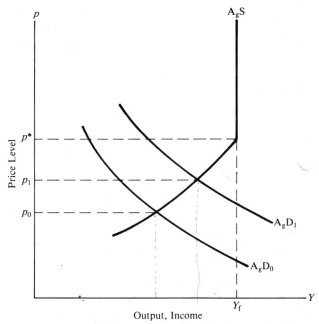

Figure 19.3   Effects of government stimulus when downward inflexible money wage rates assumed and economy is at less than full employment

Now suppose that the federal government undertakes a fiscal and/or monetary stimulus. The aggregate demand schedule would shift from AgD_0 to AgD_1. The market clearing price rises to p_1 so that in the mainstream liberal model, inflation can occur at less than full employment. It also indicates that a price level rise at less than full employment is associated with an increase in real income. This occurs because a rising price level lowers real wage rates, increasing labor demand, thereby lowering unemployment and increasing production.

There are two major differences between the conservative and mainstream liberal theories of demand-induced inflation.

1. Conservatives contend that inflation only occurs at full employment production, while mainstream liberals contend that inflation at less than full employment is possible.

2. Conservatives contend that the inflation process is associated with no change in equilibrium real income. However, mainstream liberals contend that, because inflation helps circumvent inflexible money wage rates, it enables the economy to expand at less than full employment.

For an inflation *rate* to be maintained, there must be a *continuous* increase in aggregate demand. A continuous growth of the money supply or a continuous growth of fiscal stimuli could accomplish this. Most mainstream economists do not believe that a continuous growth of fiscal stimuli is likely —especially when full employment is neared.[4] At that point, they claim it is probable that political pressure against further federal expansion would occur. This would be reflected in a lowering of the share of production generated by the government and/or reductions in government deficits. In support of this contention, mainstream liberals note that, except for the peak period of the Korean and Viet Nam Wars, the share of total government spending in real GNP has remained fairly constant during the entire post-World War II period.

Cost-Push Inflation Within Mainstream Models

Up until this point, we have identified changes in the price level with shifts in the aggregate demand schedule. This form of inflation is called *demand-pull* inflation. When inflation is due to shifts in the aggregate supply schedule, it is called *cost-push* inflation. Cost-push inflation is impossible within the conservative model once disequilibrium adjustments are accounted for.[5] Recall that

---

4. Robert J. Gordon, *Macroeconomics* (Boston: Little, Brown, 1978), p. 188n.

5. Discussed later in this chapter are the possible shortrun disequilibrium outcomes when workers do not immediately correctly estimate the future price level rise. In this case, employment could deviate in the shortrun from the longrun full employment rate. However, if we assume that workers eventually correctly adjust their price expectations, then, in the longrun, employment would be at its full employment rate regardless of the price level.

in that model, because of the rapid adjustment of money wage rates to supply-demand conditions, the real wage rate reflecting full employment is quickly established. In this case, regardless of the price level, full employment production is attained, and the aggregate supply schedule is price inelastic.

Mainstream liberals, while still considering labor markets to be competitive, believe it is possible for money wage rates to be sustained when unemployment exists. Money wage rates that are inflexible downward are either union wage rates or legal requirements, such as federal minimum wage rates. If these minimum money wage rates were to rise, then the aggregate supply schedule would shift.

Suppose we begin with labor supply and demand curves depicted in Figure 19.4a. Full employment (N_f) would occur at real wage rate w^*. Suppose the minimum money wage rate is w_0. Figure 19.4a indicates that at price level p_0, the real wage rate $w_0/p_0 = w^*$ so that N_f is demanded. If the price level declines below p_0, the real wage rate would rise above w^* and demand will decline below N_f. For example, at price level p_1, the real wage rate would be w_0/p_1. At real wage rate w_0/p_1, only N_1 labor would be hired, which reflects Y_1 production (Figure 19.4b). By continuing to select price levels below p_0, holding the money wage rate at w_0, the aggregate supply schedule $AgS(w_0)$ in Figure 19.4b is derived.[6]

Now suppose that the minimum money wage rate rises to w_1. Only if the price level is as high as $p^* > p_0$ could the real wage rate decline to w^* so that full employment N_f would be demanded. At price level p_0, the minimum money wage rate would be w_1/p_0, at which only N_2 labor would be hired, resulting in production Y_2. If the price level declined to p_1, the real wage rate would decline to w_1/p_1, hiring would decline to N_3, and production would decline to Y_3.[7] By continuing to select price levels below p_0, holding the money wage rate constant at w_1, aggregate supply schedule $AgS(w_1)$ is derived. Given AgD_0, the price level rises from p_1 to p_4 and production declines from Y_1 to Y_4 as a result of the rise in the minimum money wage rate from w_0 to w_1. If the minimum money wage rate rises each period, then the price level would rise each period. In this way, cost changes could explain inflation.

Most mainstream liberals, however, are quick to point out it is unlikely that cost-push inflation could continue for long when unemployment exists.[8] As Figure 16.4 indicates, a minimum money wage rate increase results in lay-offs and higher prices. Therefore, it seems likely that many workers would be hurt by the rising minimum money rate and either convince their leaders to refrain from further money wage rate increases or reluctantly begin shifting to

---

6. Let $w^* = 10$. If $w_0 = 12$, then when $p \geq 1.2$ the money wage rate can adjust so that $w/p = 10$. If $p_1 = 1.1$, then the *lowest* real wage possible is $w_0/p_1 = 12/1.1 = 10.9$.

7. If $w_1 = 13$ (with $w^* = 10$), then only if $p \geq 1.3$ can the real wage rate adjust to its equilibrium value. With $p_0 = 1.2$, the lowest real wage rate possible is $13/1.2 = 10.8$; and with $p_1 = 1.1$, the lowest real wage rate is $13/1.1 = 11.8$.

8. Gordon, *Macroeconomics*, p. 192.

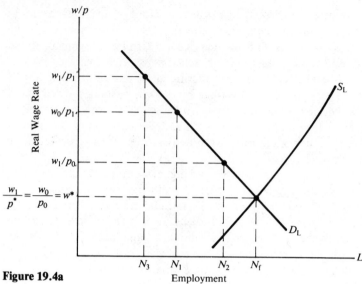

Figure 19.4a

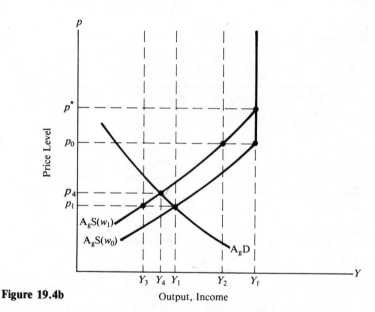

Figure 19.4b

Figure 19.4 General equilibrium with change in money wage rate

the nonunionized sector.[9] But a shift of workers to the nonunionized sector
would lower money wage rates there, and offset the continued money wage
rate increases in the unionized sector. Similarly, mainstream liberals claim that
as unemployment of low wage workers mounts, due to continuous raises in the

federal minimum wage rate, the government would be encouraged to temper these raises.[10]

19.2 LEFT-LIBERAL EXPLANATIONS OF INFLATION

Left-liberals reject the underlying mainstream notions that labor and output markets can be analyzed using competitive assumptions. In particular, they claim that productivity does not completely determine labor demands, nor does individual choice explain labor supply decisions. Hence, wage determination cannot be accurately described within a supply-demand framework. In the output market, left-liberals tend to believe that prices are determined by a profit markup rule, and that the size of the markup only slowly and imperfectly adjusts to changes in aggregate demand. Hence, supply and demand in the output market does not accurately predict prices.

Let us briefly describe the profit markup model. If we assume for the moment that each firm's costs other than labor can be neglected, we can write the pricing equation:

$$p = (1 + \beta)w/(Q/N)$$

where

β = average profit margin per unit
Q/N = average output per worker
w = average money wage rate per worker

---

9. The claim that a rise in the minimum wage rate has a negative impact on employment rates can be disputed. Let us assume that the initial effect of the rise is to redistribute income from profits to low wage workers, and that this stimulates aggregate consumption. This would imply that there would be a shift in the aggregate demand schedule, which would at least partially compensate for the initial negative employment effect of the shift in the aggregate supply schedule.

The negative employment impact is lowered even more if we assume that the demand for labor is inelastic (inelastic AgS schedule) and/or the impact of monetary variables on aggregate demand is small (inelastic AgD schedule).

If the overall negative effect on employment rates is small, then low wage workers would actually benefit from a rise in the minimum wage rate. While the average number of weeks per year of employment would decline, this would be more than compensated for by the higher weekly wage. It is better to work 40 weeks per year at $150/week than to work 45 weeks per year at $120/week. This is especially true since a large number of low wage workers have a fixed income objective. With a higher wage rate, they have to work less hours to fulfill their income objective so that the employment decline would be partially offset by a declining supply.

10. Of course, if the federal government is committed to maintaining employment it could offset the unemployment effects of the wage rate increases through stimuli to aggregate demand. This would "accommodate" the labor demands and lead to a wage-price spiral. However, this would indicate that inflation was a result of the government's policy of aggregate demand expansion, rather than the labor policy of raising institutionally-determined money wage rates. Later in this chapter there will be a full discussion of this thesis that a monetary-induced expansion is a response to wage demands.

$$\dot{p} = (1 + \dot{\beta}) + \dot{w} - \dot{Q}/N$$

Given this relationship, the inflation rate

$$\dot{p} = (1 + \dot{\beta}) + \dot{w} - (\dot{Q}/N)$$

where

• denotes the rate of change per year

This indicates that there are three factors that determine the rate of inflation: (1) the rate of change of the money wage rate, (2) the rate of change of the profit margin, and (3) the rate of change of labor productivity.

Money Wage Rates

Left-liberals claim that money wage rates, rather than real wage rates, are the primary determinant of labor contracts. They do not argue, as mainstream liberals, that this results from money illusion. Rather, it results from the ability of firms to distribute part of the risk of production towards workers. In an uncertain world, in which production has a significant gestation period, producers accept uncertainty. One of the major uncertainties faced is the effect of inflation on sales price relative to costs. If all labor contracts were negotiated in real terms, then all of the risks of production would be borne by producers.[11] Workers, by accepting longterm contracts in terms of money wage rates, accept a certain portion of the firm's uncertainty.

Most left-liberals claim that the primary influence on the money wage rate is the level of unemployment. If the economy is near full employment, workers are more likely to struggle for and win higher money wage rates. They will be more likely to struggle because their risks are less when unemployment is low. Even if their employers take retaliatory actions (firings, suspensions, etc.), workers can more easily find another position when the economy is near full employment. Workers are more likely to win because producers have a great deal to lose from a strike when unemployment is low. At high unemployment, firms are usually producing at less than full capacity. This implies that they can meet sales by producing only a portion of the year, for example, nine months. In this situation, a three-month strike would have practically no effect on the firm's sales or costs since workers would be substituting strike activity for lay-offs. However, if employment is high and firms are operating at near full capacity, they risk losing sales and/or raising costs due to a strike. In order for sales to be maintained during the strike, firms must have sufficient inventories (which is unlikely since the firm was operating at near full capacity just to meet their current sales). Even if firms had sufficient inventories, or were able to delay deliveries, after the strike they would have to employ workers at overtime rates in order to rebuild inventories and/or meet delayed orders.

---

11. Basil J. Moore, "A Post-Keynesian Approach to Monetary Theory," *Challenge* 21 (Sept./Oct. 1978): 46.

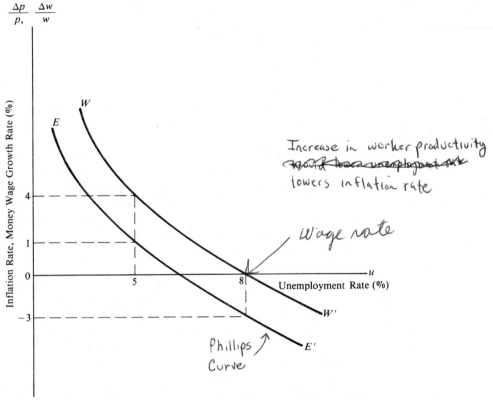

Figure 19.5   Phillips Curve—Assuming productivity growth rates and profit margins are constant

If wage rate settlements were solely a function of the unemployment rate, then it would be possible for there to be a stable relationship between wage rate settlements and the unemployment rate. This relationship is denoted by WW ' in Figure 19.5. It is downward sloping, indicating that at higher unemployment rates, wage settlements are lower. For example, when unemployment is 8%, workers are too fearful and employers too strong, so there is no rise in money wage rates. At 5% unemployment, workers are more confident and firms are more fearful, therefore, money wage rate settlements rise at 4% per year.

If changes in the profit markup and labor productivity were independent of the unemployment rate, then WW ' would completely reflect the trade-off between inflation and unemployment. For example, suppose that the profit markup is unchanged and that there is a 3% per year rise in labor productivity. In this case, EE ' represents the relationship between the unemployment and inflation rates. It is a mirror image of the wage rate-unemployment rate

schedule (WW ') since at each level of unemployment the inflation rate is 3%
lower than the change in money wage rates. The inflation-unemployment
relation will be called the Phillips Curve.[12]

Profit Margins

Within the economics profession, there are substantial differences of opinion
as to the effect of the business cycle on profit margins. In general, mainstream
liberals ignore the concept of profit margins since it reflects a noncompetitive view of market decision-making. However, they implicitly claim that
profit margins vary inversely with the unemployment rate. Their contention
rests upon their claim that the profit share of national income varies inversely
with the unemployment rate. They argue, "Firms lay off workers less than in
proportion to the reduction in sales when demand decreases; this means that
when unemployment goes up, profits fall faster than wages. . . . On the other
side of the business cycle firms have little rehiring to do when sales pick up, so
the added revenues go mostly into the profit share."[13]

This mainstream view implies that changing profit margins shift the Phillips Curve in a predictable manner. Let EE' in Figure 19.6 represent the initial
Phillips Curve with a constant profit margin. During an expansion, this
schedule implies that the inflation rate would rise due to greater wage demands
(*a* to *b*). However, if the economy also experiences rising profit margins, then
there would be a further price rise due to a shift of the Phillips Curve to FF'
(*b* to *c*). On the other hand, during recessions, inflation rates would decline not
only because of dampening wage demands (*a* to *b'*), but also because of falling
profit margins (*b'* to *c'*). Hence, if profit margin adjustments followed this
pattern there would an increase in the sensitivity of the rate of inflation to
aggregate spending fluctuations. The *longrun* Phillips Curve would be steeper.
A steeper Phillips Curve implies that reductions in aggregate spending (recessions) would reduce significantly the inflation rate.

Many left-liberals, however, reject the mainstream contention that profit
margins vary inversely with the unemployment rate. Some left-liberals assume
that the profit margin is not significantly influenced by the business cycle so
that it remains constant over the cycle.[14] Others argue that profit margins
actually increase during recessions. Kalecki, on the basis of observation during

---

12. Named after A. W. Phillips, who was the first economist to demonstrate the
relationship in his article, "The Relation Between Unemployment and the Rate of
Changes of Money Wage Rates in the United Kingdom, 1861–1957," *Economica* 25
(Nov. 1958): 283–99.

13. Joseph J. Minarik, "Who Wins, Who Loses From Inflation?" *Brookings Bulletin* 15 (Summer 1978): 6.

14. Moore, "Post-Keynesian Approach," p. 50.

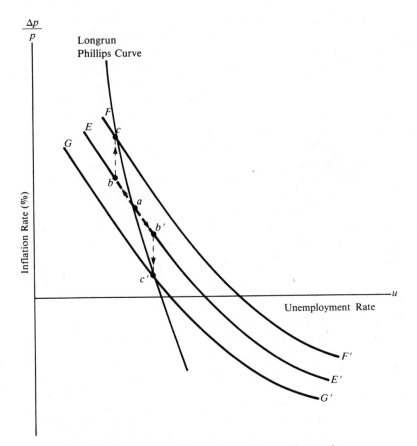

Figure 19.6   Phillips Curve—Effect of changing profit margins

the 1930s, claimed that recessions, by driving the weaker firms out of the industry, decrease the amount of competition.[15] With less competition, the remaining firms are able to increase their profit margins.

More recently, left-liberals have developed an alternative theoretical basis for their contention that profit margins increase during recessions.[16] This alternative explanation begins by assuming that firms do not try to maximize profits, but achieve a target profit rate. This target rate is determined by the profit rate patterns observed in other firms of similar size, market power, and type of product, and adjusts very slowly to changing economic conditions.

---

15. Michal Kalecki, *Selected Essays* (Cambridge, U.K.: Cambridge University Press, 1971), pp. 50–51.

16. Howard M. Wachtel and Peter D. Adelsheim, "How Recession Feeds Inflation: Price Markups in a Concentrated Industry," *Challenge* 20 (Sept./Oct. 1977): 7.

Second, it is assumed that in the concentrated industries (those in which firms have some ability to set prices) demand tends to be inelastic. Therefore, these firms can increase prices and achieve higher sales revenues.

These two assumptions, which fundamentally depart from the usual competitive assumptions, imply that changes in profit margins will vary directly with the unemployment rate. When unemployment is low, firm sales are high. In this case, a small profit margin is capable of attaining target profit rate objectives. However, with high unemployment and low sales, firms must raise their profit margins in order to attain target profit rates.

Whatever the merits of these theoretical explanations, recent data seems to indicate that profit margins vary directly with the unemployment rate. In a study of over 100 manufacturing industries, Howard Wachtel and Peter Adelsheim found that during 1950–72, there was a rise in margins in high concentrated industries during three of the four recessions.[17] The authors dismiss the exception (1969–70) by arguing that the recession was small and, coming after an eight-year expansion during which profit margins increased by over 15%, firms didn't feel it was necessary to quickly adjust profit margins. To buttress their contention that rising profit margins during recessions is a general condition of U.S. manufacturing, Wachtel and Adelsheim note that medium and low concentration industries are increasingly following the pricing pattern of the concentrated industries. For example, during the 1969–70 recession, both the average-low and medium concentrated industries raised their profit margins.

If profit margins increase during recessions, then inflation rates will not decline by as much as the wage rate-unemployment rate schedule predicts. Shifts in the Phillips Curve will somewhat compensate for the declining wage demands. On the other hand, expansions would not create as much inflation as the wage rate-unemployment rate schedule predicts, since part of the wage increases would be offset by declining profit margins. Hence, if profit margin adjustments followed this pattern there would be a decrease in the sensitivity of the rate of inflation to aggregate spending fluctuations. The *longrun* Phillips Curve would be flatter. With a flatter Phillips Curve declines in aggregate spending (recessions) would not significantly affect the inflation rate.

Labor Productivity

According to mainstream economists, as the economy approaches full employment, the capital stock cannot be expanded quickly. With a relatively fixed capital stock, mainstream economists contend that the law of diminishing returns would indicate that average labor productivity would decline. Moreover, this decline occurs because the last hired workers are considered to be the

---

17. Ibid., pp. 6–13.

least productive. Thus, mainstream economists suggest that, for purely technical reasons, average productivity declines as output increases.

Left-liberals also believe that labor productivity varies inversely with the unemployment rate, but for an entirely different set of reasons. They reject the marginal productivity argument since "unlike land or capital, workers are human beings whose output is affected by their feelings, attitudes, and morale."[18] According to this viewpoint, labor productivity is determined by sociological as well as technical reasons. As full employment is approached, along with wage increases, workers are able to win workrule changes, which lower their productivity. Hence, according to left-liberals, at higher levels of employment, labor productivity declines due to changing power relations between labor and capital rather than for purely technical reasons.

The left-liberal explanation for the inverse relationship between labor productivity and unemployment rates is reinforced by the target profit rate argument described in the last section. According to that argument, as full employment is neared, firms can attain their target profit rates with lower profit markups. Therefore, they would be more likely to accede to workrule changes, which lower labor productivity, during high employment periods than when employment and sales are low.[19]

Endogenous Money Supply

The left-liberals' explanation of inflation emphasizes the effects of changing money wage rates over the business cycle. They believe that the resulting inflation rates dictate government monetary policy. When unemployment is low, higher labor costs and declining productivity raise unit production costs. In order to meet these higher costs, firms are forced to increase their debt. If the monetary authorities refuse to expand credit, some firms will be caught in a cash-flow squeeze and go bankrupt. Other firms would be forced to rely upon money substitutes, which causes a disruption of financial arrangements as well as added inflationary pressures. Rather than allowing these economic disruptions to occur, monetary authorities are likely to expand the money supply.

The case in which monetary authorities *accommodate* the wage demands of workers is illustrated in Figure 19.7. With initial aggregate schedules AgD_0 and AgS_0, general equilibrium occurs at price level p_0 and production Y_0. An increase in the minimum money wage would shift the aggregate supply schedule to AgS_1, raising the price level to p_1 and lowering production to Y_1. How-

---

18. Moore, "Post-Keynesian Approach," p. 46.

19. Radicals do not believe that changes in money wage rates and relaxation of workrules necessarily occur together. In particular, as discussed in Chapter 17, radicals argued that during the late 1960s, in response to wage increases, corporations increased the intensity of labor.

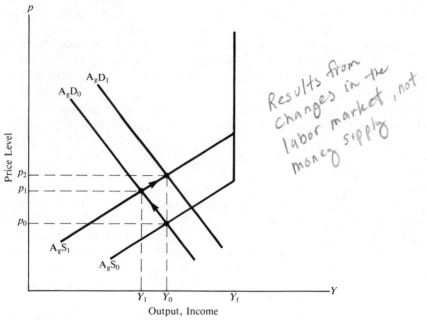

Figure 19.7   Effects of rise in minimum money wage rate when government monetary policy accommodates

ever, if the government accommodates the wage demands, it would create a monetary expansion sufficient to maintain the original level of production (Y_0). Hence, they would undertake a monetary expansion sufficient to shift the aggregate demand schedule to AgD_1, which would raise the price level still further to p_2.

This process implies that the money supply is determined by the past growth rates of money wage rates. Therefore, left-liberals agree with mainstream economists that there is a correlation between the money supply growth and the inflation rate. However, left-liberals claim that it is the inflation rate that dictates monetary policy, not visa versa. Moreover, left-liberals claim that even if monetary authorities attempt to undertake a monetary policy that would counter inflationary pressures, it would be impossible. The major outcome of a monetary constraint would be to create chaos in the financial community. Firms requiring expanded credit would switch from traditional sources of credit (M_1) to near money sources.

Even if substantial contractions would occur because of the monetary constraint, the results would be undesirable.[20] It would be the smaller firms and the more competitive industries that would be squeezed out of the tradi-

20. Moore, "Post-Keynesian Approach," p. 51.

tional money sources because financial institutions protect their best customers—the larger concentrated industries. In this case, those firms and industries in which the wage pressures are most pronounced would be insulated from the adverse effects of monetary policy. They would have little reason to alter their wage settlement and pricing policies. Reflecting this viewpoint, many economists believe that monetary constraints have little effect on reducing inflation rates, and only cause the collapse of the housing market and accelerate the failure of small businesses.

19.3 CRITIQUES OF THE LEFT-LIBERAL VIEWPOINT

The left-liberal viewpoint claims that it is possible to continuously lower the unemployment rate by allowing the inflation rate to rise. In this case, if the government is willing to allow a certain inflation rate, it could sustain any unemployment rate objective. In particular, the left-liberal theory claims that the government could sustain very low unemployment rates if it was willing to allow a high rate of inflation. Some left-liberals believe that this necessary inflation rate need not be inordinately high. For example, Michael Piore believes that because of the large reserve of secondary workers, wage rate increases do not necessarily have to be high at low overall unemployment rates.[21] Others, such as Wachtel and Adelsheim, contend that firms would not raise prices much during periods of rapid expansion since they could lower profit margins and still fulfill target profit rates.

Both mainstream and radical economists reject the notion that there is a sustainable trade-off between inflation and unemployment rates. In particular, both groups believe that very low rates of unemployment cannot be sustained in a private market economy, regardless of the willingness of the government to accept high inflation rates. This section will develop the basis for this contention and indicate the important differences between the radical and mainstream explanations.

Mainstream Economists

The first part of this chapter developed the foundation of the mainstream contentions concerning the source of inflation. It indicated that there is a natural rate of unemployment to which the economy would gravitate. This rate could be sustained with a stable price level (no inflation). Also, since it was impossible to lower the unemployment rate below the natural rate, output at this level would reflect maximum possible production.

21. According to Piore, the supply curve for labor is completely elastic so that there is no wage rate increase in response to expanded labor demand. See Michael J. Piore, "Inflation and Unemployment: An Alternative View," *Challenge* 21 (May/June 1978).

Conservatives believe that all markets would adjust to bring about this natural rate, but mainstream liberals claim that there are certain impediments to the adjustment process in the labor market. The existence of institutionalized downward inflexible wage rates implies that full employment cannot always be attained through private market adjustments. However, a sufficient price level rise could offset labor market impediments. Therefore, after some inflation (until the price level rose sufficiently), full employment can be sustained with stable prices.

The mainstream analysis could be considered a longrun analysis since it incorporates fully all market adjustments. Mainstream economists believe that in the shortrun, because of incomplete adjustments, it is possible for the unemployment rate to momentarily fall below its natural rate. This possibility is demonstrated in Figure 19.8.

Suppose we assume that workers negotiate longterm (more than a year) contracts in money wage rates. Workers must predict the future price level in order to determine the real wage rate during the life of the contract. Let us begin by assuming that workers correctly predict the actual future price level. Specifically, let us assume that the actual future price level (p^a) just equals the predicted future price level (p^e) which is p^*. According to Figure 19.8, the labor supply schedule would be S_0 and, given labor demand D_0, equilibrium employment would be E^*. At equilibrium real wage w_0^*, the money wage rate negotiated would be w_0 (since $w_0/p^* = w_0^*$). At equilibrium employment, according to mainstream economists, the number of jobseekers just equals the number of vacancies, so that the natural unemployment rate prevails.

What if, due to a sudden money supply expansion, the actual future price level was higher than expected (i.e., $p^e/p^a < 1$)? In particular, suppose that $p^e = p^*$ while $p^a = p^{**}$. Since workers continue to believe that the future will be p^*, they continue to supply the same labor at money wage rate w_0.[22] However, during the life of the labor contract, because the actual price level rises to p^{**}, the real wage rate which prevails, w_0/p^{**}, is below the expected wage rate, w_0/p^*. During the life of the contract, employment E^* would be forthcoming at a lower real wage rate than in the previous case. Hence, if workers inadvertently negotiate for lower real wage rates than they expect, their supply schedule during the life of the contract shifts downward to S_1. With the shift in labor supply schedule, equilibrium employment expands to E^{**} and unemployment would decline below its natural rate.

In this manner, it is demonstrated that if the price level rises faster than expected, actual real wage rates decline and employment expands. This process indicates that rising inflation rates can be compatible with unemployment rates declining below the natural rate.

---

22. This assumes that once workers negotiate to work at money wage rate w_0, they would continue to supply all labor demanded by firms at that money wage rate, regardless of the actual price level, for the life of the contract.

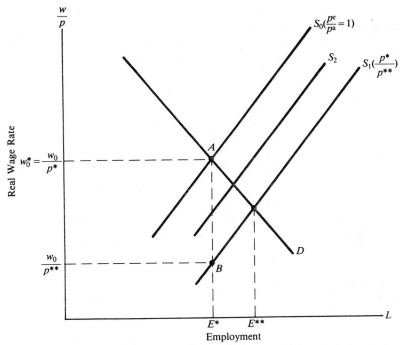

Figure 19.8 Labor market equilibrium when expected prices (p^e) do not necessarily equal actual prices (p^a)

Mainstream economists do not believe that unemployment below the natural rate can be sustained. They claim that once workers realize that the inflation rate has risen, they will adjust upward their future price expectations. As they increase their future price expectations, they will narrow the gap between the actual and expected future price level. This shifts the labor supply schedule during the life of the contract upward to S_2. According to this *adaptive expectations hypothesis,* eventually workers would correctly anticipate future price levels, which would shift the labor supply schedule back to S_0.[23] At that point, unemployment would return to its natural rate.

It is certainly possible that a further increase in the inflation rate due to a still more rapid expansion of the money supply would again be underestimated. Once again, there would be a momentary decline in the unemployment rate below its natural rate. However, once labor fully anticipates the future price increases, real wage rates rise and the unemployment rate would again ·

---

23. Adaptive expectations is one explanation of how expectations are formed. It supports the contention that, in the longrun, there is no trade-off between unemployment and inflation. See Milton Friedman, "The Role of Monetary Policy," *American Economics Review* 58 (March 1968); Edmund Phelps, *Inflation Policy and Unemployment Theory* (New York: Norton, 1973).

return to its natural rate. This indicates that only if inflation rates *accelerate* upward would it be possible for workers to consistently underestimate future prices so that unemployment could be below its natural rate.

This process indicates that the observed trade-off between unemployment and inflation rates is a *shortrun* phenomenon. According to the mainstream accelerationist theory just described, after the natural rate is attained, money supply expansions cause inflation rates to rise, and are not fully anticipated by workers. Actual real wage rates decline and unemployment declines below its natural rate. Thus, an inverse relationship between inflation and unemployment rates is possible (movement from A to B in Figure 19.9). However, mainstream economists claim that eventually workers are able to adjust to the rising inflation rates. As they more accurately anticipate future price levels, their actual real wage rate increases, and the equilibrium unemployment rate increases back towards its natural rate (B to C). Eventually, workers fully anticipate future price levels so that negotiated employment levels again reflect the natural unemployment rate.[24]

This analysis indicates that there is no longterm trade-off between inflation and unemployment rates below the natural rate of unemployment. It indicates that once inflation rates are fully anticipated, any inflation rate is compatible with the natural unemployment rate. For example, in Figure 19.9, either inflation rate F_0 or F_1 is compatible with the natural unemployment rate u^*. It also indicates that the unemployment-inflation rate relationship moves in a clockwise fashion during the latter phase of economic expansions.

Radical View

Radicals claim that because of decentralized decision-making and competitive pressures capitalism is subject to periodic crises. These crises usually cause high levels of unemployment until corrections occur. These issues have been discussed in previous chapters. Radicals contend that even if economic planning is instituted so that these excessive fluctuations were reduced, capitalism would still require a minimum necessary level of unemployment. This unemployment is necessary in order to discipline labor and stabilize profits. This is the reserve army thesis. For this reason, radicals also reject the left-liberal view that there is some permanent trade-off between inflation rates and unem-

---

24. Some extreme conservatives believe that this mainstream analysis still leaves too much room for government intervention, particularly if it is assumed that the adjustment process under adaptive expectations is lengthy. These economists have developed *rational expectations* models which posit a different method by which decision-makers form expectations. According to the rational expectations models, the adjustment process is so rapid that no room is left for government intervention. For a discussion of the rational expectations model see A. M. Santomero and J. J. Seater, "The Inflation-Unemployment Trade-off: A Critique of the Literature," *Journal of Economic Literature* 16 (June 1978): 527–29.

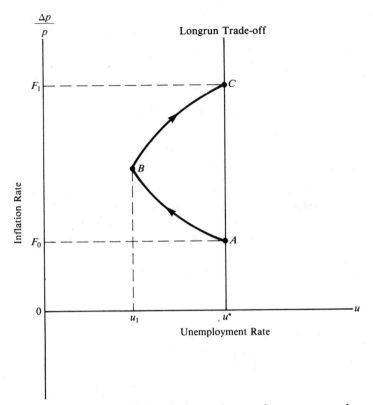

Figure 19.9   Movement of inflation and unemployment rates when price expectations lag actual price changes

ployment rates. Radicals, like mainstream economists, contend that unemployment rates below some minimum rate cannot be sustained, regardless of the willingness of the economy to accept high inflation rates. According to radicals, however, this minimum necessary unemployment rate is dictated by the requirements of a capitalist system rather than any "natural" laws.

Radicals agree with left-liberals that inflation rates tend to increase as unemployment declines due to class struggle. They agree with left-liberals that there are no *technical* reasons why employment could not be substantially expanded, even when the official unemployment rate is 4%. As noted in Chapter 2, besides those people officially counted as unemployed, there are millions of individuals whose attachment to the labor market can be dramatically increased—discouraged workers, part-time workers, etc. Therefore, radicals reject the notion that there is a *natural* unemployment rate.

Radicals contend that the minimum necessary unemployment rate is based on political and economic considerations. According to radicals, capitalism in its parliamentary democracy form, requires that labor "voluntarily" enter into hierarchical exploitative relationships with their employers. Radicals contend that an industrial reserve army is required to maintain the voluntary stability of such exploitative and hierarchical relationships. Chapter 16 indicated that when the industrial reserve army is too low, profits are squeezed, bankruptcies occur, capital investment is halted, and an economic contraction begins. Thus, *because of the specific requirements of capitalism,* there is some barrier below which unemployment cannot fall.

Changes in the Minimum Necessary Industrial Reserve Army

At the simplest level, radicals believe that what mainstream economists call the *natural* rate should be called the *minimum necessary size* of the industrial reserve army. The size of the minimum industrial reserve army is determined by factors fundamentally different from those which supposedly determine the natural rate.

According to the mainstream view, the natural rate reflects technical, demographic, institutional, and cultural factors. Conservatives argue that since women and teenagers search longer for jobs and are more inclined to remain voluntarily on unemployment insurance, demographic changes together with institutional arrangements have caused the natural rate to rise during the 1970s. Mainstream liberals emphasize cultural and technical factors in their explanation of changes in the natural rate. In particular, mainstream liberals believe that technological change has increased mismatches in the labor market. Automation has increased the mismatches between skills and available jobs, while industrial relocation has increased the mismatch between job location and where workers live. These mismatches have increased (what economists label) *structural unemployment.*

As Chapters 2 and 17 indicated, radicals claim that political factors are the most important determinants of the necessary size of the industrial reserve army. They suggest that the "success" of the fascist economies during the 1930s in maintaining full employment was due to their ability to substitute legal requirements for voluntary arrangements in determining labor market outcomes. After World War II, radicals contend that Western democracies were able to sustain historically lower unemployment rates because of the social contract negotiated between organized labor and capital. Organized labor leaders agreed to maintain labor discipline and refrain from actions that would threaten profitability. Capital agreed to maintain economic growth and low rates of unemployment in the organized labor sectors. The rise of the minimum necessary industrial reserve army during the 1970s was caused by the breakdown of the social contract. Capital was unable to fulfill its part of the contract because of the intensification of foreign competition, which necessitated a slowdown in production and real wage growth rates. Organized labor was unable to fulfull its part of the contract because of its declining influence in the overall labor market.

The growth of influence of previously disenfranchised groups of workers and capitalists hastened the breakdown of the social contract. Since the 1950s, women and black workers have demanded a greater share of the economic pie, while new money has begun to compete for a greater share of economic and political power. Therefore, even if organized labor and old money could agree to maintain the social contract, disenfranchised workers and new money could hinder its implementation.

Profit Rate Movements

According to the natural rate theory, only when workers underestimate future price increases can the economy expand below its natural unemployment rate. Declining real wage rates would imply that profit margins would be increasing. Since the economy is expanding, sales would also be increasing. Higher profit margins and sales imply that profit *rates* would also be rising. This indicates that, according to the mainstream theory, when the economy is below its natural rate, expansions should be associated with rising profit rates.

Radicals claim that during the *early* phase of the economic expansion, when unemployment rates are still high, firms raise prices in order to return to their historic profit margins. Workers are weakened by the previous downturn and are unable to raise money wage rates as fast as prices increase. This does not necessarily lead to a deterioration of the economic position of workers because of the change in working hours. During the early phase of economic expansions there is a substantial increase in average workweeks. Though real wage rates are declining, the increase in workweeks enables the real income of workers to rise. According to radicals, this is the phase of the expansion during which rising employment results in rising profit rates.

As the economy continues to expand, the strength of the working class increases and they begin to demand higher wage increases. This creates added pressures for capitalists since they can no longer meet labor demands through increases in the workweek. During this *latter* phase of the expansion, radicals contend that rising employment results in lower profit margins as firms experience the full employment profit squeeze. Thus, profit rates begin to decline during this phase of the economic expansion.

It is in this latter phase of the expansion when unemployment rates are already low that mainstream and radical economists differ. According to mainstream economists, profit rates are increasing when the economy expands below its natural rate. Radicals contend that profit rates would decrease during this period.

Both viewpoints also differ as to what causes unemployment rates to begin to increase. According to mainstream economists, the rise in real wage rates no longer allows marginal workers to be profitably hired. This causes a contraction in marginal firms and marginal ventures. However, according to mainstream view, when the contraction begins the profit rates are above historical average rates. Therefore, there is still an overall buoyancy to the eco-

increases

nomy when it begins to contract towards its natural rate. Some cutbacks are occurring, but the typical firm is still experiencing above normal profits. Eventually, when the unemployment rate declines-back to its natural rate, the typical firm's profit rate declines back towards its historical norm.

The radical view is strikingly different. It suggests that during the latter phase of the expansion the profit rate begins to erode. Only when the core firms are financially affected, when the profit slide has been sufficient to create instability within the typical not marginal firm, will a contraction begin. This contraction will coincide with profit rate declines below historical average rates. It will coincide with actual and near bankruptcies of major firms—with a massive takeover movement where the stronger firms are able to buy up the weaker firms.

As already discussed in Chapters 16 and 17, the profit rate data from the late 1960s gives a clear confirmation of the radical explanation. However, this profit rate data is not compatible with the natural rate theory. According to mainstream economists, the actual unemployment rate continuously declined below its natural rate from early 1965 through late 1969. According to the mainstream view, this should have been associated with declining real wage rates due to unanticipated inflation and resulted in rising profit rates. However, mainstream economists found that during this period the profit rate continuously declined.

The mainstream view implies that at the end of the growth of employment, the profit rate should begin to decline but still be above historical average rates. However, again, their own data contradicts the natural rate theory of inflation. By 1969, the profit rate fell below 9%, well below its historic average of close to 12%. Moreover, during the 1969–70 contraction, the profit rate rose rather than declined.

19.4 CONCLUSION

This chapter developed competing explanations of inflation. Mainstream economists contend that inflation is essentially the result of continued growth of the money supply at full employment. This view is modified somewhat by mainstream liberals who believe that, in the shortrun, inflation could be the result of fiscal stimuli or shifts in institutionally-determined wage rates, and can occur at less than full employment.

Left-liberals contend that the principal determinant of the rate of inflation is rising money wage rates. Due to higher money wage rates, firms desire expanded credit to meet their production requirements. To meet these credit needs, monetary authorities increase the money supply. Thus, according to left-liberals, the money supply is endogenously determined by the growth of money wage rates. Moreover, left-liberals contend that monetary authorities would be ineffective and inequitable if they attempted to stop inflation through a restriction on credit. They would be ineffective because the major corporations can easily circumvent monetary policy, and they would be inequitable since the adverse effects would be only felt by small firms and households.

Left-liberals contend that through the workings of the labor market, higher wage rate increases result from decreases in the unemployment rate. This inverse relationship implies that there is also an inverse relationship between the unemployment rate and the inflation rate, known as the Phillips Curve. Left-liberals tend to believe that the Phillips Curve is relatively flat so that inflation rates are not very sensitive to aggregate demand fluctuations. Hence, very low levels of unemployment would only require slightly higher rates of inflation. Moreover, according to this view, recessions would not significantly reduce the inflation rate.

Mainstream and radical economists do not accept the left-liberal thesis that by accepting higher inflation rates unemployment rates could be permanently lowered below some minimum rate. Mainstream economists contend that below the natural rate, workers have underestimated the future price level. Once they begin to correctly estimate inflation, real wage rates rise and unemployment increases back to its natural rate. Radical contend that market economies require a minimum reserve army in order to discipline labor. If unemployment increases back to its natural rate. Radicals contend that market eco-Eventually, the profit decline causes the economy to contract, which corrects the unemployment rate.

Radical and mainstream economists offer dramatically different explanations for the minimum unemployment rate and how to interpret the effects of economic corrections when the economy is momentarily below this rate. Mainstream economists contend that this minimum rate is determined by demographic, institutional, cultural, and technical factors. Radicals contend it is determined by political factors. Mainstream economists suggest that an expansion below the minimum rate is associated with rising profit rates, however, radicals contend that it is associated with declining profit rates. Mainstream economists believe that the subsequent contraction is associated with continued prosperity. Radicals believe that it is associated with widespread bankruptcies and industrial reorganization. This chapter concluded by noting that profit rate data from the late 1960s is more supportive of the radical than the mainstream view.

CHAPTER TWENTY

INFLATION: ECONOMIC EFFECTS AND CORRECTIVE POLICIES

Inflation has two possible effects on society. First, inflation may have a direct effect on real production and employment. In Chapter 19, according to the mainstream liberal view, a mild demand-induced inflation could raise real production and employment. In this case, some sections of the population would benefit from inflation through its production and job-creation effects. On the other hand, according to the conservative view, inflation has no longterm influence on production or employment. Real full employment production would be generated, regardless of the rate of inflation.

Even if total production, total income, and total employment is unchanged, inflation could still create costs to groups in society because of adverse redistributional effects. It is possible that the real income of some groups increases while the real income of other groups declines, even though inflation leaves real total income unchanged. This chapter will detail the possible production and redistributional impacts of inflation. It will enable us to specify under what assumptions individual groups may be hurt or may benefit from inflation.

To the extent that inflation is considered harmful, there are policies which can be adopted to limit price increases. One important set of such policies, called incomes policies, will be discussed in this chapter. These policies enable the government to determine income payments rather than allowing them to be determined by natural market forces. It is important to realize that the objective of incomes policies may not be the same for all advocates.

Mainstream liberals perceive of incomes policies as a method of reducing inflation *without* affecting real production. These economists see the imposition of incomes policies as superior to using a recession to eliminate inflation. For them, incomes policies are a shortrun inconvenience that is unnecessary in the longrun.

Left liberals perceive of incomes policies as one component of state planning. They believe that because of the inability of mature capitalist economies to self-adjust, and because of the increased risk associated with capital invest-ment, the U.S. economy has increasing tendencies toward volatility and stag-nation. According to this viewpoint, only continuous planning can enable the U.S. economy to sustain steady longterm growth.

Neither conservatives nor radicals advocate incomes policies. Conserva-tives reject controls because they believe they seriously affect the efficiency of the market system, and that inflation does not affect real income. They believe that the redistributional impact of inflation can be solved without the use of government controls.

Radicals do not believe that state planning can resolve the contradictions that are inherent in a capitalist society. Moreover, they contend that one objec-tive of the current move towards planning is a struggle for power between the two major capitalist groups, rather than any concern for improving economic efficiency. Specifically, radicals contend that, in the current period, incomes policies and state planning are part of an attempt by old money to regain its dominant position and reduce the power of new money.

20.1 THE ECONOMIC EFFECTS OF INFLATION

In this section, we will discuss how inflation affects the income of various groups in society after taking into account both the production and redis-tributional impacts. In order to precisely identify the difference between various theories, the private sector will be divided into three distinct groups: low-wage workers, high-wage workers, and capitalists. A second assumption made is that we will analyze the inflation process when the economy is rela-tively close to full employment and expanding—when it is in the latter phase of an economic expansion. While this ignores the effects of inflation during con-tractions, such as 1974–76, it does discuss the period in which inflation is most pronounced, and in which inflationary pressures are initiated. Moreover, much of the inflation during the 1974–76 period is usually explained by one-time increases in food and energy prices.

Conservative Viewpoint

According to conservatives, the economy would operate at full employment regardless of the inflation rate. Therefore, the only effects of inflation are its redistributional impact. Conservatives usually claim that the main redistribu-tional impact is a shift of income from the private sector to the federal govern-ment due to the progressivity of the federal income tax. Table 20.1 illustrates the conservative contention.

In year t (base year), gross income of a typical household is $1000. It is assumed that after a standard deduction of $500, all remaining income is taxed at 50%. Column 5 indicates that in succeeding years, with rising income, the

Table 20.1
The effects of inflation on real disposable income and real taxes

Year (1)	Money Y (2)	Money Y_d (3)	Money T (4)	T/Y (5)	Price level (6)	Real Y (7)	Real Y_d (8)	Real T (9)
t	1000	750	250	.25	1.00	1000	750.0	250.0
$t+1$	1100	800	300	.27	1.10	1000	727.2	272.8
$t+2$	1200	850	350	.29	1.20	1000	708.3	291.7
$t+3$	1300	900	400	.31	1.30	1000	692.3	307.7
$t+4$	1400	950	450	.32	1.40	1000	678.5	321.5
$t+5$	1500	1000	500	.33	1.50	1000	666.7	333.3

Legend: $T = .5(Y - 500)$, Real $Y = Y/p$, Real $Y_d = Y_d/p$, Real $T = T/p$.

proportion of income going to taxes, T/Y, rises. Thus, the tax structure is progressive.[1]

Now suppose that over this five-year period all gross income increases were completely offset by price level increases. This is reflected in column 6, where each year the price level rises by 10% to completely offset the yearly 10% increase in gross income (column 2). For this reason, real gross income, Y/p, remains constant at 1000 throughout the period. However, columns 8 and 9 indicate that real disposable income and real taxes do not remain constant at 750 and 250, respectively. In each year, real disposable income declines while real taxes increase. Hence, due to the progressive nature of the tax schedule, inflation redistributes real income away from private households in favor of the government.

Even if the conservative contention that real private sector income declines because of inflation is correct, it is not necessarily true that there is a decline for each individual group of households. For example, Table 20.2 indicates that it is possible for real private sector income to decline (from 1000 to 954), but that real income still rises for one group of households (Group C). Let us look more closely at the possibility that inflation has a differential impact on various household groups.

Economists believe inflation has a differential redistributional impact on wage and nonwage income so that the effect of inflation is dependent upon each household's source of income. Most studies find that wage income and transfer payments (social security, unemployment, welfare transfers) grow at the same rate as inflation after a slight time lag. Therefore, the gross earnings of low-wage and high-wage workers tends to keep pace with inflation. The

---

1. The tax would also be progressive if the marginal tax rate ($\Delta T/\Delta Y$) is increasing.

Table 20.2
Impact of inflation on real income

Households	Money income, 1978	Money income, 1979	Price index	Deflated income, 1979
Group A	$200	$220	1.10	$200
Group B	700	710	1.10	645
Group C	100	120	1.10	109
All Households	1000	1050	1.10	954

Price Index = (1979 Price Level)/(1978 Price Level).
Deflated Income 1979 = (Money Income 1979)/(Price Index).

economic position of these groups is also affected by the way in which inflation changes the real cost of debt. Due to inflation, debtors can pay off loans with cheaper dollars. In particular, homeowners, who are a significant percentage of high-wage workers, can pay off mortgages with inflated dollars. Hence, the real cost of their debt is reduced by inflation.

The effects of inflation on nonwage income and creditors are different. Often, there is a time lag before interest rates rise, so the real value of interest payments can decline during periods of rising prices. Even when interest payments rise faster than the inflation rate, financial wealthholders are adversely affected by inflation. When interest rates rise, the value of bonds held declines. The net effect for most financial wealthholders is that inflation cuts the value of their assets by more than it increases current interest payments. It is also believed that the rise in dividend payments is slower than the rate of inflation. Hence, the economic position of households which are creditors and/or receive a major portion of their income from nonwage sources is adversely affected by inflation. These tend to be high-income households.

A Brookings study summarized the differential redistributional impact of inflation as follows,

At the very lowest incomes, households for the most part are better off or unaffected by inflation; . . . Middle income households are still mostly unaffected since the burden of rising income taxes is offset by home appreciation. The results for upper income households are totally different. . . . greater real income taxes, lagging corporate retained earnings, and especially the depreciation of the face value of dollar-denominated interest-bearing securities [bonds] combine to make upper income households the big losers from inflation.[2]

2. Joseph J. Minarik, "Who Wins, Who Loses from Inflation?" *Brookings Bulletin* 15 (Summer 1978): 8.

Mainstream Liberals

According to the mainstream liberal theories presented in Chapter 19, there are two ways in which real wage rates decline during the latter phase of economic expansions. First, inflation reduces real wage rates when money wage rates are set by institutional arrangements, particularly minimum wage laws. Second, during this period, rising prices are not fully anticipated by workers, so they contract for lower wage rates. Mainstream liberals emphasize how lowering of real wage rates increases employment. They claim that the employment effects are especially large for low-wage workers, who had higher unemployment rates as a result of minimum wage laws, and some of whom are now able to obtain high-wage employment because of the economic expansion.

The mainstream liberal theories also implied that profits would rise during the latter phase of the economic expansion. Price increases cover the rising marginal cost. However, since prices also rise for previous production, *average* profits per unit output (profit margins) increase. Each existing firm would experience rising sales and rising profit margins so that profit rates increase. Higher profit rates mean larger dividends and capital gains, which implies that capitalist households would benefit from inflationary expansions.

For these reasons, mainstream liberals have been historically quite "soft" on the fight against inflation. For many years they even argued that mild inflation (2%–3% per year) was actually beneficial to society. As we have seen, these benefits are (1) the breaking down of minimum wage barriers, which hindered employment of low-wage workers; (2) unanticipated real wage declines, which enabled upward mobility for some low-wage workers; and (3) rising profit rates, which encouraged capital investment.

Left-Liberals

In Chapter 19, we found that, according to left-liberals, inflation results from increasing bargaining power as full employment is approached. In particular, left-liberals suggest that it is high-wage workers, who are in strong unions, that are able to win greater wage demands during the latter phase of economic expansions. These economists suggest that money wage increases for low-wage workers do not keep pace with the high-wage unionized workers. Moreover, since left-liberals reject marginal productivity arguments, they don't believe that there would be a significant expansion of low-wage employment resulting from the decline in real wage rates for this group of workers. Thus, according to left-liberals, it is high-wage workers rather than low-wage workers who are the beneficiaries from inflationary expansions.

Left-liberals also believe that capitalists benefit from inflationary expansions. With rising sales, left-liberals expect that firms would slowly raise their target profit rates rather than fully adjust downwards their profit margins. For these reasons, left-liberals often suggest that the inflation process enables corporations and unions to benefit at the expense of the rest of society.

It should be mentioned that many economists believe concentrated industries are more aggressive at raising prices during periods of rising demand than the foregoing left-liberal analysis claims. These economists contend that during periods of rising demand concentrated industries significantly raise prices independent of costs. This view is labeled *profit inflation*. One leading econometrician, Michael Evans, claimed that "much of the post-World War II inflation can be explained only with reference to profit inflation."[3]

Radicals

According to the radical thesis, during the latter phase of economic expansions, inflation benefits all workers but hurts capitalists. Workers benefit because besides increased employment, there is also a rise in real wage rates due to the increased bargaining power of all workers. Capitalists are hurt because they are unable to pass the complete wage increase along to consumers. As Jacob Morris has argued,

> *Price increases have a very uncertain impact on the market structure of individual industries and firms, even in so-called monopoly and oligopoly sectors. Thus, for example, an increase in steel prices may help overcome inertia of steel users and stimulate them to explore the possibilities of substitution for steel of plastics, cement, glass fiber, aluminum, and so on. Or alternatively, it may open the way for a substitution of imported foreign steel for domestic steel.*[4]

Summary

Table 20.3 summarizes the effects that income distribution has on each group of household's income according to each of the viewpoints. We found that the simplistic conservative viewpoint implied that *all* private sector groups are hurt by the redistributional impact of inflation. While it is true that inflation does shift real income from the private sector to the federal government, we found that a more detailed analysis indicates that only the capitalist households are adversely affected by this redistribution.

All of the other three viewpoints suggest that inflation has a significant impact on employment. Mainstream liberals contend that low-wage workers are the chief beneficiaries of the employment impact, while capitalists gain from rising profit margins and sales. Left-liberals contend that low-wage workers are the real losers from an inflationary expansion. There is little employment impact for this group and, due to their weak position, they cannot

---

3. Michael Evans, *Economic Activity* (New York: Harper and Row, 1970), p. 293.
4. Jacob Morris, "The Crisis of Inflation" *Monthly Review* 25 (Sept. 1973): 9.

Table 20.3
Impact of inflation on various groups of households

Viewpoint	Capitalist	High-wage workers	Low-wage workers
Conservative (simple)	−	−	−
Conservative (detailed)	−	0	0
Mainstream Liberal	+	0 or −	+
Left-Liberal	+	+	−
Radical	−	+	+

effectively bargain for higher wages. Instead, left-liberals contend that high-wage workers in powerful unions and corporations benefit. Radicals contend that during the latter phase of the economic expansion all workers benefit from increased bargaining power at the expense of corporations who are not able to completely pass along higher costs to the consumer.

20.2 INCOMES POLICIES

According to the Phillips Curve framework, there will be a level of inflation corresponding to each level of unemployment. If at low unemployment rates the inflation rate is considered intolerable, then supplementary government policies, which could shift the Phillips Curve to the left, are necessary to reconcile full employment with stable prices. The most often used supplementary policy has been direct government intervention in the wage-price process. Since this intervention ultimately determines the shares of national income going to wages and other factors of production, it is called an "incomes policy."

Incomes policies had been used in the United States during the Korean and Second World Wars, but the Kennedy administration was the first to use it during peacetime. In 1962, Kennedy introduced wage-price guideposts. These guideposts recommended that the rate of increase of money wages be limited to the overall national rate of productivity increases, and price increases should only occur in industries with below average productivity increases. By using these guideposts, the Kennedy administration hoped it could raise employment without incurring intolerably high inflation rates.

Wage-Price Controls, 1971–74

During the early 1970s, the Nixon administration instituted wage-price controls that covered a broad range of industries and labor markets. These controls went through four phases (Phase I–Phase IV) and were abandoned in 1974.

Conservatives and mainstream liberals are opposed to controls on theoretical grounds. Both groups believe that inflation is due to aggregate demand expansions (demand-pull). Therefore, inflation can be controlled by government constraints on economic expansion. Conservatives believe that the growth of the money supply should be lessened, while mainstream liberals believe government budget surpluses would eliminate inflation.

Since both groups believe that private markets are generally well-working, they both contend that wage-price controls would create serious market distortions.[5] One cause of distortion is that while domestic prices are frozen, the international price is not. In this case, controls induce many firms to shift sales from domestic to foreign markets. For example, during the Nixon controls, the disparity between the domestic and international price of fertilizer resulted in large exports and domestic shortages. Domestic fertilizer shortages lowered output per acre, and was considered by some observers to be one cause of food price inflation. Similar movements abroad were seen for polystyrene (an essential petrochemical for plastics), tubular goods (tubing, casings, and pipe used in oil drilling), copper, and scrap steel.

Second, certain price increases in a competitive economy are *necessary* in order to signal producers as to changing consumer preferences. However, price controls keep prices frozen at prior demands, thus hindering production adjustments to changing demands. For example, during the 1971–74 controls, profit margins were frozen at levels reflecting the 1969–71 period. In the steel industry, the result was a severe shortage of less profitable steel-reinforcing bars, while in the paper industry controls discouraged the substitution of lightweight paper products for the favored heavier-weight paper.

Left-liberals believe that inflation is primarily due to rising wage rates and resulting profit increases, so controls are an effective means of limiting inflation. Since left-liberals believe that monopoly power rather than competitive forces dominates output markets, they tend to minimize the distortions that controls create. Left-liberals do not believe that inflation rates are very sensitive to aggregate spending fluctuations. Therefore, they do not believe constraints on economic expansions would significantly reduce the rate of inflation. Moreover, since many left-liberals also contend that income distribution determines longterm growth stability, they believe that incomes policies are necessary to sustain balanced growth.

Mainstream liberals often point to the shortages and distortions which occur during controls, as evidence that controls don't work. Left-liberals contend that problems associated with controls are magnified when controls are viewed as *temporary*. When controls are temporary, they create destabilizing

---

5. See C. Jackson Grayson, Jr., "Controls Are Not the Answer" *Challenge* 17 (Nov./Dec. 1974).

expectations. Firms build up inventories during controls, creating shortages because they are willing to wait until after the lifting of controls to sell. Hence, left-liberals contend that it is speculation rather than natural market forces which create most of the imbalances during periods of temporary controls. Therefore, they contend that by making controls *permanent,* much of the inefficiencies and distortions can be eliminated.

The radical viewpoint on controls begins from two basic premises. First, the federal government serves the economic interest of the big capitalists. Therefore, if wage-price controls are instituted, they must be seen as a vehicle to raise the rate of profit rather than a means of limiting profits. Second, wage-price controls create serious market distortions since radicals generally believe that competitive forces are significant. More important than the costs in efficiency due to controls are the political and ideological costs. The more controls are used, the more apparent it becomes to individuals that the political and economic arenas are one and the same. Economics spends a great deal of time demonstrating how economic outcomes are dictated by efficiency considerations which underly market supply and demand. Once controls are instituted, it becomes clear that political power will determine economic outcomes rather than efficiency considerations. Therefore, radicals contend that the institution of controls takes away the veil of exploitation and exposes the role of power in determining outcomes. Were this to occur, there would no longer be Democratic and Republican Parties, but parties, like in Europe, which openly reflect economic interests. Hence, the imposition of control would only occur when there is a *serious crisis.* The imposition of controls in 1971, therefore, reinforces the radical contention that the declining rate of profit during the late 1960s created a serious crisis for capitalists.

Recall that the radical thesis argues that during the late 1960s rising wage demands and overinvestment combined to reduce the rate of profit of U.S. corporations. Historically, capitalism has corrected for profit problems through either sufficiently automating or having a recession reduce wage pressures. In 1970, neither of these alternatives was feasible. With the fragility of support for the war in Viet Nam and a viable Civil Rights movement, it was impossible for a politician to risk a significant recession. It was also impossible for many corporations to automate because the declining profit rate had created serious debt problems. Therefore, radicals contend that the only alternative available to capitalists at the time was the use of controls to lower wages. Price controls were added merely to make controls politically palatable and give them a superficial impression of impartiality.

Big business support for controls was reflected in a number of ways. The Committee on Economic Development (CED), an elite corporate policy group, recommended controls and widely publicized a film, suitable for undergraduate economics, which graphically illustrated their viewpoint. *Fortune,* the leading elite corporate magazine, editorialized for controls in the spring of 1970. However, the clearest statement of the intentions of the 1971–74 controls came from Arnold Weber, former executive director of the Cost of Living Council: "Business had been leaning on [Secretary of the Treasury] Schultz and [Chairman of Economic Advisers] McCracken to do something about the economy, especially wages. The idea of the freeze and Phase II was to zap labor, and we did."[6]

Radicals contend that with the end of the war in Viet Nam and the demise of the Civil Rights movement, it was possible, by 1974, to again use high unemployment as a means of limiting wage pressures. Moreover, in order to stimulate capital expansion, economic planning is more efficient than controls. Therefore, at that point, controls were lifted, a deep recession occurred, and discussion of government intervention centered on economic planning rather than new controls.

Tax-Based Incomes Policy (TIP)

One alternative to wage-price controls is tax-based incomes policies (TIP). TIP does not attempt to replace market mechanisms but rather to influence them through a system of rewards and/or penalties. Instead of dictating wage settlements, the government would set up an incentive system which would encourage compliance with specific wage guidelines. For example, suppose that the government sets 5% per year as the limit for wage increases. According to TIP, firms could exceed that level but would pay a penalty, such as a higher corporate profits tax rate. By penalizing corporations, the government would discourage excessive wage settlements. Some advocates of TIP have also recommended that subsidies be given to those firms which negotiate wage settlements below the government guidelines. These firms would have a reduction in their corporate tax rate.

Corporations could still decide to raise wages above the rate set by government guidelines so that the inflexibility of controls is avoided. TIP would allow employers and workers to respond to market forces and adjust relative wages when an industry is faced with labor shortages.

With the persistence of high inflation rates, mainstream liberals began to seriously consider the need for new approaches to fighting inflation. Following George Perry,[7] they claimed that while a recession could eventually dampen inflation, the cost in jobs and income would far outweigh the benefits from such a program. Thus, TIP became a viable alternative.

---

6. *Business Week* (April 27, 1974), p. 108.

7. "According to Perry, an extra point of unemployment would lower the inflation rate by only about 0.3 percentage point after one year and by 0.7 percentage point if maintained for three years. The extra point of unemployment would cost over a million jobs and some $60 billion of real production each year." *Brookings Papers* (1978): 241.

In 1978, a major government study by Larry Dildine and Emil Sunley attempted to measure the administrative costs associated with TIP.[8] They recommended that these costs could be reduced if:

1. The program would be limited to only the largest corporations.

2. Penalties alone, rather than a system of rewards and penalties, be used.

3. A flat penalty for noncompliance be used, rather than a penalty that is higher for each percentage point of wage increase above the guidelines.

Even if these recommendations were incorporated, some mainstream liberals, such as Joseph Pechman, still believe that TIP could not be administered equitably or efficiently. One problem Pechman cites is the inappropriateness in using each firm's *overall* wage rate increase to measure compliance.[9] Suppose that a firm has an overall average wage rate of $5 per hour in 1978. If the guidelines limited yearly wage rate increases to 5%, the firm would have to hold its overall wage rate to $5.25 to meet the government's guidelines. Let us assume that the firm decided to negotiate a 12% wage rate increase with all its employees. Does this mean that the company would be penalized? Not necessarily.

While the average wage rate for existing production would rise to $5.60 per hour, the firm could avoid a penalty by buying up firms which have a smaller average wage rate. For example, suppose it bought a firm, one-half its size, which has an average wage rate of $4 per hour. The expanded company would then have an overall average wage rate of $5.20 per hour, equal to $(\frac{1}{3} \times 4) + (\frac{2}{3} \times 5.6)$. If the overall average wage rate was used as the measure of compliance, the firm would *qualify for a reward* for holding wage rates below the government guidelines.

On the other hand, suppose that a firm gave 3% yearly wage rate increases to all its workers. Would this automatically guarantee that the firm's average labor costs would increase at a rate below the government's 5% guidelines? Not necessarily. Suppose that the firm has two production lines. Line A and Line B have average wage rates of $4 and $8 per hour, respectively. If production is equally split between the two lines, then the firm's overall wage rate is $6 per hour. The 3% wage increase raises the average wage rates to $4.12 and $8.24 per hour in Lines A and B, respectively. Suppose that during the year, the demand for Line A declined while the demand for Line B in-

8. Larry Dildine and Emil Sunley, "Administrative Problems of Tax-Based Incomes Policies," *Brookings Papers* (1978): 363–89.

9. Joseph Pechman, "Can TIP Work?" *Challenge* 21 (Nov./Dec. 1978): 51–52.

creased, so that Line B became 60% of the firm's production. In this case, the overall average wage rate of the firm would increase to $6.59 per hour, $(0.6 \times 8.24) + (0.4 \times 4.12)$. If the overall wage rate is used to measure compliance, then the firm's 10% rise would result in its being penalized.

These examples indicate that any change in the firm's production mix would distort the actual wage rate increases negotiated. Pechman contends that the inability to accurately adjust for changes in production mix and other problems make TIP unworkable.

Despite Pechman's criticisms, when the Brookings Institute held a panel discussion during Spring 1978, the majority of economists present favored government institution of some form of TIP. They considered TIP to be superior to either mandatory controls, which Pechman favored, or to the use of traditional fiscal and monetary restraint. The majority attitude was summed up by Henry Wallich, "Of course, nobody likes TIP per se. It is really a question of the alternatives."[10]

In October, 1978, President Carter, following the consensus developed at the Brookings Conference, announced a modified TIP proposal to the nation.[11] The centerpiece of the Carter Program was a 7% wage guideline. The penalty for noncompliance was not some legislated change in corporate tax rates. Instead, Carter stated that noncomplying firms would be penalized through loss of government contracts and/or favorable government arrangements. To encourage compliance, Carter proposed real wage insurance legislation. If a group of workers negotiated a wage settlement with less than a 7% yearly increase, they would be protected against adverse effects of high inflation. Specifically, if the inflation rate was above 7% per year, then these workers would have decreased federal tax liabilities. In this way, workers would have some assurance that by complying they would not risk accepting a lower real wage rate.

Many analysts perceived the Carter Plan as another set of *voluntary* guidelines rather than a new form of government controls. Radicals, however, believe that his proposal is just the start of extensive government economic controls. They predict that in coming years the set of penalties (and subsidies) will be more explicit and institutionalized.[12] However, radicals do not believe that the primary objective of TIP is to limit inflation. Radicals contend that TIP is part of a program to raise profits and to reestablish the dominant position of old money.

---

10. Quoted in *Brookings Bulletin* 15 (Summer 1978): 3.

11. The characterization of Carter's proposal as a variant of TIP can be found in an editorial entitled, "A TIP at Last," *NY Times* (Nov 27, 1978), p. A18.

12. This prediction assumes that old money will be successful in its fight with new money. However, it is certainly possible that new money will become strong enough to combat all attempts at government economic planning.

20.3 CONCLUSION

This chapter analyzed the impact of inflation during the latter stage of an economic expansion on household income. The evidence strongly indicates that low-wage workers benefit by the continuation of an inflationary expansion, even after adjusting for the impact of price increases. Low-wage workers have little loss of real income from the distributional impact of inflation. Both the radical and mainstream liberal viewpoints contend that low-wage workers have higher employment from the expansion.

The evidence also seems to indicate that capitalist households are adversely affected by the continuation of the expansion. Due to the progressivity of the federal income tax and the lagged increase in rentier income, inflation has an extremely adverse distributional impact on capitalist households. Some of the viewpoints contend that inflation has a positive effect on gross profits, thereby at least neutralizing the adverse distributional impact of inflation. However, these viewpoints tend to underestimate the amount of competition, especially given the intensification of foreign competition since the mid-1960s. Thus, even without accepting the full radical analysis, it is possible to argue that the continuation of an economic expansion adversely affects the real income of capitalist households. Finally, it would appear that high-wage workers benefit from the continuation of an economic expansion.

This chapter also summarized the historical experience of the United States with incomes policies. The distinction between mandatory controls and TIP proposals was indicated. TIP proposals were found to be the major new alternative proposed to reduce inflation without a costly economic slowdown. During the coming years, we will be able to determine whether TIP will become an extensively used and effective means of government economic intervention.

CHAPTER TWENTY-ONE

SUMMARY AND CENTRAL THEMES

This book has presented a diverse set of macroeconomic theories, relating to both inflation and employment, as well as individual aspects of the economy—growth, consumption, investment, and the role of money. In order to provide some sense of organization, the book divided the economics profession into four distinct groupings: mainstream economists, composed of conservatives and mainstream liberals; and left-economists, composed of left-liberals and radicals. In each of the areas of inquiry we found that these groups had different analyses. These distinctions were reflected in the overall assessment of the workings of a private market economy. This chapter will summarize each group's emphasis, as well as the policy implications of each theory.

Throughout the book certain general characteristics typified each group's viewpoint. Each group had a clear assessment of the importance of competition, profits, and economic conflict. We will present a summary of these assessments. The final section of the chapter will discuss the reason for adopting an eclectic viewpoint throughout the book.

21.1 GENERAL ASSESSMENTS OF THE ECONOMY

Conservatives

In this book conservatives, monetarists, and laissez-faire advocates have been used as interchangeable terms. This usage reflects the primary emphasis of conservatives that a private market economy is self-correcting, and thus requires no government intervention. According to this viewpoint, private market mechanisms will automatically correct the economy if a shock to the system shifts it away from its stable full employment growth path.

This conservative contention is based upon a number of distinct assertions. First, conservatives, building on the permanent income hypothesis (Chapter 6), claim that household spending is not very sensitive to changes in current income. Thus, they claim that the simple income multiplier,

1/(1–MPSP), is small. Second, household and business spending is assumed to be very sensitive to interest rate changes so that the full income multiplier is quite small, regardless of the degree to which the money market is interest sensitive. Third, and most important, conservatives contend that even if the full income multiplier is significant so that shocks to the system are not self-contained, price flexibility insures that full employment spending is eventually generated. If a shock created substantial unemployment, prices would decline. Declining prices would increase the real money supply which, by creating an excess supply of funds, would result in lowering interest rates. Lower interest rates would then induce increased consumer and business spending (Chapter 12).

The inclusion of growth and inflation into the analysis creates no problems for the conservative faith in the self-correcting ability of a market economy. According to conservatives, balanced growth is sustained, regardless of the savings behavior of households (and businesses). If households choose to save more, then interest rate adjustments would induce corporations to invest more, and capital-labor ratios would adjust so that no imbalances between capital and labor utilization rates occur. According to conservatives, inflation can only occur at full employment if the government attempts to overheat the economy. With no government intervention, other than increasing the money supply in a fixed manner, the economy could avoid inflation while maintaining balanced full employment growth.

Mainstream Liberals

Mainstream liberals claim that the conservative viewpoint overstates the case for reliance on private market mechanisms. Mainstream liberals suggest that expectations may have a destabilizing effect on household spending (Chapter 6), particularly on the timing of durable goods purchases (Katona's views, Chapter 13). Mainstream liberals also believe that business investment is subject to substantially more volatility than suggested by conservative models of investment behavior. Whereas conservatives contend that the interest rate is a dominant explanatory variable (Chapter 9), mainstream liberals believe that the accelerator principle (Chapter 13) significantly explains certain types of capital investment behavior, such as changes in the value of inventories. Hence, mainstream liberals contend that the simple income multiplier is quite substantial. Moreover, they believe the money market is quite interest rate sensitive so that the full income multiplier is also large. Thus, according to mainstream liberals, the effects of economic shocks are not immediately self-contained.

As already mentioned, many conservatives are now willing to concede that shocks to the system can result in a substantial deviation from a full employment growth path. Their emphasis has, therefore, shifted to reliance on pricing adjustments to restoring the economy. Mainstream liberals, to varying degrees, also believe that if an economy waited long enough, it is quite possible that these pricing adjustments, called the Keynes Effect (Chapter 12), could eventually restore full employment. However, a point of unity among mainstream liberals is their belief that there are substantial costs involved in waiting for the Keynes Effect to restore full employment.

Monetary policy advocates tend to have substantial faith in private market mechanisms. In particular, they agree with conservatives, that both household and business spending are highly sensitive to interest rate changes. Thus, to the extent that prices adjust the real money supply, monetary policy advocates believe that the Keynes Effect is quite strong. Unlike conservatives, monetary policy advocates believe that adjustments in the pricing system are too slow to be relied upon. Monetary policy advocates contend that because of the lagged response of workers' expectations to changing market conditions, negotiated money wages are not lowered quickly during economic contractions. However, once workers realize that conditions have changed, money wage rates and prices will adjust accordingly, allowing the strong stimuli of the Keynes Effect to restore the economy. This process was embedded in the MPS Model's prediction of the effect of a government spending shock (Chapter 8).[1] In that model, the full income multiplier after 20 months is 2.4. After that point, price and wage effects begin and the size of the multiplier declines to less than 1.0 by the end of 36 months.

Fiscal policy advocates have substantially less faith in private market mechanisms. In general, they believe that household and business spending is not very sensitive to interest rates, especially shortterm rates (Chapter 11), so they believe the Keynes Effect to be quite weak (Chapter 12). Moreover, they question the degree to which wage rates and prices will *ever* adjust downward, even after workers' expectations concerning the state of the economy have changed. Thus, while not rejecting the *possibility* that private market mechanisms could restore the economy, they believe it would be unlikely to occur over any reasonable amount of time. Not surprisingly, fiscalists contend that the size of the income multiplier is still quite large after three or four years.

Monetary policy advocates believe that the Keynes Effect is strong, but fiscal policy advocates believe it to be weak. Hence, fiscal policy advocates believe that the costs to society of government inaction are far greater than do monetary policy advocates. If economists thought that, through government intervention, *all* costs could be eliminated, then there would be unity among mainstream liberals in their support for intervention. However, government intervention could eliminate all costs only if it could be implemented simultaneously with the economic shock.

---

1. Modigliani has openly criticized the work of the strict monetary policy advocates (St. Louis Federal Reserve Bank). However, the whole thrust of his work has been to emphasize the powerful effects of monetary policy and in his belief that the Keynes Effect is strong.

Monetary policy advocates believe that the economic losses are greatest during the first two years after an economic shock. After that point, they contend that private market mechanisms will restore the economy through the Keynes Effect. They believe that due to time lags (Chapter 8), it will also be two years before discretionary government intervention begins to restore the economy. Thus, according to monetary policy advocates, the economic losses to society from an economic shock are not significantly reduced by the use of government discretionary intervention. Instead, monetary policy advocates believe that automatic stabilizers are the major way in which the government can improve the stabilizing power of the economy.

Fiscal policy advocates believe that the Keynes Effect is so weak that even after adjusting for time lags, government discretionary intervention is effective in reducing the economic losses to society from economic shocks. Unlike monetary policy advocates and conservatives, they believe that households will adjust their spending plans significantly in response to shortterm fluctuations in disposable income (Chapter 6). Thus, fiscal policy advocates claim that tax cuts can quickly and vigorously restore the economy.

In summary, because they believe the Keynes Effect is strong, monetary policy advocates contend that though economic losses from economic shocks are significant and warrant some type of government intervention, they do not believe them to be large enough or prolonged enough to justify government *discretionary* intervention. On the other hand, fiscal policy advocates believe the Keynes Effect to be weak and shortterm government tax cuts are an effective spending stimulus. They contend that the economic losses are too large and prolonged to rely on the private market when government discretionary intervention could rapidly and vigorously restore the economy.

The differences between monetary policy advocates and conservatives become even more muted when issues of full employment, growth, and inflation enter into the analysis. On all of these issues, monetary policy advocates and conservatives are in virtual agreement. As indicated in Chapter 2, most mainstream liberals accept the notion of a natural unemployment rate and its link to demographic, institutional, and technical factors. Thus, along with conservatives, they contend that during the 1970s the natural unemployment rate rose to $5\frac{1}{2}$–6%. In this case, unemployment rates of 7–8% do not appear to be very costly to society.

In Chapter 14, it was argued that mainstream liberals believe that growth requirements adapt to the savings decisions and population growth rates only after a significant time lag. Thus, capital-labor ratios do not immediately adjust to sustain full utilization of both capital and labor resources. The size of the time lag, however, varies. Monetary policy advocates generally believe it to be smaller than fiscal policy advocates. The belief among monetary policy advocates that growth does not create important problems for the management of a market economy is quite widespread. It is reflected in the latest texts written from the monetary policy advocacy position, which either eliminate the topic of growth entirely or only present the conservative theory of rapidly adjusting technology.[2]

In Chapter 19, it was noted that mainstream liberals accept the conservative notion that there is no longterm tradeoff between price stability and lower unemployment rates. Mainstream liberals and conservatives contend that it would be impossible to lower unemployment below its natural rate for long, regardless of the willingness of the government to accept higher inflation rates. Again, the chief difference between mainstream liberals and conservatives is over the speed of adjustment of the labor market. According to conservatives, there would be a rapid adjustment. However, mainstream liberals contend that due to the lag in worker expectations, the adjustment process could take a substantial period of time. Once more, monetary policy advocates, having more faith in private market mechanisms, believe that the adjustment process would be relatively rapid, which minimizes the differences they have with conservatives on this issue.

The analysis here might seem at odds with the general presentation throughout the book. In most cases, mainstream liberals are presented as a relatively unified group, rather than significantly split on the need for government intervention. Moreover, the general presentation leaned more heavily to what has been described as the monetary advocacy position. There are two reasons for the lack of detailed distinction throughout the entire text. First, given the broad range of viewpoints discussed, it was decided that as a "first approximation" the difference between the monetary policy advocates and fiscal policy advocates was not sufficient to warrant any emphasis. As Chapter 10 indicates, mainstream liberals have major differences from conservatives and left-economics, which are more primary than their internal differences. Second, within the last decade the majority of economists who subscribe to the mainstream liberal position have shifted towards the monetary policy advocacy position. By the end of the 1970s, the major government macro-policy advisory panel—the Brookings Group—had moved away from advocacy of discretionary fiscal policies. Also, the leading theoretical figure had become Franco Modigliani and his MPS Model rather than James Tobin or the Wharton Model. Moreover, those economists who could be expected to renew the credibility and acceptance of the fiscalist position have withdrawn (at least temporarily) from the ideological struggle. James Tobin, since his 1972 AEA Presidential Address, has been largely inactive in defending the fiscalist thesis. Lawrence Klein, whose Wharton Model and earlier work was a leading force for the fiscalists, has also made no response to the upsurge in the attack on this position. Indeed, in his 1977 AEA Presidential Address, Klein chose to discuss a noncontroversial subject in macroeconomics—the need to incorporate input-

---

2. Robert Gordon, *Macroeconomics* (Boston: Little, Brown, 1978) and Rudiger Dornbusch and Stanley Fischer, *Macroeconomics* (New York: McGraw-Hill, 1978) only present the neo-classical growth model.

output information—rather than discuss the more controversial major issues. Finally, the major new macroeconomic texts have presented the monetary policy advocacy position as the dominant alternative to a completely laissez-faire approach.

Left-Liberals

Left-liberals contend that economic imbalances are likely to occur and be substantial because of the high volatility of capital investment. Chapter 13 indicated that left-liberal theories of capital investment emphasize the structural properties of investment goods—their bulkiness and longevity. These theories discount the importance of interest rate movements in regulating the capital intensity of production. Instead, technological innovations play a major role in determining the timing of capital spending.

Due to this volatility, left-liberals reject the notion that equilibrium tendencies are a major characteristic of market economies. Instead, left-liberals contend that cyclical movements of a predictable nature are the major characteristic of market economies. Thus, left-liberals have little faith in policies, such as automatic stabilizers, whose major objective is to strengthen and reinforce private market mechanisms. Left-liberals believe that only through planning, which *replaces* reliance on private mechanisms, is balanced full employment growth possible.

Not only do left-liberals have little faith in reliance upon market mechanisms, they believe that at times these mechanisms can be destabilizing. For example, suppose that there is an initial divergence from full employment growth. The Paradox of Profits model (Chapter 7) indicates it is possible that corporate adjustments to their wage policies could increase the divergence. If spending fell short of full employment requirements, corporations could decide to cut back money wage rates. Without a compensating capital spending increase, there would be a decline in aggregate spending. Thus, the initial spending shortfall could be increased as a result of market adjustments.

Left-liberals contend that it is likely that imbalances between growth requirements and actual capital spending plans would occur in unplanned market economies. These imbalances are likely because, according to left-liberal economists, technology does not allow for rapid and/or significant adjustments in capital-labor ratios. Without rapid and significant adjustments, it is impossible for production to adjust so that simultaneous full utilization of labor and capital is maintained (Chapter 14). Moreover, left-liberals contend that adjustments of business future investment decisions could intensify these imbalances. Firms would reduce future investment, for example, if capacity requirements were less than the actual capital stock. However, lay-offs and household spending declines would result from the decision to cut back capital spending. If these spending declines are large enough, then excess capacity could increase even though capital spending was reduced. Thus, market adjustments worsen the initial economic imbalance.

In both these cases, business decisions result in greater instability because individual firms are unable to incorporate the indirect effects of their decisions. Specifically, individual firms can incorporate the *supply* effects—lower wages imply lower supply costs or capital investment decisions affect productive capacity—but not the *demand* effects of their decisions. Lowering wages during a contraction destabilizes the situation if the dominant effect is a decline in purchasing power of workers. Rather than raising profits, lowering wages would result in not only lower employment and sales but also lower profits. Similarly, a contraction by lowering sales might induce firms to lower their planned investment. However, the effect of cutting back investment could be to further lower sales as construction workers must cut back their purchases. Hence, firms could create a larger gap between productive capacity and actual sales by reducing investments during contractions. According to left-liberals, these destabilizing effects of individual decision-making can only be avoided through government intervention in the wage setting and investment process—through government planning.

Finally, unlike mainstream economists, left-liberals contend that inflation creates serious problems for a market economy. According to left-liberals, labor markets create wage pressures well before full employment. Due to the necessity of the banking system to accommodate the increased financial needs of firms, monetary policy validates these wage demands (Chapter 19). Thus, the discipline of the market (creating a contraction to retard wage demands) is lacking so that these wage pressures can be sustained at below full employment. This analysis implies that there is a relatively stable trade-off between inflation rates and unemployment rates. It is thus possible to reduce unemployment if, and only if, the country is willing to accept high rates of inflation. The problem it creates is that a market economy is forced to choose between price stability and high levels of employment.

The contrasts between the left-liberal and mainstream views of the economy are very striking. Whereas mainstream economists view the economy as basically stable and significantly self-regulating, left-liberals contend that the economy is volatile and subject to destabilizing tendencies. Mainstream economists believe that equilibrating tendencies dominate. Left-liberals suggest that cyclical tendencies are the primary characteristic of unplanned market economies. Mainstream economists contend that growth and inflation pose only minor problems, but left-liberals contend that they create major problems for unplanned economies, which have full employment as an objective.

These contrasting views are most clearly reflected in the differences in policy recommendations. Mainstream economists recommend that government intervention be made at most on an ad hoc basis in order to reinforce the stabilizing tendencies present in the private sector. This may include automatic stabilizers, as well as some discretionary fiscal policy. Left-liberals, on the other hand, contend that economic planning is an essential component of government intervention since the private sector cannot be relied upon.

Radicals

Radicals agree with left-liberals that a private market economy is quite volatile and that market mechanisms often intensify this instability. Radicals also agree that growth imbalances play a central role in the cyclical process that characterizes market economies. However, radicals do not believe that government planning is capable of eliminating economic problems. Radicals contend that besides the technical problems, which planning might overcome, capitalism is subject to irreconcilable contradictions. The two major contradictions are the conflict between (1) labor and capital over the distribution of income, and (2) capitalists over the market shares of sales.

Unlike left-liberals, radicals contend that there is still a substantial amount of competition among capitalists. This competition takes the form of fighting over market shares in individual industries (Chapter 16) and the struggle between interest groups for control of government economic policies (Chapter 3). These struggles make it impossible for capitalists to agree on some planning formula. The conflict over planning formulas is particularly sharp if, as radicals claim, production is characterized by uneven development (Chapter 15). In this case, economic planning would be viewed as an attempt by the declining firms (interest groups) to protect their market shares rather than a means of eliminating the inefficiencies of an unplanned market. According to radicals, Carter's energy program was an example of the interrelationship between government economic planning and the struggle between competing corporate interest groups (Chapter 3). For this reason, radicals contend that tendencies towards overinvestment (Chapter 16) that are inherent in an unplanned economy cannot be avoided.

The fundamental conflict in a capitalist society is between labor and capital. Radicals contend that a market system requires labor to voluntarily enter into a hierarchical exploitative relationship with capital. According to radicals, the only way such relationships can be sustained without the use of force is by maintaining a reserve army of the unemployed. Thus, according to radicals, sustained full employment is incompatible with stable political and economic relationships. The class struggle model (Chapter 16) claims that sustained full employment causes a decline in profit rates, forcing smaller and weaker firms into bankruptcies or unfavorable mergers. Bankruptcies and lower profit rates discourage capital spending so that a recession results. This recession, by enlarging the depleted reserve army, regenerates the profitability necessary to undertake a new expansionary phase.

The radical view thus perceives recessions and increased industrial concentration as inevitable consequences of the capitalist growth process. The most distinguishing feature of this viewpoint is that problems are intensified by government attempts to avoid recessions by maintaining aggregate spending. Without a recession, the full employment profit squeeze is extended, and overinvestment tendencies continue. Therefore, government stimulation, such as during the war in Viet Nam (1966–69), only intensifies the contradictions and makes future adjustments more severe.

Left-liberal and radical economists have different theories of inflation. Radicals reject the left-liberal contention that there is a trade-off between inflation and unemployment rates. Radicals, like conservatives, believe that low unemployment rates are impossible, regardless of the willingness of society to accept high inflation rates. Radicals contend that the existence of an industrial reserve army is fundamental to the stability and vitality of capitalism. It is, therefore, impossible for a market economy to sustain unemployment rates below the minimum necessary size industrial reserve army.

21.2 THE UNDERLYING STRUCTURE OF MACRO-MODELS

The previous section highlighted the general characteristics of the models presented by each of the four groups of economists. It indicates that they disagree in their assessment of the stability of a laissez-faire economy. These disagreements are reflected in the differing government policy recommendations offered by each group. This section indicates that these differences can be related to the underlying structure of each group's model. Each model's structure will be determined by:

1. The choice of major factors which influence individual decision-makers.

2. The importance given to profits.

3. The extent and effects of competition.

4. The extent and effects of conflict between economic classes.

Major Factors That Influence Decision-Makers

Regardless of the decision-maker (firm or household), conservative economists emphasize the role of individual choice, dictated by personal preferences and relative prices, in determining economic outcomes. This individualistic outlook was fundamental to the conservative explanation of the natural unemployment rate (Chapter 2), theories of household spending (Chapter 6), and theories of investment (Chapter 9). In each case, constraining factors, such as institutional arrangements, technical change, or access to debt instruments, were ignored. While mainstream liberals incorporated some of these constraining factors, they, too, place primary emphasis on the role of individual choice.

Left-liberals minimize the importance of individual choice. Instead, they emphasize the role of technological factors and institutional arrangements in determining economic outcomes. Thus, left-liberals emphasize the structure of income distribution in determining the national savings rate (Chapter 7) and structural factors in explaining capital spending decisions (Chapter 13). Left-liberals also contend that because of technological inflexibility, imbalances between labor and capital stock utilization rates are likely to occur (Chapter 14).

Radicals also reject the importance of personal preference and relative prices in determining economic outcomes. Radicals agree with left-liberals that institutional arrangements and technological changes are important. However, radicals believe that the struggles waged by capitalists against labor and against other capitalists are the fundamental factors that influence economic decisions. Whereas left-liberals believe that the lack of planning is responsible for persistent unemployment, radicals believe this persistence is the consequence of the political and economic requirements of capitalists—their need for a reserve army. Also, left-liberals seek planning to eliminate inefficiencies, while radicals contend that the current move towards planning is the attempt of one group of capitalists (old money) to use the state to fight off a challenge to their predominance from another group of capitalists (new money), as discussed in Chapter 3.

The Role of Profits

One of the striking features of all mainstream models is the lack of importance they place on profits. As Chapter 4 indicates, the basic model of mainstream economics assumes that profits can be ignored when describing the major factors that influence aggregate spending and employment. Some mainstream macroeconomic texts briefly mention the *possibility* that the distribution of income between wages and profits could affect the level of spending. However, none bring wage and profit categories into their formal models. Thus, mainstream economists do not consider the distribution of income between wages and profits to be significant in determining aggregate spending. Also, virtually all mainstream models totally ignore the rate of profit when discussing the factors that influence aggregate spending.

In contrast, almost all left-economic models place great importance on either the distribution of income between wages and profits or on the profit rate. Left-liberals emphasize the effect of income distribution on determining aggregate consumption (Chapter 7), as well as its influence on the conditions for stable full employment growth (Chapter 14).

Those radicals who emphasize an underconsumptionist model also place importance on the distribution of income (Chapter 18). The radical underconsumptionist model indicates why imbalances are likely to be a result of underconsumption rather than overinvestment. Also, they indicate how class conflicts influence the distribution of income.

Radicals who apply the orthodox marxian theories emphasize the effect of changes in profit rates on business decisions. They contend that due to unequal access to debt instruments, smaller and weaker firms cannot maintain their competitive position. In this case, the economic process generates unequal development (Chapter 15). When the average rate of profit declines, unequal development implies that these disadvantaged firms would either go bankrupt or be subject to takeovers by the larger firms. Thus, according to these radicals, the average profit rate is a critical index of economic vitality, and its decline foretells the coming of economic contractions and intensified conflicts between competing capitalist groupings.

Competition

Conservatives contend that competitive forces are quite strong and enable the economy to self-correct for any deviations from its full employment growth path. If a spending shortfall occurs, interest rate changes induce both consumption and capital investment to increase. If these increases are insufficient to regenerate full employment spending, then the price level declines. Through deflation, further spending increases are stimulated until full employment spending occurs. Moreover, no imbalances are created if households change their savings rate. For full employment spending to be maintained, the rate of capital investment must also adjust. According to conservatives, interest rates and wage rates adjust so that the new capital investment rate combines with the available labor supply, thereby maintaining full utilization rates of both capital and labor. Thus, self-correcting mechanisms are so strong that conservatives claim no government intervention is necessary.

Mainstream liberals agree with conservatives that market forces have a stabilizing influence on the economy. However, they do not believe that these forces are strong enough to be totally relied upon. Mainstream liberals contend that the Keynes Effect and deflation are slow and too weak during recessions to quickly bring about full employment spending (Chapter 12). Also, they contend that adjustments in the capital-labor ratio to accommodate changes in full employment investment are slow since existing capital is not malleable (Chapter 14). Thus, mainstream liberals contend that the role of the government is to reinforce and speed-up the stabilizing mechanisms of the private market.

Left-liberals do not believe market forces are very strong. They usually cite the lack of competition and the inflexibility of technology as the major reasons. They contend, moreover, that major adjustments are often destabilizing. This view is embedded in the Paradox of Profits model (Chapter 7), as well as the Harrod-Domar growth model (Chapter 14). Hence, left-liberals contend that market mechanisms are weak and destabilizing and cannot be relied upon.

In some left-liberal models, such as Galbraith's, a tendency to stagnate is never overcome by the private sector. In others, such as Schumpeter's or

Kondratieff's, external shocks are necessary before the next wave of expansions occurs. Thus, many left-liberals suggest that without government intervention there is a permanent tendency to underproduction and unemployment. These left-liberals contend that only government planning can enable a private market system to sustain full employment.

Radicals contend that competitive forces are quite strong. They believe that the struggle among capitalists over market shares is a central facet of capialism. Unlike conservatives, radicals contend that competitive market forces are destabilizing. Conservative theories of household and business spending assume that decision-makers can take a long view because of their access to debt instruments. In this case, a slight decline in the cost of borrowing (interest rates) induces decision-makers to speed up their purchases of durable consumer goods and capital goods. Radicals contend that households and firms can ill afford to take a long view during economic contractions. Radicals suggest that most households have limited access to debt instruments, and that their futures are too uncertain to adjust their spending upward when interest rates decline during recessions.

Similarly, radicals suggest that competitive pressures compel many firms to strive for shortterm liquidity during economic contractions rather than increase their expenditures on capital goods. Radicals contend that the very nature of capitalism makes longterm planning by individual decision-makers impossible during economic contractions. Thus, they reject the conservative notions that household and business spending self-corrects during economic contractions.

Radicals tend to agree with left-liberals that, in the shortrun, market adjustments tend to destabilize the economy. Certainly, the drive for liquidity implies that a precipitous decline in spending is to be expected once the profit rate declines significantly. Most radicals disagree with the stagnationist tendency that is prevalent among many left-liberal and neo-marxian models. Those radicals who adopt the views of orthodox marxists contend that, in the longrun, the recession will correct the rate of profit and, in so doing, reverse the economic process. A rising profit rate encourages capital spending to increase, which propels the economy upward until the next overinvestment and profit squeeze cycle. Therefore, while radicals believe that competitive forces are strong, they contend that only in the longrun would they have a stabilizing influence.

Class Conflict

The fundamental importance placed on class conflict by radicals distinguishes their viewpoint from all the others. It is only the radical thesis that contends that capitalists reject full employment objectives and that unemployment plays a *functional* role within a capitalist system. According to radicals, the stability of capitalism in its democratic form requires that labor voluntarily enter into an exploitative hierarchical relationship with capital. If full employment occurs for any length of time, workers upset their relationship with capital. There are three specific ways in which radicals claim instability in the work process is created by sustained full employment. First, according to the class struggle thesis of Raford Boddy and James Crotty (Chapter 16), wage demands outpace the ability of capitalists to raise prices. Thus, full employment creates a profit squeeze. Second, according to the political business cycle theory of Michal Kalecki (Chapters 2 and 16), full employment reduces the work discipline in the factory. In response, Kalecki claims that capitalists will encourage the state to slow down the economy, increase the industrial reserve army and, thus, reestablish the conditions necessary for stability in the work process. Third, according to the dirty jobs theory of Michael Piore and Herbert Gans (Chapter 2), capitalism requires many workers to accept low-paying unsafe jobs that have little prospects for continuous employment. Radicals contend that the existence of a reserve army is necessary to coerce workers to accept these dead-end dirty jobs.[3]

Conservatives reject any notion that conflict between groups occurs in a market economy. They reason that since all contracts are voluntary, market transactions only occur if they are mutually beneficial. Conservatives also contend that competition makes it impossible for any individual firm to take advantage of households, either as workers or as consumers. According to this viewpoint, the benefits of increased production and employment accrue to households, with firms being the vehicle through which consumer and worker preferences are transmitted. Thus, there can be no question of class conflict over full employment objectives within the conservative framework.

Mainstream liberals do not as easily reject notions of exploitation and conflict. They concede that imperfections in the market allow some firms to exploit households as consumers and/or workers. They concede that in certain

---

3. Recently I began giving my daughter some religious training. I decided that Passover was a reasonable opportunity since it is the historical account of a successful slave revolt. Starting a few months ahead of time, Sara and I went to the public library and found appropriate picture books on ancient Egypt and slavery in the United States. Happily, Sara was excited by the pictures of pyramids and the sketches of American slave life. She was particularly struck by the picture of a handbill advertising the sale of a slave named Sarah.

At about that time, Public Broadcasting showed the film, "Last Grave at Dimbaza," depicting the economic conditions of blacks living in South Africa. When, during the next month, the jewelry store in town advertised in a mail circular that they were now selling casements for the South African government's Krugerrand coin, Sara thought that this was wrong. We decided that she should take the circular to school during "Show and Tell" so that she could explain to her classmates why their parents shouldn't buy Krugerrand coins.

Then one day Sara came to me and asked in an equivocal voice, "Rose isn't our slave, is she?" As should be clear, Rose is the woman who cleans our house once a week. Since Rose is white, it clearly indicates that Sara thought anyone who must do menial labor must be a slave; i.e., must be coerced into performing "dirty" jobs.

industries labor settlements are determined by relative bargaining strength rather than productivity measures. However, they minimize the extent to which capitalists use an industrial reserve army to exploit labor. For example, Arthur Okun assumes that capitalists take a longterm view of labor-management relations (Chapter 16). According to Okun, capitalists realize it would be counterproductive to lower wages during periods of high unemployment. By lowering wages, capitalists risk losing their best workers to other capitalists. Thus, Okun contends that the concept of an industrial reserve army regulating wages is outmoded.

Mainstream liberals contend that even if capitalists benefit from steady unemployment, they are not powerful enough to influence government economic policies. According to mainstream liberals, giant corporations are no longer controlled by capitalists. Instead, inside managers are the individuals who exercise control over these firms. Without the ability to dictate corporate political strategies, mainstream liberals claim that capitalists can only exert influence as individuals, rather than as owners of multi-billion dollar companies (Chapter 3).

Left-liberals suggest that class conflict is intense only in highly competitive industries. In these industries (domestic industries in Chapter 15), they agree with radicals that exploitation and abuse is often necessary for survival. However, left-liberals believe that the noncompetitive sector is growing and becoming the dominant political force within the business community. It is the big (noncompetitive) corporations, not the small (competitive) firms, that exert influences on government economic policies.

According to left-liberals, the noncompetitive sector is not concerned with maximizing profits. Instead, firms in this sector select target profit rates and are more interested in maximizing sales and technical efficiency. Left-liberals contend that target profit rates are easier to fulfill during periods of economic growth and high employment. Thus the big noncompetitive corporations actively encourage full employment because it maximizes sales and because it facilitates the attainment of profit objectives. But if the large corporations favor high employment, then they have little conflict with labor over government full employment objectives. Therefore, left-liberals argue that the obstacles to full employment are not political but technical. Left-liberals contend that big corporations favor government planning because it is the only way a private market economy can sustain economic growth and high employment.

Table 21.1 summarizes the distinctions between competing economic frameworks presented in this section.

21.3 ECLECTICISM AND THE STUDY OF ECONOMICS

Chapter 1 indicates that statistical techniques could not be expected to offer evidence that would allow economists, in a value-free manner, to judge the relative merits of competing theories. One of the reasons for this inability was

Table 21.1
Major characteristics of competing economic frameworks

Characteristics	Conservative	Mainstream liberal	Left-liberal	Radical
Underlying factor	Choice theory of individual behavior		Structural and institutional	Economic conflict
Competition	Strong and stabilizing	Weak and stabilizing	Weak and destabilizing	Strong and destabilizing
Profits	No influence on spending		Income distribution	Average profit rate
Conflict	No group conflict exists		Exists but not central	Exists and central

that critical factors could not be measured in a value-free manner. This was demonstrated in Chapter 2, where the measure of unemployment was discussed. There we found that each group of economists could find a measure of unemployment compatible with its viewpoint. For example, conservatives could find a measure of unemployment that implies that the economy is almost always close to full employment. Left-economists could find a measure that implies that there is always significant unemployment in an unplanned market economy. We also found that other critical variables had viable alternative measures. Chapter 10 indicated that there were numerous measures of the supply of money, including M_1 and M_2. Chapter 11 indicated that the interest elasticity of the money market varies significantly with the choice of interest rate. Finally, the measure of the average profit rate is not straightforward, hence, numerous alternative formulations are possible. Reflecting these alternatives, the government currently estimates 7 measures of the unemployment rate, 5 measures of the money supply, and 4 measures of the interest rate, while a Brookings study listed 14 measures of profits. Thus, four of the most critical factors in macroeconomics are subject to widely differing measures, and explanations for movements in the economy are often influenced by measurement selection.

Another problem with the use of testing is that competing theories often cannot be statistically distinguished. For example, the conservative theory that money supply changes determine the inflation rate cannot be distinguished statistically from the left-liberal view that inflation rates determine money supply changes. Both theories posit the same statistical correlation but opposing assessments of the causal relation (Chapter 19). Similarly, the conservative notion of a natural unemployment rate cannot easily be distinguished from the radical contention of a minimum necessary industrial reserve army. In each case, however, the choice of theory critically affects evaluations of a market system.

These examples only highlight the difficulty of selecting appropriate tests, measures of variables, and time period of observations when testing competing theories. For this reason, rather than emphasizing statistics, this text was structured so that the theoretical foundations of competing theories are delineated.

Eclecticism—choosing what is considered the best from different systems—is one possible approach taken by individuals in attempting to develop a complete macro-model. As individuals, we are all free to integrate any combination of subtheories in order to develop our own conception of the workings of the entire system. This could include a conservative investment function, a left-liberal consumption function, a radical measure of unemployment, and so on. Certainly, one can find examples of individual economists whose overall views reflect an eclectic outlook. Therefore, it is not always possible to compartmentalize individual economists into one of four groupings.

The major purpose in studying these diverse theories, however, is not to shape our own assessment of the economy. It is to understand the language of government policy debates. Whatever the underlying motives of its participants, government policy debates are "conducted in a vocabulary supplied by economists and through professional economic spokesmen." This book provides you with the ability to understand not only the technical characteristics of policies espoused, but also to identify (1) its foundations, (2) general viewpoints, and (3) competing views.

This book contends that economic theories are fundamentally interrelated with views on the overall workings of a market system. This differs markedly from the usual approaches that consider racism and government corruption to be determined by noneconomic factors. In this book, government corruption such as the Watergate scandal (Chapter 3), and social problems such as exploitation of disadvantaged workers (Chapter 15), were directly related to the workings of a market system.

Finally, this book attempts to reduce the uncritical acceptance of views espoused by "experts." All too often, theories adopted and measures selected are accepted solely because it is alleged that they reflect some consensus choice of experts. Often they are accepted because of unawareness of alternative theories and measures. After reading this book, you should be better prepared to critically evaluate economic presentations.

GUIDE TO SYMBOLS

Symbol	Explanation
Δ	The change in a magnitude. Example: ΔY is the change in real income between one period and another.
α	Capital-output ratio: $\alpha = K/Y$.
π	Profit rate.
ΔA	Autonomous change in spending.
$A_g D$	Aggregate demand schedule.
$A_g S$	Aggregate supply schedule.
b	Marginal propensity to consume.
b_p	Marginal propensity to consume out of profits.
b_w	Marginal propensity to consume out of wages.
B	Net business income.
c	Constant capital of an individual firm.
C	Total constant capital. (See page 320.)
C	Consumer spending. (See page 70.)
C^a	Actual consumer spending.
C^p	Predicted consumer spending.
C_d	Consumer spending on durable goods.
C_{nw}	Consumer spending out of nonwages.
C_p	Consumer spending out of profits.
C_w	Consumer spending out of wages.
CU	Currency household deposit in commercial banks.
C1–3	Three assumptions which underly the neo-classical competitive theory.
D1–3	Three assumptions underlying the neo-classical demand for labor.
DD	Demand deposits.
E	Employed workers.
ER	Excess bank reserves.

G	Government spending.
GNP	Gross national product.
H	High-powered money.
i	Market interest rate.
i_L	Market longterm interest rate.
i_n	Keynesian normal interest rate.
i_S	Market shortterm interest rate.
I	Gross private investment.
I_a	Actual gross private investment.
I_i	Unintended inventory investment.
I_n	Net private investment.
I_r	Net replacement investment.
IS	Goods market equilibrium curve.
ISH	Income shares hypothesis.
k	Wage share of total income: $k = W/Y$.
K	Capital stock of investment goods.
L	Labor stock.
ΔL	Balanced budget income shift.
L_f	Full employment labor.
LCH	Life cycle hypothesis.
LM	Money market equilibrium curve.
LR	Legal reserves.
m	Marginal propensity to spend.
m_d	Real demand for money: $m_d = m_{sp} + m_t = M_d/p$.
m_s	Real money supply: $m_s = M_s/p$.
m_{sp}	Real speculative demand: $m_{sp} = M_{sp}/p$.
m_t	Real transaction demand: $m_t = M_t/p$.
M_1	Money supply concept, includes currency held by public and commercial bank demand deposits.
M_2	Money supply concept, includes currency held by public and commercial bank time deposits and demand deposits: $M_2 = M_1 +$ time deposits.
M_d	Nominal demand for money.
M_m	Money market multiplier.
M_s	Nominal money supply.
M_{sp}	Nominal speculative demand for money.
M_t	Nominal transactions demand for money.
M_y	Simple income multiplier.
M_y^*	Full income multiplier.
MEC	Marginal efficiency of capital for a firm.
MEI	Marginal efficiency of investment.
MP1-3	Three assumptions made by economists who believe only money matters.

MPC	Marginal propensity to consume.
MPC_{nw}	Marginal propensity to consume out of nonwages.
MPC_p	Marginal propensity to consume out of profits.
MPC_w	Marginal propensity to consume out of wages.
MPI	Marginal propensity to invest.
MPS	Marginal propensity to save.
MPS_{nw}	Marginal propensity to save out of nonwages.
MPS_w	Marginal propensity to save out of wages.
MPSP	Marginal propensity to spend.
MPT	Marginal propensity to tax.
n	Growth rate of laborforce.
NW	Nonwage household income.
p	Price level.
p^a	Actual price level.
p^e	Expected price level.
P	Profits.
ΔP^T	Total change in profits.
PC	Pocket currency.
PIH	Permanent income hypothesis.
$\bar{r}$	Marxian proportionality constant; the ratio of productive capacity in the capital goods industries to productive capacity in the consumer goods industries.
r_n	Internal rate of return on private investment.
R	Government transfer payments.
ΔR	Income redistribution between wages and nonwage income.
R1-5	Five assumptions underlying marxian reproduction schema.
RIH	Relative income hypothesis.
RR	Reserve requirement.
s	Surplus value of an individual firm. (See page 320.)
s	Marginal propensity to save. (See page 273.)
S	Total surplus value. (See page 320.)
S	Savings. (See page 78.)
S_b	Business savings.
S_{nw}	Nonwage savings.
S_w	Savings out of wages.
S1-2	Two assumptions underlying the neo-classical theory of labor supply.
t	Marginal propensity to tax.
T	Government tax receipts.
TIP	Tax-Based Incomes Policy.
U	Involuntary unemployed workers.
U'	Voluntary unemployed workers.

v	Variable capital of an individual firm.
V	Total variable capital. (See page 320.)
V	Transactions velocity of money. (See page 179.)
w	Money wage rate.
w^*	Real wage rate: $w^* = w/p$.
W	Total wages.
ΔW^T	Total change in wages.
X_n	Net exports: exports minus imports.
Y	Total real production.
Y^*	Highest previous level of real production.
Y_d	Household disposable income.
ΔY_d^T	Total change in disposable income.
Y_f	Full employment production.
ΔY_I	Induced change in total production.
Y_p	Permanent income.
Y_s	Potential supply of production.
ΔY_T	Total change in production.
Z_d	Equilibrium level of aggregate demand.

INDEX